Power and Politics After Financial Crises

Power and Politics After Financial Crises

Rethinking Foreign Opportunism in Emerging Markets

Edited by

Justin Robertson
Assistant Professor, Department of Asian and International Studies, City University of Hong Kong

palgrave
macmillan

First published 2008 by

PALGRAVE MACMILLAN
Houndmills, Basingstoke, Hampshire RG21 6XS and
175 Fifth Avenue, New York, N.Y. 10010
Companies and representatives throughout the world

PALGRAVE MACMILLAN is the global academic imprint of the Palgrave Macmillan division of St. Martin's Press, LLC and of Palgrave Macmillan Ltd. Macmillan® is a registered trademark in the United States, United Kingdom and other countries. Palgrave is a registered trademark in the European Union and other countries.

ISBN-13: 978-0-230-51697-7   hardback
ISBN-10: 0-230-51697-1   hardback

This book is printed on paper suitable for recycling and made from fully managed and sustained forest sources. Logging, pulping and manufacturing processes are expected to conform to the environmental regulations of the country of origin.

A catalogue record for this book is available from the British Library.

A catalog record for this book is available from the Library of Congress.

10   9   8   7   6   5   4   3   2   1
17   16   15   14   13   12   11   10   09   08

Printed and bound in Great Britain by
CPI Antony Rowe, Chippenham and Eastbourne

Contents

List of Tables and Figures

Tables

Figures

List of Acronyms

ADB	Asian Development Bank
AHTFCG	Ad Hoc Task Force on Corporate Governance
BIAC	Business and Industry Advisory Committee
BN	Barisan Nasional
BSAG	Business Sector Advisory Group on Corporate Governance
BCB	Central Bank of Brazil
BRSA	Banking Regulation and Supervision Agency
CDS	credit default swaps
CE	Central Europe
CEE	Central and Eastern Europe
CEF	Caixa Economica Federal
CEO	Chief Executive Officer
CIO	Chief Information Officer
DWSR	Dollar-Wall Street Regime
EM	emerging market
EMBI+	Emerging Market Bond Index
EMEs	emerging market economies
EMU	European Monetary Union
ESF	exchange stabilization fund
EU	European Union
FDI	foreign direct investment
FIG	financial-industrial group
FSAP	Financial Services Action Plan
FX	foreign exchange
GDP	gross domestic product
GNP	gross national product
GLC	government linked corporation
GSP	Growth and Stability Pact
ICA	Industrial Coordination Act
ICGN	International Corporate Governance Network
IFI	international financial institution
IMF	International Monetary Fund
IGP	General Price Index
IOSCO	International Organisation of Securities Commissions
IPCA	Extensive National Consumer Index
IPE	International Political Economy

ISI	import substitution industrialization
M&As	mergers & acquisitions
MNE	Multi-national enterprise
NEP	New Economic Policy
NGO	non-governmental organization
NIFA	new international financial architecture
NPO	non-performing loan
OECD	Organization for Economic Co-operation and Development
PROER	Program of Initiatives for the Restructuring and Strengthening of the National Financial System
PT	Workers' Party, Brazil
ROSC	Report on the Standards and Codes for corporate governance
SAP	Structural Adjustment Program
SDIF	Saving Deposit Insurance Fund
SEA	Single European Act
SGCG	Steering Group on Corporate Governance
SME	small and medium enterprise
TBS	Turkish banking sector
TL	Turkish Lira
TUAC	Trade Union Advisory Committee
UNMO	United Malays National Organisation

Preface

The themes of foreign opportunism and nationalistic resistance recur in nearly every international economic crisis, but the accompanying analysis often lacks both historical and theoretical depth.

The authors in this volume were assembled to take part in a project that would (i) broaden the frameworks available to assess foreign economic behaviour in the wake of economic and financial crises in developing countries and (ii) combine rigorous attention to theorizing international interests in combination with empirical tests covering several years of developments after crises.

Supported by the structure presented in the opening chapter, the book exposes readers to alternative theoretical perspectives on important empirical cases. For example, one author offers a French regulation perspective on international banking in emerging markets, whereas foreign banks are defended in another chapter as essentially liberal institutions in developing economies. We believe that such an approach is a strength of the book.

For comments and ideas along the way, I would like to thank Andrew Baker, Hugh Robertson, Paola Robotti, Ben Thirkell-White and a reader arranged by the publisher. I would also like to extend my thanks to the Palgrave team for their professionalism and efficiency.

Justin Robertson

Notes on Contributors

Andrew Baker is a Senior Lecturer in political economy in the School of Politics, International Studies and Philosophy at the Queen's University of Belfast. He is author of *The Group of Seven: Finance Ministries, Central Banks and Global Financial Governance* (2006) and co-editor of *Governing Financial Globalization: IPE and Multi-Level Governance* (2005). He has published in journals such as *Global Governance, Review of International Political Economy* and *New Political Economy*.

Korsan Cevdet is an Executive Manager, Group Risk Management, at the Commonwealth Bank of Australia. He has worked in the financial services industry for 10 years in Canada and Australia. His research interests include Turkish foreign and security policy, economic development in Turkey, EU–Turkey relations, and the Cyprus conflict.

Robert Cull is a Senior Economist in the Finance and Private Sector Development Team of the Development Research Group of the World Bank. Much of his published research has focused on the evolution of public and private institutions to resolve financial market failures, including the effects of privatization and foreign entry on developing countries' banking sectors. His most recent research is on the performance of microfinance institutions and the design and use of household surveys to measure access to financial services. He is also co-editor of the *Interest Bearing Notes*, a newsletter reporting on financial and private sector research.

Giselle Datz is Assistant Professor at the School of Public and International Affairs at Virginia Tech. She was a visiting fellow of the Transnational Project at the University of Chicago (2006). Her work on sovereign debt restructurings and credit ratings has been published in the *Third World Quarterly* (2004) and in *Deciphering the Global* (2007). She is currently researching the relationship between private and public interest in pension fund financing.

Mahrukh Doctor is a Lecturer in Political Economy at the University of Hull, Visiting Adjunct Lecturer at the Bologna Center of the Johns Hopkins University (SAIS), and Research Associate at the Centre for Brazilian Studies, University of Oxford. She has also worked as an economist at the World Bank focussing on energy and industry operations in Latin America. She holds a doctorate from the University of Oxford.

Luiz Fernando de Paula is an Associate Professor of Economics at the State University of Rio de Janeiro (UERJ). His publications include more than 60 articles on banking, financial fragility, economic policy, post-Keynesian theory, and on the Brazilian economy, in books and scientific journals.

María Soledad Martínez Pería is a Senior Economist in the Finance and Private Sector Development Team of the Development Research Group of The World Bank. Her published work has focused on understanding the causes and consequences of foreign bank participation in developing countries. Her other areas of research interest include: banking and currency crises, depositor market discipline, and, more recently, measuring access to finance, and the impact of remittances on financial development. She holds a BA from Stanford University and a PhD from the University of California, Berkeley.

Maria Pia Riggirozzi holds an Economic and Social Research Council (ESRC)-funded Postdoctoral Fellowship in the Department of Politics, University of Sheffield. She completed a PhD at the University of Warwick and has worked as a researcher on the ESRC-funded project on Governance After Crisis.

Or Raviv is a PhD candidate at the University of Sussex, England. His research interests include the rise of private forms of authority in global and European governance. He is particularly interested in, and has published several pieces on, the politics of financial market making in Europe.

Justin Robertson is an Assistant Professor in the Department of Asian and International Studies at the City University of Hong Kong. He is an Associate of the Centre for the Study of Globalisation and Regionalisation and the Southeast Asia Research Centre. He is the co-editor of *Diplomacy and Developing Nations: Post-Cold War Foreign Policy-Making Structures and Processes* and he is currently researching changing forms of business in the global political economy.

Neil Robinson is a Senior Lecturer in the Department of Politics and Public Administration at the University of Limerick, Ireland. His research interests include the political economy of post-communism, in particular of Russia, and state formation in Russia. His recent publications include *Russia: a State of Uncertainty* (2002), *Reforging the Weakest Link: Global Political Economy and Post-Soviet Change in Russia, Ukraine and Belarus* (editor, 2004) and *State-Building: Theory and Practice* (co-editor, 2007).

Andrew Rosser is a Senior Lecturer in Development Studies at the University of Adelaide. His previous work on the politics of corporate governance reform has appeared in *Third World Quarterly* and in *Reforming Corporate Governance in Southeast Asia: Economics, Politics and Regulation* (2005).

Ben Thirkell-White is a Lecturer in International Relations at the Univeristy of St Andrews. His research is centred around the political economy of development finance including: the political economy of Southeast Asia, the politics of IMF policy-making, and critical theoretic approaches to global governance. His most recent books are *The IMF and the Politics of Financial Globalisation* (Palgrave Macmillan, 2005) and *Critical International Relations Theory after 25 Years* (co-edited with Nicholas Rengger, forthcoming).

1
Introduction: Key Theoretical Divides and Directions

Justin Robertson

Economic shocks and crises inflict severe pain on the less well-off in societies with the lower and middle classes often bearing the brunt of restructuring (see Chapters by Cevdet and Riggirozzi). While social costs demand our full attention, crises are also particularly important events for the larger debates over economic ideas that they set in motion. Moments of crisis show economic paradigms in clear view and the ensuing contest of models opens up the possibility of economic change (Gourevitch 1986). In the case of developing and emerging markets, these contests highlight power structures and relationships in the international and the domestic political economy. In theory, international actors should gain greater leverage in crisis-weakened developing countries, even though some domestic forces are likely to try their best to resist foreign interventions.

Set in this context, the papers in this volume explore whether financial and economic crises in developing countries redefine the place of foreign business and Western economic norms and practices in these markets. The contributors largely agree that current body of research presents too polarized and simplified an analysis of economic crises in the developing world. The volume draws attention to the divide between foreign and domestic approaches in understanding international economic behaviour in the wake of crises and attempts to take steps beyond it.

In the 1990s and early 2000s, a range of emerging markets and developing economies suffered major economic setbacks.[1] With a multi-year empirical record to serve as a testing ground, it is now possible to turn to a theoretically-informed and comparative assessment of the aftermath of crises in these economies. The contributors direct their attention to identifying the interests of foreign political and business actors in emerging markets and evaluating whether these interests prevail after crises. While there were many highly critical, almost conspiratorial, interpretations of the role of foreign actors in the outbreak of the Asian crisis (Gowan 1999: 128), the contributors were not asked to examine foreign actions preceding crises. Regardless of whether or not there is deliberate foreign involvement in the build-up to a crisis, the post-crisis environment should present market reform and business opportunities for outside actors and this is the starting point for the book. The question is how exactly foreign firms and governments respond to – some say take advantage of – changed conditions.

The example of Turkey's decision to allow an opening to foreign capital is characteristic of countries in economic crisis and raises a set of questions that frame the analysis in this book. Like most countries negotiating with the International Monetary Funds (IMF) in the middle of a financial crisis, Turkey's May 2001 letter of intent committed the country to liberalizing the foreign investment regime and accelerating privatization. How much of this policy direction was dictated from the outside? If so, was the source of this pressure foreign capital or foreign technocrats? Were the openings to foreigners implemented as intended or resisted? Did Western investors capitalize? These questions emphasize our focus on the role of foreign actors following crises and whether they act coherently in emerging market settings. We then incorporate domestic politics and ask how domestic structures and processes mediate the pressures and preferences of foreign actors. We derive conclusions through the analytic framework set out in this chapter and through careful consideration of some of the most important actors (US Treasury, foreign banks, domestic and international creditors), issue areas (corporate governance) and emerging markets (Argentina, Brazil, Central European countries, Indonesia, Malaysia, Russia and Turkey).

The foreign–domestic faultline in studying crisis outcomes

Like many spheres of analysis in International Political Economy (IPE), there are competing narratives of whether foreigners capitalize on crises in developing countries based on either the primacy of domestic or international processes. On the one hand, crises in the developing world have perennially been linked to external factors and interests. Most recently, when leading developing economies faltered during the late 1990s and early 2000s, numerous analysts attributed the market downturns to international factors and perceived opportunism in foreign responses (Bello 1998; Cumings 1999; Higgott 1998; Johnson 2000; Wade 1998; Weiss 1999). On the other hand, analysts from a domestic political economy tradition have held up the socio-political structures of developing countries as sufficiently complex to temper outside pressures, even during periods of severe economic distress (Beeson 2002; Jayasuriya 2001; Robison *et al.* 2000; Rodan *et al.* 2001; Rosser 2003a; Whitley 1999). The analysis in this volume suggests the need for a more complex understanding of post-crisis economic change than provided by positions based on Western political actors and capital united to press new foreign ownership on developing countries or by contrast a unified set of domestic elites resisting globalization and liberalization.

The introduction begins by briefly elaborating the arguments based on foreign power and domestic politics. In the wake of emerging market crises, there are frequently examples of high-profile domestic firms that fall under foreign ownership and this outcome is attributed to a strategic form of international political power that forces emerging markets open so that foreign capital can aggressively pursue business opportunities.[2] In most cases, the connotation is negative involving self-interested international actors and exploitive foreign investment.

Foreign economic and commercial power is a longstanding image of the international economy. It captured attention in post-war Europe, the Latin American debt crisis and the emerging market crises of the last decade. In particular, it has almost become lore that 'the great global asset swindle' (Hahnel 1999) has been perpetuated on developing countries in crisis. Even widely used IPE texts now give prominence to the claim that US corporations took advantage of the Asian crisis (O'Brien and Williams 2004). The politics of foreign economic power can also be seen in advanced economies. German political elites have attacked foreign private equity funds and a provocative article foresees an oncoming US crisis in which foreign companies like Toyota capitalize on a precipitous decline in the value of the US dollar and stock market to take over blue-chip US companies at fire sale prices (Fallows 2005).

Another explanation of crisis outcomes emphasizes domestic sources of resistance. The importance of domestic structures is the subject of a rich scholarly tradition (e.g. Gershenkron 1966) discussing the experiences of richer and poorer countries alike. As a recent example, it took a decade, for example for government and banking officials in one of the world's wealthiest countries, Japan, to recognize that continued lending to failing companies could neither resuscitate these companies nor resolve the underlying weaknesses of the country's banking system.

Resistance at the domestic level can be seen either as a form of rent-seeking or as a step towards progressive economic policy. For some, this is domestic governments and capitalists failing to 'modernize' their foreign investment environments and business practices: family control of firms, overvalued assets, the rollback of reforms and special treatment of debtors hold back any wave of restructuring and foreign penetration. As an investment banker remarked: 'Korean entrepreneurs would rather drive their company into bankruptcy than sell' (*FT* 2003). For others, domestic actors are rightfully protecting the interests of domestic constituencies. The Royal Bank of Scotland serves as an example of the benefits of continuing local control.[3]

Framing crisis outcomes as the result of either prevailing foreign power or obstructive domestic politics is treated as too rigid a classification in this book. To encourage a more rigorous theoretical and empirical assessment of emerging market crises and foreign economic interests, the introduction serves two purposes. First, I set out a number of choices that analysts are confronted with when trying to build theory in this area. These concern: the level of analysis, the coherence and commitment of international actors, the motivations of Western foreign policy-makers, the rationale for domestic interventions and the economic impact of foreign investment on developing markets. Secondly, I present a typology of five perspectives that can be used to explain foreign behaviour after crises.

Mixed patterns below the surface

Pointing to the weaknesses of models of foreign power, Baker writes in his chapter that 'the notion that the United States has a single one-dimensional policy driven by an overarching strategic commercial interest is certainly a distortion'. In their chapter, Doctor and Paula add that the looming power of foreign capital in Brazil is an 'oversimplified, if not self-important, view'. Building on these criticisms, this section offers several counter-intuitive examples from today's international economy to make the point that simple labels of economic processes mask more complex underlying trends. The notions of both far-reaching foreign control in the wake of crises or, by contrast, broad-based domestic resistance ignore mixed patterns of foreign and domestic interaction.

First, consider France and Japan, two economies typically categorized as statist with a focus on labour, national champions and regulation. Ironically, both countries now host some of the most sophisticated elements of global finance. Ten years ago, if one had surveyed opinion leaders, few would have foreseen that France would become a key staging point and battleground for the private equity industry, one of the most important contemporary trends in international business. Similarly, lost in the widespread analysis of a rising China and a declining Japan is the emergence of one of the world's top private equity and investment banking markets in Japan.

Secondly, Spain's recent economic history presents a paradox for the analysis of crises. In the aftermath of recent international economic crises, Spanish companies proved to be among the world's most adept foreign investors and yet domestically, national champions continue to be sheltered – often in the very sectors that Spanish companies have exploited overseas. Capitalizing especially on crisis openings in emerging markets, Spanish energy, financial and telecommunications firms took aggressive international steps during the 1990s. Spanish financial institutions, in particular, assumed dominant positions in Latin America with these institutions now estimated to be responsible for nearly 10 per cent of the region's gross domestic product (GDP) (Mathieson and Roldós 2001: 22). Within Spanish borders, by contrast, domestic stakeholders have fiercely challenged, as one example, a German company's repeated bids to acquire one of Spain's successful, internationally-oriented companies, Endesa in the energy sector. When Spanish politicians trumpet the necessity of keeping a company Spanish-owned, the concept of strategic national sectors clearly appears across a range of countries. Spain exemplifies the mixed signals between internationalization and domestic protection so often apparent in the world economy.

Thirdly, China further illustrates the interrelationship between the domestic and the international political economy. China's closely managed domestic economic policy is complemented by a vital foreign sector making it difficult to claim that one supersedes the other. Clearly, it is difficult to wrest control of Chinese companies in industries with either state ownership or strategic designation by the state. Nor have any of the recent public listings of Chinese state enterprises put them under threat of new controlling ownership. Furthermore, there is characteristic Chinese adaptation and emulation in response to global economic trends. While there are strong words of criticism of foreign private equity funds in other developing countries, China's business and political elites are far from passive: they are quietly taking steps to foster a domestically-owned private equity industry.

Foreign companies are, nonetheless, a dynamic and important part of the Chinese economy. On the basis of their extensive investments, companies such as Honda, Motorola and Nokia generate approximately two-thirds of all Chinese exports. Led by investment banks and private equity funds, foreign financial institutions are also making inroads to match foreign manufacturing in China. Finally, and anecdotally, many ambitious young people in China today express a desire to pursue studies at US Ivy League universities, suggestive of the power of American entrepreneurship. In sum, while great efforts are made domestically to shape

China's political economy, there are sufficient elements of liberalism and market access for foreign firms such that domestic control is not absolute.

Several guiding principles for the analysis in this volume can be drawn from these country examples. We try as much as possible to avoid any binary domestic-international divide by looking below the surface at deeper processes in emerging markets and the relative positions of foreign and domestic actors. Even Argentina and Russia, the exemplars of domestic trajectories in the volume, are countries still actively engaged with global financial markets. We also expect that there will be variable patterns of foreign market pressure and market activity originating from a range of sources – certainly more than just American firms and policy-makers.

Major theoretical divides and directions

In constructing arguments about the relationship between developing countries, economic crisis and the international economy, decisions need to be explicitly or implicitly taken on several theoretical fronts. This section sets out a number of theoretical choices facing analysts of crises (see Table 1.1). Being conscious of these divides and the different theoretical avenues in which they lead facilitates comparison and evaluation of perspectives on emerging markets recovering from crisis.

Level of analysis: international or domestic

While it is difficult to neatly pull apart domestic analyses from international analyses, competing research agendas in IPE tend to weight international and domestic factors as explanatory variables and present evidence for persistent national differences in the international economy or for a movement towards common global practices. Foreign corporate and

Table 1.1   Key theoretical choices: five pairings

Issue	*Theoretical position*	*Theoretical position*
Level of analysis	International	Domestic
Coherence and commitment of international forces	Coordinated grand strategy	Disjointed and short-term interests
Foreign economic policy-making	Commercially-oriented	Ideologically-motivated
Domestic politics	Rent-seeking	Progressive
Impact of foreign investment	Predatory	Efficiency-enhancing

political power drives change in internationally-oriented models of crises whereas deep-rooted institutional structures anchor local political economies in models at a domestic level of analysis. While one might have hoped that recent financial crises would have provided definitive support for either a convergent or a divergent world economy, this has not been the case. For example, can we look back at the Asian crisis as having planted the seeds of convergence in the region? In critical cases, such as Korea, the issue remains disputed with some authors arguing that national champions are a relic of earlier statist strategies (Pirie 2005) and others maintaining that national champions continue to be an integral part of policy-making (Weiss 2003).

Many of the authors in this volume reconsider commonly-held international-level arguments and present new perspectives: Baker on the capacity of the US Treasury Department, Cull and Martinez-Peria, as well as Cevdet, on foreign bank entry after crises, Datz on creditor heterogeneity, Rosser on organized labour and international economic negotiations, Doctor and Paula on the exaggerated impact of crises and Raviv on aggressive European financial capital. Other authors sharpen and refine domestic-oriented analysis with close attention to the experiences of Argentina (Riggirozzi), Indonesia and Malaysia (Thirkell-White) and Russia (Robinson).

At the domestic end of approaches, Riggirozzi depicts Argentina undergoing a domestic-driven period of change after its crisis. The use of the word 'national' is telling in her analysis. There are innumerable references to national structures and processes in the post-crisis context: national development policies, national industry, national interest groups, national production and, above all, national pathways to crisis recovery. For Riggirozzi, domestically-determined agendas have supplanted the internationally-influenced economic policy of Argentina during the 1990s. Argentina is not a country cut off from the world, but rather one in which domestic actors have held their ground in intensive, often acrimonious, relations with foreign creditors, firms and institutions.

At the international end of approaches, I argue (Robertson 2007) that any analysis of foreign economic interests in developing countries should start with an international level of analysis and the composition of those interests to ensure that they have been accurately portrayed. Too often, the blame for low levels of foreign investment in developing countries is placed squarely on domestic shoulders, even though international business strategies and interests may be far more important than any domestic variables. Reversing this logic, Doctor and Paula (Chapter 7) caution against overplaying the importance of financial crises and international corporate behaviour, noting that these factors played a secondary role in Brazil's decade-long process of corporate restructuring.

Raviv uses an international level argument to explain when foreign investors do position themselves aggressively in emerging markets. In the case of Central Europe, only international factors, namely the nature of the international economic system and the specific characteristics of European capitalism, can explain the dominant place of foreign financial capital. First, business, government and consumer debt in mature economies is reaching a ceiling and their relative promise in emerging markets propels foreign financial firms into these economies. Secondly, the continuing role of banks as the central financial institution in the European region explains how Western European commercial banks won the largest share of the Central European market. While critics simplistically associate Citibank with the multi-faceted American financial industry (Robertson 2007), they would be closer to the mark in identifying European banks as key actors in crisis settings. Capitalizing on their commercial strengths, Erste, KBC, Unicredito and other European banks took over controlling shares of Central European banks.

Rosser and Datz draw together international and domestic analysis in interesting ways in this volume. Rosser examines new international economic standards by separating the formulation of these standards from their implementation in domestic settings. Domestic and international forces interact with each other in both spheres but it is an open question whether internationally agreed conventions are implemented fully at the domestic level. Even if global capital is sufficiently coherent to write the international rules of capitalism, a point discussed in the next section, it is domestic institutions that interpret and implement international standards. As two authors recently concluded of the Basel Accord, 'it is only as relevant as [domestic] regulators decide to make it' (Steil and Litan 2006: 25). In Rosser's framework, neither international forces nor domestic forces seem to entirely achieve their objectives. On corporate governance, for example, neoliberal standards have been toned down because of pressure from internationally-organized labour and then have struggled to be implemented as designed in many emerging markets. Outcomes can only be understood through the interaction of the domestic and the international, although Rosser's stance appears to be that ultimate power rests at the domestic level.

Datz's chapter is another example of combining domestic and international levels of analysis. Her argument shares the introduction's skepticism that outcomes are ever as clear-cut as either foreigners gain and domestic actors lose or vice versa. After Argentina's economic crisis, neither domestic actors nor foreign creditors were the outright 'winners.' At the domestic level, the national government and domestic investors displayed more sophistication than expected. Local pension funds are one of the untold stories of this crisis and Datz points to their successful navigation through tumultuous times using shrewd financial strategies. By the same token, not all foreign investors suffered during Argentina's downturn. The theoretical point is that 'gains and losses depend on where one stands and holding which kind of security' (Datz, Chapter 4). While many Italian investors incurred enormous losses in Argentina, a small but important group of foreign investors demonstrated that substantial profits can be realized from strategic investments in emerging market debt.

Keeping the focus on international level explanations, the next subsections draw attention to competing interpretations of two post-crisis issues: (i) whether international forces act coherently and with long-term commitment to emerging markets and (ii) whether commercial or ideological factors are more important sources of foreign government action.

Coherence and commitment of international forces: coordinated grand strategy or disjointed and short-term interests

Much of the attention at the height of emerging market crises centres on what is believed to be concerted foreign pressure. It is claimed that American-led consortia, such as a 'Wall Street – US Treasury complex' (Bhagwati 1998), direct crisis management. These conceptions of coherent and coordinated long-term international strategies stand in contrast to arguments of more disjointed and short-term foreign economic and commercial interests in emerging markets.

As the world's dominant economy since the 20th century, it is not surprising that theories of coercive foreign power usually start with the US The US state has frequently been conceived of wielding a long-term strategic foreign economic policy. For example, in the wake of war-time economic destruction, the US had the foresight to construct an Asian region that integrated the economies of Japan and the Southeast Asian nations (Bowie and Unger 1997: 28) and in post-war Europe, US officials intervened intensively and 'had a great deal to do with decisions as to who was advanced into crucial positions of leadership in government, business and the labour market' (Block 1987: 89).

Comparable arguments are made today. For example, America's response to the Asian financial crisis was linked to the long-term objective of reducing Japanese influence on China's economy (Cumings 1999: 18) and several years later, the US is now in the midst of devising a 'grand strategy' in Asia of empowering countries that it assumes will counter Chinese power in the future, such as India, Indonesia and Vietnam (Twining 2006). Authors such as Gowan (2004) are convinced that the US state is preoccupied with forestalling China's emerging regional role. These analyses frequently use verbs like 'engineer' to characterize US foreign policy towards developing economies. The implications are clear: (i) there is an accepted and shared interest for American government and business and (ii) this interest is deliberately acted upon to destabilize other markets and advance American interests.

Rosser's argument has some limited parallels to this position. His chapter describes how the Organization for Economic Co-operation and Development (OECD) was given a mandate to work on corporate governance reform in emerging markets. Where did this mandate come from? Here we find coherence among international economic actors. Foreign capital and OECD members exhibited near unity on the importance of corporate governance as a 'new' issue in global economic governance and how it should be dealt with in policy terms. The shared voice of foreign capital and economic ministries was not, however, unchecked since there was a valiant attempt by Western labour groups to challenge the corporate governance agenda. While organized labour gained greater access to decision-makers, its outsider status was confirmed when the OECD corporate governance codes matched the Anglo-American economic model. For these reasons, there is a degree of coherence and commitment attributed to international actors in Rosser's discussion of corporate governance negotiations.

On the whole, the evidence in this book supports an alternative perspective on foreign power in which the notion of a single 'Western' or 'foreign' economic interest is challenged. Instead, foreign leverage is exercised through a number of uncoordinated actors, some of which have only short-term horizons. A self-centred major power during times of crisis could ruthless pursue international gain, but it could also mean an inward-looking country whose policy-making apparatus is neglectful and distracted (Winters 2000) and whose firms are preoccupied with the home market. Contrast America's post-war economic interventions in Asia and Europe, which were seen as strategically planned and costly, with the response to Russia's post-Cold War transition, which Sachs (1995: 60) called the 'greatest foreign policy failing in decades' because it was so poorly planned and financed.

The wide range of international business and foreign policy responses necessitate disaggregating foreign actions in the study of crises. The business community, in particular, is rarely considered united. This argument is best captured by Block's research on competing and short-sighted capitalists who do not have 'a fully developed strategic conception of what the state should do' (Block 1991: 396). Blustein's investigative journalism on US policy in response to Indonesia's economic crisis provides some unexpected support for this argument. Behind aggressive US efforts to break up the Suharto business empire was apparently the lobbying of American and Indonesian labour and religious groups (Blustein 2001: 101). In other words, what numerous commentators assumed was a business-driven and neoliberal-oriented US foreign policy was, in fact, mobilized by non-governmental organizations (NGOs).

Among the various examples in this collection that put the coherence of international actors into question, Datz's concept of adaptable agendas bears mentioning. To be adaptable implies that foreign investors are not closely wedded to the market policy demands made of emerging markets by international financial institutions (IFIs) and leading powers. Instead, financial investors are overwhelmingly driven by the need to deliver returns, which elevates market opportunities above any other criteria, including IFI pronouncements. Datz denies that there is any overarching system in which previously non-compliant countries are excluded from flows of global capital. Pairing Datz's findings for the finance sector with Walter's (2000) important work on multinational corporations, one can conclude that foreign capital has exhibited a willingness to invest in countries with illiberal foreign investment practices so long as there are growth prospects. In Suharto's Indonesia, foreign firms rushed to find political patrons that would provide them market access and protection (Thirkell-White, Chapter 9). In Argentina today, foreign firms are ignoring the unsettled foreign investment climate and committing to the fast-growing construction and manufacturing sectors (Riggirozzi, Chapter 6).

Foreign governments also often carry out foreign economic policies based on short-term interests and commitments. To suggest that foreign actors attempt to 'dismantle' other forms of capitalism implies that a coherent, long-term economic strategy exists, which misconceives the depth of commitment within leading governments, not least the US government, to guide reform efforts in emerging markets. When one looks inside the US Treasury Department, one finds an institution lacking the size and resources necessary to involve itself deeply in other countries. By no means is the Treasury Department passive and impartial. The Treasury Department is the dominant American economic institution during international crises, paying relatively little attention to the commercially-oriented arms of government and articulating strong views on liberalization internationally. But the extent to which the Treasury Department advocates US business abroad is debatable (see next sub-section), its human resources are stretched and leadership skills fluctuate (Baker, Chapter 2) and in the Asian crisis, its engagement lasted less than one year (Robertson 2007) – a far cry from long-term guided intervention.

The lack of long-term planning in emerging markets is also evident in the private sector. Datz's adaptable financial investors (Chapter 4) need flexibility and thus commit to generally short-term investments. Short-term performance assessments further limit long-term financial strategies. The bond industry, for example, takes at most a one-year market outlook, and usually a much narrower time horizon. In a revealing example of global finance's short-term memory, foreign investors bought Argentine bonds almost the day after the country's default. Datz would tell us that if short-term gains present themselves in emerging markets, international finance will find its way there.

More broadly, the generalized US firm is oriented to short-term results to a greater extent than its competitors internationally (Doremus *et al.* 1998). This is in large part a result of the power of capital markets and the focus on earnings for shareholders. Even US private equity funds, which are purposely moving away from a quarterly framework, are ultimately short-term investors in emerging markets and usually try to divest their acquisitions within several years. Most economists argue that international banks are long-term investors in emerging markets (Cull and Martinez-Peria, Chapter 3). Other analysts counter that foreign banks are likely to reduce their ties when crises strike. Cevdet's chapter suggests that foreign companies, on the whole, and particularly foreign banks, are risk-averse and tend to concentrate their business activities in their home base during economic turmoil. In light of this perceived tendency among foreign banks, Cevdet advocates creating financial systems based around strong locally-owned institutions, through domestic mergers if necessary. Cevdet's analysis is an implicit rejection of a Singapore-style economy founded on foreign multinationals as a model for the majority of developing countries.

Foreign economic policy-making: commercially-oriented or ideologically-motivated

A widely cited view is that Western foreign policies towards emerging markets are closely aligned with Western commercial interests. In the wake of crises, Western sectoral interests press governments to address their long-standing market access grievances in developing countries. A different explanation traces Western market opening pressures to the ideas and beliefs of policy-makers. Theorizing international responses to emerging market crises usually entails favouring either Western business or Western economic ideology as the principal impetus for market opening. These are distinct positions, although it is sometimes hard to separate them. For instance, Wade's writings carry a strong instrumentalist standpoint but then this author also exposed a World Bank whose work is primarily influenced by American economics training and ideology (Wade 2002).

The firm-driven understanding of foreign policy-making draws links between business preferences and policy outcomes. Although more attention is devoted to the ideological argument in this section, two further examples highlight commercially-oriented foreign policy outcomes. First, Braithwaite and Drahos (2000) argue that global investment and trade policy is derived, in large part, from the lobbying of a small club of US Chief Executive Officers (CEOs). Secondly, the American Chamber of Commerce, US car manufacturers and other corporate interests engaged in direct political involvement during the Asian crisis, including drafting parts of Korea's IMF agreement and determining Thailand's foreign investment and privatization regimes, according to Bello *et al.* (1998: 48, 68, 103).

The power of ideology is one rare international economic issue on which leading economists Stiglitz (2002) and Wolf (2004) agree. The key actors for these authors are government officials and technocrats, not business executives. Both Stigtliz and Wolf contend that an unshakable commitment to the free market among practitioners is a primary determinant of the manner in which international economic integration moves forward. As Wolf (2004: 246) writes, 'it was not corporations that pushed liberalization and privatization but governments (and behind them, intellectuals) convinced that this was in the interests of their countries'.

The economic ideologies of Western policy-makers are apparent in three respects. First, these officials believe that there is a single correct framework for financial and economic liberalization in emerging markets. American and IMF officials are genuinely intellectually committed to these beliefs (Chapters 2 and 9) and believe that their interventions contribute to economic development in emerging markets. The US government, in particular, has long called for developing countries to welcome foreign investment in all sectors with a particular emphasis on eliminating restrictions on the size and number of foreign banks, which it believes will improve domestic productivity.

Secondly, the frame of reference for senior policy-makers at points of crisis is the belief that market-oriented policies can restore economic confidence. Characteristically, when asked about the mindset of the US Treasury Department in the midst of the Asian crisis, a former senior official responded, 'we were motivated by the question "what will make these economies work?"' (anonymous interview). Only policies that advance macroeconomic discipline, openness and transparency can send the appropriate signals to the market. Accordingly, one could look at IMF programs and detect a sincere belief in the principle of transparency (Thirkell-White, Chapter 9).

Third, ideologically-driven US officials are relatively unconcerned about foreign business outcomes. Market credibility as a policy objective supersedes and differs from market access for foreigners (Baker, Chapter 2). Part of the ideological commitment to foreign participation entails establishing equal treatment for domestic and foreign firms. Public statements by US officials during the Asian crisis made frequent reference to a level playing field, which was, in fact, a far greater theme than opportunism in the US Trade Representative's testimony to Congress (Barshefsky 1998) so frequently cited by critical scholars. US officials maintain, for example, that facilitating market access for foreign banks is separate from privileging US business (Summers interviewed in Blustein 2001: 47; Truman interview). A Treasury Department official employed this logic in explaining that whether American firms manage the resolution of non-performing loans (NPLs) is wholly secondary to the process itself: 'we don't care by what means they do it, we just tell developing economies that they have to get rid of their NPLs' (Buckley interview). Senior US economic officials appear to believe that there is sufficient competition in most international markets to ensure that firms from one country or region do not dominate.

Treating government officials as independent actors presupposes a degree of state autonomy from capital. Doing so challenges accounts of commercially-oriented foreign policy-making. Analyses of crises in emerging markets based on opportunistic foreign firms with political access contradict the less cited but important argument made in comparative politics that economic crises, in fact, heighten the autonomy of the state (Jenkins 2000). Crises are unique periods of economic turbulence where the state centralizes decision-making authority. It is in more normal economic times, not crisis times, that capital gains political voice.

International economic policy is also a more autonomous sphere than domestic economic policy. Whereas business is often directly involved in drafting domestic American legislation, for example dealing with agriculture or communications, US foreign policy-makers are more removed from the business community. The relationship between Wall Street and the US Treasury is ad hoc and disjointed (Baker, Chapter 2) and there is scant evidence of lobbying by individual US companies to shape American foreign policy towards emerging markets in crisis (Baker, Chapter 2;

Thirkell-White, Chapter 9). US government officials, in turn, place little commercially-oriented pressure on IFIs (Robertson 2007) and extend less direct support to US firms overseas than their European counterparts (Vernon 1998: 127). In short, the captured state model of foreign policy-making differs significantly from analyses that point to the ideological bases of foreign responses to crises in the world economy.

Domestic politics: rent-seeking or progressive

Accounts grouped under the label of resistant domestic politics presume that domestic institutions can withstand pressures emanating from global structures and actors. One important divide in this type of analysis concerns whether domestic interventions serve productive economic purposes or instead the interests of political and corporate elites. We find examples of both of these positions in the aftermath of crises.

In the first perspective, vested interests and political elites work together to ensure that rents from liberalization flow in their direction. This is the argument that domestic institutions have channelled power and patronage historically. In particular, domestic conglomerates emerged in developing countries through preferential treatment from state officials (Rosser, Chapter 5). Crises are unable to disrupt this dynamic. In Thailand, for example, despite fears of diminished wealth and privilege, 'the top 1,000 elites fell on a cushion during the crisis, not a rock, because of their social and political power' (Krongkaew interview).

The politics of privatization and corporate governance in post-crisis Indonesia and Thailand are representative examples. According to one informed observer (Crispin interview), Thailand's privatization process in the wake of the Asian crisis was at best partial and more typically entailed 'privatization for Thais,' meaning that small stakes were sold to pro-government elements of the private sector. Politically-connected debtors are often influential enough to distort bankruptcy codes in emerging markets. In Indonesia's case, vested interests worked through many channels so that it was virtually impossible for the state to enforce debt or to place companies in meaningful bankruptcy proceedings (Thirkell-White, Chapter 9).

Another variant of domestic political economy analysis is that domestic channels are put to use for national economic development. Domestic politics represents more than the capture of rents. Weiss has eloquently presented the theoretical and practical case that states are capable of crafting advanced industrial policy. Well-designed policies, especially towards science and technology, can shape economic outcomes in emerging markets (Weiss 2003).

The research on Argentina and Turkey in the volume is consistent with this model. The sense one gets from Riggirozzi's analysis is of a country where nearly all domestic constituencies rallied around a new economic model and where government actions were purposive and effective. The post-crisis Argentine state has been socially progressive on price controls and welfare policy and yet still managed to bolster domestic demand and produce trade and fiscal surpluses. In financial policy, the Argentine government displayed independent policy-making capacity by wisely leveraging local pension funds as a source of credit and the broader stance on debt repayment proved politically popular (Datz, Chapter 4). Similarly, overcoming its historically weak public policy, the Turkish state has committed to a liberal, transparent and regulated financial sector and its more stable banking sector of the mid-2000s reflects a progressive form of domestic political economy (Cevdet, Chapter 11).

Impact of foreign investment: predatory or efficiency-enhancing

Despite its widening global reach, foreign investment continues to be a contentious political issue. From the withdrawal of a Middle Eastern company's takeover of US ports to the failure of Siemens to complete Russian acquisitions (Robinson, Chapter 10) to the protection of national pharmaceutical champions in France, planned foreign investments across diverse sectors and economies are regularly withdrawn or rejected due to domestic concerns and sensitivities.[4]

The politicized nature of foreign investment is further evident in the analysis of completed deals. Again, crises bring debates over foreign investment to the fore, especially the relationship between foreign investment and economic development in developing countries. Negative labels are usually attached to foreign capital after crises because of a perceived failure to contribute to the real economy. As mergers and acquisitions (M&As) grow in the world economy, particularly in finance and real estate, some authors (e.g. Weiss 1997) argue that few employment and production gains are generated, especially in comparison to new greenfield investments. While it is not Datz's objective to evaluate the economic impact of new types of finance, the clear impression that her chapter provides is of strategic-minded capitalists trading bonds in relative isolation from the real economy.

The competing argument is that foreign investment in developing economies is, in most cases, welfare-enhancing. In the discipline of Economics, the consensus is that foreign investment encapsulates new ideas, management and technology and that this dynamic package of assets is particularly needed in countries struggling with a financial or broader economic crisis. Economists highlight the irrationality of protecting badly indebted local companies:

> every [Korean] won of investment that goes into failing firms is a won that productive firms cannot access. Every won of investment that goes to the zombies helps perpetuate dead-end jobs with no future and impedes the creation of new jobs with vastly better prospects (Noland 2002).

The evidence to support this case includes a major study of acquisitions in post-crisis Thailand that found that foreign firms impacted positively on Thai competitiveness (Brimble 2001) and Graham's (2005) finding that many of the recent successes in the Korean automotive sector can be traced back to the post-crisis entry of foreign corporations. The case study of Brazil in this volume concludes that, on the whole, foreign firms brought new technology to the country and, above all, introduced competition to the market, which forced Brazilian companies to become more efficient.

Finance is an instructive example of the competing positions on foreign investment. While finance is undoubtedly a vital mechanism in economic growth, foreign investment in the financial sector has proven divisive. Critics charge foreign financial institutions with capitalizing on crises to wrestle management and ownership control of banking industries. At its worst, Hertz (2004: 88, 138) takes foreign 'debt vultures' to task for their mercenary-like pursuit of legal loopholes to press bankrupt owners to give up even their non-business assets. Other more moderate analysts have specific qualms about the foreign banking community, whether the 'carelessness' of commercial banks in the run-up to financial crises (Wolf 2004: 282) or the conflicts of interest created by foreign investment banks when they evaluate risks in emerging markets (Blustein 2005). Advocates respond that foreign banks bring new and much needed banking practices to emerging markets, and rarely capture dominant market share. The debate is played out in this book, particularly in the competing approaches that Cull and Martinez-Peria and Raviv use to analyse foreign financial ownership in developing economies.

The entrance of foreign banks into developing countries is often associated with financial policy reforms enacted after crises. For example, Mexico's economic troubles in the early 1990s spurred an opening that has almost completely reversed the prior domestic ownership of the financial sector. Latin America and Eastern Europe saw their banking assets under foreign ownership double and triple, respectively, during the late

1990s and early 2000s (see Chapter 3). Using a comprehensive database, Cull and Martinez-Peria's chapter confirms the importance of economic crisis as an independent variable and documents how foreign participation in emerging markets increases after crises.

More importantly, how does the foreign financial industry contribute to the economic development process in developing countries? Cull and Martinez-Peria present a detailed literature review, including the latest research based on firm-level data, and a sophisticated empirical test that are consistent with an efficiency-enhancing interpretation of foreign bank operations in emerging markets. Cull and Martinez-Peria are not hardened neoliberal ideologues: these are researchers from the World Bank bringing significant empirical evidence to bear on the issue.

The Cull-Martinez-Peria model is clearly liberal and it is one in which competition is perhaps the most important dynamic. The entry of foreign banks pressures domestic banks to perform better and competition from foreign groups drives profit margins down at domestic banks. The story here is not one of efficiency for efficiency's sake. The argument is that efficiency gains flow through the system in the form of better terms for loans, wider branch networks and other advantages for businesses and consumers. Cull and Martinez-Peria's discussion is balanced by the recognition that there are conflicting findings in the economic research on foreign bank activity. Some economists have concluded that the benefits of foreign banking have been mixed for small domestic firms, for Latin America as a region and for credit levels in the aftermath of crises. For the last finding at least, the authors have a plausible hypothesis: it is not foreign banks per se that bring down credit levels, it is the prevalence of distressed assets among the holdings of domestic banks acquired by foreign owners.

Raviv reaches a different conclusion, calling foreign banks predatory actors in emerging markets. By this, he means that foreign banks take over local financial systems at low cost and their interest-based income model contributes little to productive forces in the economy. Raviv raises a number of specific criticisms. First, he sees poor credit provision as endemic to international banks, rather than as an exceptional feature of financial crises. Using measurements such as the ratios of private sector credit to GDP and foreign bank credit to the small business sector, he argues that the much anticipated efficiency gains promised by foreign banks and their supporters never materialized in Central Europe. Secondly, he notes that both individuals and governments in the region are more reliant than ever on the policies and practices of foreign banks.

Private equity funds taking positions in emerging markets represent another key feature of recent emerging market crises. New financial vehicles in the global economy, such as hedge funds and private equity funds, are being placed under close scrutiny. Critical voices associate private equity funds with a disregard for company values, employees and communities and a sole preoccupation with buying low and exiting with a profit – hence the insinuation of 'vultures.' The contrary position highlights how private equity groups have turned around numerous struggling companies, such as Japanese and Korean banks. The funds argue that inefficient domestic companies would drain state resources and ultimately collapse were it not for their involvement. While private equity deals generally involve job losses at the outset, a top executive with private equity fund Newbridge questions the logic of the critics: 'coming in and stripping the assets of a company and selling off the assets and firing all the people . . . if you figure it out, you can't make much money doing that' (IHT 2006). Private equity funds are only the most recent example of the perennial divide on the merits of foreign investment between those convinced either of its predatory nature or its efficiency-enhancing qualities.

A typology of analytic frameworks

With these theoretical divides and choices in mind, this section outlines five different perspectives on the outcomes of financial crises in developing countries. The widely referenced models of foreign economic power and resistant domestic politics are briefly restated, but the typology's primary contribution is to broaden the range of analytic frameworks. The perspectives are presented according to those which are more internationally-oriented (Foreign Power, Uneven Foreign Involvement, System Overhaul without Foreign Benefit) and those which are more domestically-oriented (Resistant Domestic Politics, New Domestic Winners, or at Least Some Old Domestic Losers).

Foreign power

According to the foreign power hypothesis, foreign governments and institutions intervene in the domestic economies of developing countries during crises to advocate market opening and international business enters in an unprecedented fashion. Building on the theoretical distinctions set out earlier, this is an international level argument based on coherent and committed public and private actors operating within a commercially-oriented foreign policy framework.

American power stands out as a focal point. There are two distinguishable interpretations of US influence: one is more finance oriented and bound up with the nexus between financial firms, the US government and international policy-makers and the other is more oriented to production with an image of US corporations taking over prime assets in foreign economies experiencing a crisis. Thirkell-White develops this point in his chapter and argues that the first interpretation should be taken more seriously.

In suggesting that crisis openings in developing countries are met with a forceful push by foreign capital, Raviv can be roughly placed in this typological category. Financial capital is what counts most in Raviv's analysis. Specifically, European financial services took advantage of a particular moment in time, in which crisis served as a key variable, to capture dominant market share of Central European banking sectors. Raviv conceives of a world economy that has become finance-based and in which core financial institutions seek out interest-based transactions globally. This process is now entrenched in Central Europe and Western European banks have been the undisputed winners. The high revenues and profits of these foreign banks look set to continue as consumers and households in the region take on even more debt. In particular, the global real estate boom has reached Central Europe and mortage lending has become a highly profitable line of banking for European financial institutions in these countries.

Foreign political power is inextricably part of the rise of international banking in Central Europe. Foreign political power has been exercised by the European Union (EU), an organization that Raviv tells us has embraced neoliberalism since the 1980s. The combination of financial deregulation and market access pressure on new EU entrants emboldened Western European financial capital and enabled its penetration into Central Europe. Raviv has a more complex analysis of foreign economic power than many writers in this typological category, recognizing, not least, that the sources of power extend well beyond simple notions of American neo-economic imperialism. Indeed, Raviv helpfully reminds us that Western Europe's predatory financial role in Central Europe only repeats a historical pattern of the late 19th and early 20th centuries. His chapter is one step towards answering Baker's call (Chapter 2) for more empirically and historically grounded tests of the foreign economic power thesis.

Uneven foreign involvement

An uneven pattern of foreign economic involvement in the developing world is another possible outcome of crises. The argument is that there are a variety of foreign actors with diverse interests at play in emerging markets and a corresponding lack of coherence and coordination between foreign firms and foreign policy-makers. While some foreign elements may behave aggressively, many others are likely to be cautious or absent. Rejecting pervasive foreign opportunism in Brazil, Doctor and Paula (Chapter 7) conclude that 'if anything, the macro-economic volatility ensuing from the crises served to deter investment'. This is not surprising in that crises generate both incentives and disincentives for foreigners in developing economies. Managers of multinational and finance companies are unlikely to simultaneously declare their intention to 'enter!' emerging markets in crisis, just as supposedly mobile global capital is unlikely to move en masse to 'exit!' jurisdictions with rising costs and regulations (Garrett 1998: 76).

The larger theoretical point is made well by Bergsten *et al.* (1978: 497) when they note that FDI by American firms 'does not have a single, pre-ponderant net impact of any kind on the economy of the United States, the functioning of the international economic system or the foreign policy goals of the United States'. In studying the consequences of crises, foreign economic interests need to be disaggregated. A disaggregated form of analysis makes it possible for some Koreans to acknowledge the post-crisis contributions of foreign car companies while keeping a wary eye trained on private equity funds (*Asia Times* 2006).

There are several examples of differentiated analyses of foreign eco-nomic behaviour in this volume. Doctor and Paula contrast the outcomes in the financial and manufacturing sectors in Brazil. While foreigners captured market share in manufacturing, they did not do so in banking. It was only in select manufacturing sectors, such as automotive parts, that Brazil's economic crises, and the tight monetary policy they neces-sitated, shifted financing and technological terms in favour of foreign business. In her chapter, Datz draws out the varying strategies of foreign creditors responding to the Argentine crisis with a particular focus on the minority of investors who correctly read the bond market.

Two propositions on uneven foreign economic engagement can be derived from these types of analysis. First, close attention should be paid to the nature of assets available in emerging markets following crises. For example, many of Southeast Asia's advanced industries already feature a substantial foreign presence (Chapter 9), whereas Russia's outdated indus-trial sector holds minimal interest to foreign investors (Chapter 10). In neither of these cases could the argument reasonably be made that inter-national firms were set to takeover the crown jewels of the economy.

Secondly, analysts need to recognize the variable interests of interna-tional business. In this volume, Baker rightly faults critical theories of American corporate power for crudely combining US financial and commercial interests. What is certain is that financial crises have high-lighted one important new trend in international business. Long established multinational corporations have been joined as foreign investors by a new set of business actors, namely private equity funds and ever expanding investment banks. In fact, among the most active crisis investors in recent emerging market crises have been US investment banks and private equity funds, not blue-chip US multinational corporations that we normally associate with driving the international economy.

While private equity funds carry a technical sounding name and resonate only faintly with the general public, their operations are politically and economically significant. These are not finance companies shifting hot money around; private equity funds own and manage local companies and, thereby, participate directly in the domestic economies of emerging markets. East Asia has become one of the most active hosts in the world for private equity and certainly the most active region among emerging markets. The Asian crisis served as a turning point. While some observers expected 'Main Street' to enter the region, the real story of this crisis was the aggressive deal-making of relatively unknown US firms, such as Cerberus, Lone Star, Newbridge Capital and Warburg Pincus (Robertson 2007).

The international successes of US private equity funds and investment banks reflect American strengths in specialized finance. US firms hold a particular comparative advantage in corporate and financial restructuring, having built proficiencies dating from the US savings and loans crisis of the 1980s and American-owned accounting, auditing, consulting, investment banking and law firms are among the leading business services providers internationally. The politics of crisis, then, links an economic downturn in the US to crises in emerging markets decades later.

However, to make sense of larger foreign business patterns in the aftermath of emerging market crises, the net must be cast wider than American capital. Companies from Europe and Asia often stand at the forefront of business activity in emerging markets, even when it is American policy-makers that most aggressively push foreign investment liberalization. Thus, after Korea and Thailand further opened to foreign capital in the late 1990s, European capital made particularly strong moves. European-headquartered firms, such as BASF, Carrefour, Norske and Philips, were more engaged in industrial sectors, more willing to enter into shared ownership and more oriented to medium and long-term profits than US companies (Robertson 2007).

International banking offers similar examples. It was European banks ABN-Amro, HSBC and Santander that acquired Brazilian banks during recent crises (Doctor and Paula, Chapter 7) – not American banks. Likewise, the regional specializations of banks in the international economy puts into question the notion that US banking multinationals cross the globe to dominate emerging markets. The presence of Spanish banks in Latin America has already been discussed. Cull and Martinez-Peria (Chapter 3) provide evidence for other cases of regionalized banking: Austrian banks in Eastern Europe and Central Asia, Scandinavian banks in the Baltic states and Greek banks in the Balkans.

System overhaul with minimal foreign benefit

In this last international-level perspective, foreign interventions are judged to be motivated by threats to international financial stability and the need to rescue domestic financial systems. Neither crude opportunism nor widespread foreign takeovers are evident in the aftermath of crises. This is, in particular, the practitioner's view of financial crises in emerging markets. Discussions with international economic officials demonstrate that they self-identify themselves 'as technicians engaged in the task of correcting faults in the international financial system' (Baker, Chapter 2). The argument is that the innumerable technical assistance projects launched in the wake of financial crises by international institutions, foundations and Western powers are largely altruistic: they are designed to strengthen the fundamentals of domestic economic systems and not to liberalize markets for foreign multinationals.

The case for systemic interventions is bolstered by a content analysis of US Congressional hearings on the Asian crisis (US House of Representatives 1998). These hearings devoted little time to addressing the commercial prospects for American companies. Secretary Rubin's testimony focused almost entirely on restoring Asian financial stability for the sake of the American, Asian and international economies (Rubin 1998).

Foreign banks are actors in this perspective as well. This is where foreign banks are seen to be delivering efficiency, as much as profit-making, to developing countries. Thus, private equity fund Newbridge Capital should be assessed, first and foremost, on how it reshaped banking in Korea, such as declining government requests for chaebol financing and innovating on small business lending. Its high return on investment is relevant but secondary in the larger picture. The larger picture is that Chile, Hungary, Korea, Mexico and Poland represent countries where more dynamic and sophisticated financial sectors have emerged from post-crisis reforms and foreign bank entry (Wolf 2004: 286–7, World Bank 2000a: 86).

Resistant domestic politics

The next two positions locate the sources of political and economic change – or, in the first case, lack of change – at the domestic level. Reference has been made to the first position of resistant domestic political economy throughout the introduction. Put simply, developing countries pursue domestically-determined economic policies and relations with foreign actors, even in the face of crisis. As captured in the language of a 'bitter political struggle' between local and international forces (Rosser, Chapter 5), domestic politics is theorized as a terrain on which there is active resistance to pressure from the outside world. The national economic orientations of Argentina and Russia (Chapters 6 and 10) and the increased interventions of the post-crisis Malaysian state (Chapter 9) exemplify outcomes consistent with this perspective.

Most of the examples of domestic resistance thus far have been drawn from the world of politics where political elites slow down or reverse market reforms. Attention will now be paid to the business world and how economic crises are associated with the continuing dominance of domestic conglomerates. The wider argument has been made that globalization correlates with rising numbers of oligopolies and monopolies (Scholte 2000: 130). This type of analytic framework challenges assumptions about business concentration in a supposedly freer global economy. For example, even though Hong Kong practises arguably the most liberal international economic relations of any economy in the world, this has not stood in the way of domestic conglomerates capturing dominant market power.

In emerging markets, the hypothesis is that economic liberalization and conglomerates are compatible. Hence, Indonesia's liberalization program of the 1980s and 1990s actually reinforced the position of powerful politico-business families (Thirkell-White, Chapter 9) and a similar dynamic unfolded in Brazil, Chile and Mexico (Goldstein and Schneider 2004). If, contrary to the expectations of the foreign power model, the same corporate players in developing countries survive and prosper after financial crises, then one response might be that business and government elites used strategic political resistance against foreign market pressures and business competitors.

Thailand, Russia and Malaysia are examples of countries where domestic firms have strengthened their business positions after economic crises. Taking advantage of weakened competitors, Thai conglomerates, such as CP, Malemont, Shin and Thai Military Bank deepened their already close ties to the state in pursuit of business expansion after the Asian crisis (Phonpaichit and Baker 2001). Russian business groups have also been solidifying market share in the wake of turbulent economic times. Robinson (Chapter 10) illustrates that successive economic crises could not shake loose domestic control of Russia's vital oil sector and less than 5 per cent of the Russian oil industry is foreign owned. Robinson describes a rational and calculating state that keeps foreign firms at bay. Gazprom is the most prominent example of the widening spheres of some Russian businesses. With clear political support and 51 per cent state ownership, Russia's largest energy company is becoming a true conglomerate with holdings in entertainment, media and transportation. Illustrative again of state power, much of the economic space in Malaysia created by the fall of former business empires has been filled by government linked corporations, which are now responsible for nearly 40 per cent of the stock market's value (Thirkell-White, Chapter 9). In Malaysia, Russia and Thailand, therefore, political power has been harnessed on behalf of business conglomerates.

Others would see the same outcome – the continuing power of domestic conglomerates after crises – as a result of natural market strengths rather than political bargaining. There is support for this argument in the chapter on Brazil. The authors not only tell us that Brazilian banks remain domestically dominant, but that leading local banks have earned this market status through efficient operations. Domestic banks are arguably even more productive than foreign banks and they led the post-crisis restructuring of the Brazilian banking industry. Öniş (2006) recounts a similar story in terms of Turkey's crisis where expectations of new private sector power bases centred on smaller companies failed to materialize and efficient larger conglomerates advanced even further. The Brazilian and Turkish experiences point to market competition as the key factor, rather than political favouritism.

New domestic winners, or at least some old domestic losers

The argument in this final domestic-level perspective is that substantial market change follows most crises in the developing world, in contrast to the image of hostile domestic politics, and yet many of the winners are new local firms, rather than foreign capital. The starting assumption is that crises are points in time when pre-existing forms of political economy can be transformed, especially the close relationship between capitalists and the state.

Thirkell-White (Chapter 9) draws attention to the genuine interest in change within developing countries and efforts to break new ground in business-government relations. For example, the rise of a favoured politico-business class in Malaysia had by the late 1990s generated significant resentment. While his chapter ultimately seems to suggest that neither Indonesia nor Malaysia underwent a radical domestic realignment after the Asian crisis, this episode still highlighted the scope of domestic forces that seek socioeconomic change. This implies that not all domestic firms are neatly lined up behind the status quo, as depicted in models of resistant domestic political economy. Thirkell-White puts this point well: 'one should be as skeptical of claims made by large politically-connected corporations about the national interest as one might be about the IMF's claims to be a neutral technocratic advisor.'

Despite only modest changes to their domestic landscapes, common to both Indonesia and Malaysia was the demise of capitalists associated with the Mahathir and Suharto regimes. These developments are consistent with the notion of 'old losers,' that long-standing elites are among those who suffer political and financial loss. As a journalist concluded of Indonesia, 'if you saw the crisis as a moral drama where the virtuous got rewarded and the others got punished – well, it did happen in Indonesia' (*Asiamoney* 1999). Numerous high-profile Indonesian business leaders lost their companies and the conglomerates that survived the crisis resurfaced weakened and indebted.

Thirkell-White reorients analysis of Malaysia's crisis away from an overplayed representation of foreign corporations pitted against domestic interests. For Thirkell-White, the real political contests occurred between domestic actors. Hard questions were asked and groups mobilized in the post-crisis period to both challenge and defend the place of Malay preference in the country's political economy. Just as this volume advocates breaking down foreign economic interests, this is another form of disaggregation: to break down 'the domestic'. Rosser's framework fits here as well. It would be conceptually impossible in his model for there to be a universal model of domestic resistance. Domestic forces are almost always divided between more liberal and more resistant coalitions.

The financial crisis brought down several powerful businesses and created some limited space for new domestic capitalists in Malaysia. International and Malaysian observers nearly all mistakenly expected that companies and business leaders associated with politicians would outlast the Asian crisis. A set of business groups had gained strength through affiliation and privileges granted by Mahathir, Anwar Ibrahim and especially Daim Zainuddin (Gomez 2003). In the face of deep domestic opposition to crisis bail-outs, Mahathir opted to let these Malay tycoons deal with the market without government support. Nearly all the tycoons, including key pre-crisis figures, such as Tajuddin Ramli, Halim Saad and Rashid Hussain, failed during the crisis. By early 2001, no Malay businessperson held a significant stake in any of the top ten companies in Malaysia (Gomez 2003). While it is politically significant that tycoons have fallen out of the business elite in Malaysia and Indonesia, it should be pointed out that many of these individuals protected their personal wealth.[5]

Several additional examples point to new domestic sources of corporate power in the wake of economic crises. Some of the business literature (van Agtmael 2007) has highlighted how financial crises have separated innovative emerging market companies, such as Aracruz, Samsung and Yuen, from their uncompetitive and often politically-dependent domestic counterparts. Rarely does a country's political economy undergo as rapid change as Argentina in recent years. Its crisis signaled the decline of financial capital and the empowerment of domestic industrial and export-oriented sectors (Riggirozzi, Chapter 6). Representatives from these 'new domestic winners' recently formed an influential association named the Productive Group. In Brazil, several domestically-owned industries, such as ceramics, shoes and textiles, successfully reacted to crisis conditions and limited foreign penetration, while the Brazilian food processing industry exemplifies domestic firms keeping pace even when foreign entrants do penetrate the market (Doctor and Paula, Chapter 7). In Korea, Graham (2005) employs the logic of new domestic winners in arguing that strong Hyundai automotive results in the years following the Asian crisis are a function of the Hyundai car unit's newfound independence from the larger chaebol.

Conclusion

Economic crises quite naturally spark intensive scholarly and journalistic attention and, at their height, polarize analysis. This chapter has provided a number of ways to systematically evaluate the relationship between crises in developing countries and foreign commercial and economic interests. The chapters that follow take advantage of the intervening years since the turbulence in emerging markets of the late 1990s and early 2000s to engage empirically with the post-crisis record. In making distinctions among the interests of foreign and domestic governments and firms, the contributors demonstrate that international opportunism and domestic resistance are not fully satisfactory theoretical frameworks. The concluding chapter points to the underlying importance of international processes after crisis, noting that emerging markets continue to be exposed to foreign economic ideas and to multinational and financial companies. While recognizing the strength of domestic political and economic forces, the conclusion questions the degree to which domestic forces actually disrupt the international economy. Taken as a whole, the book stands as one important attempt to rethink foreign and domestic responses to one of the major features of the world economy, episodic financial crises in developing and emerging economies.

Notes

1. For sake of ease, I use developing world, developing countries and emerging markets interchangeably to refer to middle income developing nations. Turkey and Eastern European countries are normally referred to as emerging markets but their GDP per capita places them on a par with Brazil, Malaysia and other developing countries.
2. Some of these foreign acquisitions turn into highly profitable operations while others are divested several years later with substantial returns. For example, Banamex, the bank Citigroup acquired in Mexico, regularly reports net income of over $1 billlion annually, and US private equity funds have registered over $1 billion gains on several divestments of Korean banks purchased during the Asian crisis.
3. 'Instead of being a regional office of an American bank,' Hutton (2006) writes, the Royal Bank of Scotland resisted foreign acquisition, which 'keeps alive an idea of Scotland and Edinburgh as one of the world's financial playmakers rather than a subcontractor'.
4. The United Kingdom is the exception where the reigning philosophy is 'if someone offers you a good price for anything, you sell it' (Karel Williams of Manchester University quoted in Rice-Oxley 2006).
5. A common theme of crises is that former members of the business elite are able to transfer their money outside the country. Examples would include Indonesian funds placed in Australia, Hong Kong and Singapore and the $16 billion of domestic deposits moved outside of Argentina during 2001 (Setser and Gelpern 2004).

Part I
International Actors and Issue Areas

2
Financial Crises and US Treasury Policy: The Institutional and Ideational Basis of American Capability

Andrew Baker

Precisely what capability does the United States Treasury, as the key US government agency with responsibility for the conduct of American international financial policy, have to control and manipulate the management of financial crises in various parts of the world? In particular, to what extent has the US Treasury acted in a strategic and instrumental fashion, conducting policy that has affected a shift in the ownership of assets in countries experiencing financial crisis in the direction of US private financial and commercial concerns? Several voices from different backgrounds and perspectives have associated episodes of financial crisis, disturbance and distress with the strategic exercise of US power. The basic tenure of this strong American power thesis is that there is a powerful Wall Street–US Treasury financial regime that controls global institutions, such as the IMF, and has the power to determine the future of weaker economies through credit manipulation and debt management strategies (Bello 1998; Bhagwati 1998; Strange 1998; Wade and Veneroso 1998; Gowan 1999; Gills 2000; Stiglitz 2002; Harvey 2003; Soederberg 2004). This regime has been variously referred to as the Treasury–IMF complex (Bhagwati 1998), the Dollar–Wall Street Regime (Gowan 1999), Washington–Wall Street alliance (Peet 2003), Wall Street–Treasury financial regime (Harvey 2003), Wall Street–Treasury–IMF complex (Wade and Veneroso 1998) and Wall Street–Treasury Complex (Cohen 2003). In short, a sufficient number of authors have identified the existence of this state–society coalition and alluded to its influence in international financial governance for claims about US financial power and capability based on the realization of Wall Street preferences and American interests to be taken seriously.

Nevertheless, the full extent and parameters of US power in financial governance have rarely been related to the reality of how financial crises are actually managed and handled by US Treasury officials on a day-to-day basis. By focusing on the every day experiences and realties encountered by Treasury officials, I aim to shed light on some of the constraints the US government faces in handling financial crises, as well as the opportunities such crises afford. I will argue that the exercise of US power, although undoubtedly evident in the handling and resolution of financial crises, is less pronounced, more constrained and crucially less strategic and instrumental than it is often assumed in the strong American power thesis literature. The practical realities of US policy in response to financial crises are not entirely captured by generalized notions of opportunistic, strategic and instrumental American power. While the strong American power thesis does offer an approximation of sorts of how US power and interests play out in financial crises, the reality is somewhat more complex and the principal determinants of US policy less straightforward than strong American power accounts of the political economy of financial crises assume.

Strong versions of the American power thesis are essentially a caricature. Like all caricatures, they have some degree of accuracy, but they still represent a somewhat simplified version of events. The rest of this chapter develops this argument. The first section provides a broad overview of the strong American power thesis literature. The remaining sections identify and discuss the principal constraints on the US Treasury: the institutional mandate and function of the Treasury (including relations with other organs and agencies of central government), reigning ideology, knowledge and beliefs, the nature of Treasury–private sector relations and finally the problem of resource scarcity.

The strong American power thesis

There are several variants to the strong American power thesis, but the basic premise is the same. The United States, as the world's leading financial power, benefits asymmetrically from financial crises, behaves opportunistically and strategically in the resolution and handling of crises to ensure the maximum benefits for its own commercial concerns in terms of the ownership of assets and market entry, and in some cases even acts to instigate, or at least not prevent such crises, as it benefits from volatility and a 'flight to quality' through financial inflows into its own financial system, which in turn finance twin fiscal and trade deficits (Strange 1998; Gowan 1999).

Peter Gowan probably goes furthest in developing the strong American power thesis. For Gowan (1999) the Asian financial crisis was a direct result of US statecraft and the instigation of a strong dollar policy in 1995. According to this perspective, currency fluctuations were used to increase the indebtedness of Southeast Asian corporations, which led to increased borrowing from foreign financial institutions, before US hedge funds wrenched lines of credit back into Anglo-Saxon financial centres causing a credit crunch, bankruptcies and a spate of currency crises. This was seen as part of an orchestrated strategy on the part of the so called Dollar–Wall Street Regime (DWSR), whereby the Treasury Department exploited its connections with Wall Street to catalyse market movements in accordance with strategic US interests. The market power of Wall Street is seen to be bound up with a handful of large hedge funds and is viewed as a *de facto* extension of US state power. In this way, currency movements and the growth in indebtedness were orchestrated by a DWSR as part of a strategy of economic statecraft designed to prise open Asian markets and secure increased US ownership of assets in the Southeast Asian region, while increasing the inflow of foreign funds into the US stock market. As I have argued elsewhere (Baker 2006b), Gowan is certainly right to argue that Wall Street is a liquidity driven market whose constant re-supply of funds from abroad is essential to offset low levels of domestic savings and keep the domestic economy booming. American governments do have some interest in financial volatility as this maintains the vast inflow of foreign funds into New York in the form of a 'flight to quality'. However, it is quite another thing to assert that the United States was able to manipulate the dollar at will and engineer the Asian financial crisis, so as to secure improved US access to Asian markets.

One does not need to go as far as Gowan to accept a strong American power thesis. Several other voices, while not necessarily accepting the argument that the US instigated, or orchestrated the Asian crisis for its own purposes and strategic gain, do maintain that the US operated in an opportunistic fashion in the aftermath of the crisis. Their general argument is that the US used the urgent need for liquidity in Asian financial systems to impose conditionality on Southeast Asian economies through IMF structural adjustment programmes with the intent of prising open Asian markets to a hitherto unprecedented extent.

A more sober assessment for example, is that the handling of the Asian crisis resulted in the intensification of the perception throughout Asia that the IMF remained an instrument of US power (Higgott 1998; Hughes 2000; Katada 2001; Bowles 2002; Tadokoro 2003; Kirshner 2004). This was also accompanied by a sense in Asia that wealth losses were not allocated fairly and that workers and local entrepreneurs bore a larger share of the crisis than foreign investors, who were bailed out on favourable terms in return for the minimal concession of rolling over some loans (Higgott 1998).

Indeed, there is much to be said for this argument that the United States used the Asian financial crisis to lever open Asian financial markets. Taking this argument a stage further, market opening policies were seen to be motivated by the opportunity this provided for major international banks, amongst them US banks such as Citibank, to begin to make major inroads into the region's banking sectors. Moreover, deflated asset prices were seen to afford discount purchasing opportunities to US multinationals, which were seen to be the major beneficiaries of 'fire sales' (Higgott 1998). Similarly, an 'ideas battle' was also seen to be key to the Asian crisis (Higgott 1998), with the United States opportunistically seeking to dismantle the Asian developmental state model and impose neo-liberal norms on a reluctant Asia (Gills 2000). Based on this kind of logic, some authors made bold predictions. Notably, Robert Wade (1998) suggested that the Asian crisis would lead to the biggest transfer of assets from domestic to foreign owners in recent world history.

But it is not just scholars from a critical IPE perspective who were implying that a US centred agenda of market opening was at work in Asia. The liberal trade economist Jagdish Bhagwati (1998) made the argument that a Washington–Wall Street network had relentlessly propelled the international financial system and the IMF toward the goal of capital account convertibility, so as to enlarge the arena in which Wall Street could make money. Similarly, the World Bank's Chief Economist at the time of the crisis, Joseph Stiglitz, later recorded surprise at how strong IMF and US Treasury criticisms of Asian countries were, and argued that IMF prescriptions reflected the interests and ideology of the Western financial community – while denying that this was necessarily part of some sort of conspiracy to deliver cheap assets into the hands of Western investors (Stiglitz 2002).

The gaps and limitations of the strong American power thesis

With such a diverse range of voices identifying US power and interests behind the international response to the Asian financial crisis, there is likely a degree of substance behind strong American power accounts of the crisis. However, one notable gap in this literature, particularly in critical IPE accounts, is that the story of the Asian financial crisis is told from an Asian perspective, as a deliberate anecdote to mainstream neo-classical analyses that prevailed in US and Western elite policy circles (Higgott 1998). There were obvious reasons for proceeding down this route, and it served a valuable purpose, but it also meant that accounts of what was driving US policy were often generalised, lacking in sufficient detail and with an inadequate appreciation of how US officials actually operated and the considerations on which they based their actions. Consequently, appreciation of the extent of American capability to drive the response to the Asian financial crisis and to act strategically and instrumentally is seriously compromised. Furthermore the majority of this literature, as Robertson (2007) has observed, was written too soon after the crisis, to allow a longer term perspective on the extent to which American penetration of Asian markets has been successful (for an exception see Beeson 2002).

Several, often conflicting, impulses guide US policy at moments of financial crisis. These conflicting imperatives have to be balanced and reconciled, but the notion that the United States has a single one-dimensional policy driven by an overarching strategic commercial interest is certainly a distortion. In particular, the simplistic notion that the US government successfully acts on behalf of US business interests in its handling of financial crises is flawed for two principal reasons. First, such a line of argument is based on a crude aggregation of US financial and commercial interests that is not sustainable in practice, while the strength and coherence of Treasury-private sector relations is overestimated. Secondly, the strong American power thesis misrepresents and simplifies the reality of financial crises as they are experienced by Treasury officials. Their first priority and their principal institutional function is to stabilize and halt a crisis, namely to stop the haemorrhaging of capital and boost liquidity levels. This objective is interpreted as a technical task and assumes primacy over other more strategic objectives. The following sections consider some of the forces and considerations that were interacting in the formulation of US Treasury policy and impacting upon the calculations and strategy of US Treasury officials. Together, these factors demonstrate that the exercise of US power in response to financial crises, although still pronounced, is subject to more constraints and is less straightforward than is often assumed.

The institutional mandate and position of the US Treasury Department

It is widely accepted that the Treasury Department is the lead agency in generating US international financial policy. Two particular responsibilities are key to Treasury power in international financial policy. The first of these is control of the exchange stabilization fund (ESF), a war chest for purposes of foreign exchange market interventions and currency stabilisation. In normal times, the Treasury would have relative discretion and autonomy in the deployment of ESF resources. However, at the start of the Asian crisis, Congress had curbed ESF funding following the Mexican bail out of 1995 through the so-called D'Amato restrictions. The second responsibility is that the Treasury is the principal representative of the US government to the IMF – international lender of last resort and financial fire fighter that provides liquidity to countries experiencing capital flight. US policy towards the IMF is formulated by the Treasury Secretary, who represents the US government at IMF ministerial meetings. Moreover, the US National Executive Director at the IMF, who represents the US on the IMF's board of directors – the body that oversees the day to day running of the Fund – although independent in principle, is in practice answerable to Treasury officials. US IMF policy might be overseen and implemented by the Executive Director, but policy is generated by the US G7 deputy and the Treasury Secretary (Baker 2006a). Long serving Treasury officials are unable to recall an occasion when the Executive Director openly defied the deputy, or took independent action (confidential interview February 1998).

As the largest shareholder and financial contributor to the IMF, US Treasury policy is sometimes simply read as IMF policy. It may be true that it would be unlikely for a matter to be deliberated at the IMF board without US Treasury approval (Woods 2000). Consequently, the Treasury has something approaching a power of veto on IMF matters, but this does not mean the US always get its own way on IMF policy. Treasury officials acknowledge that IMF staff views tend to be similar to their own, but they are quick to deny that the IMF is merely the handmaiden of the US and emphasize that other states can influence the IMF, while IMF staff themselves have some degree of independence (confidential interviews with officials, February and March 1998). In this sense the Treasury cannot control the IMF. The Managing Director of the IMF enjoys a significant degree of independence and Treasury officials would see their role as supporting the Managing Director in his activities (Interview with official February 1998). For example, in the lead up to the announcement of the $55 billion package of IMF assistance for South Korea in December 1997, Michel Camdessus was engaged in intensive negotiations with the South Koreans. US involvement came through a telephone call from Rubin to Camdessus, urging him to maintain a tough negotiating stance and emphasising the importance of a strong programme (Rubin and Weisberg 2003: 234). This stance appears to have been motivated by a very real US fear that Camdessus may have responded to intense South Korean pressure for a much weaker package. Suasion, encouragement and moral support for a tough IMF negotiating stance were the principal means through which the US exerted influence in the initial negotiations between the Fund and Asian countries.

Later in December 1997, Treasury official David Lipton was the first US government official to visit Kim Dae-jung in Seoul following his election victory to ascertain his commitment to a programme of market based neo-liberal economic reforms. Certainly the Treasury encouraged Dae-jung to procced in this direction and provided the carrot of a US supported private sector bail-in and the rolling over of loans as an incentive for a commitment to a reform programme. Larry Summers also visited Indonesia in January 1998, but the dialogue with President Suharto only lasted an hour and Suharto dominated the conversation. Ultimately, the package drawn up for Indonesia was put in place by Camedssus in consultation with Indonesian officials, especially respected economist Widjoyo Nitisastro, who led the negotiations and devised some of the more controversial structural reform measures (Rubin and Weisberg 2003: 247).

While control of the ESF and representing the US government at the IMF are the two principal levers open to the Treasury to conduct US international financial policy, it is difficult to define the precise nature of Treasury power and responsibility. The reason for this is that the precise role of the Treasury in international financial affairs is not tightly defined, and Treasury authority fluctuates over time in accordance with the individuals in key positions – their own reputation, and at any one time the relations with and between the White House, the State Department, the Department of Defense and the Council of Economic Advisers. Under Summers and Rubin, Treasury gained a reputation as an intellectual powerhouse that to a large extent defined many of the major policy trajectories of the Clinton Administration during the high water mark of neo-liberal globalisation (Harvey 2003). This was largely due to the commanding personalities and formidable intellect of that Treasury team and a Democrat electoral campaign that prioritized economic policy successes. In contrast, the Bush administration engineered a partial securitization of foreign economic policy due to perceived security threats, and the re-emergence of a military industrial complex challenging neo-liberal corporate America (Harvey 2003; Higgott 2003). In accordance with this, the Treasury under Paul O'Neill enjoyed nowhere near the same standing, authority, autonomy and role in foreign policy making as the Summers-Rubin Treasury, but part of this was also because O'Neill lacked the market credibility and experience that Rubin enjoyed.

Most crucially, however there is a general sense that the Treasury has a responsibility for maintaining international financial stability and should assume principal responsibility for formulating US policy for managing international financial disturbance. Indeed, in the case of the Asian crisis, Treasury officials almost universally cited that their first priority was to stop the crisis and work out what would be most effective in restoring market confidence. Stopping the contagion and restoring normal markets and economic recovery was the overriding Treasury priority, not least because of fears of the effects contagion would have for the world economy more generally and for US economic performance (confidential interviews with officials, February and March 1998). For example, the Treasury was of the view that contagion had a ripple effect. US commercial and investment banks that had little exposure to South Korea, could still find themselves troubled if they had heavy exposure to Japanese banks that were in turn heavily exposed to South Korea (Rubin and Weisberg 2003: 231).

Treasury officials contended that the most assured way of stopping capital flight was reform in crisis affected countries that restored market confidence. In other words, the principal impetus behind US policy was not a long term strategy designed to deliver market opening and cheap assets for US commercial concerns, but a sense of duty among Treasury officials that their fundamental responsibility and most pressing concern was to stop the crisis and its ripple affects, and the subsequent beliefs officials held about the most effective means of doing this. Ultimately, such was the institutional culture at Treasury, with the prominence of professionally trained economists, that Treasury officials by and large viewed themselves as technicians engaged in the task of correcting faults in the international financial system and constituent national financial systems.

Accordingly, Treasury and the foreign policy arm of the Clinton administration viewed the crisis from quite different perspectives. Madeline Albright's principal concern was the relationship with important military allies such as South Korea, and the reaction the crisis might draw from North Korea. The State Department line was that the handling of the crisis by Treasury was paying insufficient attention to geo-political concerns and Albright and her staff argued strongly for financial assistance being dispatched quickly to South Korea through the ESF. For Treasury the priority was economic stability which in turn would ensure any geo-political goals could be accomplished. The Treasury view was that any financial assistance had to be dependent on an adequate commitment to reform by the South Korean government. Providing money without such a commitment would in the Treasury view not only reduce their leverage in getting the country to adopt a programme that would work, but also undermine the likely economic success of any financial aid package. For Treasury Secretary Robert Rubin:

> The immediate imperative was to overcome the crises in the various countries. In our view that needed to be done in the context of market based economics and globalization, which had served developing countries well, and meant re-establishing the confidence of domestic and foreign creditors and investors (Rubin and Weisberg 2003: 255).

Despite Treasury's lead role, the US policy response to the Asian situation was formulated through an intra-agency process consisting of a daily conference call between Treasury, NEC, NSC, State, Defense and Commerce. However, trade and commerce officials, who were far more attuned and sensitive to the needs of American business were very much on the margins of this process and their efforts to draw Treasury attention to direct commercial concerns in crisis affected countries were on the whole rebutted. Instead, the Treasury focus was on what would work and which faults needed to be corrected to restore market confidence. This in turn was largely viewed as a process of technical reform.

Throughout the handling of the crisis the Treasury was hampered by the refusal of Congress to pass legislation for an $18 billion contribution to a total $90 billion increase to Fund resources. As more countries fell victim to the spreading financial market contagion, these resources were urgently needed. Congressional failure to pass the legislation to increase IMF funding had two significant impacts on the Treasury. First, at a time when the Asian financial crisis was at its peak, Treasury officials were involved in a time consuming and energy sapping exercise to persuade Congress to pass the legislation. One senior official estimated that in the first half of 1998, 50 per cent of his staff's time was spent testifying to Congress, whereas in normal times this would be closer to 20 per cent. Consequently, Treasury officials were distracted from the task of responding to the Asian crisis as their attentions were diverted towards fighting an exhausting domestic political battle. This limited the energies which Treasury officials could devote to IMF country programmes. Secondly, Congressional refusal to make the money available undermined US ability to influence Fund staff and reduced the weight and credibility of US officials involved in deliberations on future Fund policies. Other governments, and the IMF itself, were less inclined to listen to the views of a state that had failed to keep to its stated financial obligations. Ultimately, while the institutional mandate and culture of the Treasury caused officials to view the response to the crisis as a technical matter of correcting faults and restoring financial stability, Treasury autonomy to act was restricted by an uncooperative Congress and a strong IMF that enjoyed more independence than is often assumed.

Ideology, knowledge and beliefs

Identifying the fundamental intellectual propositions, beliefs, ideas and normative values that informed the decisions and actions of leading Treasury officials is essential to a balanced understanding of what drove the US policy response to the Asian economic crisis. The overriding belief held by senior Treasury officials was that liberalized capital markets were good for the global economy and overall global welfare, with the benefits believed to show up in higher rates of growth, wages, returns to capital and standards of living (Summers 1999). It was from this basic premise that all policy proceeded. Consequently, the use of capital controls, beyond some limited support for Chilean style controls on short-term inflows into banking systems, was never seriously contemplated (Summers 1996; Cohen 2003). Throughout the crisis, support for and protection of the principle of open capital markets was the starting point and defining feature of US policy. Moreover, this basic assumption about the merits of financial liberalisation meant that the US response to financial crisis invariably centred on the restoration of market confidence in the country concerned through national market friendly reforms – what Paul Krugman has termed 'the confidence game.' (Krugman 1999; Cohen 2001). Playing the 'confidence game' involves the implementation of policies that have market 'credibility', such as commitment to monetary and budgetary rectitude and structural reform of financial and labour markets (Balls 1998; Baker 2005) Automatically, therefore, the emphasis in the crisis resolution approach of the US Treasury was on the reforms implemented by national authorities in crisis affected countries, and in return for such pledges and commitments, financial assistance was provided multilaterally through the IMF, or bilaterally from Treasury funds in accordance with the principle of 'conditionality', as financing was released in stages, conditional upon the implementation of a reform package.

The Treasury position has been that financial crises are triggered by a loss of confidence by market players (Rubin and Weisberg 2003: 258).

Such a loss of investor confidence can be caused by underlying macroeconomic or structural problems, or a sudden re-evaluation by investors of the attractiveness of a country. In the Asian case, the Treasury view was that the distorted nature of Asian markets was one of the problems and that relationships between banks and corporate borrowers were too close, while self dealing, protectionism, corruption and lack of transparency were serious problems that impeded rational investment. The practice of 'direct lending,' whereby government officials would tell banks to whom to extend credit, was a cause of particular concern (Rubin and Weisberg 2002: 233–4). Eradication of this practice was certainly a priority for the Treasury as was the limiting of foreign investment and competition, which was seen to inhibit market discipline and protect certain firms from failure. All of these 'faults' meant in Treasury eyes that investors and creditors were suddenly surprised by the revelation of concealed problems (Rubin and Weisberg 2003). The repeated theme in US Treasury policy was to place the onus onto governments in crisis affected countries: 'only when sound policies were pursued would confidence – and capital investment – return and economic recovery take place' (Rubin and Weisberg 2003: 219).

Basic neo-liberal beliefs emphasising the value of macroeconomic discipline, market restructuring, regulatory reform and enhanced transparency were the principal lens through which the financial crises of the late twentieth century were viewed by the US Treasury. These views do, to an extent, have a certain political convenience (Baker 2006a) because the US and its economic constituencies have been the principal beneficiaries of a liberalized financial order (Cohen 2003), and because such beliefs also enable the principal responsibility for resolving crises to be deflected onto national authorities in affected countries (Blyth 2003). We should not, however, underestimate the degree to which senior officials at the Treasury hold a genuine intellectual commitment to the beliefs behind this position. That is to say neo-liberal ideas are not promoted by the Treasury simply because of a strategic, instrumental political calculation that they are in US interests, but ultimately as a consequence of a basic intellectual faith in the efficiency of free markets (Bleaney 1985; Blyth 2003). This basic intellectual faith in liberalized capital markets and their economic virtues was at the root of the Treasury response.[1] Free markets were viewed as a superior form of economic organisation. Enhanced transparency and better information were consequently seen as the best solution to tackling market distortions because markets were expected to react to information more rationally and revise prices accordingly, if the information they received was more timely, accurate and frequent (Best 2005; Baker 2005). On the basis of these beliefs Treasury policy emphasized enhanced transparency, macroeconomic discipline and structural reform as the principal elements of reform to be implemented in crisis affected countries following the Asian crisis.

In accordance with such an intellectual commitment to these basic beliefs, the three top international officials at the Treasury during the Asian crisis all had professional economics training and were to all intents and purposes professional economists. They arrived at policy decisions on the basis of intellectual deliberation and an assessment of available data based on their familiarity with certain economic theories, models and concepts. This is not to say that political considerations were entirely absent from discussions, merely that assessments of the economic evidence and perceptions of what constituted good economics, i.e. those policies most likely to restore market confidence and to have market credibility, assumed primacy over more strategic political objectives or calculations.[2]

Deputy Secretary Lawerence Summers and Under Secretary David Lipton were Harvard trained PhD economists of a neo-classical orientation, with Summers an award winning academic economist, before he moved to a position at the World Bank. Lipton spent eights years at the IMF, dealing with countries in financial distress. One place further down the hierarchy, at Assistant Secretary, Tim Geithner held an MA in International Economics and East Asian Studies from John Hopkins. Even Treasury Secretary Robert Rubin had completed a thesis on hyper-inflation in Brazil, before becoming an arbitrage trader and later partner at leading Wall Street institution Goldman Sachs. This economic background was integral to the professional identity of Treasury officials as economists and they couched policy debates and decisions in the language of economics. Throughout the Asian crisis, the Treasury sought to continuously emphasize the technical economic aspects of handling the crisis to both the President and the State Department, repeatedly arguing that financial crises could not be viewed solely in geo-political terms (Rubin and Weisberg 2003). Rubin's own view is that his Treasury team was comprised of 'extraordinarily well qualified figures in the field of international economics . . . our group would sit around for hours and intensely debate the merits of this or that policy option the way people might in an academic seminar' (Rubin and Weisberg 2003: 229).

Economic beliefs and ideas were clearly a key motivating force driving Treasury policy, but to what extent were these ideas instrumental constructs, employed and put into practice because they benefited US commercial concerns? Hypothetically at least, financial liberalisation should benefit European and Japanese institutions as much as US ones, and Treasury officials routinely make this point, when pressed on the issue (confidential interviews with officials, February and March 1998). Indeed, as Robertson has pointed out, an ideational attachment to liberalisation and free markets can just as easily produce outcomes detrimental to the position of US corporations. Korean bank privatisations for example, saw the American owned Cerberus outbid by Korean banks, but the US Treasury was happy with the outcome, precisely because it brought the withdrawal of the Korean government from the banking sector (Robertson 2007). In this case, the principal impetus for Treasury policy was not concern for commercial opportunities and gain for US institutions, but ideological and ideational – a determination to minimize the role of government intervention and to let market forces take their course. These kind of reforms were seen as the most reliable route to the restoration of market confidence and to enhanced economic efficiency and performance, which were viewed as the priorities by Treasury officials, rather than any potential gains for American firms as a consequence of 'fire sales'.

Clearly the availability of cheap assets brought about by the crisis and subsequent policies of privatisation, regulatory and financial market reform did offer opportunities for foreign investors. However, many of the bold predictions concerning the transfer of assets into US hands, made by strong US power interpretations of the Asian crisis, did not materialize. As Robertson (2007) points out, the majority of assets that became available in Korea and Thailand were principally in areas such as chemicals, machinery and retail banking, in which US firms did not compete in the international economy. Ultimately, US pressure for liberalisation in Asia often resulted in significant market share going to other foreign firms, rather than American enterprises. In other words, strong US pressure for reform in Asia was not necessarily part of an orchestrated, self interested campaign, but rather was the result of a genuine Treasury belief in the value of neo-liberal policies as a means to resolving the crisis and restoring market confidence.

In this respect, the initial, almost reflexive, response of the US Treasury to the Asian crisis was to de-cry 'crony capitalism' in an effort to cement the dominance and superiority of American values. This response was generated almost instinctively by officials who were committed to and schooled in beliefs and methods emphasising the benefits of freer markets and foreign competition. However, there was also a more strategic, opportunistic motivation evident at the ideational level, in the sense that the Asian crisis represented an opportunity to discredit the Asian developmental state model and present neo-liberal development strategies as the 'only alternative'. This in turn was expected to strengthen the IMF's negotiating capacity and the institution's capacity to impose conditionality in the region and to dispense advice to policy makers, who not only required a source of capital, but whose position had seemingly been weakened and undermined by a failing economic model and a series of policy and regulatory failures.

While these rather simplistic calculations clearly influenced the initial US response in terms of the discourse surrounding the crisis, the US Treasury position did soften over time as the crisis unfolded, and as deliberations with G7 partners proceeded, particularly as Japanese concerns registered with US officials as the crisis continued (Baker 2006a). A more sophisticated position emerged in which the Treasury maintained that the developmental state model was flawed, but that the reckless behaviour of international investors and an international financial system characterized by inadequate transparency had also contributed to the crisis. A review of the international financial architecture followed, including some emphasis on the principle of private sector burden sharing and experimentation with collective action clauses. An ideational faith in market friendly reforms so as to enhance market confidence was however a consistent intellectual influence on US Treasury policy in the handling of the Asian crisis. Moreover, this was reflected in IMF policy towards Asia, indicating significant Treasury influence on post-crisis restructuring in Asia. However, the biggest single reason for Treasury influence on the Fund was the correspondence in the beliefs held by IMF staff and Treasury (Momani 2005). Ultimately, reforms and policies were advanced out of a genuine faith in their merits as a solution to financial disturbance in Asia, rather than for strategic, calculated material gain for American firms.

Treasury–private sector relations

Clearly Treasury's capacity to control the process of responding to financial crises is subject to a number of ideational and institutional constraints. However, the principal weakness in the Treasury–Wall Street thesis on American power is the overestimation of the harmony and coherence of Treasury–Wall Street relations. Whether this is expressed in terms of Treasury capacity to orchestrate and steer Wall Street hedge funds in a form of hedge fund warfare (Gowan 1999), or the notion that the Treasury is almost entirely beholden to Wall Street (Wade 1998; Bhagwati 1998), there is a tendency for the closeness of Treasury–Wall Street relations to be overstated.

First, Treasury–Wall Street consultations are more informal, ad hoc and less well established than is frequently assumed. The Treasury–Wall Street complex thesis simply assumes a closeness between New York and Washington, yet the social basis of this apparent network is never probed in any rigorous systematic fashion.[3] The motivations and mind sets of Treasury officials and how they reach decisions need to be subjected to closer scrutiny if the Treasury–Wall Street complex thesis is to be taken seriously. Too often this state-society coalition is simply assumed to exist and questions of how it is constituted, the extent to which various Wall Street interests have captured the Treasury at any one given time and of how Wall Street interests come to be represented in Treasury foreign policy, if indeed they are, are overlooked. Future research needs to dissect the claims of the Treasury–Wall Street complex and subject them to closer scrutiny. Secondly, there is insufficient differentiation between different economic sectors in the assessment of what constitutes US commercial interests in most strong American power accounts.

Taking the first of these problems, channels of communication with Wall Street institutions are surprisingly ad hoc. In crisis situations, individual Treasury officials do have informal conversations with some of the larger institutions. Such informal conversations are primarily information gathering exercises (confidential interview with official, February 1998) and the existence of these Treasury–Wall Street interactions should not be interpreted as evidence that Treasury policy was being designed by the needs and demands of Wall Street. Neither are they indicative of an all powerful Treasury strategically guiding Wall Street decision-making in a *de facto* extension of economic statecraft. Treasury Secretary Robert Rubin outlined the circumspect and cautious nature of Treasury Wall Street communications as follows:

> During all my time at Treasury, I was very conscious of market sensitivity and avoided discussing Treasury matters with friends in New York, many of whom still worked in the financial markets. . . . But Treasury and Fed officials do need to understand what market participants are thinking, which requires listening carefully to what people are saying, as well as monitoring what markets are doing (Rubin and Weisberg 2003: 278).

Market communications often take an altogether more generalized form, with officials seeking to monitor trends and price movements for signs of excess and to subsequently identify the psychology and thinking that is the cause of such volatility. What results from such a loose monitoring process is a form of symbolic communicative diplomacy, in which officials express their concerns to markets in public statements that make references to how market movements relate to economic data and future projections (Baker 2005, 2006a, b). The other side of these symbolic state-market communications is the so-called 'confidence game' in which public authorities put in place certain policies and institutional frameworks to engender market confidence and obtain credibility with investors (Krugman 1998; Sassen 2002; Baker 2005). This form of symbolic diplomacy and strategic signalling has undoubtedly provided Wall Street and international investors more generally with a significant means of influencing public authorities in the US and beyond and it has been highly effective in producing market friendly policy and regulatory arrangements. This 'confidence game' has also been the principal means of Wall Street influence and is at the root of Wall Street and US financial power. However, direct Wall Street lobbying of the Treasury on specific issues is relatively rare and the Treasury is unlikely to respond directly, although this is not to say that Treasury officials do not have a general sense that market opening and free markets are in US interests and contribute to world and US economic growth.

Treasury communications with Wall Street did intensify on the issue of rolling over loans, extending due dates and converting short-term obligations to longer-term ones in the case of South Korea in late 1997. Banks however did not act on their own and Treasury had to act as a catalyst. Chase Manhattan, Morgan Stanley and Citibank all eventually got together and organized US banks that had exposure in Korea (confidential interview with official, February 1998), but they made this decision reluctantly and would have been unwilling to take this action without Treasury pressure. In reality, the Treasury had relatively little leverage to induce the banks to co-operate beyond moral suasion explaining that rolling over loans would be in their collective self interest and threatening to name and shame reluctant parties (Rubin and Weisberg 2003: 238). Such examples illustrate the difficulties Wall Street institutions had in co-operating and defining a collective self-interest.

In this respect, the notion that some sort of Treasury–Wall Street complex comprises a coherent US foreign policy-business nexus is a simplification. In reality, Wall Street–Treasury interactions are ad hoc and disjointed. Notwithstanding the intra-agency consultative process in which it participates, the Treasury enjoys a significant degree of autonomy from wider social forces, and tends to act on the basis of technical views about what will work in a particular set of circumstances. There is no doubt that the Treasury is closer to the concerns of the US financial services industry than other socio-economic interests, but these interests are themselves diverse and the extent of that closeness is generally overestimated. For example, Treasury officials were dismissive of the efforts of the US Trade Representative to draw attention to the commercial interests that the US had in Asia, choosing instead to focus on technical questions of crisis management and resolution. More generally, the Treasury received relatively little in the way of direct lobbying from business on the question of managing the Asian crisis and Treasury officials often felt isolated in their appreciation of the potential damage financial contagion could wreak, particularly in the face of a recalcitrant and sceptical Congress.

The notion of strategic US opportunism in Asia engineered by a Wall Street-Treasury complex is further undermined when we consider the kind of sectors Asia specialised in and the opportunities they represented. By and large the cheap assets that could be acquired in Asia were in assembly intensive manufacturing production line activities, whereas US foreign direct investment (FDI) has increasingly specialised in technology and science intensive areas – aerospace, pharmaceuticals and finance. Asia represented limited opportunities in these areas. Consequently, US firms did not buy up significant shares of banking and industrial sectors in Asia, and European firms acquired more businesses in post-crisis Korea and Thailand than other foreign firms (Robertson 2007).

US benefits in Asia after the crisis primarily accrued to investment banks such as Goldman Sachs, JP Morgan, Merill Lynch and Morgan Stanley which offered a variety of services in the aftermath of the crisis, handling privatisations and public offerings, overseeing sales of distressed assets, mergers and corporate restructurings. Private equity funds marshalled by GE Capital and Goldman Sachs also bought up assets in a series of short-term investments before selling them for significant return, but this kind of activity eventually led to falling levels of total US FDI (Robertson 2007). Crucially however, such instances of commercial US opportunism were not part of an orchestrated strategy by the Treasury and the US government, rather they were simply an element of the individual commercial strategies of certain American equity funds and investment banks.

Ultimately, references to an influential Treasury–Wall Street complex are something of a caricature. There can be no doubt that the Treasury and Wall Street both represent significant centres of influence in contemporary global financial governance, but the extent and strength of any alliance is a great deal more informal and incidental than is often appreciated. There is relatively little in the way of continuous channels of communication or institutionalized lobbying between the Treasury and Wall Street. Wall Street's power primarily results from the ideas and beliefs leading policy makers hold about financial and economic governance in an era of globalization and the emphasis these ideas place on policy makers obtaining credibility with international investors and the subsequent 'confidence game' that results. It is the socially constructed imperatives of symbolic signalling between authorities and markets that brings policy and institutional frameworks into line with the broad preferences of Wall Street for macroeconomic discipline, liberalized financial systems, minimal government intervention and regulatory regimes based on transparency.

Resource scarcity

A particular constraint on the Treasury in the handling of the Asian crisis was the problem of scarce resources. Not only was Treasury impeded by the actions of Congress – the restrictions placed on the ESF and refusal to pass IMF legislation – but after more than a decade in which the virtues of small government had been pledged, Treasury resources were far from limitless. By 1998, there were between 80 and 90 officials working in the Treasury's international section (confidential interview with official, February 1998), although the immediate team focused on the financial crisis in Asia was smaller still and centred around the office of the Deputy Assistant Secretary for international monetary and financial policy – the largest and most important sub division within the international section of the Treasury. Nevertheless, the Treasury had at most 40 officials to cover the range of issues thrown up by the Asian financial crisis and IMF policy, and the section also had to compete with five other sub divisions for resources and personnel.

Resources were stretched as more and more countries were affected by contagion and also by time consuming negotiations with Congress to pass legislation to increase IMF funding. Treasury capacity to micromanage the response to the Asian financial crisis was therefore severely restricted by budgetary and human resource constraints. Certainly the limited number of officials the Treasury was able to devote to issues arising from the crisis compared unfavourably to the IMF and meant that the Treasury did not have the capacity to control, or approve every last detail in country programmes. For example, throughout the Asian crisis Korea was viewed as the most significant Asian market, and the most important for US interests (confidential interview with Federal Reserve official, March 1998), yet the Treasury never had more than three officials focused on Korea at any one time and by the autumn of 1998 attention had switched to Latin America, leaving one official playing little more than an occasional monitoring role in relation to the progress of the Korean reform programme (Robertson 2007).

Treasury resources were stretched to the maximum by the spate of financial crises in 1998, and the image of the all powerful Treasury, orchestrating and restructuring the global political economy in its own image is divorced from reality. Treasury officials dealt with numerous issues simultaneously, often on a rotating basis. Attention and priorities shifted to reflect a volatile and rapidly changing financial world and resources were consequently spread thinly. An image of the Treasury running to stand still is closer to reality. In this regard, Treasury Secretary Robert Rubin's constant refrain that the tools for dealing with crisis were not 'as modern as the markets' captured the essence of Treasury's resource problems.

Conclusions

In response to the first question posed at the outset of this chapter, there can be little doubt that US influence featured prominently in the management of the Asian financial crisis, even if this is often overstated in strong versions of the American power thesis, or at least the constraints on the US government have often been underestimated. US power and pressure were repeated features of the response to the Asian crisis, but the Treasury did not dictate the conditions in IMF programmes. The Treasury did however lend support to IMF staff and encouraged them and the Managing Director to drive a hard bargain in negotiations with crisis affected countries. In this respect, the Treasury engaged in an interactive, deliberative process with Fund staff and with other major creditor governments in designing IMF rescue packages and the conditionality attached to them. The principal source of Treasury influence on the Fund and its officials was through a shared world view, which meant Fund policies and approaches tended to meet with Treasury approval and were compatible with the intellectual prejudices of Treasury officials, rather than through more explicit Treasury pressure or control of the Fund. Treasury views carried weight because of the personal reputations and intellectual capability of its officials, as much as because of IMF funding arrangements and US contributions, although this factor is obviously far from irrelevant in IMF politics.

The chapter has also pointed out how at key points in the crisis, Treasury capability and capacity to drive a market re-structuring process in Asia was undermined by the actions of Congress and the problem of resource scarcity. Nevertheless, the Treasury was the key US actor in formulating a response to the crisis and enjoyed a relative degree of autonomy from wider societal forces in formulating the US policy response. In this respect, the biggest influences on Treasury policy were the overriding ideas and beliefs of leading officials and what they perceived to be the most feasible technical solutions for averting the crisis and stopping capital flight – generally neo-liberal market based reforms.

In relation to the second question, the ideas and beliefs that guided the actions and decisions of Treasury officials were not simply instrumental, or strategic constructions. Treasury officials appeared to have a genuine intellectual faith in the value of what might be loosely termed neo-liberal ideas and policy prescriptions, as described in the third section of this chapter. The implementation of those ideas has given rise to a specific set of social and political interactions that can be termed the 'confidence game', in which governments in crisis affected countries have to implement a series of market friendly reforms in order to attain 'market credibility'.

The discussion in this chapter has also revealed that we need to be wary of the claims of the strong American power thesis concerning the operation of the so-called Treasury–Wall Street complex. The Treasury operated on the basis of a general calculation that open markets were good for the world economy, world growth, US growth and generally represented opportunities for US enterprises. Nevertheless, US firms did not benefit disproportionately from market opening and restructuring in Asia, while instances in which Asian companies obtained assets ahead of American firms, were still applauded by the Treasury for ideological reasons, because they brought a retreat in state intervention. Moreover, European companies, rather than American firms, were the biggest beneficiaries given the nature of investment opportunities in Asia. The American opportunism that was evident in Asia appeared to be the result of the individual commercial strategies of leading US investment and equity funds, rather than as a consequence of a grand strategy orchestrated by the Treasury.

Finally, the Treasury–Wall Street complex thesis generally overestimates the closeness of relations between the Treasury and Wall Street and the degree of co-ordination that takes place between the two. Communications are surprisingly disjointed, informal and ad hoc, and in this respect, the notion of a Treasury–Wall Street complex is something of a caricature.

Treasury views do count, and on the whole they are generally favourable to Wall Street institutions, but this is not because of some tightly woven state-societal pact, or close knit institutionalized iron triangle. Relatively little formal lobbying of the Treasury by commercial interests took place over its handling of the Asian crisis. Rather, as we have seen, the ascendancy of neo-liberal ideas, in both the Treasury and the IMF, has been the most significant determining factor on the form the policy response to the Asian financial crisis took. A Treasury–Wall Street complex of sorts may exist, but it is not a coherent network orchestrating and setting international financial policy, with clear pre-conceived policy priorities and strategies. Wall Street does appear to have very general preferences for macroeconomic discipline, market re-structuring, regulatory reform and enhanced transparency, but it is the ideas about finance that advocate such policies, and result in a form of 'confidence game,' as a series of socially constructed power relations, that has been the most powerful force in bringing about these preferences. Moreover, these ideas are held by the Treasury, not because they reflect Wall Street preferences, or because the Treasury operates on behalf of Wall Street, but because of a genuine intellectual commitment to them based on officials' formal economics training.

Notes

1. Of course this raises question as to whether economic ideas and supposedly technical knowledge are ever entirely value free. Crucially, however, Treasury officials rationalized their commitment to policies in terms of economic theories and ideas, rarely if ever making the connection with US commercial interests.
2. This is to not to say that judgements reached were anything less than subjective, or that the decision to prioritize market confidence as the principal economic policy goal was not a political decision in its own right. For a discussion of this in the context of macroeconomic policy, see Baker (2005).
3. Serious political science has had relatively little to say on Treasury–Wall Street relations, the basis and nature of them in relation to international financial policy, although more popular commentaries have broached the subject see Phillips (1994).

3
Crises as Catalysts for Foreign Bank Activity in Emerging Markets

Robert Cull and María Soledad Martínez Pería

Introduction

Since the mid-1990s, banking sectors in many developing countries have experienced some important transformations. Key among them has been a rapid increase in the degree of foreign bank participation. Between 1995 and 2002, the average share of banking sector assets held by foreign banks in 104 developing countries rose from 18 per cent to 33 per cent.[1]

Many studies have examined the causes and implications of foreign bank participation. The contribution of this chapter is to survey the existing literature and to focus on the role of crises in serving as a catalyst for the entry of foreign banks into developing countries. The empirical analysis that follows shows that countries that experienced a banking crisis from 1995 to 2002 tended to have higher levels of foreign bank participation than those that did not. Moreover, foreign participation tended to increase as a result of crises rather than prior to them. However, post-crisis increases in foreign participation did not tend to coincide with improved provision of credit to the private sector, in part because foreign entrants often acquired distressed banks with a high share of loans that needed to be written off. By contrast, in countries where the level of foreign participation was relatively high and stable, private credit levels were significantly higher than in other countries before, during, and after crises.

The chapter is organized as follows. The first section examines the trends in foreign bank participation among developing countries. The second section reviews the existing literature on the causes and implications of foreign bank participation. The third section examines the relationship between crises and foreign bank participation in developing countries and the last section concludes.

Trends in foreign bank participation

Statistics on the average share of banking assets held by foreign banks in developing countries over the last decade disguise important regional differences, as well as differences within each region. This section describes levels and trends in foreign bank participation across regions and also discusses the degree to which recent changes in foreign bank participation are common to most countries in each region or are driven by only a few.

As shown in Figure 3.1, between 1995 and 2002 foreign bank participation increased primarily in Eastern Europe and Central Asia, Latin America, and Sub-Saharan Africa. By 2002, close to 40 per cent of assets in all three regions were in the hands of foreign banks. On the other hand, in Asia and in the Middle East and Northern Africa, foreign bank participation remained low – close to 10 per cent of banking sector assets – and stagnant throughout the period.

Even among the three regions where the share of assets held by foreign banks has been rising there are some differences both in the levels of foreign bank presence and in the speed with which it has increased in recent

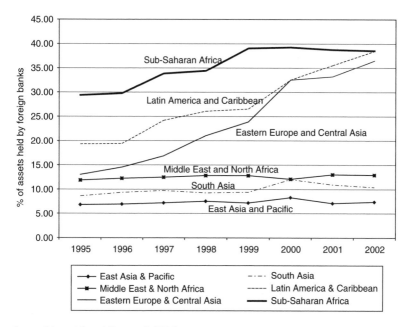

Source: Adapted from Micco *et al.* (2006).

Figure 3.1   Foreign bank participation across regions, 1995–2002

years. For example, whereas the average level of foreign bank participation during 1995–2002 was highest in Sub-Saharan Africa, both the absolute and relative increases in the share of assets held by foreign banks have been most significant in Eastern Europe and Central Asia and in Latin America. The share of assets held by foreign banks in Sub-Saharan Africa rose by 9 percentage points from 30 per cent in 1995 to 39 per cent in 2002. This represents a 1.3 times increase. In Eastern Europe and Central Asia the share of assets held by foreign banks roughly tripled from almost 13 per cent in 1995 to 39 per cent in 2002. In Latin America, foreign bank participation nearly doubled, going from 19 per cent to 37 per cent over this period.

In Africa, many of the foreign banks have been operating since colonial times, whereas entry in Eastern Europe and Latin America has been more recent. Most of the entry of foreign banks in Eastern Europe and Central Asia has resulted from the privatization of state-owned banks following the fall of communism in the region. The largest five foreign banks with operations in Eastern Europe and Central Asia are KBC Bank (Belgium), Erste Bank (Austria), HVB Group (Austria), Société Générale (France) and Unicredito Italiano (Italy). There are regional specializations of some foreign banks: large Scandinavian banks like Swedbank and Skandinavska Enskilda have the markets of the Baltic States, and Greek banks such National Bank of Greece, Piraeus Bank, Alpha Bank, and Emporiki Bank of Greece are present in the Balkan countries. At the same time, Austrian banks – Erste Bank, HVB Group and Raiffeisen – control large shares of banking assets in most Eastern European and Central Asian countries, with the exception of the Baltic States. In Latin America, entry has been driven by foreign bank acquisitions of domestic banks. In particular, two Spanish banks – Banco Santander Central Hispano and Banco Bilbao Viscaya Argentaria (BBVA) – have been particularly aggressive in acquiring banks in the region. However, other non-Spanish banks such as Citibank from the US and HSBC from the UK also have an important presence in the region.

East Asia had the lowest levels of foreign bank participation throughout the period 1995–2002 and also exhibited the smallest increase. The share of assets held by foreign banks was close to 7 per cent throughout the entire period. In terms of levels of foreign bank presence, South Asia follows East Asia as the region with the lowest levels of foreign bank participation. In South Asia, the share of assets held by foreign banks was almost 9 per cent in 1995 and rose to 12 per cent in 2000 only to drop to 10 per cent by 2002. Finally, foreign bank participation in the Middle East and North Africa was close to 12 per cent in 1995 and barely rose to 13 per cent by 2002.

Table 3.1 presents detailed information on the share of assets held by foreign banks in each of 104 developing countries. This allows us to

Table 3.1 Foreign bank participation in developing countries, 1995–2002

Table shows the share of assets (as a % of total banking sector assets) held by foreign banks

	1995	1996	1997	1998	1999	2000	2001	2002
Developing countries	*18.1*	*18.5*	*21.2*	*22.6*	*24.5*	*28.9*	*30.5*	*32.7*
East Asia & Pacific	*15.0*	*14.5*	*15.1*	*14.6*	*12.6*	*8.2*	*7.7*	*11.7*
Cambodia						8.5	8.3	7.9
China	0.0	0.0	0.0	0.0	0.0	0.0	0.1	0.2
Indonesia	4.4	4.7	5.8	6.0	3.0	5.7	4.1	3.9
Korea, Rep.	2.1	2.1	2.2	5.0	4.7	7.6	4.9	9.2
Malaysia	24.9	24.9	25.0	26.0	23.1	25.4	22.7	22.8
Mongolia					0.0	7.1	11.3	45.3
Papua New Guinea	71.7	67.0	70.3	63.9	63.1			
Philippines	7.9	8.2	8.5	8.3	8.6	9.4	9.8	8.3
Thailand	7.2	6.9	7.1	6.5	10.2	9.0	7.3	6.7
Vietnam	1.4	1.8	1.7	1.0	0.8	1.0	1.0	0.9
Europe &	*13.0*	*13.3*	*14.7*	*18.2*	*21.1*	*28.4*	*32.7*	*35.7*
Central Asia								
Albania						10.9	15.6	19.7
Armenia			17.6	24.6	34.9	49.3	60.1	59.1
Azerbaijan	0.0	0.0	0.0	0.0	0.0	0.0	0.0	
Belarus	0.0	0.0	0.0	7.2	4.3	3.8	8.4	9.5
Bosnia and Herzegovina		5.3	6.5	7.4	12.4	34.0	46.1	45.1
Bulgaria	8.2	10.3	10.3	19.5	30.9	70.1	55.5	51.7
Croatia	9.8	13.6	14.1	14.6	15.8	19.1	20.6	42.1
Czech Republic	14.2	10.6	13.7	17.3	31.0	48.9	61.4	58.7
Estonia	80.7	78.9	72.1	74.0	73.5	73.1	73.0	72.7
Georgia		10.6	7.7	6.4	4.8	20.0	35.8	36.2
Hungary	22.4	23.1	42.1	62.9	67.8	63.5	63.3	58.7
Kazakhstan	12.6	10.6	15.8	18.7	18.6	11.7	12.6	20.0
Kyrgyz Republic						30.3	33.3	20.8
Latvia	17.8	30.4	32.7	35.3	37.0	37.6	38.6	38.8
Lithuania	18.9	28.4	35.5	36.9	41.8	62.5	92.2	91.3
Macedonia, FYR	28.4	27.1	25.8	23.3	23.6	47.8	43.8	41.8
Moldova		1.6	1.8	1.8	2.5	7.9	18.8	18.3
Poland	3.7	8.4	13.8	27.1	34.1	37.8	50.7	49.3
Romania	0.0	0.2	0.5	12.9	17.2	25.9	27.0	26.5
Russian Federation	2.0	1.4	2.7	2.1	4.5	11.5	13.7	15.6
Serbia and Montenegro						0.0	0.0	0.0
Slovak Republic	8.7	11.9	18.0	20.4	21.5	54.6	56.6	81.5
Slovenia	6.8	6.5	6.4	6.5	6.1	10.3	14.3	25.8
Turkey	0.4	0.3	0.3	0.4	0.5	0.9	1.8	1.8
Ukraine	0.0	0.0	0.0	0.0	2.3	5.8	6.2	6.8
Uzbekistan			0.0	0.0	0.0	0.6	0.6	0.8

(Continued)

Table 3.1   (Continued)

	1995	1996	1997	1998	1999	2000	2001	2002
Latin America &	*19.3*	*19.4*	*24.3*	*25.0*	*25.4*	*29.6*	*30.2*	*33.2*
Caribbean								
Antigua and Barbuda						0.0	0.0	0.0
Argentina	25.6	28.1	36.7	40.0	39.6	47.8	44.2	37.5
Bolivia	42.7	40.5	39.7	44.4	44.2	40.9	39.4	39.4
Brazil	9.0	9.7	14.4	15.1	17.3	26.4	30.4	27.9
Chile	31.0	35.3	36.0	37.6	38.8	38.4	40.0	44.8
Colombia	6.3	10.9	15.9	18.0	16.4	25.8	21.1	17.4
Costa Rica	0.0	0.2	0.6	5.1	5.0	18.0	18.4	18.8
Dominican Republic	11.1	10.8	9.9	2.0	17.5	16.2	17.7	17.5
Ecuador			26.0	27.4	28.2	0.0	0.0	0.0
El Salvador	1.0	1.8	2.9	8.3	8.3	13.6	13.5	14.2
Guatemala	6.0	5.6	6.1	6.3	7.0	8.4	8.6	8.1
Guyana	0.0	0.0	24.7	27.5	26.7	23.5	23.6	23.1
Haiti				0.0	0.0			
Honduras	2.3	2.1	2.1	1.5	1.5	4.4	5.0	5.8
Jamaica	24.3	21.2	32.9	35.8	21.9	18.9	19.3	50.3
Mexico	2.3	4.3	7.2	7.5	9.9	28.5	30.0	61.9
Nicaragua	0.7	1.4	3.0	3.9	3.8	5.1	4.3	4.4
Panama	59.7	54.9	51.5	50.8	48.4	64.9	64.2	58.1
Paraguay	69.3	56.2	73.9	76.8	77.2	79.9	81.7	83.3
Peru	51.7	59.5	63.1	66.1	64.8	66.1	66.7	86.4
Trinidad and Tobago	14.0	13.5	16.2	17.1	17.7	11.2	10.4	10.4
Uruguay	24.3	14.2	18.1	24.4	30.6	91.8	95.5	94.5
Venezuela, RB	4.8	17.4	29.1	33.7	34.3	20.7	30.2	26.6
Middle East &	*11.9*	*12.3*	*12.5*	*12.8*	*12.8*	*14.4*	*15.9*	*18.8*
North Africa								
Algeria						59.0	67.5	60.0
Egypt, Arab Rep.	4.0	6.0	6.1	6.1	6.2	6.9	6.4	7.1
Iran, Islamic Rep.						0.0	0.0	
Jordan	12.8	12.4	12.9	12.8	12.8	13.5	13.7	13.3
Lebanon	29.6	29.4	29.4	31.5	31.2	30.5	28.9	28.0
Libya						0.0	0.0	
Morocco	18.6	19.3	19.5	19.8	20.4	16.9	17.3	16.4
Oman	0.0	0.0	0.0	0.0	0.0	0.0	8.0	8.7
Tunisia	10.8	11.0	11.5	11.7	11.9	12.1	14.9	14.8
Yemen, Rep.	7.3	7.8	8.2	8.0	7.3	5.0	2.0	2.4
South Asia	*8.6*	*9.4*	*9.7*	*9.3*	*9.4*	*12.0*	*10.9*	*10.4*
Bangladesh	0.0	0.0	0.0	0.0	0.0	0.0	0.0	0.0
India	0.9	1.1	1.3	1.3	1.3	1.7	1.4	0.5
Nepal	38.9	41.7	42.0	39.4	40.0	52.8	46.7	45.4
Pakistan	1.4	1.5	2.3	2.4	2.4	3.4	4.3	6.0
Sri Lanka	2.2	2.5	3.1	3.2	3.3	2.3	2.4	0.3

Table 3.1   (Continued)

	1995	1996	1997	1998	1999	2000	2001	2002
Sub-Saharan Africa	30.2	28.7	32.4	33.1	37.4	45.3	45.3	45.0
Angola							38.1	43.0
Benin		49.4	48.2	46.0	46.0		51.8	53.1
Botswana	79.6	79.5	79.7	80.7	83.0	84.2	84.7	84.0
Burkina Faso				44.4	43.8	24.4	29.4	30.4
Burundi	39.2	37.3	37.6	37.2	36.4	16.2	23.6	21.5
Cameroon			65.4	64.0	63.9	54.9	56.7	59.0
Cote d'Ivoire	20.3	19.7	20.0	23.8	53.6	58.3	62.8	61.8
Ethiopia	0.0	0.0	0.0	0.0	0.0	0.0	0.0	0.0
Ghana	28.4	29.9	53.8	53.9	57.6	64.7	52.1	52.8
Kenya	26.6	27.6	27.6	29.4	28.6	31.6	34.4	36.0
Lesotho						84.9	86.1	86.3
Madagascar	42.3				63.3	62.1	61.4	62.0
Malawi		8.9	8.2	8.1	8.9	33.7	27.5	27.9
Mali	41.1	41.3	40.6	40.3	40.8	57.6	49.9	48.9
Mauritius	9.5	19.7	22.5	32.8	42.4	24.6	25.3	24.7
Mozambique		22.0	38.4	40.6	44.8	60.0	72.2	72.5
Namibia	45.2	42.6	35.5	33.8	35.3	47.4	68.6	66.9
Niger						51.0	51.1	43.7
Nigeria	10.1	10.1	10.1	9.5	12.5	15.0	10.5	11.2
Rwanda		22.4	22.8	21.1	23.7			
Senegal		43.1	42.5	42.6	42.8	42.3	40.9	39.1
Seychelles		12.6	13.1	13.6	13.8			
Sierra Leone			0.0	0.0	0.0	31.6	32.2	29.5
South Africa	0.3	0.2	0.2	0.2	0.2	11.4	10.4	10.8
Sudan	0.0	0.0	0.0	0.0	0.0	3.0	2.9	4.7
Swaziland						79.1	74.7	71.1
Tanzania		26.0	31.5	31.5	34.6	63.5	64.3	64.3
Uganda	39.7	38.5	36.3	69.8	76.0	53.8	53.9	55.4
Zambia	55.2	52.9	93.6	57.2	61.1	69.7	68.4	66.6
Zimbabwe	45.8	46.9	49.8	47.3	58.2	51.5	33.8	33.3

Source: Adapted from Micco *et al.* (2006).

examine more closely whether the regional trends described above were driven by most or only some of the countries in each region. In Sub-Saharan Africa, the increase in foreign bank participation was a fairly widespread phenomenon. Foreign bank participation increased in 22 out of the 30 African countries for which we have data on foreign bank participation. In Eastern Europe and Central Asia, the increase in foreign bank participation observed over the last decade was also quite pervasive. Out of 25 countries in the region for which we have data, the share of assets held by foreign banks increased in 22 of them. In Latin

America, foreign bank participation increased in 17 out of 23 countries in our sample. On the other hand, in the Middle East and North Africa region, the share of assets held by foreign banks increased significantly only in the case of Oman. Similarly, Nepal and Pakistan were the only two countries in South Asia where foreign bank participation increased between 1995 and 2002. Finally, with the exception of Mongolia, where the share of assets held by foreign banks rose significantly, in most other countries in East Asia, the share of assets held by foreign banks remained constant or declined over the 1995–2002 period.

Overall, the data on foreign bank participation suggest that regional trends in foreign bank presence were common to most countries within each region, with the share of assets held by foreign banks rising in Eastern Europe and Central Asia, Latin America and Sub-Saharan Africa, and remaining constant or declining in East Asia, South Asia, North Africa and the Middle East.

Survey of the causes and implications of foreign bank participation

This section reviews the literature on the causes and implications of foreign bank participation in developing countries. We summarize the existing evidence on the effects of foreign bank presence on efficiency, bank competition, stability, and access to credit.

What drives foreign bank participation?

To date the existing literature on foreign bank entry discusses the following factors as potential drivers of foreign bank participation: (a) banks' desire to service their customers abroad – the so called 'follow the clients' motive, (b) host-specific factors including market opportunities and regulatory barriers and (c) economic and cultural ties and institutional and regulatory similarities between home and host countries.[2]

An early strand of the literature on the decision by foreign banks to operate overseas focused on the experience of developed countries (especially the US) with foreign bank entry and bank internationalization during the 1970s and 1980s (see Goldberg and Saunders 1980, 1981a, b; Ball and Tschoegl 1982; Nigh *et al.* 1986; Cho *et al.* 1987; Hultman and McGee 1989; Goldberg and Johnson 1990; Goldberg and Grosse 1994; Fisher and Molyneaux 1996). A majority of these studies find support for the hypothesis that banks go abroad to service their domestic clients with overseas operations. While the evidence on the 'follow the clients' motivation seems solid when it comes to developed countries, there is less consensus as to its importance in driving foreign bank participation in developing countries. Most of the early studies that explored this hypothesis included few developing host countries in their sample. Furthermore, in one case where separate estimations were conducted for the sub-sample of developing countries (see Miller and Parkhe 1998), the authors could not find a significant link between FDI by non-financial firms and foreign bank activities in those countries.

Relative to the 'follow the clients' motivation, there is consistent evidence for the importance of local market opportunities in driving foreign bank participation. Using data on the location choices of 143 banks with at least one shareholding abroad across 28 countries (including 6 developing countries: Czech Republic, Hungary, Korea, Poland and Turkey), Focarelli and Pozzolo (2001) find greater foreign bank entry in countries where the expected rate of economic growth is higher. Analyzing 2,300 international bank mergers that took place between 1978 and 2000 in developed and developing countries, Buch and DeLong (2004) find that foreign banks tend to go to larger yet less developed economies, where there is the prospect for economies of scale and future growth opportunities. Similarly, looking into the FDI of German banks across 190 countries during the second half of the 1990s, Buch and Lipponer (2004) find that, other things equal, German banks are attracted to larger markets (in terms of GDP).

Many studies have also documented the importance of regulatory barriers in acting as an obstacle to foreign bank entry. In their study of international bank mergers, Buch and De Long (2004) find that banks operating in more regulated environments are less likely to be the targets of international bank mergers. Similarly, Focarelli and Pozzolo (2001) find that foreign banks prefer to invest in countries with fewer regulatory restrictions on bank activities. Looking at the foreign asset holdings of international banks that report data to the Bank for International Settlements, Buch (2003) finds that regulations are important in influencing the international asset choice of banks. Finally, focusing on the specific case of German banks' foreign assets holdings across countries, Buch and Lipponer (2004) find that if countries impose controls on cross-border financial credits, they receive less FDI from German banks and banks also perform fewer cross-border financial services in those countries.

The evidence on the importance of geographical proximity and economic and cultural similarities in driving foreign bank participation is quite overwhelming. Studies such as Buch (2003), Galindo *et al.* (2003),

Buch and De Long (2004), Buch and Lipponer (2004), and Claessens and Van Horen (2006) have shown that bilateral distance, sharing a border, speaking a common language, and having common colonial ties are all factors that influence foreign bank entry. There is also some evidence that similarities in the legal, regulatory and institutional environment matter, but there is less agreement as to whether absolute differences or differences vis-à-vis competitors are important. Galindo *et al.* (2003) argue that absolute legal, regulatory and institutional differences across countries can increase entry costs and reduce the participation of banks in foreign countries. Using bilateral foreign banking data for 176 countries, the authors find results that support their hypotheses. On the other hand, Claessens and Van Horen (2006) argue that what is important in driving foreign bank participation is not the difference between the institutional environment in the host and source country, but rather the difference taking into account the institutional quality of the competitors from other source countries. Using data for most banks in all developing countries, the authors find that absolute levels of institutional differences between the host and source countries do not matter once they control for the relative advantage the source country has compared to its competitors from other countries operating in the same host.

To summarize, there is substantial evidence that factors such as market opportunities, regulatory barriers in the host countries, along with economic, cultural and institutional similarities between home and host economies, influence the decision of banks to operate overseas. Contrary to the wealth of evidence on these factors, the role that crises can play in bringing about foreign bank participation has only been discussed anecdotally. For example, in discussing the rise in foreign bank participation in Argentina, Brazil and Mexico, Peek and Rosengren (2000) mention the Tequila Crisis in Mexico and Argentina and the 1999 Brazilian crises as catalytic events. Moreno and Villar (2006) also point to the experience of Mexico in stating that foreign bank entry might be stimulated by the need for countries to recapitalize their banking systems in the aftermath of crisis. Similarly, Tschoegl (2003) discusses the importance of crises in bringing about the subsequent entry of foreign banks in emerging markets focusing on 12 countries. Yet, solid empirical evidence on the role of crises is lacking. The goal of this chapter is to fill the gap in the literature by exploring the statistical association between crises and foreign bank participation. We turn next to the implications of foreign bank participation for the degree of competition, efficiency, stability and access to credit in the host countries.

What is the impact of foreign bank participation in developing countries?

Competition and efficiency

The promises of efficiency improvements and greater competition in the banking sector are perhaps the main arguments brought forth by proponents of foreign bank entry. As detailed below, with the exception of research that focuses on Latin America where the evidence is mixed, existing studies on the impact of foreign bank participation on efficiency and competition largely support the claim that foreign banks operating in developing countries are more efficient than domestic banks (i.e. have lower overhead costs), charge lower spreads, and help promote bank competition by pressuring other banks to lower their costs and their spreads.

Claessens *et al.* (2001), Claessens and Lee (2003), and Claessens and Laeven (2003) offer cross-country evidence of the benefits of foreign bank participation in terms of efficiency gains and greater competition. Using data for 80 countries from 1995 to 1998, Claessens *et al.* (2001) find that foreign bank participation is associated with a reduction in profitability, non-interest income and overhead expenses of domestic banks – results which they interpret as indications of greater efficiency and competition due to foreign bank participation. In a follow-up paper, Claessens and Lee (2003) focus on financial systems in 58 low-income countries. They find that the increased presence of foreign banks benefited the local banking sector by reducing financial intermediation costs making the banking system more efficient and robust. Following the Panzar and Rose (1987) methodology to obtain a parameter that quantifies the degree of competition in the banking sector in 50 countries between 1994 and 2001, Claessens and Laeven (2003) find that systems with greater foreign bank entry and with fewer activity and entry restrictions are more competitive.

A variety of country and regional case studies complement the cross-country literature on the impact of foreign bank participation on efficiency and competition. Using bank accounting data from Philippines for 1990–98, Unite and Sullivan (2002) investigate how foreign bank entry and increased foreign ownership of banks in that country affected bank efficiency and competition. The authors find that greater foreign bank entry reduced the interest rates and operating expenses of domestic banks, but not their profitability. They conclude that foreign competition forced domestic banks to be more efficient. Denizer (2000) studies the impact of foreign bank participation in Turkey between 1980 and

1997. The study shows that foreign bank entry had a positive impact on competition in the sector as witnessed by the decline in profits and overhead costs. Looking at the performance between 1995 and 2001 of 219 banks from a sample of ten countries in Central and Eastern Europe, Uiboupin (2004) offers evidence consistent with the notion that foreign bank entry increased competition in those countries.

In the case of Latin America, however, the evidence on the impact of foreign bank entry on bank competition and efficiency is mixed. Studying the competitive effect of foreign entry in Colombia, Barajas *et al.* (2000) find that foreign entry improved the efficiency of the domestic banking system by reducing nonfinancial costs. Focusing on Argentina, Chile, Colombia, and Mexico, Martinez Peria and Mody (2004) find that foreign bank participation did not affect spreads directly, but caused a drop in administrative costs. In the case of Mexico, foreign bank participation has not been found to increase competition and efficiency. Haber and Musacchio (2005) show that the entry of foreign banks led, instead, to a retrenchment in lending and no improvements in efficiency and competition. They argue that this is related to the fact that Mexico had an extremely concentrated banking system both before and after foreign bank entry. Focusing also on the case of Mexico, Schulz (2006) shows that foreign bank entry had no effect on administrative costs and employment levels. He too argues that this lack of impact on the overall efficiency of the sector can be explained as a result of limited competitive pressures. Finally, using data for eight Latin American countries, Levy Yeyati and Micco (2007) find that foreign bank penetration weakened competition in the region as measured by the H statistic proposed in Panzar and Rose (1987).

All in all, the evidence on competition and efficiency suggests that foreign bank entry can bring potential gains in this area except in environments which limit competitive forces such as when bank concentration is high, bank activities are restricted, and bank entry and exit is difficult.

Stability

The rise in importance of foreign banks in developing countries has led to an intense debate on the pros and cons of foreign bank participation in terms of its impact on banking sector stability. Those opposed to foreign bank participation argue that because foreign banks have weaker ties to developing nations and have more alternative business opportunities than domestic banks, they are more likely to be fickle lenders. Furthermore, there is also the potential that they could import shocks from their home countries. On the other hand, in favor of greater stability is the notion that foreign banks are typically well diversified institutions, with access to many sources of liquidity that will be less affected by shocks.

Though some studies have found that foreign banks can respond to shocks from their home countries (Goldberg 2002; Martinez Peria *et al.* 2005), a larger number of studies have found that they tend to be more stable lenders than domestic banks, in particular during periods of crisis in the host countries. Looking at the behavior of banks in Argentina and Mexico during the 1994–95 Tequila crisis, Goldberg *et al.* (2000) find that foreign banks generally had higher loan growth rates than their domestically-owned counterparts. Peek and Rosengren (2000) reach a similar conclusion after examining direct and cross-border foreign bank lending in Argentina, Brazil, and Mexico during 1994–99. Using bank level data for the late 1990s for Argentina, Chile and Colombia, Crystal *et al.* (2001) show that foreign banks on average exhibited higher loan growth rates than domestic banks. Examining the behavior of foreign and domestic banks in Malaysia during the 1997–98 Asian crisis, Detragiache and Gupta (2006) find no evidence that foreign banks abandoned the local market during the crisis. Finally, De Haas and van Lelyveld (2006) examine how foreign and domestic banks in ten countries of Central and Eastern Europe (CEE) reacted to business cycle conditions and host country banking crises from 1993 to 2000. Their results show that while during crises domestic banks contracted their credit, foreign banks maintained their credit supply.

Overall, the evidence available so far suggests that foreign banks can have a stabilizing influence on credit markets in developing countries, at least where financial sector depth is concerned. Next we turn to the impact of foreign bank participation on financial sector breadth or reach.

Access to credit

The extent to which foreign banks contribute to greater access to credit, in particular for small firms, in developing countries is perhaps the most controversial aspect of the process of foreign bank participation. Those opposing this process ague that foreign banks are likely to 'cherry pick' the most profitable and transparent customers. On the other hand, those in favor of foreign bank entry point out that foreign banks have access to a larger pool of loanable funds that can help them sustain higher levels of lending. Also, proponents of foreign bank participation argue that even if foreign banks focus on the most transparent firms, this process can enhance access to credit by smaller firms by forcing domestic banks to move down the market. The existing empirical evidence on the impact of foreign bank participation on access to credit is to date mixed.

Using data for 61,295 firms with 195,695 loans from 115 different banks in Argentina, Berger *et al.* (2001) find that smaller and more opaque firms are less likely to obtain loans from large or foreign-owned banks. Using data for 89 low income and lower middle income countries, Detragiache *et al.* (2005) find that a larger foreign bank presence is associated with shallower credit markets and slower credit growth. Focusing specifically on the case of Pakistan, using a panel of 80,000 loans over 7 years, Mian (2006) finds that foreign banks have shied away from lending to 'soft information' firms such as those that are small, located in rural areas, not affiliated with business groups, or seeking first-time loans and long-term relational financing.

Other studies have presented evidence that foreign bank participation may not always be pernicious for access to credit in host developing countries. Using bank-level data from Argentina, Chile, Colombia and Peru during the mid-1990s, Clarke *et al.* (2005) investigate whether bank origin affects the share and growth of lending to small businesses. While they find that on average foreign banks seem to lend less to small businesses, they also uncover significant differences between small and large foreign banks. In fact, at least in these countries, large foreign banks often surpass large domestic banks in their share and growth of lending to small businesses.

Some researchers have taken important steps towards incorporating firm-level data in their analyses. Giannetti and Ongena (2005) employ a large panel of almost 60,000 firm-year observations on listed and unlisted companies in Eastern Europe to investigate the impact of foreign bank lending on firm growth and financing. They find that foreign lending stimulates growth in firm sales, assets, and leverage. They conclude that large firms benefit more from foreign bank presence, but even small companies profit from foreign bank entry. Combining responses from a survey of over 3,000 firms operating in 35 developing countries with data on the degree of foreign bank presence across these countries, Clarke *et al.* (2006) find that all enterprises, including small and medium-sized ones, report facing lower financing obstacles in countries having higher levels of foreign bank presence, though the effect is smaller for small firms.

In summary, the evidence on the implications of foreign bank participation for access to credit suggests that foreign banks are generally less inclined to lend to small and opaque borrowers relative to domestic banks. Nevertheless, there is also evidence that their presence can have overall positive effects on access to credit, even if foreign banks themselves are not lending to small firms.

Foreign bank participation and crises

This section studies the link between foreign bank presence and crises. We begin by presenting data on the prevalence of banking crises and on the post-crisis levels of foreign participation across regions. Then, we use regressions to test whether countries that had crises also had higher levels of foreign participation in banking, and find that they did. Next, we offer panel regressions with country-level fixed effects that allow us to control for unobserved country characteristics and enable us to pinpoint better the timing of the increases in foreign bank presence. In this way, we can assess whether foreign participation occurred in response to banking crises. Finally, we offer panel regressions that test whether higher levels of foreign participation coincided with increased provision of credit to the private sector.

Crises and foreign bank participation: general patterns

Banking crises are a fact of life in developing economies. Since the mid-1990s, 77 crises episodes have taken place in 72 developing countries, including at least one country in each region of the developing world. Crises represent enormous challenges to policy-makers in developing countries and the costs of dealing with crises (e.g. paying for deposit losses, recapitalizing banks, and building banking systems that are more resilient to shocks) can be very large. Crises during the 1990s and early 2000s took their toll on developing economies and the data in Caprio and Klingebiel (2003) illustrate that in ten countries, out of thirty for which statistics are available, the fiscal cost of crises amounted to at least 15 per cent of GDP as a result of banking crises. Moreover, most crises have macroeconomic roots and take place in environments where governments have already difficult fiscal situations. Table 3.2 shows the average budget deficit to GDP in each region three years before and three years after crises. This table illustrates how even before the start of crises, governments in most regions were already running budget deficits, a fact that should have hampered their ability to deal with the cost of these episodes subsequently.

Yet, crises also represent opportunities for developing countries since they prompt governments to think differently and creatively about the problems they confront. In many developing countries, crises have

Table 3.2   Average budget to GDP before and after crises

Region	Average budget deficit to GDP 3 years before (%)	Average budget deficit to GDP 3 years after (%)
East Asia & Pacific	0.20	−1.24
Eastern Europe & Central Asia	−3.94	−4.18
Latin America & Caribbean	−3.94	−3.17
Middle East & North Africa	−7.08	−2.34
South Asia	−7.55	−5.95
Sub-Saharan Africa	−2.88	−3.64

Source: World Development Indicators (World Bank) and International Financial Statistics (IMF).

Table 3.3   Banking sector restrictions, 1995–2002: crises and non-crises countries

Country	Banking restrictions*
East Asia & Pacific	
Crises countries	3.5
Non-crises countries	3.21
Eastern Europe & Central Asia	
Crises countries	3.02
Non-crises countries	3.56
Latin America & Caribbean	
Crises countries	2.72
Non-crises countries	2.79
Middle East & North Africa	
Crises countries	3.25
Non-crises countries	3.47
South Asia	
Crises countries	3.81
Non-crises countries	2.88
Sub-Saharan Africa	
Crises countries	3.18
Non-crises countries	3.6

Note: *This table shows average values of a measure of banking sector restrictions for countries that had crises between 1995 and 2002 and those that did not. For each country, we take the average value of the index over the period. The index was developed by the Heritage Foundation with values from 1 to 5 where higher values indicate greater restrictions. This index considers: the ease with which foreign banks can open branches and subsidiaries, government interference in the allocation of credit including government ownership of banks, the ability of private banks to operate without government regulation such as deposit insurance, and the ability of banks to provide a wide range of financial services (including real estate and securities transactions, and insurance).

encouraged governments to deregulate their banking sectors and to allow the entry of foreign banks. Table 3.3 shows average values of a measure of banking sector restrictions across countries that had crises between 1995 and 2002 and those that did not. The index takes values from 1 to 5 with higher values representing greater restrictions. With the exception of Asia, countries that have experienced crises tended to be more open subsequently than countries that never experienced a crisis.

Though many studies have discussed the catalytic role that crises can play in promoting foreign bank participation in developing countries, few have offered systematic evidence to this effect. We begin by plotting the share of foreign bank assets in each region in a five year period following crises occurring between 1995 and 2002. Because crises did not occur in the same years in all countries, we date as 't' the first year of the crisis for each country and we take the average share of foreign bank participation at that point in time for each region. We compute regional averages for each year after the crisis within a five year window in the same manner.

We see from Figure 3.2 that crises in Africa, Latin America, and in particular, in Eastern Europe and Central Asia have been followed by an increase in foreign bank participation. On average, the share of assets held by foreign banks in Eastern Europe and Central Asia increased from 10 to 32 per cent within the five year period following crises. In Africa, foreign bank participation increased from an average of 32 per cent to almost 45 per cent five years after crises. In Latin America, the increase was smaller, with foreign bank participation increasing from 28 to 32 per cent.

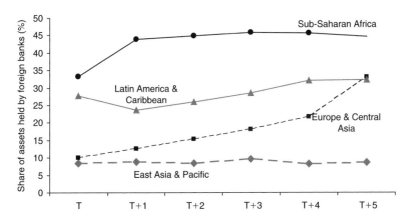

Source: Adapted from Micco *et al.* (2006).

Figure 3.2   Foreign bank participation across regions following banking crises

Crises and foreign participation: cross-country regressions

To further assess the role that crises play in promoting foreign bank participation we estimate equation (1), in which we regress the change in foreign bank participation between 1995 and 2002 on a dummy for whether countries had crises over this period along with a number of controls:

$$\begin{aligned}
\Delta\, Foreign\, Bank &= \alpha + \beta_1 Crisis_i + \beta_2'Macro_i + \beta_3 Banking\, Index_i \\
Participation_i &\quad + \beta_4 Property\, Rights\, Index_i + \beta_5 Market\, Size_i \qquad (1)\\
&\quad + \beta_6 Initial\, Foreign\, Participation_i + \beta_7'Regional \\
&\quad\ Dummies_i + \varepsilon_i.
\end{aligned}$$

$\Delta\, Foreign\, Participation$ is the change in the share of banking sector assets held by foreign banks in country i between 1995 and 2002. *Crisis* is a dummy variable equal to one if a country experienced a systemic banking crisis at any point during the period of study as defined in Caprio and Klingebiel (2003). *Macro* is a matrix of two variables, inflation and total output growth, intended to capture the attractiveness of an environment for prospective foreign entrants. Inflation is averaged over the period; output growth is the total change in real output from 1995 to 2002.[3] We expect foreign bank participation to increase with GDP growth because it reflects opportunities for the profitable provision of financial services (especially lending), and to decrease with the level of inflation because it reflects uncertainty and, perhaps, macroeconomic mismanagement by the government. Both of those factors make medium and long-term lending problematic.

The *Banking Index* is taken from the Heritage Foundation which reports a yearly assessment of the level of banking restrictions in a country. Among the restrictions that the Heritage Foundation considers in constructing this index are the ease with which foreign banks can open branches and subsidiaries; government interference in the allocation of credit, including government ownership of banks; the ability of private banks to operate without government regulation such as deposit insurance; and the ability of banks to provide a wide range of financial services (including real estate and securities transactions, and insurance). We would expect that more restrictive environments would be less receptive to foreign bank participation. For their part, foreign banks would also likely find it unattractive to enter restrictive environments. Thus, we expect a negative association between the *Banking Index* and *Foreign Participation*.

Property Rights Index measures the level of protection of private property in a country. Like the *Banking Index*, it ranges from 1 to 5 with lower values indicating better protection of property. In constructing this measure, the Heritage Foundation considers the extent to which the government protects and enforces laws to protect private property, the likelihood that the government will itself expropriate property, the existence of a commercial code, and the speed and efficacy of the judiciary in resolving contractual disputes. We expect foreign banks to be more prevalent in countries that better protect private property, and thus a negative relation between the index and foreign bank participation in the regressions that follow. Two advantages of the Heritage indexes are that the underlying methodology has been consistent over time and the country coverage is wide. We can therefore construct a balanced panel that captures the same concepts over time for a wide array of countries.

In some specifications we include a measure of market size, namely the log of GDP averaged from 1995 to 2002. Controlling for the quality of the macroeconomic environment and banking sector, foreign banks might find larger markets more attractive, and thus we expect a positive relationship between the log of GDP and foreign bank participation. We include the share of banking sector assets held by foreign-owned banks in 1995–96, *Initial Foreign Participation*, in some specifications to test whether foreign bank participation grew more rapidly in countries that had little foreign bank presence at the outset of the period. The intuition is that the process of foreign bank entry was already complete in countries with high foreign participation shares. We would therefore expect a negative relation between the level of foreign participation in 1995–96 and the subsequent change in foreign bank participation.

Finally, we include regional dummy variables in some specifications. As illustrated in the figures above, the level of foreign bank participation and its response to banking crises varied across regions, with relatively high levels in Africa, Latin America, and Eastern Europe and Central Asia as compared with East Asia and the Pacific, the Middle East and North Africa, and South Asia. Post-crisis increases in foreign bank participation also tended to be steeper in Africa, Latin America, and, especially, in Eastern Europe and Central Asia. We include the regional dummies to control for some of these differences in the evolution of foreign participation. We note, however, that these dummies are also likely to rob the banking crisis variable of some explanatory power since the occurrence and severity of crises also evince a regional pattern. We, therefore, view the models that include the regional dummies as a stricter test of the relationship between crises and foreign bank participation.

The main result from Table 3.4 is that countries that had banking crises tended to have larger increases in foreign bank participation than

Table 3.4 Cross-country regressions for the % change in foreign bank participation, 1995–2002

Explanatory variables	1	2	3	4	5	6	7	8
Banking crisis	0.1126	0.1114	0.1000	0.0745	0.1045	0.1168	0.0921	0.0777
	[2.24]**	[2.16]**	[2.02]**	[1.58]	[2.31]**	[2.30]**	[2.16]**	[1.70]*
Inflation	0.0006	0.0006	-0.0007	-0.0008	0.0004	0.0004	-0.0009	-0.0009
	[1.12]	[1.09]	[1.14]	[1.18]	[0.78]	[0.68]	[1.30]	[1.28]
GDP growth	0.0109	0.0109	0.0122	0.0123	0.0086	0.0088	0.0108	0.0111
	[2.57]**	[2.45]**	[2.88]***	[2.83]***	[1.78]*	[1.82]*	[2.34]**	[2.42]**
Banking index	-0.0571	-0.0574	0.0059	0.0075	-0.0760	-0.0789	-0.0208	-0.0156
	[1.27]	[1.26]	[0.15]	[0.21]	[1.63]	[1.68]*	[0.50]	[0.38]
Property rights	0.0215	0.0224	-0.0212	-0.0092	0.0208	0.0136	-0.0185	-0.0113
	[0.61]	[0.61]	[0.66]	[0.30]	[0.59]	[0.39]	[0.60]	[0.38]
Log average GDP 95–02 (constant GDP)		0.0006		0.0274		-0.0160		0.0156
		[0.04]		[1.48]		[0.98]		[0.94]
Initial foreign owned bank share (95–96)					-0.2398	-0.2959	-0.2722	-0.2298
					[1.64]	[1.83]*	[1.86]*	[1.62]
Dummy (East Asia & Pacific)			-0.2699	-0.3393			-0.8050	-0.3386
			[2.81]***	[2.93]***			[3.50]***	[3.41]***
Dummy (Europe and Central Asia)			0.1263	0.1008			0.0755	0.0691
			[1.93]*	[1.44]			[1.02]	[0.92]
Dummy (Latin America & Caribbean)			0.0199	-0.0128			-0.0277	-0.0372
			[0.31]	[0.20]			[0.38]	[0.51]
Dummy (Middle East and North Africa)			-0.1174	-0.1513			-0.1741	-0.1848
			[2.26]**	[2.83]***			[3.04]***	[3.13]***
Dummy (South Asia)			-0.1089	-0.1723			-0.1649	-0.1927
			[1.79]*	[2.22]**			[2.13]**	[2.20]**
Constant	0.1614	0.1464	0.1480	-0.4926	0.2698	0.6823	0.3112	-0.0801
	[1.61]	[0.39]	[1.52]	[1.11]	[2.21]**	[1.57]	[2.51]**	[0.20]
Observations	78	77	78	77	78	77	78	77
R-squared	0.13	0.12	0.36	0.39	0.17	0.18	0.41	0.42

Notes: Robust t statistics in brackets, * , ** and *** denote significance at 10%, 5% and 1%.

those that did not. The banking crisis coefficient is significant at the ten per cent level or better in all but one specification. In that model (column 4), it just misses significance. These findings confirm and expand upon those of Mathieson and Roldós (2001), who found a significant positive association between banking crises and various measures of foreign participation and foreign ownership of banks for fifteen countries over a shorter period (1995 to 1999). They find that, controlling for many of the same factors that we do in Table 3.4, foreign bank participation in 1999 (defined as we do) was 9.2 percentage points higher in countries that had a banking crisis. In our models, which are estimated over a much wider set of countries, foreign participation increased by 7.5 to 11.3 percentage points between 1995 and 2002 for countries that suffered a banking crisis.

As hypothesized, GDP growth is significantly positively related to foreign bank participation. In the specifications that include regional dummies (3, 4, 7, and 8) inflation is negative, as hypothesized, though the coefficient does not achieve significance. In almost all cases, neither the banking restrictions index nor the insecurity of property rights index is significant. The exception is the banking restrictions coefficient in model 6, which has the expected negative sign. The insignificance of the banking and property rights indexes might be because better (i.e. lower) scores on those indexes also indicate a healthier environment for private domestic banks, making it more difficult for foreign banks to enter and compete.

The initial level of foreign bank participation is negative and approaches or achieves significance in all specifications in which it is included (columns 4–8), which suggests that it is a relevant control variable. The coefficients for the regional dummies reflect the foreign participation patterns described above, with Asia and the Middle East lagging the omitted region, Africa. As anticipated, the inclusion of the regional dummies, and also market size and initial foreign participation, reduces the significance and magnitude of the banking crisis variable to some extent. However, in our most complete specification (column 8), the coefficient is significant at ten per cent and its magnitude (7.8 percentage points) is only slightly smaller than for the less complete models. The results in this sub-section indicate that, all else equal, banking crises are associated with increased foreign bank participation. Admittedly, however, cross-sectional regressions are not ideal for assessing whether crises actually caused those increases because of the potential for relevant omitted country characteristics that might drive both foreign bank participation and crises.

The timing of foreign bank participation: regressions with country fixed effects

To address the concerns with cross-country regressions and to better understand the timing of changes in foreign bank participation as a result of crises, we conduct panel estimations following equations (2) and (2′) below:[4]

$$\textit{Foreign Bank Participation}_{it} = \alpha_i + \beta_1 Crisis_{it} + \beta_2' Macro_{it}$$
$$+ \beta_3 Banking\ Index_{it} + \beta_4 Property \qquad (2)$$
$$Rights\ Index_{it} + \beta_5 Market\ Size_{it}$$
$$+ \beta_6' Year\ Dummies_{it} + \varepsilon_{it}.$$

$$\textit{Foreign Bank Participation}_{it} = \alpha_i + \beta_1 Crisis_{it} + \beta_2 Post\text{-}Crisis_{it}$$
$$+ \beta_2' Macro_{it} + \beta_3 Banking\ Index_{it}$$
$$+ \beta_4 Property\ Rights\ Index_{it} \qquad (2')$$
$$+ \beta_5 Market\ Size_{it} + \beta_6' Year$$
$$Dummies_{it} + \varepsilon_{it}.$$

In Table 3.5, columns (1)–(4) reflect the specifications following equation (2) where the crisis dummy identifies periods of crisis *vis-à-vis all* other periods (i.e. post and pre-crisis periods are lumped together). In the specifications that exclude the year dummies (columns 1 and 2), the level of foreign bank participation is 6–7 percentage points lower in crisis years. When we introduce the year dummies in columns (3) and (4), the reduction in foreign bank participation is only 2.2–2.4 percentage points, but the crisis variable remains significant at the 10 per cent level.

Columns (5)–(8) of Table 3.5 correspond to equation (2′). In this case, we separately control for crisis and post-crisis periods. When we do this, the crisis coefficient in models (5)–(8) is insignificant except for the positive, marginally significant coefficient in model (5). These results indicate that foreign banks did not reduce their participation in crisis years. Moreover, the positive significant coefficients for the post-crisis dummy in models (5)–(7) indicate that the steep increase in foreign participation occurred after crises had passed. In model (8), the post-crisis dummy is positive, but it does not achieve significance. Again, however, there are good reasons to exclude the year dummies from these specifications, in which case the most relevant model is (6), which shows a strong association between foreign participation and the post-crisis dummy. In addition, in model (8) the bank crisis dummy is negative and nearly significant. We can therefore nearly reject the null that the crisis and post-crisis dummies are equal to each other (F-statistic 2.13, p-value 0.12) for that model.

Table 3.5 Regressions with country fixed effects for the share of banking sector assets held by foreign banks

Explanatory variables	1	2	3	4	5	6	7	8
Banking crisis	-0.067 [4.41]***	-0.058 [4.63]***	-0.024 [1.80]*	-0.022 [1.85]*	0.059 [1.90]*	0.018 [0.74]	0.000 [0.01]	-0.035 [1.52]
Post-crisis					0.094 [6.85]***	0.075 [5.73]***	0.032 [2.41]**	0.019 [1.43]
Inflation		-0.024 [1.76]*		-0.043 [3.38]***		-0.002 [4.85]***		-0.001 [3.32]***
GDP growth		0.014 [1.26]		-0.034 [2.97]***		-0.003 [1.87]*		-0.001 [0.80]
Banking index		-0.002 [5.11]***		-0.001 [3.22]***		-0.025 [1.86]*		-0.042 [3.34]***
Property rights		-0.003 [2.06]**		-0.001 [0.60]		0.011 [1.04]		-0.034 [3.01]***
Dummy 1996			0.001 [0.09]	-0.008 [0.51]			-0.001 [0.08]	-0.007 [0.45]
Dummy 1997			0.029 [2.03]**	0.019 [1.22]			0.024 [1.57]	0.022 [1.35]
Dummy 1998			0.043 [3.12]***	0.027 [1.66]*			0.037 [2.50]**	0.029 [1.78]*
Dummy 1999			0.059 [4.38]***	0.045 [2.88]***			0.053 [3.59]***	0.048 [2.99]***
Dummy 2000			0.107 [7.34]***	0.104 [6.38]***			0.1 [6.24]***	0.104 [5.98]***
Dummy 2001			0.12 [7.77]***	0.12 [6.79]***			0.113 [6.70]***	0.123 [6.61]***
Dummy 2002			0.134 [7.67]***	0.134 [7.05]***			0.126 [7.35]***	0.135 [6.84]***
Constant	0.274 [46.13]***	0.338 [6.99]***	0.197 [16.45]***	0.451 [8.61]***	0.193 [10.62]***	0.292 [5.97]***	0.185 [10.28]***	0.455 [8.32]***
Observations	713	640	713	640	713	647	713	647
Number of countries	102	99	102	99	102	99	102	99
R-squared	0.04	0.13	0.25	0.32	0.09	0.14	0.25	0.31

Notes: Robust t statistics in brackets, *, ** and *** denote significance at 10%, 5% and 1%.

In short, models (5)–(8) indicate that foreign banks did not retreat during crises, and increased their participation in the aftermath of crises. Thus, the negative crisis coefficients in models (1)–(4) are attributable to the high levels of foreign participation in post-crisis years rather than low levels in crisis years (relative to pre-crisis years).

Many of the control variables are more highly significant in the fixed effects regressions in Table 3.5 than they were in the cross-country regressions in Table 3.4. For example, inflation is significantly negatively related to foreign participation in all models in which it appears, as hypothesized. Similarly, the coefficients for restrictions in banking and the insecurity of property rights are significant and negative in multiple specifications. However, GDP growth is not robustly associated with foreign bank participation, and the negative significant coefficient in model (4) is unexpected. This could be due to collinearity between GDP growth and other regressors (most notably inflation).

Discussions about whether foreign banks have behaved opportunistically in response to crises are often inconclusive because they hinge on how opportunism is defined. For example, if one defines as opportunistic a foreign bank profiting from its participation in stable periods and retreating during crises, the results in this section indicate that banks have not behaved opportunistically. However, our results could be consistent with foreign banks acquiring cheap domestic banking assets as a result of crises, which could be viewed as opportunistic. We refrain from drawing that conclusion for two reasons. First, the acquisition of distressed banking assets by foreign interests is often viewed as beneficial by regulators and supervisors coping with the aftermath of a crisis. Indeed, those officials often look to foreign investors to help re-capitalize their banking sectors because they lack other options due to the fiscal constraints discussed above. Second, the post-crisis increase in foreign participation might not be due to acquisitions or de novo entry, but to more rapid growth of the assets of the pre-crisis roster of foreign banks relative to domestic ones.

Foreign participation, crises, and private credit

One potential negative by-product of crises is the destruction of information generated via long-term relationships between borrowers and failed banks. Even in the case where banks are not closed but are merged or acquired, a disruption in lending relationships might result from the restructuring and reorganization that typically takes place within banks following mergers and acquisitions. Since they are at a relative disadvantage in local knowledge, foreign banks, and particularly recent entrants, might not be well suited to reconstituting such relationships. Thus, while our evidence indicates that the asset share of foreign banks has increased after crises, it does not necessarily follow that greater participation has gone hand in hand with more lending. In this section, therefore, we examine whether foreign bank participation coincided with increased provision of credit to the private sector, especially after crises. We use fixed-country-effects specifications similar to those in Table 3.5, except that the level of private credit relative to GDP is the dependent variable:[5]

$$\begin{aligned} Private\ Credit_{it} = \alpha_i &+ \beta_1 Post\text{-}Crisis_{it} + \beta_2 FOB\ share_{it} \qquad (3)\\ &+ \beta_3 Post\text{-}Crisis{*}FOB\ share_{it} + \beta_6{'}Macro_{it}\\ &+ \beta_6 Banking\ Index_{it} + \beta_7 Property\ Rights_{it}\\ &+ \beta_8 Market\ Size_{it} + \beta_9{'}Year\ Dummies_{it} + \varepsilon_{it}. \end{aligned}$$

The positive significant coefficients for the post-crisis variable in columns 1 and 2 of Table 3.6 indicate that private credit levels tend to be higher in the aftermaths of crises, which could be taken as a sign of recovery. In addition, the positive, significant coefficients for *FOB Share* in those specifications indicate that increased foreign participation is associated with higher levels of private credit (relative to each country's average private credit level over the period). However, the negative significant coefficient for the *FOB*post-crisis* interaction is similar in magnitude to the positive *FOB share* coefficient. Thus, the positive association between foreign participation and the extension of credit to the private sector pertains only to the pre-crisis and crisis periods.

Because these results might be driven by how we specified the post-crisis dummy variable, columns (5) and (6) use the crisis and post-crisis dummies that we used in Table 3.5 in the regressions above. Inclusion of both of those dummies provides a more precise comparison between private credit levels in the pre-crisis, crisis, and post-crisis periods. Though the crisis dummy is positive and weakly significant in one specification, the post-crisis dummies remain positive and highly significant, indicating that the increase in private credit levels occurred in the post-crisis period. The pre-crisis and crisis periods tend to be statistically indistinguishable from one another. With the inclusion of the crisis dummy the foreign bank participation variable remains positive, though it loses some significance. The *FOB*post-crisis* interaction remains negative and highly significant. If anything, the results in columns (5) and (6) provide a stronger suggestion that, in the aftermath of crises, high foreign bank participation levels are associated with lower private credit levels.

Does this imply that foreign banks pull back from lending as a result of crisis? Not necessarily because, as noted above, it could be that foreign banks are acquiring distressed banks with relatively weak loan portfolios. Many of those loans are written off in restructuring exercises prior to the sale of banks to foreign investors, and thus the reduction in private credit is a mechanical accounting exercise rather than a reflection of slow post-crisis credit growth. The negative, significant results for the *FOB*post-crisis* interaction could be picking up these selection effects.

To test for that possibility, we try to distinguish between established banks and recent entrants by introducing a new variable: the interaction between the level of foreign participation at the beginning of the sample period and the post-crisis dummy. If *FOB share* is close to *initial FOB*, the level of foreign participation has remained relatively constant throughout the sample period. In those environments, we hypothesize that foreign banks are better established. By contrast, environments where foreign participation is much higher than it was initially are likely to be characterized by the recent acquisitions of distressed banks described above. We expect therefore that the negative association between foreign participation and private credit in the post-crisis period will be smaller (in absolute value) in countries where initial and post-crisis foreign participation levels are close to one another. In other words, if our conjectures are correct, we expect a positive coefficient on the *initial FOB*post-crisis* interaction.

In columns (3) and (4) of Table 3.6, we include the initial FOB interaction in specifications with only one crisis variable, the post-crisis dummy. That dummy remains positive and significant. *FOB share* remains positive in those specifications, while the *FOB*post-crisis* variables remains negative. Both are highly significant. As hypothesized, the *initial FOB*post-crisis* interaction is positive and significant. When *FOB share* and *initial FOB* are equivalent, the two interaction terms roughly cancel out one another. In those cases, there is no post-crisis reduction in private credit, and thus the positive association between *FOB share* and private credit holds for all periods (pre-crisis, crisis, and post-crisis). The same pattern holds when we introduce the crisis dummy in columns (7) and (8). In short, these results are consistent with the idea that post-crisis reductions in private credit in countries with high levels of foreign bank participation are due to the recent acquisitions of troubled domestic banks. We cannot, however, rule out the possibility that the newly arrived banks are simply poorer financial intermediaries for the private sector. In environments where foreign banks are better established, there is no such reduction. Indeed, foreign participation appears

Table 3.6 Regressions with country fixed effects: dependent variable, credit to the private sector/GDP

Explanatory variables	1	2	3	4	5	6	7	8
Banking crisis	0.046 [3.56]***	0.047 [3.35]***	0.038 [2.97]***	0.040 [2.92]***	0.048 [1.77]*	0.045 [1.64]	0.045 [1.69]*	0.043 [1.56]
Post-crisis					0.043 [3.18]***	0.045 [3.10]***	0.037 [2.85]***	0.039 [2.82]***
FOB share	0.086 [2.49]**	0.069 [2.02]**	0.127 [3.35]***	0.122 [3.03]***	0.064 [1.82]*	0.056 [1.59]	0.121 [3.13]***	0.117 [2.88]***
FOB × post-crisis	-0.094 [2.79]***	-0.094 [2.74]***	-0.208 [3.82]***	-0.214 [3.83]***	-0.084 [2.49]**	-0.085 [2.46]**	-0.202 [3.68]***	-0.208 [3.69]***
Initial FOB × post-crisis			0.202 [3.62]***	0.209 [3.68]***		0.198 [3.53]***	0.198 [3.59]***	0.205
Inflation	0.000 [0.23]	0.000 [0.32]	0.000 [0.91]	0.000 [0.40]	0.000 [0.63]	0.000 [0.14]	0.000 [0.79]	0.000 [0.30]
GDP growth	-0.003 [3.54]***	-0.003 [3.22]***						
Banking index	0.003 [0.37]	0.002 [0.23]	0.002 [0.36]	0.002 [0.31]	0.002 [0.29]	0.002 [0.26]	0.002 [0.27]	0.002 [0.24]
Property rights	-0.016 [2.01]**	-0.016 [2.01]**	-0.014 [1.79]*	-0.014 [1.76]*	-0.015 [1.92]*	-0.015 [1.87]*	-0.015 [1.89]*	-0.015 [1.85]*
Concentration		-0.090 [2.41]**		-0.063 [1.81]*		-0.059 [1.67]*		-0.058 [1.65]
Constant	0.282 [9.39]***	0.352 [7.99]***	0.267 [9.14]***	0.313 [7.34]***	0.258 [7.65]***	0.303 [6.49]***	0.245 [7.38]***	0.288 [6.13]***
Observations	559	541	554	536	554	536	554	536
Number of countries	79	79	79	79	79	79	79	79
R-squared	0.09	0.1	0.1	0.11	0.09	0.09	0.11	0.12

Notes: Robust t statistics in brackets, *, ** and *** denote significance at 10%, 5% and 1%.

to have a positive effect on private credit provision regardless of the occurrence of crises.

One might object to our characterizing all environments where foreign participation remained relatively constant as having relatively well-established foreign banks. In some countries, foreign participation remained negligible throughout the period, and thus foreign participation should have had little or no effect on private credit levels. To test whether it is countries with low, stable levels of foreign participation that are responsible for the results in Table 3.7, we restrict the sample to countries that exceeded various thresholds of initial foreign participation (5 per cent, 10 per cent, and 20 per cent). Because it splits the sample into groups of roughly equal size, the results for the 10 per cent threshold appear in Table 3.7. Qualitative results are similar for the 5 per cent and 20 per cent thresholds.

The pattern of significant results found in Table 3.7 – i.e. positive for *FOB share*, negative for *FOB*post-crisis*, and positive for *initial FOB*post-crisis* – is only found for countries that had initial foreign participation above 10 per cent (Table 3.7, columns (1) and (2)). For countries with initial participation less than 10 per cent (columns (3) and (4)), none of the foreign bank participation variables is significant. Therefore, the results in Table 3.6 are being driven by countries that had reasonably high levels of foreign participation, and, within that group, the positive relationship between foreign participation and private credit is due to those with participation levels that remained relatively constant over time. The results in Table 3.7, therefore, provide additional support for the idea that, in the aftermath of crises, better established foreign banks provide more credit to the private sector than recent foreign entrants, perhaps because those entrants tend to acquire distressed banks. For countries with low levels of participation, the foreign ownership variables explain little variation in private credit levels, as one would expect.[6]

To summarize the results from this section, we find that countries that experienced at least one banking sector crisis from 1995 to 2002 tended to have more foreign bank participation than those that did not. Moreover, the timing of the increases indicates that foreign participation often increased in response to crises. However, post-crisis increases in foreign participation do not appear to be associated with improved provision of private credit. We hypothesize that this could be because recent foreign entrants tend to acquire distressed banks with loan portfolios in need of deep restructuring (i.e. write-offs). We cannot, however, rule out the possibility that the new entrants are simply poor intermediaries for the private

Table 3.7 Split-sample tests, regressions with country fixed effects, dependent variable is credit to the private sector/GDP

Explanatory variables	Sample Initial FOB >= 10%		Sample Initial FOB < 10%	
	1	2	3	4
Banking crisis		−0.006		0.054
		[0.35]		[1.73]*
Post-crisis	0.022	0.022	0.067	0.067
	[0.85]	[0.84]	[3.84]***	[3.85]***
FOB share	0.12	0.121	0.102	0.098
	[2.79]***	[2.68]***	[1.51]	[1.45]
FOB × post-crisis	−0.224	−0.225	−0.14	−0.126
	[3.16]***	[3.11]***	[1.55]	[1.38]
Initial FOB × post-crisis	0.233	0.234	−0.663	−0.752
	[3.27]***	[3.23]***	[1.21]	[1.30]
Inflation	−0.001	−0.001	0	0
	[3.34]***	[3.28]***	[0.83]	[0.83]
GDP growth	−0.002	−0.002	−0.003	−0.003
	[1.25]	[1.25]	[2.82]***	[2.39]**
Banking index	−0.016	−0.016	0.022	0.022
	[2.18]**	[2.18]**	[1.87]*	[1.86]*
Property rights	0.013	0.013	0.03	−0.033
	[1.17]	[1.17]	[2.62]***	[2.73]***
Concentration	−0.067	0.066	−0.053	−0.035
	[1.37]	[1.36]	[1.07]	[0.69]
Constant	0.271	0.274	0.328	0.29
	[5.93]***	[6.04]***	[4.82]***	[3.96]***
Observations	285	285	251	251
Number of countries	43	43	36	36
R-squared	0.2	0.2	0.13	0.15

Notes: Robust t statistics in brackets, *, ** and *** denote significance at 10%, 5% and 1%.

sector. By contrast, countries with reasonably high and stable levels of foreign participation tend to have higher private credit levels than others before, during, and after crises.

Conclusions

This chapter has described the recent trends in foreign bank ownership in developing countries, summarized the existing evidence on the causes and implications of foreign bank presence and re-examined the link between banking crises and foreign bank participation. We find that foreign bank participation has risen strongly in two regions of the world: Eastern Europe and Central Asia and Latin America. Foreign bank presence has increased in Africa as well, but at a generally slower pace than in the other two regions. By contrast, foreign bank participation has remained stagnant or even declined in East and South Asia and in the Middle East and North Africa.

The literature on the drivers of foreign bank participation points to factors such as market opportunities, and cultural, regulatory and institutional similarities. In terms of the implications of foreign bank participation, the existing evidence suggests that foreign banks tend to foster efficiency and competition in the sector (except in cases of high banking concentration or when restrictions on banking activities are present), bolster banking sector stability, but may or may not improve access to credit.

Our empirical analysis shows that countries that experienced a banking crisis from 1995 to 2002 tended to have higher levels of foreign bank participation than those that did not. Additional regressions indicate that foreign participation tended to increase as a result of crises rather than prior to them. However, those post-crisis increases in foreign participation did not coincide with improved provision of credit to the private sector. We speculate that this was because foreign entrants acquired distressed banks with a high share of loans that needed to be written off. By contrast, in countries where the level of foreign participation was relatively high and stable, private credit levels were significantly higher than in other countries before, during, and after crises.

Notes

We are grateful to Soledad Lopez for outstanding research assistance. The views expressed in this chapter are those of the authors and not those of the World Bank.

1. These statistics come from Micco *et al.* (2006), arguably the most reliable time series, which is constructed from Bankscope data. We exclude developed countries and off-shore centers. If we take the average over the 72 countries for which information exists for each year between 1995 and 2002, the average participation in developing countries is not substantially different. It rose from 17 to 31 per cent.
2. These factors are also highlighted by Clarke *et al.* (2003). The main difference is that we cite evidence based primarily on foreign entry into developing countries. They primarily refer to literature on foreign bank activities in the US and other developed countries.
3. The construction of these variables is intended to minimize the influence of yearly observations that are outliers. In the fixed effects regressions in the next section, which are of necessity based on yearly observations, we remove

observations for inflation and output growth on the tails of their respective distributions (<1st percentile, >99th percentile).

4. Both in (2) and (2′), α_i represents the average level of foreign bank participation for country i over the period. Thus, coefficients in both equations indicate departures from country-specific mean participation levels that are associated with changes in our explanatory variables. Because we include country fixed effects in the regression, we can no longer include regional dummies as these do not vary over time. We can, however, include year dummies, which we do in some specifications. Because crises occurred in waves, the yearly dummies are likely to reduce the explanatory power of the banking crisis variable. It is therefore questionable whether they should be included. Finally, both in (2) and (2′), we include similar macro and institutional controls to those included in the cross-section regressions discussed above. There is one important difference between equation (2) and (2′). In equation (2), the banking crisis variable is a dummy equal to one if a country was in crisis in a given year as defined by Caprio and Klingebiel (2003). For pre- and post-crisis years, the dummy is equal to zero. Thus, the banking crisis coefficient in equation (2) picks up a simple comparison between crisis and non-crisis years. Pre- and post-crisis years are lumped together as non-crisis years. To test separately whether crisis periods differ from pre-crisis and post-crisis years, we estimate equation (2′). In that equation, we include a new crisis variable equal to one from the onset of the crisis onwards. Furthermore, we introduce a post-crisis dummy equal to one beginning in the year after Caprio and Klingebiel (2003) determined a crisis to have ended. The coefficient for the new crisis variable measures the level shift in foreign bank participation relative to the pre-crisis period, while the post-crisis dummy reflects the shift relative to the crisis period.

5. In equation (3), we include the post-crisis dummy variable on its own (i.e. without the crisis dummy) because that is the most likely period for recovery in lending. *FOB share* is the share of banking sector assets held by foreign-owned banks. This variable is included to test whether foreign bank participation was associated with higher levels of credit to the private sector. We also interact *FOB share* with the post-crisis dummy to test whether the association between foreign bank participation and private credit remained the same after crisis. In some specifications, we include the share of banking sector assets held by the top 3 banks in each country because sector concentration could lead to higher interest rates and less lending.

6. It is interesting to note that the post-crisis dummy is significant only for the countries that had low levels of initial foreign participation, suggesting that the recovery in lending in those environments is due primarily to domestic banks. In countries with high levels of initial participation, the post-crisis dummy is insignificant, indicating no such rebound. Again, however, the positive significant coefficient for *FOB share* indicates that private credit levels are higher during both crisis and non-crisis periods (at least, that is, for countries with relatively stable foreign participation levels). In this sense, foreign bank participation can be viewed as a stabilizing influence on private credit levels.

4
Adaptable Agendas: Private Creditors and the Politics of Debt in Emerging Markets

Giselle Datz

Financial crises in the 1990s and early 2000s exposed the vulnerabilities of emerging economies in an age of financial liberalization. From Mexico to Russia to Argentina, contagion effects were directly felt or, as in the case of the latter, the series of external shocks that marked the 1990s decade ended up amounting to monetary and fiscal pressures that kept feeding one another in an unsustainable pattern. Indeed, the Argentine crisis that escalated in 2001 led to the largest default on sovereign debt to date. Four years later, the debt restructuring process entailed a larger reduction in repayment than any other process of its kind since the 1980s.

The outcome of the Argentine default largely contradicts analyses that detect a lack of room of maneuver on the part of emerging market economies *vis-à-vis* financial markets. Argentina was not severely 'punished' by international financial markets due to its suspension of debt payments. No sustained credit crunch was endured by the country after its debt restructuring. Though not active in financial markets right after defaulting on its debt, Argentina did manage to acquire positive debt upgrades when the restructuring was concluded in 2005, and its exchanged sovereign bonds (for the defaulted ones) have registered spreads comparable with those of countries that weathered crises without defaulting, such as Brazil.[1] Because of this counter intuitive outcome, Argentina's debt restructuring process presents a fruitful empirical window into understanding private (financial) behavior at the height of a severe crisis as well as in its aftermath.

I argue that despite the fact that sovereign defaults are episodes of non conformity with financial market expectations, debt restructuring operations – even when they involve high reductions in repayments – highlight patterns of private and public *adaptable agendas* which escape a static understanding of debtor–creditor relations based on fixed gains and losses between the defaulter and its creditors. Bonds change hands especially in the eve of an official debt restructuring. The case of Argentina made it clear that some investors – most notably hedge funds – may buy defaulted bonds from their original bondholders for a bargain price, join the debt exchange and profit substantially from the increase in value the bonds enjoy after the transaction is completed. Hence, no longer are we talking about a set bargaining situation in which an organized group of creditors sits at one side of a table and debtors at the other. The market for sovereign debt is a dynamic and mostly liquid one – i.e. where bid and ask offers abound for bonds that can be easily transferred from one owner to another.[2] In order to understand gains and losses, it is fundamental to capture the specific temporal horizons of players involved as well as their strategic tools in a macroeconomic context marked by liquidity (or the lack thereof) that, in turn, determines risk appetite or aversion.

Ultimately, this study reveals that Sovereign lending, which has historically paid off on average, has continued to do so, despite today's more volatile and integrated global financial markets. Not all creditors win, admittedly. Yet, savvy financial players do maneuver in a realm of gains when dealing with emerging market bonds. In turn, debtor countries have, for the most part, begun to understand the complexities of the bond market at home and abroad. Hence, foreign as well as local opportunities for gains in debt restructuring processes may well prove at once more investor-specific and more prevalent in the current age of financial globalization.

The remainder of this chapter is organized as follows. The first section presents some of the discontinuities we see today in debt restructurings compared to old patterns. In the second section the notion of adaptable agendas is explained, focusing on industry-specific incentives for sovereign bondholders. The case of Argentina is presented in section three, where key lucrative opportunities for foreign investors are identified before the December 2001 default, between then and the date of the official debt restructuring in 2005, and from that time on. The last section discusses the implications of this evidence for the study of sovereign debt in particular and of some key trends in IPE in general.

Restructuring sovereign debt: old process, new tools?

It is well known that for every boom in lending to developing countries there follows a bust of varying intensity and scope, but of a challenging nature. Default and debt restructurings have always affected countries in a stage of development, some of which are now the richest economies in the world (Reinhart *et al.* 2003). There is every reason to believe that defaults will not become an extinct trend, but there is also reason to bet on some significant changes that may affect the debt market and, consequently, policy-making in emerging economies.[3]

In analyzing recent debt crises, it is clear that an important departure from previous decades (most markedly the 1930s and 1980s) has been the development of new financial markets and mechanisms that have accelerated lending processes. The 1989 Brady Plan promoted the securitization of bank loans from defaulting countries, transforming them into 'Brady bonds' sold in international financial markets. This development was key to the rapid rise in outstanding emerging market bond debt. While in 1993 most net external financing to developing countries came from loans from official creditors (US$42 billion), in 2006 a greater piece of capital inflow was associated with private debt and equity, totaling a record of $647 billion. Principal repayments to official creditors in fact exceeded disbursements by $75 billion in 2006.

Consequently, the investor base on emerging market debt has broadened. In the early 2000s, public and private pension funds, endowments and other conservative institutional investors turned their attention to emerging markets' financial instruments. In a generally low return global environment, emerging markets were an option for consistently high returns for money managers. In fact, emerging market bonds broke previous flow records in 2005 with investors committing $10 billion to these investments, three times the amount they invested in 2004. The JP Morgan index for emerging market sovereign bonds (the EMBI+) registered total returns of 11.8 per cent in 2005. This is more than 400 per cent the amount of returns of an investor buying US Treasuries with seven to 10 years maturities, which registered a total return of 2.6 per cent. Latin America, a region particularly plagued by capital 'exit' threats, was one of the biggest beneficiaries of this boom in inflows (*The Financial Times*, 2 January 2005).

Not only were bond yields attractive to investors, but the quality of the assets offered by emerging markets also became more palatable. About half the outstanding bonds issued by emerging economies are now rated investment grade, up from about 30 per cent in 2001. That has a lot to do with successful policies to build up foreign reserves, which emerged as a key lesson from the financial crises of the 1990s. In 2005 spreads on sovereign bonds dropped to historic lows, averaging 306 basis points, compared to 423 basis points in 2004 (World Bank 2006a).

Moreover, speculative investors took advantage of low interest rates in financial centers to borrow cheaply and invest in riskier but higher yielding assets in, for example, Turkey, Hungary, South Africa and Iceland – a strategy known as carry trade (*The Financial Times*, 26 July 2006). In 2006, despite much turbulence in emerging markets due to interest rate increases in the US, recovery has been experienced as the Federal Reserve has rested its increases at a safe rate for emerging markets of around 4.7 per cent annually (*Clarin*, 5 November 2006). As of the end of 2006 sovereign bonds continued to attract investors despite recent crises and risks that still endure as an intrinsic feature of these assets.

As it concerns sovereign bankruptcy arrangements, the recent shift in financing from bank debt to 'hot' money flows into the stock and bond markets of debtor countries paints a new and more complex picture. Rather than the restricted discussions among bankers and diplomats at the Paris and London Clubs of official and commercial bank creditors, respectively, debt restructuring processes now involve obtaining the consent of a majority of bondholders who for the most part lack a forum for negotiations. Once a crisis unfolds it becomes more difficult to identify and contact creditors. Creditors' wealth is less related to the evolution of a specific country that owes them money, so they tend to have significantly less long-term interests alignment with borrowers than was the case with commercial banks during the 1980s (Marx 2003: 6). Compared to the 1930s era of bond-financing, creditors nowadays form an even more diverse and scattered group operating in a realm of financial volatility heightened by herd behavior[4] on the part of investors and by the technological ability of financial transactions to be executed in split seconds.

Not only is it useful to recognize the diversity of international creditors now involved in debt restructuring negotiations, but it is also important to highlight the role of domestic creditors in the process. This is indeed a new variable usually neglected in studies of debt crises in the 1990s in relation to the 1980s (and previous periods for that matter). In the past, when governments borrowed money from residents they usually used local currency under local law; when governments borrowed money from foreigners, the debt was denominated in foreign currency and followed foreign laws, to be interpreted in foreign courts (mostly New York's or London's). Nowadays, however, it is increasingly inaccurate to separate domestic creditors of foreign debt from other creditors in the bargaining process, or ex ante in the political calculations in favor of default. The increasing sophistication of domestic financial systems and the liberalization of capital flows have allowed for private local investors to seek both internationally and domestically attractive investment options. Sovereign bonds have emerged as appealing securities in which to invest given their high rates of return (a function of their risk level). This is especially the case with local pension funds that are prohibited to invest significantly in foreign equity, and find themselves with a very large pool of money under their care and limited domestic investment options.

Despite substantial changes in financial markets, the more volatile nature of lending to emerging markets, and the absence of a formal mechanism (say endorsed by the International Monetary Fund and/or the US Treasury), lately, Ecuador, Pakistan, Russia, Ukraine and Uruguay have all been able to restructure their bonds in default or quasi-default in record time. In each of these cases 'substantial debt-service relief and even sizable debt forgiveness' were obtained 'through the use of exchange offers, often accompanied by bondholder exit consents that encourage the participation of as many investors as possible in the take-it-or-leave-it settlements' (Porcecanski 2006: 278). This is a significant departure from two prevalent views in the literature on the relationship between states and financial markets.

On the one hand, the IPE literature in the last decade or so produced several studies that emphasized the lack of room for emerging market economies to maneuver given the highly reactive nature of moody financial flows (Armijo 2001; Mosley 2003, Soederberg 2005). Underlying analyses about the threat of 'sudden stops' (Calvo *et al.* 2003) – i.e. brusque reversals in capital inflows – was the idea that markets tend to 'punish' economies where fiscal and/or monetary parameters are (perceived as) unsustainable. It would follow, then, that defaulting on debt owed to scattered (domestic and international) bondholders would meet with a severely negative reaction in terms of future credit access on the part of sovereign debtors. However, that was not the case in recent debt restructurings where access to credit markets was reestablished relatively soon after the Argentine exchange of defaulted bonds for new ones. More impressive, as noted above, are the low spreads sovereign bonds of all emerging markets (including many of those which dealt with restructurings) have been registered especially in 2005–2006.

On the other hand, analyses of the Argentine debt restructuring in particular, that point to the asymmetric power on the side of the debtor to impose its conditions on unorganized creditor groups (Scott 2006) – and even on the IMF (Cooper and Momani 2005), neglect to tells us more about creditor heterogeneity and how particular group of lenders did profit from the restructuring even if the debt reduction involved in the exchange of defaulted bonds for new bonds was substantial (about 75 cents on the dollar).

It is worth noting that given its focus on private investors, this chapter does not deal in detail with the role of the IMF in the Argentine crisis. Its involvement, however, was significant prior to the default, but not so marked during the debt restructuring. It is logical to recognize that the

Fund would not be part of a portrait of adaptable agendas when it comes to accepting debt reductions. As Porcecanski (2006) contends, while private lenders will take losses and move on, the IMF and official lenders have shown themselves unwilling to grant debt forgiveness, preferring instead to reschedule maturing obligations.

The argument presented here is that not only is it the case that sovereign debtors are able to find room to move in a context of highly volatile financial operations, but – more importantly – that debtor–creditor relations in the early 2000s (as evidenced in the case of Argentina, but potentially beyond it) are marked by interactions that do not reveal zero-sum games. That is, at different stages of the process opportunities emerge for both the debtor and some of its creditors to strike favorable deals. Crisis are then undeniably socially and economically (if not also politically) costly situations, but they are also windows of opportunities for some financial players, holding particular assets and/or able to deal with the crisis-affected government in ways that derive gains from public measures to delay or ameliorate economic chaos.

Furthermore, financial innovation may well broaden this group of potential 'winners' from financial crises, who may either profit from strenuous circumstances or well insure themselves from possible losses. In fact, an element still new to the analysis of debt crises, which is bound to play a critical role in the future, is a novel type of (credit) derivatives, called credit default swaps (CDS).[5] These work as an insurance mechanism for investors in sovereign debt, compensating bondholders for defaults and other adverse credit events. This hedging provision, allows for more investment in emerging market assets, which has important implications to the pricing and supply of debt capital to developing countries.[6] According to the World Bank, 'by transferring to other market participants some of the credit risk that banks incur in their lending and trading activities, credit derivatives have altered, perhaps fundamentally, the traditional approach to credit risk management' (World Bank 2006a: 44). CDS can bring liquidity to illiquid credit markets and thus enable any type of credit exposure that investors want (*Euromoney*, December 2001). In fact, the growth in this market has been explosive; credit derivatives are now worth more than $12 trillion in terms of the notional amount of debt covered by CDS[7] (*The Financial Times*, 6 March 2006). Increasingly, this industry is attracting not only commercial and investment banks, but also hedge funds, pension funds, insurance groups, commodity traders, and even more traditional asset managers, who seem impressed by the resilience of CDS to major credit market dislocations since the Asian crisis of 1997 (*Euromoney*, December 2001; Dages *et al.* 2005).

It seems reasonable to speculate that CDS will have a significant impact in analyses of gains and losses derived from debt crises and, specifically, debt restructuring processes. A brief analysis of CDS in the context of the Argentine crisis is presented below.

There is theoretical importance in studying specific financial tools. Analyses within IPE have yet to understand in detail the diverse financial strategies of institutional investors that deal with an ever expanding menu of complex securities. In order to capture the real policy impact of financial integration, it is essential to unpack the constant interrelating dynamics of the hedging game. This may well reveal that opportunities for gains abound in the market for sovereign debt insofar as they shape what are now mostly adaptable public and private agendas.

Adaptable agendas

The sophisticated realm of engagement between governments of emerging economies and international markets that configure debt restructurings does not amount to a zero-sum game. A default is not an overall loss for markets participants who have much to gain at different stages of the process. Gains and losses depend on where one stands and holding which kind of security, at what time, and facing what external liquidity conditions (Datz 2007a).

Given that portfolio allocations are chosen based primarily on the risk tolerance and investment goals of investors (Haley 2001), it is fundamental to understand what determines these portfolio allocations, once international factors (such as low interest rates in financial centers) point favorably to emerging markets as promising investment harbors.

First, it is important to clarify that it has become increasingly problematic to refer to 'financial markets' as a representation of a homogeneous group of players with common investment goals. In Santiso's (2003) assessment, there is no such thing as 'financial markets', but rather, 'there are various types of investors, different actors, from brokers and rating agencies, involved in the confidence game with divergent and frequently conflicting strategies' (Santiso 2003: 193). Beyond macroeconomic considerations, an industry-specific view of the bond market and its players reveals how their decision making is bounded by the bonus granting, index following, and behavior mimicking features within financial institutions, which ultimately determine investment choice and timing (Calvo and Mendoza 2000; Santiso 2003).

A long established practice in institutional money management is to measure performance against benchmarks, usually equity or bond indexes.

This approach has become standard in emerging markets, with many fund managers performances measured against the JP Morgan Emerging Market Bond Index (EMBI+). This index tracks on a daily basis the prices and yield of bonds issued by various emerging market countries, which rise and fall based on news, developments and interest rate trends. Each country in the index has a weighting – for example, 10 per cent for Russia, 15 per cent for Argentina, 4 per cent for Venezuela, etc. – that depends largely on the amount of bonds it has issued compared with the total issued by all the countries combined (Blustein 2005).[8] The index serves the purpose of providing a means through which funds' clients can evaluate managers' performances, which are measured against the index in a quarterly basis or even more frequently in many cases. What is problematic about the index is its potential to feed an unsustainable cycle in sovereign lending. By relying on the EMBI+, investors are encouraged to lend to those countries that are most heavily indebted – at times, unsustainably so. Despite dissatisfaction with this trend, investors admit that they have to follow the index because 'the contracts of clients frequently specify such benchmarks' (Santiso 2003: 75). Most analysts are aware that index following and benchmark imperatives contribute to herd behavior in financial markets, playing a crucial role also in explaining contagion effects at times of financial crises (Calvo and Mendoza 2000).

Mosley (2003) explains that since clients cannot directly observe the performance of fund managers – i.e. 'they do not know what information they are collecting or how they are using this information, and they cannot distinguish between managers' abilities and managers' luck – they can use relative performance outcomes to get some sense of individual market participants' efforts and abilities' (Mosley 2003: 42). In turn, fund managers respond to relative performance evaluation in a variety of ways, but most commonly by looking at similar indicators and fundamentals.[9] Indeed, once aware that they will be judged relative to the market-leading analyst, fund managers become prone to mimicking the recommendation of the market leader (Graham 1999). As explained by one fund manager, '[I]t's always better to be wrong with the market than wrong against it' (cited in Santiso 2003: 67).

Moreover, time horizons for asset managers are mostly constrained by frequent performance monitoring. Indeed, each quarter of each month fund managers deliver newsletters, monthly or quarterly reports and data on their portfolio performance according to the mandates negotiated with clients. Even if institutional clients (like pension funds and insurance companies, for example) do not generally ask for strategic shifts in allocations during a single quarter, fund managers tend to adopt strategies dominated by short-term horizons (Lachman 2004; Blustein 2005). Also, because bonuses (the part of remuneration based on performance and risk taking behavior) are more important than salary for actors in the financial industry, they tend to focus attention on short-term gains with a maximum temporal horizon of one year (as bonuses are given in a yearly base) (Santiso 2003: 109). Funds with incentive fees usually take on higher risk and pursue non-benchmark strategies. Indeed, the compensation structure of hedge funds is such that most managers receive 2 per cent of the assets they manage as a management fee and take home 20 per cent of profits as an incentive pay/fee. The idea behind this compensation structure is to motivate money managers to produce high returns within a year. The time horizon they operate in is thus extremely short, which can lead in some instances to managers taking undue risks especially at the end of each year. Hence, what we see today in contemporary financial markets are prevailing short term horizons and more sensitivity to risk than in the 1980s, even though the diversity of instruments and increased ability to hedge risk has given investors more flexibility to manage their assets (McGovern 2004).

An important implication emergent from these industry-specific considerations is that there is no reason to bet on the fact that money managers will 'punish' a defaulting country with a credit crunch.[10] Rather, forward looking, short-term-oriented investors are moved by the possibility of pocketing hefty returns in the short run, which means that 'punishments' based on historical or even recent records of repayment and/or default are not key to determining their investment strategies. Outside of a benign context, however, even non defaulters may 'pay' for simply being more risky options of investment than liquid instruments such as US Treasury bonds.

Anecdotal evidence is illustrative of this idea. In recounting the profitable tales of two extremely successful investors in the mutual fund management industry, *The Wall Street Journal* reported:

> . . . stumbling into his office one day in February 1995, following a late-afternoon run, . . . [Thomas Cooper] didn't expect to see his bosses, Jeremy Grantham and Eyk Van Otterloo, waiting. Before he could change out of his running shorts, they asked how much Argentine debt he owned and why he owned it. His heart sank as he explained, believing they wouldn't like the risk. He and Mr. Nemerever had bought the Argentine bonds because they deemed them cheap, beaten down in price as a result of the 1994 Mexican currency crisis spreading fear about instability to Argentina. "I expected them to tell

me to sell," said Mr. Cooper. Instead, to his amazement, they wanted to know how to get more exposure to the bonds (*The Wall Street Journal*, 5 September 2006).

It seems logical to speculate that this conversation would have proceeded similarly in 2002 (after the Argentine default, for example). Indeed, if these money managers bought Argentine bonds when their value was at the bottom and joined the debt restructuring in 2005, their tale of profits would only be enhanced by further gains, as explained below.

Therefore, although recent defaults and debt restructurings were episodes of non-conformity with financial market expectations, they did not amount to irreversible losses for *all* creditors who held defaulted bonds. In the case of Argentina, patterns of private and public adaptability can be detected, reducing 'market punishments' to a stigma perhaps more linked to Argentine President Kirchner's new populist agenda than to credit markets' dynamics. That is to say, both debtors and some creditors relied on a mix of savvy advising, an understanding of the bond market's diverse temporalities, and on 'financial engineering' to come up with a deal that presented advantages to investors as well as to the debtor government.

Private interest and public success: the Argentine debt restructuring, 2001–2006

After the decade-long rush of international capital flows into Argentina, the country was by the end of the 1990s a time bomb. The Convertibility Law that fixed the peso at a rate of one-to-one with the dollar was no longer sustainable. The costs of keeping the parity had augmented considerably after the many external shocks of the 1990s (notably the financial crises of Asia and Russia with its spillover to Brazil). No longer could the country count on the substantial income it had raised from privatizations in the past decade. On the contrary, the program for pension privatization started at the same time brought high transition costs to the federal budget. The government would not feel the relief of pension payments that had shifted to the private system in the short-term, but felt immediately the deprivation of a large amount of tax revenue, which had to be compensated via new borrowing.

As a result of mounting fiscal burdens, Argentina's consolidated public debt rose from under one-third of GDP in the early 1990s to more than 41 per cent in 1998. Much of the debt had to be serviced in foreign currency, which was made more difficult by Argentina's low export-to-GDP ratio, a product of an overvalued currency. The country's total foreign currency debt was around five times the size of its foreign currency receipts from exports of goods and services by the end of 2001 (Krueger 2002a).

Prior to the December 2001 default

On 23 December 2001, interim president Adolfo Rodrigues Saá officially announced that Argentina would suspend debt payments in what became the largest default in history to date (involving approximately $155 billion, of which $88 billion was owed to private bondholders, excluding interest). The restructuring of such a large amount of defaulted debt was also bound to become the most complex operation of its kind ever, imposing the largest cut in debt repayment to creditors. The variety of legislations and types of debt instruments involved in this debt restructuring was broad beyond precedent. Of the total bonds in default, 61 per cent were denominated in dollars, 3 per cent in Argentine pesos, 21 per cent in euros, 4 per cent in yen, and 12 per cent in other currencies (Marx 2003). Of the total debt in default residents held approximately 50 per cent.

Although the official debt restructuring of Argentine defaulted bonds was started in 2005, it was only the last phase of a piecemeal process that the government articulated strategically, and which allowed for it to deal with domestic bondholders – especially pension funds – differently than international creditors. This was a political move to offer a sweeter deal to domestic residents, given the way the government abruptly tapped into their resources when foreign credit had dried up by the end of 2001 (Datz 2007b). At that time, the government managed to 'strong arm' pension funds and local banks to accept a restructuring of $32 billion of federal bonds for new bonds at lower interest rates and longer maturities.[11] This was the largest debt swap in financial history up until that point, and became known as the megaswap (*megacanje*), which allowed Argentina to avoid default in June 2001[12] (Machinea 2002).

The operation carried out in November 2001 was to be followed by another of the kind involving foreign creditors when the zero-deficit plan was put in place by returning Minister of the Economy, Domingo Cavallo – the architect of the convertibility system. The idea was to offer domestic bondholders a chance to swap their foreign-law, foreign-currency bonds for a 'guaranteed' loan governed by Argentine law and denominated in dollars. In addition, bondholders were offered the option to recover their original bonds if any terms or conditions in the guaranteed loans were changed in the future. Guarantees in financial transactions are never a free lunch, which meant in this case that interest payments on the bonds (now loans) would be reduced by 30 per cent relative to the original rate with a cap at 7 per cent per year (Sturzenegger and Zettlemeyer 2004).

Strategically crucial for the government was that with this 'bonds for loans' swap it was possible to treat the new domestic instrument differently than the original bonds (Roubini and Setser 2004: 264; Gelpern 2005). Phase 2 of this swap operation, which aimed at restructuring debt held by external creditors (almost $58 billion in bonds), was not completed until the beginning of 2005.

With this November 2001 swap, debt service to external creditors was then maintained (Mussa 2002). However, on 16 November 2001, following a steady decline, foreign reserves dropped to $19.44 billion, almost exactly the same level as immediately before the IMF loan of September 2001 when the central bank's reserves were replenished with the disbursement of $5 billion (Blustein 2005). In December 2001, just prior to the default, the government ordered the local pension funds to transfer $2.3 billion to the national treasury in exchange for treasury bills.[13]

The Argentine crisis proved extremely lucrative for several investment banks. In the partial restructurings of 2001, large fees were paid to creditor committees' representatives, and 'almost all the investment arms of leading Wall Street firms made lucrative deals' (Santiso 2003: 193). For example, before the restructuring was concluded the *Dow Jones Newswires* reported that Adam Lerrick, chairman of the Argentine Bond Restructuring Agency (ABRA),[14] would pocket around $11.6 million in fees when the Argentine restructuring was completed (*Dow Jones Newswires*, 21 January 2005). Interestingly, despite refusing to accept the Argentine government's offer in late January, ABRA joined the debt restructuring two hours before the deal's deadline, surrendering to the then widespread notion that high participation in the debt exchange meant that no better offer would be proposed by Argentina after that restructuring process was finalized (*The Financial Times*, 27 February 2005).[15]

When it came to Wall Street financial players, even when Argentine economic 'fundamentals' pointed clearly to the problem of debt unsustainability, fund managers and analysts refrained from spelling out their concerns in investment reports – limiting them to private conversations. Blustein (2005) reports that analysts from Salomon (which renamed itself to Citigroup Global Corporate and Investment Baking Group), the fifth largest investment bank to sell Argentine bonds during the 1990s,[16] were bringing in large sums of cash to their firm out of the sale of Argentine sovereign bonds. These market players faced an explicit conflict of interest in making comments that could reduce demand on these same bonds (Blustein 2005: 62–3). Salomon was hardly alone in this scheme. Enjoying high fees from assisting Argentina with the selling of its bonds in financial markets, other banks were equally disinclined to issue negative reports on the country, deepening its indebtedness process. These banks were reputable institutions such as Barclays, Morgan Stanley, Credit Suisse First Boston, JP Morgan, and Salomon (Bonelli 2004). In July of 2001, it was reported that Argentina's $29.5 billion sovereign debt exchange deal was 'a great coup for the banks lead-managing it'. By that time, it had already become obvious that a default would have been a less costly alternative than a swap that raised interest rates on payments for a country already suffocated in debt obligations. Yet, investment bankers found an ally in Argentine economy minister (Domingo Cavallo)'s reluctance to accept the inevitability of a default. These banks pocketed billions in fees from the deal (*Euromoney*, July 2001).

A critical discontinuity in comparison with defaults past is not only the fact that debt is owed to private, scattered investors (domestic and international bondholders) today – as opposed to the commercial banks of the 1980s – but the fact that, for example, Argentine bonds that were not defaulted on (*Bodens*) were being traded even prior to any restructuring offer was announced. A thriving market for defaulted bonds (or distressed debt) exists and has grown considerably in the last decade due to its incomparable rates of return (Singh 2003).

CDS played a small but significant role in the Argentine crisis. They proved able to endure such a large default episode, which added strength to the industry. Prior to the 2001 default, Argentina counted on an IMF package at the end of 2000, which contributed to soothe investor's sentiment, given improved risk probabilities in November of that year. When it became clear that no bail out package was forthcoming and that the government was failing in imposing significant fiscal breaks in the economy, trading on Argentine default swaps stopped completely in December of 2001 (IMF 2002) – which confirms the notion that the Argentina's default was fully anticipated by the market. Most market players had sufficient time to exit the bond and credit protection market. Main sellers of credit insurance managed to hedge their books in the repo market.[17] Approximately 95 per cent of all Argentine CDS were settled by mid-February 2002 (Ranciere 2002). These dynamics contribute to the complexity of debtor–creditor interactions, and substantiate the need for a nuanced understanding of different player's strategies at different times of the debt game.

When it came to domestic politics, President Kirchner's popularity, in fact, soared as he adopted a tough stance towards the country' creditors, especially the IMF. It is worth noting that it was Saá, not Kirchner, who announced the default on 23 December 2001. Saá remained in power for only a few weeks. It would be, however, incorrect to believe that Saá was 'ousted' because of his stance on debt repayment. His default announcement at the Argentine Congress was, instead, cheered by legislators and many popular groups. Also, as far as Kirchner's popularity is concerned, despite having received 22 per cent of the votes in the presidential elections, the president would have taken 53 per cent of these votes if elections had been held in January 2004. Moreover, Kirchner's approval rating climbed to 81 per cent in January of 2004, from 76 per cent in November of 2003, an increase that is attributed to the public's support for the president's firm stance in debt negotiations (*Bloomberg* 2004). Another opinion poll carried out days before the government decided to default on about $3 billion in debt to IFIs, revealed that 83 per cent of those in the sample supported the government's decision, while 10 per cent did not and 3 per cent strongly disagreed with the government's stance. This poll also revealed that popular support for President Kirchner had reached a historic high, with an approval rate of 84 per cent of sampled opinions in March 2004 (*La Nación*, 11 March 2004).[18]

During the 2005 restructuring

On 14 January 2005, Argentina's official debt exchange was opened to exchange $81.8 billion in 152 types of bonds into $41.8 billion in debt in the form of 3 types of bonds.[19] With it the government hoped to count on a majority of bondholders to swap approximately 150 types of bonds into only three new types of bonds. Despite involving a deep reduction in repayment, the debt restructuring counted on 76 per cent of creditors' acceptance. This was far lower a level than that of other restructurings in the 1990s, but was a sound outcome given that this restructuring involved the largest repayment reduction so far (i.e. a repayment of about 30 cents on every one dollar of debt).

Only two weeks after the official swap was announced, 30 to 40 per cent of retail investors had sold their bonds (*Reuters*, 2 February 2005). While the official exchange was still in its first week, Standard & Poor's announced that it would upgrade the credit rating of the swapped Argentine bonds, which injected more confidence into the restructuring process (*La Nación*, 3 February 2005).

Also, hedge funds which joined the Argentine restructuring in 2005 at the last minute, having bought defaulted bonds at very low prices from less experienced retail investors especially in Italy, made huge profits with the debt swap (Gelpern 2005). If the debt restructuring proved a zero-sum game it was mostly to these Italian retail investors.[20] It is worth noting that this lucrative move by hedge funds does not stand in contradiction with the index following trend identified above. Given their short-term horizons and intense pressures to perform at least along with competitors, hedge funds by definition are more risk-prone investors, embedded in a lax regulatory framework. Indeed, for these types of investors, trading opportunities emerge 'from extreme market swings as well as market collapses', which prove to be a daring window of opportunity for well above-average profits (EIM Group 2006: 1).

Even local pension funds, which held 20 per cent of the defaulted bonds and became the main creditor source for the Argentine government in late 2001 when international sources of credit were all but gone, were offered a deal at the time of the restructuring that was designed to fit their investment strategies. They were the first to join the exchange, attracted by a type of bond designed to match their long-term horizons (the Cuasi Par bonds with the longest capitalization period from the three types of bonds offered), which would enter their accounting books in nominal value (not market value), preventing accounting losses.[21] According to a pension fund CEO, not only did the local pension funds refrain from incurring losses, but they even gained from the deal, especially given that their new bonds were indexed to inflation, whereas salaries and pensions lagged behind inflationary rates.[22] All in all, the goal of a pension fund is to guarantee future income in local currency (pesos) to their clients. Since privatized pension systems are new in Argentina, it is estimated that only by 2020 will the amount of inflows and pension payments be balanced out. So far, only approximately 2 per cent of the contributors receive pensions. With such a long-term horizon, the debt restructuring proved lucrative as long as pension funds can continue to capitalize on bonds attached to GDP growth, which has been impressive.[23]

After the 2005 restructuring

In September 2005, Argentina recorded its 37th consecutive month of positive growth. The economy grew at an impressive rate of 10 per cent in the second quarter of 2005 alone. In fact, Argentina has grown at an approximate rate of 9 per cent a year since 2003 (*The Financial Times*, 21 September 2005). Most agree that the extremely benign global environment following the debt restructuring has a lot to do with it. Not only was high liquidity (due to low interest rates abroad) a factor in allowing for such record growth rates, but, with high global demand, Argentine agricultural commodities found a broad demand. Moreover, then Minister of the Economy, Roberto Lavagna, stuck with a policy of fiscal austerity, leading the country to also register record highs in terms of primary fiscal surplus, which makes investment in Argentina more attractive.

In October of 2005, Argentina was not only receiving better credit ratings, but its country risk was raised to a level very close to that of Brazil (a country that despite having faced severe currency crises in 1999 and 2002, never defaulted on its large debt).[24] One year later, that outlook did not change. In mid-October of 2006, Argentine risk amounted to 291 points, the lowest number since August 1997, when it amounted to 294 points. Again, importantly, Argentine's country risk was only 100 points below the equivalent measure for Brazil (*Clarin*, 14 October 2006).

The way the Argentine government handled its relations with local pension funds is a clear product of some of the new dynamics of debt crisis and default with their respective political costs. That these costs were minimal at least in the short term is a sign of how well a government that did have room to move, maneuvered the cards in its deliberate use of pension funds as a source of domestic credit when others had dried out, and in their deliberate 'compensation' of these key domestic creditors (who held 20 per cent of the total debt in default). A top debt negotiator at the Argentine Ministry of the Economy resisted the term 'compensated' but confirmed that the funds were offered a 'very good deal'. Interviews with pension funds' CEOs and Chief Information Officers (CIOs) backed up this view from an industry perspective.[25] Moreover, ironically, those pension funds that did not hold large quantities of defaulted bonds now lagged behind their competitors in terms of average returns by the end of 2006. That is because the more bonds funds had at the time of the debt exchange, the more GDP-indexed bonds they were able to swap for the old (defaulted) bonds. As it turns out, GDP-indexed bonds – initially mocked by financial analysts as an unattractive asset – have registered extremely high returns. The idea of offering those bonds was to turn bondholders who joined the restructuring into 'partners in the Argentine economic growth'.[26] And the 'partnership' paid off. So much so that pension funds are trying to find a way to have access to purchase GDP-indexed bonds, something they cannot do under their investment guidelines, which set risk thresholds (*Clarin*, 14 November 2006).[27]

At the external front, Argentina took time after the restructuring to tap international capital markets in part because it could rely on an eager lender: Venezuela. In 2005, the Venezuelan government led by Hugo Chavez bought $3.1 billion in Argentine bonds. This was hardly a zero-sum game. Argentina gained access to credit, selling its bonds at lower interest than those (potentially) charged by the market at the time. Unsurprisingly, that was also a very profitable deal for Venezuela. Soon after purchasing Argentine bonds, President Chavez sold them to local banks, at the rate of 2,400 bolivars (the Venezuelan national currency) to the dollar, significantly above the official rate of 2,250 to the dollar.[28] All in all, the Venezuelan government sold $2.4 billion worth of bonds, at a significant profit.[29] Banks in Venezuela also gained from the transaction; free to sell the bonds abroad for dollars, they pocketed profits of around $250 million (*The Economist* 2006a).

Overall, the bonds swapped in the 2005 debt restructuring have outperformed expectations. In the first 10 months of 2006, both dollar-denominated Discount and Par bonds, originated in the official exchange, registered returns of 25 per cent and 50 per cent respectively.[30] This is a long way from the approximately 4.7 per cent interest rate set by the Federal Reserve Bank of the US (*Clarin*, 5 November 2006). And even in the category for extremely risky bonds (known as junk bonds), the gains from Argentine swapped bonds are outstanding. A recent study revealed that from the end of 1996 though the third quarter of 2006, the average index of original-issued junk bonds showed an annual return of only 5.5 per cent (*The New York Times*, 17 November 2006).

Furthermore, the political outlook also seems positive for the government that enacted the debt restructuring. In the latest legislative elections, President Kirchner gained more ground establishing himself in the Peronist party with an advantage over his main rival, former President Eduardo Duhalde.

Conclusion

An important implication of this analysis is that defaulters are not simply 'serial contract breakers'; they are players in a debt game that albeit increasingly challenging, does present opportunities and not only constraints. The menu of negotiating maneuverings available to defaulting governments in this scenario may indeed increase with the complexity of debt restructurings. Although outcomes of these processes cannot be predicted from the outset, restructurings are far from a realm of self-defeat of either the defaulting government or all of its creditors.

Moreover, when it comes to a new formal debt restructuring mechanism, evidence presented here reinforces the view that successful workouts in the future can be achieved through the ad hoc machinery (Rieffel 2003) of public-private adaptability that was prevalent in the late 1990s and early 2000s. Beyond that, it is hard to clearly specify the future of debt restructurings since there is reason to believe that financial innovations are bound to insert new elements to complex bargaining dynamics (directly or indirectly). What is clear is that scholars and policy makers need to understand more closely innovative financial instruments linked to hedging strategies, which remain to a large extent outside the realm of analysis of debt restructurings, and processes of indebtedness more generally.

In conclusion, for some financial players – domestically as well as internationally – investing in debt may become an even more lucrative (and hence recurrent) choice given new hedging techniques. In this sense, private financial innovation may well enlarge the scope of policy choice available to governments in developing countries, rather than reduce it. This is a story yet to be told.

Notes

1. Bond spreads are the difference in the price between a given bond and US Treasury bonds (viewed as risk- free assets). The larger the difference between the price of a given emerging market (EM) bond and US Treasury bonds, the higher its spread, and the further the EM bond is from a risk-free assessment.
2. Sovereign debt is the term used to describe what is public federal debt owed to local and/or international creditors in local and/or foreign currency.
3. While in the 1980s the average number of sovereigns in default was 44 and average debt in default totaled US$145 billion, in the 1990s, these numbers were 52, and US$ 177 billion, respectively. In fact, 19 per cent of all sovereigns have defaulted on their debts since the beginning of the 1990s. This represents one of the highest records in the last 180 years. Higher average default rates were only registered in the 1830s where 31 per cent of sovereign countries defaulted on their obligations, in the 1980s, when the rate was 22 per cent, and in the depression of the 1930s when the rate was 21 per cent (Beers and Chambers 2002).
4. Herd behavior – hardly a new phenomenon- occurs when a few market players' behavior (often, millionaire funds) produce a mimicking effect on the part of other investors, who run into or out of certain markets at times of financial distress (Kindleberger 1978; Chancellor 1999; Calvo and Mendoza 2000, Santiso 2003).
5. In this insurance-like deal, one party promises to pay another party a fixed sum of money if the bond issuer defaults on its bonds. In exchange for the protection, the 'insured' party promises to pay an annual fee and deliver the bonds to the other party if a default occur. CDS were traditionally an inter-dealer market, with banks purchasing credit insurance from sellers such as other banks and insurance companies. Lately, the growth is linked to investment banks structuring credit portfolios for their clients (*Euromoney*, December 2001).
6. Hedging can be defined as an 'insurance procedure' whereby an investment is made in order to reduce the risk of adverse price movements in a security, by taking an offsetting/compensating position in a related security.
7. The notional value of a derivative is the value of its underlying assets.
8. In 2001 Argentina was the biggest country to move in the index, with the weighting of the country dropping from more than 20 per cent at the beginning of the year to less than 3 per cent by the end of the year (Santiso 2003).
9. The logic underlining this idea is that a poor investment decision affects absolute performance dramatically, but, if all actors take similar action, it affects relative performance negligibly.

10. In Datz (2007a), I explain how reputational theories of sovereign default that support the idea of market punishments are inconsistent with evidence on major debt crises since the 1930s.

11. Local banks' loans to the public sector constituted about 27 per cent of the banks' assets in October 2001 (Blustein 2005).

12. However, the deal did not change negative perceptions of Argentina in the market. Country risk for Argentina, a few days later, continued to follow a downward spiral (Machinea 2002: 66).

13. This initiative raised the total investments in government paper in pension funds' portfolios to 70 per cent in that year, and would increase further in 2002 (to 76.7 per cent), as government reliance on pension fund investment increased (Kay 2003).

14. ABRA represented 20,000 European (mostly Austrian and German) retail investors holding $1.2 billion in Argentine defaulted bonds.

15. As of August 2007, no other offer was laid out to creditors of Argentine defaulted debt. Hence, those who did not join the swap still hold bonds with no market value.

16. Salomon sold $5 billion worth of bonds in the 1990s, for which the firm earned $53 million in fees from the government (Blustein 2005).

17. The repo market is the one in which two participants agree that one will sell l securities to another and make a commitment to repurchase equivalent securities on a future specified date. It is a way to borrow stock/bond for cash, with the stock/bond serving as collateral.

18. The sample included 1,200 households in different regions of Argentina.

19. These bonds were issued in four currencies (pesos, dollars, euros and yens) and followed four different jurisdictions, that of Argentina, US, England and Luxembourg.

20. Identifying who joined the swap is not a clear cut effort. In the case of pension funds and some hedge funds, their moves were traceable. But fieldwork revealed that the detailed exercise of identifying each creditor was futile. Bonds were changing hands, and some investment banks were entering the swap on behalf of some of their clients. So the computers of the *Caja de Valores* (the Argentine authority in charge of the technical procedures) could not capture but a glimpse of the 'who's who' in the final deal, which was to a large extent then made public through the media – always in general terms.

21. Government Guaranteed Loans (compulsorily bought by pension funds) were exchanged by long-term bonds, the Bodens 2014, indexed to inflation. 80 per cent of total defaulted bonds in possession of Argentine pension funds were indeed exchanged for Cuasi Par bonds (the total made available by the government), the other 20 per cent of pension funds' bonds were traded for Discount bonds, all indexed to inflation and in a package that also included the now extremely profitable bonds attached to GDP growth.

22. Interview with a pension fund CEO conducted by the author in Buenos Aires, 17 November 2005.

23. See Datz (2007) for a detailed analysis of the pension fund industry before and after the 2005 Argentine debt restructuring.

24. It is also important to note that Brazil received large loans from the IMF, especially in the 2002 debacle preceding the Presidential election of Lula da Silva.

25. These interviews were conducted by the author in Buenos Aires in November 2005.
26. Author's translation.
27. In early analyses of the Argentine default, analysts noted that Nacion (the pension fund that accepted the 'pesification' of their assets after the default, when other pension fund firms did not) had profited and attracted more contributors than its competitors (Kay 2003). However, in November 2006, Nacion was being outperformed exactly by those pension funds that, by not accepting the pesification, were stuck with defaulted bonds. Those pension funds are now profiting from the high returns derived from their swapped, GDP-indexed, bonds. For further details, see Datz 2007b.
28. Since 2003 the bolivar has been pegged to the dollar.
29. The figure announced by Venezuela's finance team was $309 million. Some sources, like *The Economist*, reported on the deal but suggested skepticism in trusting the government's numbers. Indeed, according to *The Financial Times*, the profit was around $200 million (*The Financial Times*, 12 July 2006)
30. Most of these gains were enjoyed in the last four months of the 10-month period.

5
The Political Economy of International Financial Reform Since the Asian Crisis: The Case of Corporate Governance

Andrew Rosser

Introduction

Since the onset of the East Asian financial crisis in the late 1990s, Western governments and the IFIs – that is, the World Bank and the IMF – have introduced a set of initiatives aimed at promoting a so-called 'new international financial architecture' (NIFA). These initiatives have included making a more concerted attempt than in the past to encourage standardisation of financial sector regulation and practice throughout the developed and developing worlds. In particular, they have involved the promotion of international codes and standards in 12 key areas of financial policy-making: monetary and financial policy, fiscal policy transparency, data dissemination, insolvency, corporate governance, accounting, auditing, payment and settlement, market integrity, banking supervision, securities regulation, and insurance supervision. The declared purpose of these codes and standards has been to specify 'best practice' in the areas to which they relate.

In writing about these developments – and in particular Western governments' and the IFI's promotion of codes and standards – scholars of (IPE) have generally offered perspectives that reflect either a 'foreign power' or 'resistant domestic politics' approach (Robertson, Chapter 1). In this chapter, I suggest that neither of these approaches provides an adequate understanding of the political dynamics surrounding the NIFA. While the 'foreign power' approach overstates the ability of international financial capital and its allies to pressure emerging economies and developing countries into adopting and implementing market-based financial reforms, the 'resistant domestic politics' approach overstates the ability of domestic political and business elites to resist this pressure. The latter also overlooks the fact that, in some cases, these elites may for various reasons support market-based financial reform, or at least do so selectively. At the same time, neither approach considers the influence of labour, particularly organized labour from Western countries. Instead, I suggest that the NIFA is best understood, not as the simple expression of the interests of international financial capital nor as a project that is doomed to fail because of resistance from political and corporate elites in developing and emerging economies, but as a compromise between these two elements – the exact nature of which will vary from case to case depending on the interests of these elites – with a few concessions thrown in for organized Western labour.

To illustrate this argument, I examine the political dynamics surrounding the formulation of an international code of corporate governance and attempts to promote its adoption and implementation in developing and emerging economies. Corporate governance is typically seen as involving 'a set of relationships between a company's management, its board, its shareholders and other stakeholders' (OECD 2004a: 11). In this sense, it is not distinct from other key areas of financial policy and practice such as accounting, auditing, and insolvency – all of which have a significant bearing on these relationships – but, in fact, encompasses them. Among the 12 key areas mentioned above, therefore, it can be regarded as one of the most important.

The structure of the paper is as follows. In the next section, I examine the different perspectives that scholars of IPE have offered in relation to the NIFA and outline an alternative perspective that seeks to overcome their weaknesses. In the third section, I examine the politics surrounding the formulation of an international code of corporate governance and attempts to promote its adoption and implementation in developing and emerging economies, focusing on Southeast Asia. In the last section, I present the conclusions.

Understanding the NIFA

In writing about the NIFA, scholars of IPE have offered two main perspectives, the first of which is broadly consistent with the 'foreign power' approach and the second with the 'resistant domestic politics' approach (Robertson, Chapter 1). The first perspective has suggested that the NIFA is essentially an expression of the interests of international financial capital and its main allies, the US government and the IFIs. Soederberg (2001: 176), for instance, has argued that the NIFA represents 'a transnational class-based strategy to reproduce the power of financial capital in the world economy and, in effect, the structural power of the

United States'. Porter (2005) and Langley (2004a: 70) have made similar arguments although using language that is less explicitly Marxist. Scholars that have offered this perspective have often further implied that the NIFA is part of a trend towards growing convergence in the nature of global financial systems. Nölke (2004: 164), for instance, has suggested that there has been a 'strong tendency towards substantial convergence' in the nature of corporate governance regulations across the globe over the past few years.

The strength of this perspective is that it highlights the political nature of the NIFA. Some scholars have suggested that the NIFA has been an essentially technical rather than political response to the East Asian financial crisis.[1] In contrast to this suggestion, the first perspective illustrates that, regardless of the technical rationale for the NIFA, the NIFA has been a political project in that it has embodied the interests of particular class and state forces and been driven by them. In this sense, this perspective adds to our understanding of the NIFA.

The weakness of the first perspective is that it overestimates the ability of international financial capital and its allies to pressure emerging economies and developing countries into adopting and implementing market-based financial reforms. This is especially the case in so far as it implies that the NIFA is contributing to convergence in the nature of financial systems across the globe. The problem with the perspective is twofold: first, it focuses solely on the forces driving change and virtually ignores those resisting it; and second, it focuses on financial policy-making at the international level and ignores the way in which international financial policies and attempts to promote them translate into particular policy and implementation outcomes at the domestic level. By ignoring these two factors – resistance to international regulatory harmonisation and the domestic level of analysis – the perspective gives the misleading impression that market-oriented financial reform in developing and emerging economies as defined by the NIFA is more or less inevitable.

The second perspective on the NIFA that scholars of IPE have offered has emphasized the way which political and corporate elites in developing and emerging economies have resisted the implementation of international financial codes and standards. These elites, it is argued, have resisted implementation of these codes and standards because, if properly enforced, they would reduce opportunities for powerful political and corporate elites to engage in rent-seeking activities. Walter (2003: 132), for instance, has argued that while many governments in East Asian countries have adopted international prudential banking regulations, political and corporate elites in these countries have resisted the proper implementation of these regulations because they would raise the cost of finance for them by restricting lending to related parties. As such, the second perspective suggests that the NIFA is doomed to fail because of a lack of underlying political and social support within developing and emerging economies. In contrast to the first perspective's vision of growing convergence in the nature of global financial systems, then, the second perspective suggests that there will be continued divergence in the nature of these financial systems.

A major problem with the second perspective is that, just as the first perspective overestimates the ability of international financial capital and its allies to pressure emerging and developing countries into adopting and implementing market-based financial reforms, the second perspective overestimates the ability and desire of political and corporate elites within these countries to resist this pressure. It suggests that political and corporate elites in emerging and developing economies are so powerful, at least within their own countries, that they can simply ignore demands for financial reform from international financial capitalists and their allies with impunity. But, where emerging and developing countries are integrated into the global capitalist system and rely, to at least some extent, on flows of mobile capital to promote investment and economic growth, this is unlikely to be the case. In these countries, there is a structural imperative for political and corporate elites to respond to the demands of mobile capital controllers: to ignore them completely runs the risk of provoking capital flight and economic collapse and thereby undermining their own power.

At the same time, political elites in some emerging and developing countries have in some cases supported, rather than opposed, market-based financial sector reforms, at least selectively, for their own reasons. Scholars operating from the second perspective tend to assume that political elites in emerging and developing countries are inherently opposed to market-based financial sector reform. Yet, this is not always the case. Even within East Asia, the region on which Walter (2003) focuses, there is considerable variation in the extent to which the political elites favour market-oriented economic reform, reflecting the balance of power between pro-market and anti-market fractions of the domestic capitalist class (Jayasuriya and Rosser 2006). This in turn means that one cannot automatically assume that attempts by international capital and its allies to promote the adoption and implementation of international financial codes and standards in developing and emerging economies will founder as a result of resistance from domestic political and corporate elites. Where it suits them, these elites may in fact try to facilitate reform.

In contrast to these perspectives, I argue that the NIFA is better seen as (for the most part) a function of the way in which the interests of international financial capital and its allies intersect with those of political and corporate elites in developing and emerging economies. The point here is that both sets of actors exercise considerable influence over the nature of the NIFA: international financial capital and its allies through their control over the bodies that formulate international financial policies and their ability to exercise structural leverage over emerging and developing economies (through their control of mobile investment resources, particularly credit, equity funds, and foreign aid);[2] and political and corporate elites in developing and emerging economies through their influence over financial policy-making and implementation outcomes at the national level. At the same time, political and corporate elites in developing and emerging economies vary in terms of the extent to which they share the interests of international capital and its allies in promoting market-oriented financial sector reform. As such, the NIFA is not so much a clear victory for either international capital or political and corporate elites in emerging and developing countries as a compromise between them, the exact nature of which will vary from country to country.

At the same time, I also argue that the NIFA embodies certain concessions to labour, particularly organized Western labour. Neither of the above perspectives examines the role of labour in influencing international financial policy-making and attempts to promote the adoption and implementation of international financial policies in developing and emerging economies. To a large extent, this is justified: labour has played an insubstantial role in financial sector policy-making at both the international and domestic levels because its representative organizations are generally excluded from participation in the bodies that formulate financial policies. At the same time, they often lack the resources and technical skills to participate effectively in any case, particularly in developing and emerging economies. But in some cases, such organizations have been involved in financial sector policy-making processes, corporate governance being an example, as we will see in greater detail below. As such, labour deserves some attention in analyses of the political economy of the NIFA.

In sum, then, my argument is that the NIFA should be understood in terms of the way in which three sets of actors – international financial capitalists and their allies in the US government and the IFIs, political and corporate elites in emerging and developing economies, and labour, particularly organized Western labour – have shaped international financial policies and attempts to promote the adoption and implementation of these policies in emerging and developing economies. At the same time, I argue that it should not be understood as the straightforward expression of the interests of international financial capital nor as a project that is doomed to fail because of resistance from political and corporate elites in developing and emerging economies, but as a compromise between these two elements with a few concessions thrown in for organized Western labour. In the following section, I illustrate these points using the case of corporate governance.

The case of corporate governance

The political struggles that have taken place over the formulation of an international code of corporate governance and attempts to promote its adoption and implementation in developing and emerging economies have centred on the merits of the so-called 'outsider' model of corporate governance that is characteristic of corporate governance systems in the US, the UK, and Australia. The main features of this model are a high reliance on equity finance; dispersed ownership; strong legal protection of shareholders, including minority shareholders; strong bankruptcy regulations and courts; little role for creditors, employees and other stakeholders in company management; strong requirements for disclosure; and considerable freedom to merge or acquire. This model is commonly distinguished from the 'insider' model of corporate governance, the main features of which are a high reliance on bank finance; concentrated ownership; weak legal protection of minority shareholders; weak disclosure; limited freedom to merge or acquire, and, in some cases, a central role for stakeholders such as employees and creditors in the ownership and management of companies. Efforts to formulate an international corporate governance code and promote its adoption and implementation in developing and emerging economies have been widely viewed as an attempt to promote the use of the outsider model.

Actors and interests

International financial capitalists and their allies in the US government and the IFIs have been the main supporters of the outsider model of corporate governance. International financial capitalists have had a strong interest in this model for several reasons. First, they have had a strong interest in the protection of shareholders' rights because many of them have purchased shares in publicly-listed companies, both in developed and developing or emerging countries. At the same time, they have had an interest in the protection of minority shareholders' rights in particular because they have often taken minority stakes in these companies, especially in developing and emerging economies where original owners have often only sold a small proportion of their companies' shares to the public. Secondly, because international financial capitalists require reliable financial information in order to make profitable investment decisions, they have had a strong interest in high levels of disclosure and transparency on the part of publicly-listed companies. Thirdly, they have had an interest in being able to determine companies' policies, appointments and other activities, without interference by stakeholders such as employees. Fourthly, they have had an interest in greater freedom to merge and acquire in so far as this has meant that individual international financial investors, or consortiums of international investors, can more easily achieve control of companies. Finally, in so far as they have lent money to companies, they have had an interest in strong protection of creditors' rights.

For their part, the US government and the IFIs have supported the outsider model of corporate governance because of their respective relationships with international financial capital. On the one hand, international financial capital has exercised considerable structural power over these institutions, as it has elsewhere, reflecting its importance as a source of investment resources for the US and, in the case of the World Bank (which has to raise some of its funds on Wall Street) its importance as a source of funding. On the other hand, as various scholars have pointed out, there are instrumental linkages between international financial capital, the US government, and the IFIs, a phenomenon neatly summarized in the notion of an 'IMF–Wall Street–Treasury complex' (see, for instance, Bhagwati 1998). These linkages have severely constrained the autonomy of the US government and the IFIs in financial policy-making, both at the national and international levels. They have led to a situation where, as Underhill (1997: 18) has aptly put it, 'the preferences of private actors have dominated the choices of official agencies with crucial public responsibilities.'

Organized labour from Western countries and political and corporate elites from emerging and developing economies have in general opposed the outsider model, or at least its promotion as a universal model of corporate governance, although for different reasons. For organized labour from Western countries, the main concern has been to ensure that companies are held accountable, not simply to their shareholders as in the outsider model, but to society at large. At the same time, it has had a particular concern to ensure that companies are held accountable to their 'internal constituents' (i.e. employees) (TUAC 2003: 3). To this end, it has sought to defend the diversity of corporate governance systems across the globe and in particular to protect those continental European systems that permit employee participation in company management through 'works councils',[3] employee representation on company boards, and other mechanisms (TUAC 2005: 19–20). Importantly, it has at times been able to gain support for its agenda from some continental European governments. While these governments have been subject to structural and instrumental pressures from international financial capital just like the US, and have consequently also tended to support the outsider model, they have also faced strong organized labour movements, giving them a greater propensity to occasionally support employees' role in corporate governance.

For political and corporate elites in emerging and developing economies, the main concern has been to limit corporate transparency and accountability to external shareholders, at least within their own countries. In many developing and emerging economies, political and corporate elites – or more specifically, the private business empires they control – have benefited from privileged access to state facilities, monopolies and licenses as a result of corruption, collusion and nepotism. Corporate governance reforms that increase corporate transparency thus increase the risk that these elites will either be prosecuted for corruption or lose the benefits of corrupt activities. Similarly, reforms that increase accountability to external shareholders threaten to reduce their control over their corporate empires and the rents that these generate. In these cases, then, political and corporate elites have had a strong preference to retain the insider system of corporate governance rather than adopt the outsider model. In cases where political elites have not developed strong links to private business groups, however, they have had relatively little incentive to oppose corporate governance reform, at least in so far as this has entailed reform of private business groups. To the extent that it has entailed the reform of state-owned enterprises, however, their position has tended to be different, particularly in some former socialist economies where state-owned enterprise have been a key rent-seeking mechanism for the elite.[4]

A final set of actors in the political struggles over the formulation of an international code of corporate governance and attempts to promote its adoption and implementation in developing and emerging economies has been international NGOs concerned with social and environmental issues in developing and emerging economies. Like organized labour from Western countries, these actors have argued that corporate governance is not simply about the relationship between the owners and managers of companies as implied by the outsider model, but also about companies' relationships with society as a whole. But whereas organized labour from Western countries has emphasized the extent of employees' participation in company management, these international NGOs have emphasized the wider social and environmental impact of corporate activities in developing and emerging economies, particularly that of multinational corporations based in the North. In pursuing this agenda, they have received some support from labour organizations and human rights NGOs in developing and emerging economies. But the latter have not always been supportive of their agenda, in many cases seeing it as too 'Northern-driven and focused on a narrow set of issues, sectors and companies' (Utting 2003: 12). In any case, such labour and human rights organizations have tended to be weak politically, even within their own countries. This in turn has meant that to the extent that international NGOs have gained the support of NGOs and labour organizations in developing and emerging economies, they have nevertheless lacked a strong basis of social support in pursuing their corporate social and environmental responsibility agenda. This in turn has limited their ability to exercise influence over corporate governance policy-making and implementation, at both the international and national levels.

Formulation of the code

When the East Asian financial crisis occurred in 1997–98, there already existed widely accepted international standards in several areas of financial policy-making, reflecting the fact that bodies such as the International Accounting Standards Committee (now the International Accounting Standards Board), the International Federation of Accountants, and the Basel Committee of the Bank for International Settlements had long been active in producing standards in their respective areas of expertise. However, with no international organization having adopted corporate governance as its preserve, there was no comparable standard or set of standards in this area. The OECD had developed an interest in corporate governance issues during the 1990s as its Directorate of Science, Technology and Industry became increasingly concerned with how to encourage member countries to shift away from industry policy. At the same time, the Economics Department of the OECD had become concerned about promoting economic transition in Eastern Europe which, in so far as it involved the creation of a private sector, required engagement with corporate governance issues.[5] In the mid-to-late 1990s, the OECD established a Business Sector Advisory Group on Corporate Governance (BSAG) consisting of European and American corporate governance experts to report on 'what is necessary by way of governance to attract capital' (Gregory 2000: 61). Its report, which was handed down at the height of the East Asian financial crisis in April 1998, identified four principles of corporate governance on which it argued there was consensus among private sector actors – fairness, transparency, accountability, and responsibility – effectively a blend of the values underpinning the outsider and insider models (Gregory 2000: 61–2; Millstein n.d.). Had the East Asian financial crisis not occurred, the OECD may well have gone on to produce an international code of corporate governance. But at that point, corporate governance was low on the OECD's political agenda and progress was slow.

The onset of East Asian financial crisis gave the OECD's work on corporate governance great impetus. The US government, the IFIs, and many international financial investors were quick to blame the crisis on weaknesses in financial regulation and supervision within crisis-affected countries, particularly in the area of corporate governance, and began to call for urgent reform in this area (Camdessus 1997; Greenspan 1998; Mussa and Hache 1998; World Bank 1998). As the international organization most involved in corporate governance-related work, and with a long history in international standard-setting, the OECD was seen as the most suitable organization to prepare an international standard in this area. At the same time, the East Asian financial crisis changed the focus of the OECD's work on corporate governance. Whereas it had previously focused on facilitating economic restructuring in member countries and economic transition in Eastern Europe, it now became focused on promoting economic reform in developing and emerging economies. Reflecting this shift in emphasis, OECD Ministers instructed the OECD in April 1998 to 'develop, in conjunction with national governments, other relevant international organizations and the private sector, a set of corporate governance standards and guidelines' that could be used by governments across the globe as a 'benchmark' to help them 'evaluate and improve their laws and regulations' (OECD 1999: 3, 8).

To carry out the process of developing an international code of corporate governance, the OECD established the Ad Hoc Task Force on Corporate Governance (AHTFCG). This body consisted of representatives from the 29 OECD member countries as well as various international organizations and actors with an interest in corporate governance issues who were invited to participate on an 'ad hoc' basis. The latter included representatives of the IFIs; international financial regulators such as the

International Organization of Securities Commissions (IOSCO) and the Basel Committee of the Bank for International Settlements; the official advisory committee to the OECD representing Western business, the Business and Industry Advisory Committee (BIAC); the official advisory committee to the OECD representing organized Western labour, the Trade Union Advisory Committee (TUAC); and organizations representing international financial capital such as the International Corporate Governance Network (ICGN).[6] TUAC's and BIAC's inclusion reflected the established OECD practice of including official advisory committees in policy discussions on an *ad hoc* basis. Over the course of the next year, the AHTFCG held consultations with representatives of non-member governments and other parties with an interest in corporate governance issues, invited submissions from the public through an internet-based website, and held meetings with a range of corporate governance experts before preparing a draft code for endorsement by the OECD Council.

The forthcoming corporate governance code would be soft law rather than hard law, reflecting the non-binding nature of OECD guidelines and standards. Despite this, however, there was still a lot at stake for the various sets of actors discussed earlier. First, even soft law has authority, especially in so far as it influences the actions of powerful actors such as the IFIs or financial intermediaries such as debt rating agencies. Second, soft law is sometimes translated into hard law as a result of processes of regulatory harmonisation, as we have seen recently with the widespread adoption at national level of the IASB's (previously optional) international accounting standards. Third, as an OECD product, the code would apply to OECD countries, notwithstanding the fact that the primary agenda in relation to its development was to promote corporate governance reform in developing and emerging economies. Finally, the forthcoming corporate governance code would provide a key reference point in future negotiations over corporate governance policy at both the international and national levels. Certainly, TUAC understood the importance of the code to its future campaigning efforts, seeing it 'as an opportunity to raise the awareness of corporate governance issues in the labour movement and to influence standards that would help advance the interests of workers (as employees, shareholders and citizens) in a wide range of corporate governance systems (Anglo-American, European and Asian)'.[7] The various actors mentioned earlier thus had a considerable interest in ensuring that the final version of the code was broadly consistent with their values and political agendas.

Not surprisingly, then, the AHTFCG became the locus of a bitter political struggle between international financial capital and its allies, on the one hand, and its opponents, particularly organized Western labour, on the other. The consultations held by the AHTFCG were relatively limited, providing little scope for elements not represented on the AHTFCG, particularly political and corporate elites in developing and emerging economies and international NGOs working on human rights and social issues, to influence the outcome of its work. However, as an ad hoc member of the AHTFCG, TUAC was able to play a key role in shaping its work. The various members of the AHTFCG appear to have agreed that the code on corporate governance should outline the rights of shareholders and deal with issues such as transparency, accountability and the responsibilities of company boards, the main concerns of supporters of the outsider model. But there was considerable disagreement within the AHTFCG over the extent to which the code should specify the rights of stakeholders such as employees.

On the one side, TUAC argued in favour of the draft code including a chapter on the rights of stakeholders. An initial draft prepared by the OECD Secretariat included a stakeholder chapter – but it was dropped at the first meeting of the AHTFCG. TUAC argued strongly for its reinstatement. On the other side, the US, the IFIs, BIAC, and the ICGN adamantly opposed this proposal. Despite their numerical weight, however, the latter could not simply dictate the content of the forthcoming code. As a consensus-based organization, the OECD can only officially endorse policy documents if they are approved by all OECD country members. This meant that TUAC had some leverage in respect of the stakeholder chapter, at least so long as it could get at least one OECD member country on side. Much to the annoyance of the US, the IFIs, BIAC, and the ICGN, it was able to do this. The Austrian government, apparently concerned about possible inconsistency between the forthcoming code and its own corporate legislation, threatened to veto the draft standard if a stakeholder chapter was not included in the code.[8]

Faced with this situation, international financial capital and its allies conceded to the inclusion of a stakeholder chapter. Clearly, for international financial capital and its allies, the cost of not producing a corporate governance code was greater than the cost of producing one which contained some concessions to organized Western labour. At the same time, they were able to water down the content of the stakeholder chapter in subsequent negotiations within the AHTFCG. In particular, they were able to ensure that the code recommended that the rights of stakeholders be respected only if they are 'protected by law' and 'performance-enhancing mechanisms for stakeholder participation' (which TUAC interpreted to include works councils and employee representation on company boards) should be 'permitted' rather than encouraged.

The final version of the code, which was entitled the *OECD Principles of Corporate Governance* (hereafter the *Principles*) and endorsed by the OECD Council in May 1999, was thus something of a compromise. At the same time, however, it was one that clearly favoured the interests of international capital and its allies. TUAC had been able to achieve some concessions – important ones given that this was the first official international policy document to explicitly recognise the rights of stakeholders in corporate governance. But it was only able to achieve concessions. While the code incorporated a stakeholder chapter, this did not provide a strong statement in favour of the insider model of corporate governance, particularly the Continental European stakeholder variant of this model. Its content was largely consistent with the outsider model of corporate governance. Indeed, the ICGN (1999: 1) concluded that: 'Much of the document reflects perspectives promoted by ICGN representatives serving on the [AHTFCG].'

Revision of the code

Under OECD rules, the OECD was obliged to conduct an 'assessment' of the *Principles* within a few years of their adoption with a view to revising them if they were felt to be deficient in any respect. The collapse of Enron in 2002 and the occurrence of a series of other corporate scandals in the US and Western Europe soon thereafter, however, forced OECD governments to bring this assessment forward. With the nature of corporate governance systems in the US and Europe being widely criticized in the wake of these scandals, it became imperative for OECD governments and the US government in particular to do something, or at least appear to be doing something, to improve the quality of these systems. Reassessing the *Principles* provided one way in which they could do this. Ensuring broad consistency between international corporate governance regulations and national corporate governance regulations in the OECD, which in a number of cases were amended in the wake of these scandals (most notably the US where the Sarbanes-Oxley Act greatly tightened corporate governance requirements in 2002) provided another reason to revisit the *Principles*.

In calling for the 'assessment', OECD governments opened up a small opportunity for organized Western labour and other opponents of the outsider model to press for revisions that would give greater emphasis to the social responsibilities of companies and strengthen protection of stakeholder rights. Certainly, TUAC saw the 'assessment' as an opportunity to reopen negotiations on the stakeholder chapter with a view to strengthening the rights of employees to participate in management (TUAC 2003).

At the same time, the OECD also slightly widened the scope for opponents of the outsider model to participate in the assessment by conducting a more extensive consultation process than it had in 1998–99. As Jesover and Kirkpatrick (2005: 135) have observed, this process included a set of regional corporate governance roundtables organized under World Bank auspices; three major consultative meetings with broad participation; two informal meetings with representatives of key international organizations, business and labour; various other public meetings, and an opportunity for all interested parties to submit comments on an early draft of the revised code through an internet site. For the most part, political and corporate elites from Western countries did not participate in these fora: the main institutional mechanism through which they might have been brought into the revision process – the regional roundtables – were dominated by technocrats, lawyers and academic researchers hand-picked by the World Bank. In any case, they probably judged that it would be more productive from their point of view to enter the battle at the implementation stage (see below). But Western trade unions and international NGOs concerned with human rights and social issues did participate in these fora. Among the internet submissions received by the OECD, for instance were ones from the International Federation for Human Rights, the International Metalworkers Federation, the International Union of Food Workers, Union Network International, Traidcraft, and the International Confederation of Free Trade Unions (OECD 2004b).

From the outset, however, it was clear that OECD governments were not going to permit major revisions to the *Principles*, particularly ones that would strengthen the stakeholder chapter. According to a TUAC report (TUAC 2004: 8), OECD 'government representatives agreed early that the original *Principles* were simply in need of some fine tuning, and that many issues that could not be ignored should be buried within the annotations'. The US was reportedly particularly resistant to change, taking the view that the assessment 'should not reinvent the *Principles*' (as quoted in TUAC 2004: 8). In essence, this resistance reflected the fact that OECD governments were primarily interested in manufacturing an international corporate governance code that was consistent with the outsider model. The 1999 version of *Principles* already provided this and so, in the view of OECD governments, there was little need for change, notwithstanding the crisis in confidence created by the Enron and other scandals.

Not surprisingly, then, by early 2004 the Steering Group on Corporate Governance (SGCG) (the successor to the AHTFCG) had made few fundamental changes to the 1999 version of the *Principles*. The version released for public comment in January 2004, for instance, was a more substantial document than the 1999 *Principles* in three main respects – it contained a new chapter on 'ensuring an effective corporate governance framework', it contained expanded annexes, and it included a number of additional principles in different chapters – but, at the end of the day, was essentially an elaborated version of the 1999 *Principles* rather than something fundamentally different. Most notably, it contained few changes to the stakeholder chapter and almost nothing that strengthened employees' rights to participate in corporate decision-making. The main changes to this chapter were the addition of clauses protecting whistleblowers (added at the request of the US to make the *Principles* consistent with Sarbanes Oxley Act) and providing stronger protection for creditor rights (OECD 2004a). The former offered a modest improvement in protection of employees' rights while the latter offered only further protection to international financial capital.

Faced with this situation, TUAC called on its national affiliates, particularly its European affiliates, to lobby their respective governments to intervene in support of a stronger stakeholder chapter. Many OECD governments brushed this aside but several European governments proved sympathetic, particularly the French government. Just days before the revised *Principles* were to be finalized, the French government proposed changing the wording regarding 'performance-enhancing mechanisms for stakeholder participation' such that these mechanisms should be 'encouraged' rather than merely 'permitted' (Norris 2004). This led to a series of last-minute negotiations between the various OECD country members, the outcome of which was two main revisions to the stakeholder chapter. The first was the replacement of the word 'permitted' with the phrase 'permitted to develop' in relation to performance enhancing mechanisms for stakeholder participation. The second was to change the wording related to the basis of stakeholder rights such that corporate governance frameworks should not simply respect stakeholder rights 'as established by law' but also those established by 'mutual agreement' (which TUAC interpreted to include collective bargaining). Although these changes did not alter the fundamentally outsider-oriented character of the *Principles*, they did increase the concessions made to organized labour.

Adoption and implementation of the *Principles* in developing and emerging economies

Following endorsement of the *Principles* by the OECD Council in 1999, Western governments and the IFIs have pursued a number of strategies for promoting the adoption and implementation of the *Principles* in developing and emerging economies. First, and probably least import-ant, they have formed a series of regional corporate governance round-tables under joint World Bank–OECD auspices. As noted above, these roundtables provided a means by which representatives of developing and emerging economies participated in the revision of the *Principles*. But their primary purpose has been to 'ensure widespread knowledge and consideration of [the *Principles*]', provide fora for the discussion of corporate governance issues, and aid the development of blueprints for reform in each respective region (Blume 2003: 2–3). At the same time, they have provided a certain degree of legitimacy to attempts by Western governments and the IFIs to promote corporate governance reform in developing and emerging economies by making it seem as if the reform project has been based on genuine consultation with governments and interested parties in these economies.

Secondly, and more importantly, the IFIs have used their structural leverage over governments in developing and emerging economies to pressure them into introducing corporate governance reforms. The IMF, for instance, made the introduction of various accounting, auditing, and insolvency reforms that are consistent with the outsider model a feature of its rescue programs for crisis-affected countries following the onset of the Asian financial crisis and demonstrated a willingness to withhold funds from countries if its policy demands were not met (Rosser 2003b). For its part, the World Bank has sought to promote cor-porate governance reform in developing and emerging economies by funding (with the OECD) the Global Corporate Governance Forum, a multi-donor trust facility that supports 'global, regional, and local ini-tiatives that aim to improve the institutional framework and practices of corporate governance' (World Bank 2006b), and a variety of separate cor-porate governance reform programs in East Asia, Latin America and the former Soviet Union. The IFIs have also persuaded other major donors such as the Asian Development Bank to support their efforts to promote corporate governance reform in developing and emerging economies, adding to their overall structural leverage.

Thirdly, the IFIs have introduced a Report on the Observance of Standards and Codes (ROSC) for corporate governance. The IFIs introduced ROSCs in a range of different financial policy areas following the Asian financial crisis to help them monitor individual countries' progress in adopting and implementing key international financial codes and stand-ards. Because the assessment criteria used in the corporate governance ROSC has been based on the *Principles*, it has enabled the IFIs to monitor the extent to which individual countries' have reformed their corporate governance systems in accordance with its provisions. Although the ROSC has been voluntary, it has fed into negotiations between governments in developing and emerging economies and the IFIs – for instance, it has filtered into the regular Article Four consultations between these governments and the IMF (2005). To the extent that it has influenced the willingness of the IFIs to lend or provide grants to these governments, it has acted, as Soederberg (2003) has argued, as a 'disciplinary mechanism'.

At the same time, private credit rating agencies and securities firms have begun to issue corporate governance ratings, both for individual firms in developing and emerging economies and for countries as a whole, that draw upon the outsider model for their assessment criteria (Gill 2001; Standard and Poor's 2004). The corporate governance ratings issued by securities firm CLSA Emerging Markets, for instance, are based on an assessment of 57 issues under seven main categories, six of which draw upon the outsider model – management discipline, transparency, accountability, responsibility, fairness, and independence. The final category 'social awareness' is more closely associated with the 'stakeholder' system of corporate governance. The issues assessed under the 'social awareness' category include whether or not a company employs under-aged people, has an explicit equal opportunity policy, and invests in countries where leaders lack legitimacy (e.g. Myanmar).

Yet, in calculating a company's overall corporate governance score, CLSA Emerging Markets gives much greater weight to the first six categories than the 'social awareness' category – a company's score under 'social awareness' only accounts for 10 per cent of its overall corporate governance score while its scores under the other categories account for 15 per cent each of its overall score, or 90 per cent in total. Furthermore, two particular issues closely related to minority shareholder interests – whether company executives have made decisions that have favoured themselves over shareholders, and whether executives have made any decisions that have favoured majority shareholders over minority shareholders – are given relatively high weights within the independence and fairness categories. The effect of this approach is to bias the overall score in favour of the concerns of outside/minority investors and establish those elements of corporate governance associated with the outsider model as the dominant criteria for assessing corporate governance quality. In so far as financial investors have utilized these scores in making their investment decisions, they have served, just like the ROSCs, as a 'disciplinary mechanism' for developing and emerging economies (Soederberg 2003: 15).

Despite the great structural pressure on developing and emerging economies to adopt and implement the *Principles*, however, governments in these economies have made uneven progress in reforming their respective corporate governance systems in line with the *Principles*. Several studies have suggested that in general developing and emerging economies have introduced significant changes to their corporate laws and regulations in recent years to increase regulatory conformity with the *Principles*. At the same time, they have also suggested that implementation of these changes has varied from country to country: while it has been weak in most countries, it has been fairly good in some (Fremond and Capaul 2002; OECD 2003; Cheung and Jang 2005). In a study of corporate governance reform in East Asia, for instance, Cheung and Jang (2005: 1) found broad conformity between corporate laws and regulations in East Asian countries and the OECD *Principles* but a 'significant difference in terms of market perceptions of their corporate governance practices' (see Figure 5.1). In broad terms, existing ROSCs tell a similar story.[9]

Underlying this outcome has been the fact that the interests of political elites within developing and emerging economies *vis-à-vis* corporate governance reform have varied from country to country. This in turn has yielded different compromises with international financial capital and its supporters in each country with respect to the nature of their respective corporate governance systems. In countries where political elites have had close links to private corporate elites, they have tended to be opposed to corporate governance reform along the lines of the outsider

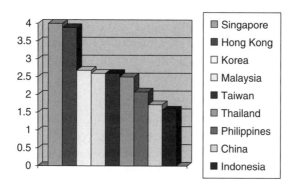

Notes: All scores are averages based on 25 observations, except for Thailand, Philippines (both 24 observations) and Indonesia (21 observations).
Source: Cheung and Jang (2005: 25).
Figure 5.1   Scores for overall corporate governance quality

model, and the result has consequently been poor implementation of recent changes to corporate laws and regulations.

In Indonesia, for instance, opposition to corporate governance reform from politico-bureaucratic elements within the state apparatus and well-connected private conglomerate owners has derailed attempts by the IFIs, the Asian Development Bank (ADB) and Western governments to promote the implementation of a new insolvency system. Within weeks of the establishment of a new commercial court to hear insolvency cases, questions were already being raised about the quality of its decisions (*Far Eastern Economic Review*, 22 October 1999). Very few cases were successful. More recently, the World Bank (2003a: 45) has suggested that the problem with the court is less the quality of its decisions in general than its decisions in particular 'high-profile' cases: The government has introduced a variety of changes to the court's operation to improve its credibility in international financial capitalists' eyes such as appointing outside *ad hoc* judges, publishing all decisions, and introducing a mandatory code of ethics. Nevertheless, these capitalists appear to have lost confidence in the court – between 2000 and 2003, the number of bankruptcy cases that the court has handled dropped from around 100 to around 30–40 per year (World Bank 2003b: 34; 2003c: 46).

In countries where political elites have not had close links to private corporate elites, they have been less opposed to corporate governance reform along outsider lines and the result, by contrast, has been relatively good implementation of recent policy changes, at least as they apply to private firms. This has been the case in Singapore, for instance, where the relationship between the political elite and local business class has been characterised historically by distance and tension, reflecting the different cultural backgrounds of the two groups and a perception on the part of the latter that the former have been unsympathetic to their interests. While the political elite in Singapore have sought to insulate so-called 'government-linked corporations' – the corporations in which the ruling People's Action Party has a considerable interest – from major corporate governance reforms, they have not attempted to do the same in relation to private business groups, promoting the implementation of reform (Rodan 2004: 50; Ho 2005). For instance, the Singaporean government has responded vigorously to a series of recent corporate governance scandals involving private companies listed on the Singapore Stock Exchange, including launching investigations and arresting key suspects (*The Edge Singapore*, 13 June 2005; Teen 2005).

In sum, then, although there have been strong structural pressures on developing and emerging economies to adopt and implement the

Principles, the extent to which they have adopted and implemented them has been determined in large part by domestic political variables, particularly the nature of the relationship between the state and local capital. The result has been an uneven process of corporate governance reform across countries.

Conclusion

In this chapter, I have illustrated that while international financial capital and its allies dominated the process of formulating and revising an international code of corporate governance and used their structural leverage and other mechanisms to promote the adoption and implementation of the code in developing and emerging economies, they did not have things all their own way. On the one hand, they had to make strategic concessions to organized Western labour in order to secure the introduction of an international code of corporate governance. This diluted the extent to which the code embodied the outsider model of corporate governance, the model preferred by international financial capital and its allies. On the other hand, they encountered fierce resistance to implementation of the code from political and corporate elites in many developing and emerging economies, resulting in an uneven process of corporate governance reform across developing and emerging economies. While some countries, such as Singapore, have made significant progress towards the adoption and implementation of the model of corporate governance entailed in the *Principles*, many others, such as Indonesia, have not, foundering on problems related to implementation.

In terms of broader debates about the nature of the NIFA, this analysis suggests that both the 'foreign power' and 'resistant domestic politics' approaches are inadequate for understanding the dynamics surrounding global financial policy-making and the implementation of global financial policies in developing and emerging economies. In writing about the NIFA, many scholars of IPE have emphasized the extent to which international financial capital has driven and benefited from its creation. Others have emphasized the ability of political and corporate elites in developing and emerging economies to resist global pressures for financial reform, particularly at the implementation stage. In this chapter, I have presented an alternative view, specifically, that the NIFA is better understood as a compromise between international financial capital and political and corporate elites in developing and emerging economies, the exact details of which vary from case to case, with a limited set of concessions made to organized Western labour. This view of the

NIFA in turn suggests that, to the extent that convergence in the nature of developing and emerging countries' financial systems is occurring, it is doing so at a modest rate and, in many cases, mainly at the level of regulation rather than practice.

Notes

I am indebted to Ricardo Gottschalk, Justin Robertson and Geoffrey Underhill and a number of others who would prefer to remain nameless for detailed comments on earlier versions of this paper. I also wish to thank students and staff in the Amsterdam School for Social Science Research at the University of Amsterdam for the helpful feedback I received on a presentation of this paper at a staff seminar. Of course, none of these people bears any responsibility for any remaining errors or omissions in the paper. That responsibility lies entirely with me.

1. See, for instance, Larsen (2002: 12). Germain (2003) has presented a similar view, although he has also pointed to the politics surrounding the creation of more inclusive international financial policy-making institutions such as the G20.
2. On the link between mobility and structural power, see Winters (1996).
3. Works councils are 'legislatively mandated bodies set up for the purpose of informing, consulting and/or negotiating with elected employee representatives on questions relating to employment and work place issues and any operational changes affecting the organization. The scope of the power and competences and works councils are usually defined by law. A works council is usually composed of elected employee representatives and in some cases of management representatives' (TUAC 2006).
4. See, for instance, Freeman (2005). See also the discussion of Singapore below.
5. Interview with Grant Kirkpatrick, Corporate Affairs Division, OECD, Paris, April 2006.
6. According to the ICGN, its members control over $US 10 trillion in assets (ICGN 2001).
7. Personal communication with informed source, September 2006.
8. The Austrian government was also concerned about language in the draft code that favoured a single tier board (characteristic of Anglo-American corporate governance systems) over a dual board structure (characteristic of corporate governance systems in many continental European countries). Interview with an informed source, Paris, April 2006 and personal communication with the same source, September 2006.
9. See, for instance, World Bank (2001; 2003a; 2004; 2005).

Part II
Country Studies

6
Argentina: State Capacity and Leverage in External Negotiations

Maria Pia Riggirozzi

The economic and political behaviour of national and international actors during the resolution of Argentina's 2001 crisis reveals complex policy processes in which the dominance of a particular actor or paradigm *vis-à-vis* other actors and paradigms is not reinforced simply by the coercive power of external lenders over borrowers but rather by the capacity of Argentine state institutions to integrate competing impulses into a policy consensus. Crisis management in Argentina has, in fact, forged a new space of dissent from global rules that became paradigmatic in terms of policy dynamics among local and external actors. This chapter looks at these patterns focusing on how the government and foreign actors, specifically IFIs and creditors, interacted in Argentina's post-crisis resolution. In this analysis, notions of power, interests and policy outcomes are central to the relations between actors, but in Argentina's case these notions were subsumed by a strong need to restore the bases for political and economic governance.

The literature on crisis and crisis resolution in Latin America has been mainly concentrated on the experience of the 1980s and 1990s when the region went through a critical debt crisis with negative effects on economic growth and social development (Nelson 1990; Haggard and Kaufman 1992; Stallings 1992; Lustig 1997). In this instance, the financial survival needs of developing countries augmented the leverage of the IFIs. However, crisis resolution recently experienced in Argentina shows a different dynamic. This departs from models of social change that overemphasize one-resource power determinism and a one-linear way of power exercise in favour of external actors. This analysis emphasizes how, in contrast to the experience of the late 1980s, the political economy of Argentina after December 2001 was foundational in many ways. In an extraordinary refocus, the national authorities managed to fragment and insulate international pressures from IFIs and private creditors and designed a national path towards post-crisis reconstruction of its political economy. As this study suggests, by relying on the national productive structure, economic recovery helped to successfully tackle the relationship between foreign influences and the adoption of a new policy model.

This chapter supports the claim that the economic crisis, as in most countries in the region, was a catalyst for political processes that deeply contested the nature of neoliberal governance. In the case of Argentina, post-crisis management has been shaped, to a remarkable degree, by state-led social and economic strategies in strong contrast to the neoliberal agenda of the 1990s. Crisis management, in effect, deviated from the externally-induced norm and, in contrast to crisis resolution in the 1980s, the role of external actors, in particular the IFIs, to impose any particular terms of a deal was critically reduced. This argument is supported by the fact that while foreign actors have played an important role in either bailing out financially or acting as primary adviser in other crises, crisis resolution in Argentina represented a nationalistic solution, contesting the international norm. To understand Argentina's response to financial crisis, this article explores the interaction between the state, international creditors and domestic actors in the attempt to institutionalize the new political economy.

The article is divided into five sections. The first section opens a general discussion on developing countries' bargaining power *vis-à-vis* international actors, contextualising the question that structures this article, that is, how much of this emphasis on the power of external actors applies to crisis resolution in the case of Argentina after December 2001? The second section examines the roots of the crisis by surveying the failures of neoliberalism as a political economic model of governance during the 1990s. The third section explores the gradual emergence of an alternative national project as a response to the crisis which erupted in December 2001. The fourth section turns the focus on the negotiations of the post-crisis government with IFIs and foreign creditors in an attempt to institutionalise a more dynamic role for the state in domestic politics. The final section offers a concluding discussion on state power and foreign interests in the reconstruction of post-crisis governance.

International and domestic factors affecting crisis and crisis resolution

The debate on developing countries' bargaining power vis-à-vis international lenders and creditors has been generally assumed to be shaped by the uneven leverage of international actors. Compelling accounts of the role of international organizations and state compliance in the current international political economy cannot ignore, even in a globalizing era, the centrality of the inequalities of power between actors (Held and McGrew 2002: 12). This perspective has been particularly influential in explaining Latin American dependency of external finance and their economic policy outcomes. Widespread consensus pointed at the reduced margin of manoeuvre of developing countries' governments in deciding economic policies when facing pressing debt crisis. For instance, it has been largely argued that credit rationing during Latin America's debt crisis in the 1980s confined the policy choice of states toward the adoption of stabilization measures according to the receipts of the IFIs, which acted as lenders of last resort (Kaufman and Stallings 1989; Stallings 1992: 43–44; Haggard and Kaufman 1994). In this case, as their financial assistance became decisive, IFI leverage was unchallenged. Straightforward explanations showed that by adapting preferences toward the implementation of structural, market-oriented reforms, Latin American countries were 'rewarded' with access to financial flows. This dynamic defined the character of domestic choices that were, in turn, associated with fiscal reforms, liberalization of trade and the general expansion of exchange rate regimes, and to generally the role of market forces and the private sector (Acuña and Smith 1996; Nelson 1990; 1994).

Yet, how much of this emphasis on the power of external actors applies to crisis resolution in the case of Argentina after December 2001? Bad policies, bad luck and bad advice have featured in explanations of the causes and consequences of Argentine crisis (Tomassi 2002). Some authors claimed that the crisis was a combination of bad policy decisions and political-institutional incentives that underpinned coalition politics and vested interests. Therefore, the blame is put on domestic causes and crisis resolution is expected to be part of 'getting policies right'. For instance, Mussa (2002) argues that fiscal deficits and the buildup of government debt were the prime causes of the Argentine collapse. Similarly, Perry and Serven (2002) and Krueger (2002b) argued that weak fiscal performance was important, and also emphasized the interaction with overvaluation caused by exchange rate rigidity under the currency board. This rigidity led the economy to a serious debt dynamic.

In contrast, Stiglitz (2002) contended that the causes of crisis are to be found in the development of a political economy based on the recommendations of the IMF and the multilateral development banks. The neoliberal project of the 1990s promoted by these organizations left the country susceptible to fiscal deficits, in particular those reforms related to privatization of social security. IFI conditionality often called for fiscal tightening that was in turn an economic liability, especially during recession times. From this perspective, bad economic advice, in addition to the pressures of the IMF which kept pumping in money in an attempt to avoid devaluation were mainly responsible for the lack of policy instruments left for the country to manage its vulnerabilities (Blustein 2005). In addition, external vulnerability meant that the real economy has been extremely unstable, with negative implications for growth, equity and domestic financial stability (Ffrench-Davies and Studart 2003).

Whether international factors or domestic factors are more important in understanding the crisis is a rhetorical question. Although there has been a large debate that either favours one or the other in Argentina, a false dissociation of the 'internal' and the 'external' can lead to a myopia that overlooks the socio-political foundations related to the interplay of actors, tensions and resistance, and sources of legitimacy supporting political-economic models that explain the political unravelling. These factors not only help to explain the lead up to the crisis but, more importantly, the political responses to international pressures in the context of crisis resolution. In this context, this study suggests that fiscal adjustment, large debt building and currency board rigidities are part and parcel of a process that involved the interaction of domestic and international political actors and interests that unfolded within a context of economic and political weakness. With this in mind, the next section focuses on unfolding patterns of the Argentine political economy since the late 1980s.

From strong neoliberal governance to state failure

Many scholars have explored how neoliberal reforms in Argentina during the 1990s modified the organizational principles of the traditional welfare system which had developed since the 1940s (for instance Cavarozzi 1994). As in many countries in Latin America during this decade, the state's capacity as the main actor to organize and distribute resources was largely affected as global finance and transnational actors became increasingly dominant in the international economy after the late 1970s. Developing countries became more and more subject to international markets and their imperatives, and thus governments' room for manoeuvre and their range of policy options were critically reduced. True, this assumption was also politically functional as many governments in developing countries found external conditionality a useful device to overcome internal opposition and accelerate unpopular reform agendas (Casaburi *et al.* 2000). That is, while globalisation restricted or 'punished' governments in developing countries that followed national economic policy these international constraints acted as a double-edged sword, helping governments to overcome domestic constraints in the implementation of neoliberal reforms. This was particularly the case in Argentina during the 10 years of the Menem administration (1989–99), and the subsequent two years of De la Rúa's presidency, between 1999 and 2001, when unpopular neoliberal reforms were carried out. These were the years of 'internationalisation' of the Argentine state by which an orthodox reform agenda was dutifully implemented following macro-economic policies and structural adjustment in tune with the exigencies of IFIs.

Crafting a domestic base of receptivity and legitimacy for these reforms was a necessary condition for the implementation of radical socio-economic change, often achieved appealing to clientelistic policies (Pastor and Wise 2004). At the same time, achieving a 'seal of good conduct' from IFIs was needed in order to attract international private capital. Argentina, under the government of Carlos Menem, embarked on a broad agreement with the World Bank and the IMF to comply with the principles of the Washington Consensus (Tussie and Tuozzo 2002: 28). In this case, while internationalisation of the state imposed limits on the discretionary capacity of the state to manage choices of economic policy, it also helped the national government to manage decision-making processes and to neutralize opposition, in particular from labour unions, to market-oriented reforms (Acuña 1995; Murillo 1997). As argued by Tedesco (2002: 474), 'Menem was able to structure a discourse around the idea of an *emergency* that needed drastic measures' in order to secure political and economic stability (also O'Donnell 1994).

As a result, after recurrent crises and inability to find a stable system of governance, Menem managed to secure a parliamentary bill, the Convertibility Law, that in 1991 brought back the confidence of international actors by pegging the national currency to the dollar. The Convertibility programme produced the longest period of political and economic stability in the country's economic history. This was helped by the access to the international financial markets and a sweeping state reform and privatization of public services (Tussie and Tuozzo 2002). Framed under constitutional law, the Convertibility virtually eliminated the possibility of it being altered as a tool of economic policy if circumstances changed.

Convertibility became the basis of the country's neoliberal economic and political governance. It did away with a number of undesirable policies that were associated with past economic failures, such as fiscal deficits, devaluations, state economic intervention, and led to a new stabilisation period in which Argentina experienced a strong economic growth, expanding from US$141 billion in 1990 to US$282 billion in 1999 (World Bank 2000b: i). The misplaced optimism of the IFIs with regard to the Argentine economy overlooked some unfolding political patterns related to corruption and the deterioration of democratic governance. According to Manzetti (2002: 6):

> during most of the 1990s, Menem's reform earned him high praise at home and abroad to the point that he was even invited to address the annual IMF/World Bank meeting in Washington as late as 1998, an honor granted to few heads of state from developing countries.

The institutionalization of a neoliberal political economy transformed Argentina's social structure during the 1990s. The process of privatization and deregulation that accompanied the neoliberal reforms moved decisions traditionally taken in the hands of the public sector to the private sector, reducing the state's participation in areas such as welfare spending and safety nets. In this sense, neoliberal politics reconfigured the state's role as manager of economic redistribution, placing market forces as the main criteria in the allocation of socio-economic resources. However, Convertibility enclosed a paradox; that is, while growth gave a temporary feeling of improvement in living standards, 'its relation to the sustainability of growth based on internally generated resources, unemployment and income distribution was given secondary importance' (IDB 2004: iii, ft 5). Decreasing involvement of the state in welfare provision led to unequal distribution of growth and an increasing problem of poverty and inequality (Grugel and Riggirozzi 2007). This was particularly so as the injections in government revenues from the sale of state enterprises started to slow down by the mid to late 1990s (Schorr 2005). It was from this point that international debt started to rise, becoming a major resource of state funding (Rozenwurcel interview). A sharp recession affected the Argentine economy in 1995, particularly stirred by the crises in emerging markets, and although growth recovered, social indexes deteriorated steadily ending in the crisis of 2001. Therefore, the distributional impact of neoliberal restructuring is critical to understand the politics of crisis and crisis resolution.

By the end of the decade, the apparent paragon of stabilisation and growth based on pegged currency and orthodox policies had no instruments through which to mediate the problems of capital flight and falling reserves that were deepened by financial crises in other emerging markets

(Rodrik 2004). Despite the increasing debate on the future prospects of neoliberalism, and the mixed records of Latin American political economic performance, any attempt to replace the Argentine neoliberal model of development looked highly unlikely. Nationally-organized interest groups, notably business groups, financial groups, individual investors, mostly comprising the politically influential middle-class, and corporate organizations have acted as veto players in relation to changes in policies, and thus played a distinctive role in delaying decisions that would modify the exchange rate regime in particular and the economic model in general (Tomassi 2002). As Argued by Escude (2002: 5), the 'success' of Convertibility mainly measured in terms of control of inflation and monetary stabilisation 'tended to cloud policymakers' [and the public] perceptions with respect to the sustainability of the regime and downplayed the growing vulnerability of the economy to a change in the external environment'. A struggle between forces for and against devaluation was at play and political and economic governance came under stress (Blustein 2005; Schorr 2005; Woodruff 2005). Delays in domestic policy reform augmented the political and economic costs of a controlled exit from Convertibility. Soon it became clear that despite the merits of Convertibility in successfully containing hyperinflation, there was no exit strategy. Ultimately the politics of neoliberalism in Argentina failed to balance the attraction of capital flows against the limits they placed on domestic governance.

On October 1999 Fernando de la Rúa, the candidate for the centre-left coalition *Alianza*, won the presidential elections with promises of reverting the economic course and ensuring transparency and democratic accountability. However, once in power the administration was unable to deal with domestic and international pressures, especially pressures to keep the economic policy based at a fixed exchange rate. These pressures became evident when, in an attempt to show political strength and commitment to stability, De la Rúa brought back Domingo Cavallo, Menem's finance minister, 'father' of Convertibility and contending candidate in the 1999 elections. The inability of the government, therefore, to provide mechanisms of adjustment led to an increasing debt, which was the precursor to the financial crisis. Argentina's public debt to GDP ratio increased from 29 per cent at the end of 1993 to 38 per cent at the end of 1998, shortly after the beginning of the recession, and to 51 per cent at the end of 2001 (Escude 2002: 5). Together these trends were reinforced by the irresponsible actions of the IMF that kept pumping in money as a way of increasing the security to financial markets and local lenders *vis-à-vis* the possibility of currency devaluation (Blustein 2005).

The economic and political pressure to stick to Convertibility led the government of De la Rúa to adopt orthodox policies and to deepen structural reforms, elements that helped gain approval for a new IMF Stand By Agreement for US$7.2 billion in March 2000. The IMF insisted on a new fiscal pact with the provinces, which not only were running extensive deficits but also were issuing quasi-monies (Cibils 2003). Other conditions involved a new law for labour market deregulation, which led De la Rua's Vice-President, Carlos Alvarez, to resign amidst corruption scandals related to bribery in the Senate House; and health and pension system reforms. Despite adjustments that included severe tax increase, restricted fiscal spending and a timid tax-sharing agreement between the provinces, recession was not averted and fiscal targets with the IMF were not met. Stagnation had persisted since 1998 and the crisis was now unavoidable. Different attempts to prevent it were ineffective as they only reinforced the polarisation between those for and against the sustainability of convertibility.

Contending strategies were developed with regard to managing Convertibility and avoiding a default at all costs in the servicing of foreign debt. Two hard lines of debate unfolded; an extreme orthodoxy which proposed advancing toward a complete 'dollarisation' of the economy, and those that insisted on the need to end Convertibility, devalue the currency and foster an export strategy based on the local economic structure (de Mendiguren interview). But the weakened government was torn between competing projects that represented different interests. The stance of the multilateral institutions and foreign creditors was compelling as they provided a new line of credit worth US$ 40 billion toward future commitments. The new credit instrument was articulated by the IMF, the Inter-American Development Bank, the World Bank, the Spanish government and other private financial institutions, and was called '*blindaje*' (armour). However, the inability to sustain the debt burden failed to change investor's perception, and the country's risk level continued to skyrocket. State capacity began to be seriously questioned domestically and internationally.

Unable to borrow at affordable rates, the government announced a 'Zero Deficit Plan', a budget cut of 13 per cent of state workers' wages and pensions plus the reduction of resource transfers to provincial governments. The IMF also agreed to a second rescue package of US$8 billion in September 2001. But not only did the Argentine economy keep deteriorating, but money also kept fleeing the country. Social unrest, labour protests and street blockage promptly followed becoming a daily affair. A movement of the unemployed (*piqueteros*) emerged in several provinces which opposed further adjustment and demanded re-nation-alisation of former state-owned companies and banks, and non-payment of the external debt (Svampa and Pereyra 2003).

Matters came to a head by mid-November when the IMF announced cancellation of its financial support. In a desperate reaction to stop the massive capital flight, the government implemented a '*Corralito*', an unprecedented measure that restricted bank withdrawals and the trans-fer of money abroad. The middle classes joined the unemployed *piqueteros* in street protests. Looting of supermarkets took place in areas of extreme deprivation. On 19 December, the president declared a state of siege. However, rather than being an effective control mechanism, this des-perate measure led more people to spontaneous street protests and wide-spread unrest (Peruzzotti 2001; Manzetti 2002). The popular slogan supporting successive public demonstrations demanded '*Que se vayan todos*' ('out with all of them') suggestive of not only the failure of the established model of governance, but rather the whole structure of policy-making and the political class (Peruzzotti and Smulowitz 2003). It rejected in particular the *Corralito*, the administrative and economic fail-ure, the social consequences of neoliberalism and the political corruption that permeated different levels of authority. In turn, popular mobilisa-tion forced the resignation of first the Minister of Economics, Domingo Cavallo, and then of the President Fernando De la Rúa on 19 December 2001. By mid-December the country was finally declared in international and national default.

In January 2002 an interim government was established by parlia-mentary rule and Eduardo Duhalde, from the Peronist Party, was elected provisional president. Duhalde, who begun his term with congressional backing proposed a recovery effort that deviated from neoliberal ortho-doxy by prioritising the revival of domestic industry over the early restor-ation of debt servicing. Consequently, one of his first political measures was to terminate the Convertibility system and let the Argentine peso drop more than one-third to reach a new point from which to start again.

Restoring state capacity

The collapse of Convertibility was part of the most profound crisis in Argentine economic history. The model initiated by Duhalde's adminis-tration in the immediate post-crisis period had three main challenges: regaining political legitimacy; achieving social peace; and recovering the macroeconomic instruments necessary to reactivate the economy (Grugel and Riggirozzi 2007). At the same time, the government was facing these challenges in very adverse initial conditions: an accumulated loss of 20 per cent of its GDP; decreased consumption of 30 per cent, investment of 54 per cent and industrial production of 30 per cent; unstable exchange and inflation rates; a critical loss of capital that flew the country in early 2001 – equivalent to 7.6 per cent of that year's GDP; a loss of 55 per cent of international reserves, levels of unemployment that reached over 23 per cent; poverty levels at over 50 per cent and extreme poverty levels of over one-quarter of the population (Ministerio de Economia 2005). In addition, other pressing aspects were related to a monetary anarchy as 14 money denominations were circulating in 11 different provinces in parallel to the peso; a highly conflictive social situation and an institutional abyss. Lack of international financial support both to the public and private domestic sectors magnified the extent of this crisis and isolation.

President Duhalde faced a critical point as he urgently had to confront social unrest associated with the country's financial instability. In facing the exhaustion of Convertibility the government was challenged by resilient pressures related to the two contending perspectives regarding 'dollarisation' of the Argentine economy or stimulating the national productive structure for the internal market. The first option implied officially replacing the peso with the US dollar at a fixed exchange rate and eliminating the Central Bank as a body issuing currency to transfer its financial assets to other bodies, intensifying the model of the 1990s. The second option proposed as a solution the devaluation of the peso stimulating export market competition based on the national industry, restructuring domestic alliances and replacing the financial sector and the privatized companies from the hegemonic centre in favour of the productive, industrial sector.

Politically, the dilemma for the interim president was that economic measures to reactivate the economy were likely to exacerbate social and political tensions. In this context, what emerged as policy response was the appeal to national resources to change the model and reconstruct political legitimacy and trust. The government put forward an agenda that compromised demands of popular movements, some of which were politically vocal after the crisis such as the unemployed workers movement, *piqueteros*; and the pressures from national and international actors demanding economic stabilisation and social pacification. As put by Tussie (2006: 11), 'the government faced the *realpolitik* dilemma of attempting to pacify powerful business interests and [its] electorates, seeking to maintain and consolidate the domestic constituencies of support to shore up [its] domestic popularity'. In this highly mobilized society the government used two tools that assured a balanced relationship between mobilisation and resistance: a new nationalistic rhetoric and a new approach to economic management. These elements helped to amalgamate and compromise interests between business and civil society at the national level, and in turn reconstruct state legitimacy and capacity. State actions accompanied a new nationalistic rhetoric, which proved an authoritative mechanism to regain some social and political control. Economically, one of the first and highly symbolic decisions of Duhalde's government was to abandon Convertibility – by converting financial contracts to peso valuations, what was called 'pesification' (Baldi-Delatte 2005) – and immediately impose a moratorium on servicing the public debt. This set the stage for stabilising the economy and was the most significant sign that the government would actively support a national pathway to crisis recovery.

The devaluation brought to the centre of the political and economic arena the export-oriented sectors and the industries that provided substitutes for foreign imports and financial resources to back up government policies. The so-called *Grupo Productivo* (Productive Group), formed by representatives from nationally-based industrial firms producing for the domestic market, was highly influential in shaping the terms of a new national economic strategy (De Mendiguren interview). The Productive Group had been lobbying the government throughout the 1990s in relation to the privatization policy and more strongly after the 1998 recession that damaged national industry. In facing the imminent crisis of 2001, the Group strongly supported devaluation policies and the reactivation of national industry by means of lowering the costs of production and fostering export and trade. Representatives from the agricultural and construction sectors supported the industrialist initiative, which not only was presented to the immediate post-crisis government but also to representatives of the IMF, the World Bank and the IDB in October 2001 (UIA 2001).

In contrast to the 1990s when the retrenchment of the state augmented the power of capital over national resources, by the mid 2000s economic recovery in Argentina had been engineered by a combination of export expansion and re-industrialisation for the domestic market that reinforced the national production structure, and the alliance of the government with the Productive Group. In tandem, a series of ad-hoc policies restored the fiscal balance supporting the reconstruction of state capacity. For instance, Duhalde's government managed to negotiate a 20 per cent tax on export earnings from agricultural commodities and hydrocarbons, which became the central source for financing social emergency programmes. Increased state income as a consequence of debt default and export-oriented growth bolstered welfare spending, political inclusion and the promise of job creation (Grugel and Riggirozzi 2007: 28). Other government policies involved subjecting privatized companies to price control over the services they provided, a decision that was particularly controversial among these stakeholders which claimed the loss of their capital as a consequence of the devaluation (Aspiazu 2002). Finally, in order to help the domestic market to thrive again, restrictions under *Corralito* were lifted.

Gradually, the economy recovered and fiscal balance was restored by the end of 2002 (Gerchunoff and Aguirre 2004: 4). A growing export sector also helped to stabilize the currency. Just as importantly, it made possible new social investments which, though modest, helped calm the situation socially by attaining social urgencies by means of distribution of food, health and workfare plans and subsidies and integrating leading groups in the implementation of social plans (Svampa and Pereyra 2003).

This political economic response effectively helped to re-legitimize and re-institutionalize the government after the crisis and, more importantly, altered the rules of the game that defined Argentina's relationship with international financial organizations and international creditors. Manoeuvring between international financial actors and domestic politics defined a key pattern in the reconstruction of Argentina's state capacity. That is, the government managed fiscal and monetary policies in order to stimulate national development policies, attending at the same time to social needs. State control was helped by means of negotiation of governability pacts with productive sectors, provincial governments and social actors delaying at the same time negotiations with international institutional and private creditors. This opened a new dynamic between material resources and power relations involving Argentina and the external actors. Argentina's political economy before the crisis was often constrained by the dependency on external funding, mainly supplied by IMF funds and private investors that helped to loosen the constraints of the strict currency board (Setser and Gelpern 2004: 7). Therefore, during the 1990s the Argentine economy, as well as others in the region, surrendered important margins of national sovereignty and transferred formal decision-making powers in sensitive areas to transnational firms and IFIs through conditional loans and country risk evaluations. As Lehman and McCoy (1992: 602) assessed:

if Latin American states refuse to offer acceptable concessions or impose severe demands on the creditors in order to placate internal political groups, [they] risk retaliation from international banks, such as attachments of foreign assets, rupture of trade lines, and cessation of lending.

In contrast, the Argentine crisis catalysed a government more responsive to the interests of domestic citizens and markets than to the interests of foreign creditors and the international capital. This was a bargaining game that revealed a different pattern from that experienced in the 1980s and 1990s. Today there is a different tendency in play; the state re-emerged as a political base to implement changes that diverge from the international norm.

Augmenting state bargaining power with international actors

Given the acute socio-political and economic turmoil surrounding the recent crisis in Argentina, it would have been commonly expected for the state to have little or no bargaining position, especially in facing international financial actors' conditions to reopening financial channels of support. However, the collapse of Argentina's economy in 2001–2002 represented a turning point that prompted audacious and well-targeted reforms aimed at reverting the neoliberal model. Moreover, crisis resolution in Argentina was actually foundational in that it managed to revert the tendency to rely on external bailout and thus on conditional funding to overcome financial crisis, and with it to avoid the political costs of further dependency. While the model of the 1990s was highly dependent on international market access and funding, post-crisis reconstruction in 2001–2002 leaned on a revitalized national economic structure supported by political decisions that led to a sustained strategy of '*des-endeudamiento*' (de-borrowing).

De-borrowing implied the renegotiation of existing debt with international institutions and private creditors without asking for any further loan and repaying debt with national reserves. The external context was also favourable to this strategy. In the previous decade the economy rested highly on external capital while the terms of trade were unfavourable for the region. After devaluation, on the contrary, the Argentine economy has benefited from improved terms of trade that together with a competitive exchange rate led Argentina to build a double trade and fiscal surpluses in a short time and thus to reduce its dependency on external sources of funding. Furthermore, while in the 1990s macroeconomic management became hostage to foreign capital inflows, abandoning any ability to adjust interest rates to fight inflation or recession, the devaluation of early 2002 was part of a hard-line strategy by which flexibilisation of the exchange rate and an expansive monetary policy were implemented regardless of access to the international financial markets. External trade and internal surplus were possible because of the immediate signs of economic growth led by sectors that benefited from the real depreciation of the peso and a gradual recovery in consumption. As a result, growth output has been sustained at an average of 9 per cent since mid-2002.

As Argentina became less dependent on fresh money from the IFIs, the balance in terms of bargaining capacity in negotiations of loan conditions and payment also inclined in favour of the Argentine government. The World Bank and the IDB, for instance, agreed to reorient their portfolios toward social priorities identified by the government and to earmark important funding for social assistance programmes (Masnatta interview). Those funds were still subject to an agreement with the IMF, but the IMF was reluctant to advance an agreement claiming that more orthodox adjustments were needed as well as a renegotiation of contracts with private creditors and privatized companies after the government's decision to devaluate the peso (see IMF 2004). The 'tough' position of the IMF has been interpreted as a stance 'to set the record straight in the face of critics who considered it had been too lenient too long with the country' (Cline 2003: 40). The IMF, in effect, refused to endorse nationalistic measures such as the regulation of utility companies and privatized enterprises which were subjected to a price freeze over the services provided following the 'pesification' of the economy, the implementation of new taxes on trade and finance and other capital controls. Negotiations stalled as neither the IMF wanted to loosen up its conditions over reforms nor did the Argentine government want to reach an agreement at the expense of adopting unpopular policies reducing social spending or rising taxes. Some argued that there was a deliberate strategy on the part of the Argentine government to 'play for time with the IMF' in order to 'procure the best arrangement possible for Argentina as part of a long-term approach to dealing with its creditors' (Cooper and Momani 2004: 310). What was at stake was a dispute over policies and approaches that was unlocked when the Argentine government threatened a new default on a payment of about $800 million to the World Bank in mid-November 2002 and of about $800 million to the IDB early in 2003. This move established a negotiation framework. Not without a normative dilemma, the IMF came in with a US$6.78 billion package for Argentina to meet immediate payment to the multilateral banks in January 2003. Given that the debts to the IMF of Argentina, Turkey and

Brazil, accounted for more than 70 per cent of its outstanding credit, the IMF could not afford to deal with another default. The January agreement gave Argentina economic breathing space which was also capitalized in the campaign for a new president.

When Néstor Kirchner took office, in May 2003, negotiations with the IMF for an enhanced loan agreement were under way. Like his predecessor, Kirchner's administration had strongly put forward a rhetoric of nationalism and anti-neoliberalism that substantiated policy decisions based on stimulating domestic demand before negotiating foreign debt payments. Economic recovery and renewed competitiveness of national-based production afforded greater state control over economic activity through government investment, social development and increased regulation of public service companies and banks, policies that not only contradicted IMF rules but also made clear that Argentina would not allow foreign creditors to dictate economic norms. At the same time, it reduced leverage of the IMF as 'lender of last resort'.

In this context, Argentina was in a strong position to determine the terms of the negotiation with the IMF and, in fact, rejected the conditions of a three-year agreement proposed by the international institution in September 2003. The three-year plan projected that Argentina would generate a 4.5 per cent of GDP primary fiscal surplus in 2004, and larger surpluses in 2005 and 2006. The IMF also requested a timeline for increases in the privatized utility rates. Finally, the IMF wanted Argentina to start making capital payments on its US$15 billion debt to the institution, in addition to keeping up its interest payments (Cibils 2003: 1). Upon these conditions, the IMF would make disbursements after an evaluation of the country's economic performance. But as Argentina firmly rejected these conditions, the IMF had to finally back down on its original demands to finally agree to a smaller condition on primary fiscal surplus (3 per cent of GDP) and no timeline for utility rate increases. The final agreement was, therefore, a consequence of a long *tit-for-tat* game in which a great deal of leverage increased on the side of the debtor, which on its road to recovery could threaten not to service debt commitments. Likewise, the risk of default put the IMF in a weaker position. As Cline (2003: 40) notes, 'the final question regarding the IMF is whether it and the other multilateral donors have now entered into the "lender's trap" in which there is a great deal of leverage on the side of the debtor because it expects no net new financing from the donor and it can threaten not to pay principal due'.

Having effectively reverted the terms of bargaining with the IMF, Argentina turned to the private creditors with which it also adopted a strong position regarding their claim for compensation over their devalued assets. The Argentine Economic Minister, Roberto Lavagna, presented a proposal for restructuring debt at the 2003 World Economic Forum meeting held in Dubai. These terms set a political benchmark for the government, stipulating that the creditors accept a 75 per cent debt reduction and no recognition of past due interest (Dhillon *et al.* 2006). Private investors immediately rejected the Dubai offer and, as a consequence, the IMF delayed the first quarterly review delaying as a consequence the first disbursement. Yet again, facing the risk of default on the IFIs, the IMF capitulated and approved the first payment. Immediately, the Argentine government, which had a US$3.1 billion payment due on March 2004, demanded that the IMF assured the procedures for the second review and that the disbursement of funds followed the schedule as agreed.

Negotiations with private creditors continued on the basis of a new settlement offered by the Argentine government on June 2004, the so-called Buenos Aires proposal. This offer proposed a final 70 per cent of debt swap and invited private creditors to voluntarily take it within a deadline set for 25 February 2005. At the end, the majority of creditors (76 per cent) accepted a final offer of 66.3 per cent debt reduction (Miller and Thomas 2006: 12). Although Argentina was still in default with 24 per cent of its creditors, the final acceptance of the debt reduction by the majority augmented Argentina's leverage against the remaining creditors, who were left in a weak bargaining position. In the context of these negotiations, and as part of the strategy of dealing with the external actors, on August 2004 Argentina sidelined the IMF announcing it would suspend further lending agreements with that institution. Once again, this move not only worked against IMF leverage but also against pressures of those private bondholders that did not accept the Buenos Aires proposal and who had hoped that IMF surveillance would be an effective instrument to induce Argentina to improve its debt restructuring conditions. By fragmenting the private creditors and the IMF conditionality, Argentina has rewritten the financial rules of the game (Cooper and Momani 2004).

By the end of 2005, the Argentine economy was growing at a steady 9 per cent average. This economic growth supported the government's radical decision to pay in full its US$9.8 billion debt with the IMF (5.5 per cent of GDP). An emergent nationalistic outlook supported by a new wave of economic growth in Latin America, led by Argentina, Chile, Brazil and Venezuela, seems to have recently influenced the decision of the Uruguayan government to follow Argentina's lead in reorienting its relationship with the IMF. This move further enhanced sovereignty and autonomy in government decisions, as the country freed itself from IMF surveillance. It augmented at the same time its margin of manoeuvre in negotiation with private creditors that were left without the umbrella of IMF to enforce their debt servicing.

The experience of Argentina's bargaining with the IMF and the private creditors since 2002 has been unprecedented not only in terms of changing the balance and the terms of bargaining but also in terms of how the international financial system works. For instance, while the World Bank requires national governments to have won the IMF's seal of approval before it funds major new projects, in Argentina funding from this and other multilateral organizations such as the IDB and the UNDP were unaffected by the bargaining games with the IMF and the international creditors. These institutions kept supporting important social programmes in the country contributing to social peace and complementing welfare spending that helped to re-legitimize and re-institutionalize state politics after crisis. From this perspective, in contrast to structural arguments that claim that power in international economic relations has moved away from states to markets (Frieden and Rogowski 1996; Haggard and Maxfield 1996; Strange 1998) post-crisis resolution in Argentina facilitated the reassertion of state control over politics and policy adjustment, as well as its negotiating capacity before the IMF and foreign creditors. As such, rather than a delegation of power and decision-making to external actors, the crisis in Argentina represented the turning point from which state authority and policy capacity were re-established. Crisis resolution thus shifted back power to domestic institutions, enabling the state to achieve its goals.

A final note on state power, interests and governance

One of the most significant aspects of crisis management in Argentina has been the determination of the government to shift the development model toward an alternative to neoliberalism. Crisis management has, therefore, been foundational in that it has forged a new space for dissent from global rules without falling into outdated, anti-capitalist economic autarky (see Grugel and Riggirozzi 2007). Crisis and adjustment cannot, in fact, be understood in any sense as exclusively national processes as governments must show credibility in their policies and decision-making not only to domestic constituencies, but also to international investors. However, in the aftermath of the crisis and after declaring a major default on its debt, rebuilding legitimacy of the domestic political economy in Argentina was prioritized over the critical task of rebuilding credibility for the financial market. What emerged was an interesting relationship between the search for international autonomy and the reconstruction of legitimacy of the national development project. Whilst the post-crisis government did not insulate the economy from the forces of global markets, it did seek to revert the terms of exchange that define Argentina's insertion and negotiation in the international political economy.

This political decision was a keystone to rebuild state power and engage with the global economy in a different way rather than by restricting national projects. State choice in this case diverted from the ideological authority of neoliberalism and sought to augment its apparent narrowed policy space. The crisis acted as an enabling force as it generated political pressures for the government to increase social protection in the context of financial isolation. Concurrently, financial isolation presented a paradox in terms of building state power and autonomy against foreign actors. In the aftermath of the debt crisis of the 1980s, market openness provided governments with access to capital, yet it also subjected them to external discipline. In this context, investors' exit capacity often provides them with political power. In this case, developing countries' powers and capacities and their policy options were limited in scope by the power of internationally mobile capital. In contrast, crisis management in the aftermath of December 2001 faced capital market reticence so the ability of the government to access and redistribute resources in line with social and economic objectives had to rely on national resources. In the midst of the Argentine abyss, the post-crisis government did not capitalize on the rules of globalisation but rather in the search of new governance spaces within the national economic structure that in turn were amplified in search for new political alliances within the region. Restructuring and integration at the international level, therefore, were results not of external obligation but of a national strategy. Policy-making autonomy was, in fact, a direct result of state capacity to regulate and control economic activity and to stand firm in international debt negotiations.

Yet, some questions emerge when considering the prospects of post-crisis stabilisation in Argentina. The undoubtedly strengthened state is here to stay, participating in the economic process in a fashion that differs from the neoliberal project of the 1990s. However, this does not mean a nationalistic, autarkic project in which nationalisation of politics and economics replace the open market legacy of the 1990s. The current scenario seems to point to a project of opened nationalism in which market-oriented policies amalgamate and compromise with state intervention. Nonetheless, the state currently relies heavily on its nationally-supported sources of income. Moreover, the 'investor-friendly policy approach' of the 1990s has been replaced by a climate in which foreign investors remain deterred by some micro-level 'anti-market' policies from the government of Kirchner, in particular those related to the implementation of price control. In this process much compromising is still to be seen between national actors and IFIs and creditors. Paradoxically, public sector-led investment growth prompted rising incomes and falling unemployment, which together with export dynamism are driving strong economic growth. This strong recovery seems to be the basis for foreign investment attraction, in particular from emerging economies such as China, and the underpinnings of the economy in the near future (UNCTAD 2006: 69). It has also situated the country as a main investor in the region. A final interesting note in this context is the nature of the foreign investors that seem to have moved from services provision toward construction and manufacturing; two of the leading areas in economic recovery. Still to be seen is the final resolution of disputes over contracts and agreements concluded among foreign investors operating in the country during the 1990s. Here again, amalgamation of interests and compromising positions will determine the extent to which the Argentine economy breaks the cycle of crisis and economic bottlenecks.

As a corollary, it can be concluded that financial crisis and crisis resolution are context contingent and that traditional explanations based on dominant positions of international actors' power need a cautious note. Foreign power in Argentina's crisis resolution has been largely mediated by national material capabilities and institutional forms that situated the state at the centre of power relations and as an anchor in the pursuing of domestically-orientated economic policies, defying established dynamics of power relations.

Note

The financial support of the ESRC Postdoctoral Fellowship is gratefully acknowledged (Ref.: A112865). This study has also benefited from the ESRC-funded project on *Governance After Crisis*. The author would like to thank Jean Grugel and Justin Robertson, as well as the interviewees cited in this chapter.

7
Brazil: Mixed Impact of Financial Crises on Manufacturing and Financial Sectors

Mahrukh Doctor and Luiz Fernando de Paula

The Brazilian economy was hit by three financial crises between 1994 and 2005, only one of which could be described as having mainly domestic origins. The first was triggered by the Mexican Crisis in 1994–95 and came shortly after Brazil's successful stabilization under the Real Plan; the second, more of a slow-drip crisis, began with contagion from the Asian (1997) and Russian (1998) crises, but then became a full-blown local crisis, which led to the maxi-devaluation of the currency in January 1999; the third crisis, of mainly local origin, was the 2002 capital and currency market instability triggered by the upcoming presidential elections. The origins, sequence and fallout for the domestic economy differed in each crisis as did its impact on foreign interests in the Brazilian economy.

Much of the academic literature on financial crises was initially preoccupied with ascribing blame, whether on bad domestic policy or financial panic in international capital markets (Chang 1999). Much less was written about the medium- and longer-term impact of financial crises on the prospects for economic growth and development. What little there was, depending on one's view of foreign participation in developing country economies, tended to focus either on the 'opportunism' of foreign responses or on more benign external 'intervention' (whether in the form of advice and funding or via the positive externalities generated by market activities of private firms). As evidence of the former interpretation, many pointed to the significant increase in foreign firms' presence in the 1990s, where local businesses were bought up in what some described as 'fire sales' in the aftermath of financial crises. Undoubtedly, in Brazil, inward FDI stocks as a percentage of GDP rose appreciably from 6 per cent in 1995 to 17 per cent in 1998 (UNCTAD 2000). However, when looking more closely at the evidence in the Brazilian case, we found that this was an oversimplified, if not self-important, view on the part of foreign/Western interests and analysts.

In the Introduction, Robertson proposed a number of perspectives for analyzing the position of foreign interests in the wake of financial crises. Given constraints of space, this chapter focuses on four aspects – two of which emphasize the domestic and the other two the role of foreign interests in Brazil. These are: resistant domestic politics, domestic winners, uneven foreign involvement and efficiency enhancing foreign investment. We find that the consequences of financial crises must be examined in a disaggregated manner – both in terms of the degree of impact relative to other processes in the wider economic conjuncture as well as in terms of specific sectors and types of financial flows. Thus, our more nuanced picture first considers the general economic policy and market context during and after the financial crisis. Next, it distinguishes between types of capital flows (portfolio capital and foreign direct investment) and types of economic activity (financial services and manufacturing industry), with the analysis focusing on the latter distinction.

Our argument is presented in two steps. First, we argue that at the micro-economic (firm and industry) level, whether in the financial or productive sectors, domestic economic processes and policy-making, discussed in section two, had a much greater impact on the changing ownership structure and investment pattern than did the fall out from international financial crises. Secondly, we show that among the various financial crises in the 1990s, the Mexican crisis had a much deeper and longer-term impact on Brazilian firms than did the Asian crisis (notwithstanding the drastic devaluation and switch to an inflation-targeting monetary regime, as explained below).

The chapter is organized in five sections. After the introduction, section two examines the general economic context in terms of macro-economic reforms and industrial restructuring; section three considers the impact of crisis on foreign and domestic firms in financial services, specifically the banking sector; section four analyses the impact on firms operating in the manufacturing sector, specifically the automotive parts industry; finally, section five discusses the overall impact of the crises on foreign and domestic firms in the context of greater internationalization of the Brazilian economy.

Economic context and financial crises in Brazil

Financial crises and macro-economic policy responses in 1994–2005

Since the beginning of the 1980s, high inflation was a major problem and indexation contracts spread all around the Brazilian economy. By 1993, inflation was almost 3,000 per cent. Starting in 1994, after the failure of a number of previous price stabilization programs, Brazil finally implemented the successful stabilization program, the Real Plan.[1] This plan differed from Argentina's Convertibility Plan in that it adopted a more flexible exchange rate anchor. It brought inflation down fast, with a combination of exchange rate appreciation, high interest rates and a huge reduction in import tariffs. However, the expansion of demand, and the overvalued exchange rate created immediate difficulties for Brazil's external sector. From 1995 to 1998, the trade balance accumulated a deficit of US$22.3 billion and the current account registered a deficit of US$105.6 billion (Table 7.1). The Brazilian economy's high degree of external financial fragility left it susceptible to short-term changes in the international situation and kept it vulnerable to currency crises.

The Mexican crisis in 1994–95 made clear that sooner or later the consequence of Brazil's external vulnerability would be a currency crisis. As a result of the 'tequila effect', foreign investment declined, thereby reducing Brazil's foreign reserves. In order to face off a speculative attack on the Brazilian domestic currency (*real*), the authorities introduced a crawling peg system to operate the exchange rate flexibly, moved tariffs upwards in some specific sectors (including the automotive industry) and increased the interest rate to nearly 65 per cent in an attempt to entice international capital. These measures effectively prevented a speculative attack on the *real* and averted a currency crisis. However, the increase in the nominal interest rate (Figure 7.1) slowed growth and increased net public debt. Such a policy also caused difficulties for businesses and the financial system suffered serious distress due to a rapid increase in the number of bad loans.

After a period of some economic normality, but with an increasing external fragility due to the current account deficit (3.8 per cent of GDP at the end of 1997), the *real* suffered another speculative attack in October 1997 because of contagion from the East Asia crisis. Once again, the annual nominal interest rate was raised from 24.5 per cent in October to 46.5 per cent in November 1997. The government also announced the implementation of a fiscal package in the hope of inspiring more confidence in economic agents. These policies were well received as evidenced by a reduction in capital outflows during the first semester of 1998 and by the fact that foreign reserves rose to US$70 billion by the end of July 1998 (up from US$40 billion at the beginning of July 1994).

However, in the third quarter of 1998, another speculative attack on the *real*, a mix of contagion from the Russian crisis plus perception on the part of market operators that Brazil was experiencing serious macroeconomic imbalances, clearly demonstrated that foreign reserves were no protection against speculation. The monetary authorities insisted on

Table 7.1 Brazil: some macroeconomic data, 1991–2005

Year	Consumer Index Price (IPCA)	GDP growth – annual %	Investment, rate (% of GDP)	Trade balance – US$m	Current account – US$m	Net public debt-over-GDP	Real average income – Sao Paulo urban region (1985 = 100)	Formal unemployment rate* – Sao Paulo urban region (%)
1991	472.5	1.03	18.11	10,580	1,408	38.1	58.5	6.7
1992	1,119.1	−0.54	18.42	15,239	6,109	37.1	61.3	8.0
1993	2,477.1	4.92	19.28	13,299	−676	32.6	68.4	7.6
1994	916.5	5.85	20.75	10,467	−1,811	30.0	65.9	7.8
1995	22.4	4.22	20.54	−3,466	−18,384	30.6	69.9	8.7
1996	9.6	2.66	19.26	−5,599	−23,502	33.3	71.5	9.2
1997	5.2	3.27	19.86	−6,753	−30,452	34.4	72.4	10.2
1998	1.7	0.13	19.69	−6,575	−33,416	41.7	71.5	10.8
1999	8.9	0.79	18.90	−1,199	−25,335	48.7	65.9	10.5
2000	6.0	4.36	19.29	−698	−24,225	48.8	62.3	10.0
2001	7.7	1.31	19.47	2,651	−23,215	52.6	56.9	11.6
2002	12.5	1.93	18.32	13,121	−7,637	55.5	51.6	11.4
2003	9.3	0.54	17.78	24,794	4,177	57.2	53.5	12.0
2004	7.6	5.18	19.58	33,693	11,669	51.8	52.3	10.0
2005	5.7	2.30	19.93	44,748	14,193	51.0	54.1	9.7

Note: *Formal unemployment rate does not include informal unemployment.
Source: IPEA data.

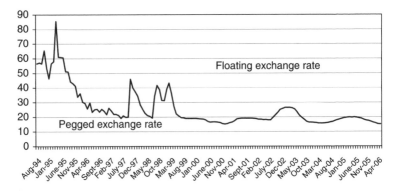

Source: Central Bank of Brazil (BCB).
Figure 7.1   Brazil: nominal interest rate (%/year)

maintaining the semi-fixed exchange rate. Further fiscal belt-tightening was announced, and the BCB raised the nominal interest rate to 43 per cent. However, disappointment with slippage in fiscal adjustment during 1998 plus a growing public debt contributed to the general feeling that Brazil remained vulnerable. The continuity of the Real Plan, at least as originally conceived, became ever less sustainable.

Investor uncertainty saw capital flowing out of the country and foreign reserves fell rapidly (by 38 per cent between September and December 1998). Although the IMF put together a US$42 billion rescue package, financial markets were unconvinced, and as a result, Brazil was unable to defend its currency. In January 1999, the exchange rate regime was finally changed. A floating exchange rate regime supplanted the semi-pegged exchange rate anchor (the main pillar of the Real Plan). Some months later, the Brazilian government adopted an inflation-targeting regime as the new anchor for prices, inspired by the British model.

A few months after the initial economic turbulence brought about by the devaluation, the economy already began to show signs of recovery. Indeed, in 1999 and 2000, GDP increased 0.8 per cent and 4.4 per cent, respectively, and the inflation rate (Extensive National Consumer Index: IPCA) rose by no more than two digits, that is 8.9 per cent in 1999 and 6.0 per cent in 2000; and the medium- and long-term inflows of portfolio capital as well as FDI rose.

However, in 2001, owing to a number of international shocks (the slow-down in the US economy, and the Turkish and Argentine crises) the Brazilian economy again began to flounder (growth fell to 1.3 per cent). The already high level of external debt rose from 24.0 per cent of GDP in

1997 to 41.2 per cent in 2001. Although the current account balance fell from US$33.4 billion in 1998 to US$23.2 billion in 2001 (Table 7.1), the ratio of the current account balance to GDP was over 4 per cent. Thus, Brazil remained vulnerable to the mood in international financial markets.

In mid-2002, when the Workers' Party (PT) candidate, Luiz Inacio Lula da Silva, began leading in opinion polls for the October presidential elections, investor fears triggered capital flight, pushing down the exchange rate. There was a 'sudden stop' in capital inflows, with many investors refraining from purchasing public securities maturing after 1 January 2003 (the start of the new presidential term). The pre-election macroeconomic instability pushed the IPCA to 12.5 per cent and GDP growth was less than two per cent in 2002. President Lula's new government moved to reassure markets, limiting further damage. The BCB increased interest rates in 2003 and the government raised the primary fiscal surplus (fiscal balance before interest payments) to 4.25 per cent in 2003 and 4.59 per cent in 2004. Inflation was 9.3 per cent and GDP growth a meager 0.54 per cent in 2003.

In subsequent years, favorable international conditions resulted in an up-surge of global capital flows with positive impacts on the Brazilian economy: an increase in demand for and prices of commodities boosted the trade surplus from US$24.9 billion in 2003 to US$44.8 billion in 2005; and exchange reserves rose from US$37.8 billion to US$53.8 billion in the same period. However, GDP growth took a 'stop-go' pattern: 0.5 per cent in 2003, 4.9 per cent in 2004, 2.3 per cent in 2005 and an estimated 3.0 per cent in 2006. Growth rates were low for Brazilian needs, and also low when compared to other big emerging countries over the same period.[2]

To summarize, the 1999 switch from an exchange anchor to a floating exchange rate regime plus inflation targeting brought no significant improvement in macroeconomic variables (see Table 7.1). However, the 2003–2005 accounts improved mainly due to increases in the trade surplus. Interest rates did not fall quickly; rather they rose in 2001 due to turbulence in international markets, and again in 2003 due to market unease with the new government.

The *modus operandi* of an inflation-targeting regime plus the adoption of a floating exchange rate under conditions of full opening of the capital account resulted in greater instability of the nominal exchange rate. In 2002–2003, a sharp exchange rate devaluation had knock-on effects on the BCB's inflation target, compelling it to increase the interest rate to avoid both capital outflows and pass through effect. This in turn caused a decline in output and employment, and increased the volume of public debt.

In Brazil, high interest rates performed multiple functions, which had important implications for the presence and influence of foreign interests. They were designed to influence and achieve inflation targets, limit exchange devaluation, attract foreign capital, encourage roll over of public debt, and reduce trade deficits by curbing domestic demand (Bresser-Pereira and Nakano 2002). On a less positive note, and also of relevance to our analysis, high interest rates in Brazil: (i) constrained economic growth, through the price of credit (loan rates) and entrepreneurs' negative expectations; and (ii) increased the public deficit due to high interest payments on bonds indexed to the overnight rate (Over/Selic). Indeed, the robust demand for hedges against exchange devaluation and interest rate changes in turbulent periods not only strongly affected Brazil's internal public debt, but also compromised the viability of longer term productive investments. In the 1998–2005 period, more than 50 per cent of the federal domestic securities were indexed to the overnight rate. Almost 30 per cent of securities were indexed to the exchange rate in 2002 (Table 7.2), but this decreased sharply thereafter.

Financial crises and industrial restructuring in 1994–2005

In addition to the high inflation mentioned in the previous section, decades of protectionism, state intervention and under-investment had

Table 7.2　Brazil: federal domestic securities – percentage share index (portfolio position)

	Exchange	TR	Inflation (IGP)	Over/Selic.	Preset	Inflation (IPCA)	Other	Total
Jun.-00	21.1	5.4	5.4	54.7	13.3	0.0	0.1	100.0
Dec.-00	22.3	4.7	5.9	52.2	14.8	0.0	0.1	100.0
Jun.-01	26.8	5.0	7.2	50.2	10.8	0.0	0.0	100.0
Dec.-01	28.6	3.8	7.0	52.8	7.8	0.0	0.0	100.0
Jun.-02	29.9	2.2	7.5	50.4	8.6	1.4	0.0	100.0
Dec.-02	22.4	2.1	11.0	60.8	2.2	1.6	0.0	100.0
Jun.-03	13.5	2.0	11.3	67.2	4.5	1.6	0.0	100.0
Dec.-03	10.8	1.8	11.2	61.4	12.5	2.4	0.0	100.0
Jun.-04	8.9	1.8	11.9	57.5	16.8	3.0	0.0	100.0
Dec.-04	5.2	2.7	11.8	57.1	20.1	3.1	0.0	100.0
Jun.-05	3.6	2.5	10.6	57.1	23.0	3.3	0.0	100.0
Dec.-05	2.7	2.1	8.2	51.8	27.9	7.4	0.0	100.0

Notes: IGP means 'General Price Index', prepared by FGV foundation.
IPCA, that means 'Extensive National Consumer Index', is the official inflation index, calculated by IBGE.
Source: BCB.

created major problems related to low productivity and competitiveness in the Brazilian economy. In the 1990s, Brazil's industrial and service sectors underwent a profound restructuring as a result of five distinct, but mutually reinforcing processes: globalization, regional integration, privatization, market liberalization and stabilization. The interaction of these processes resulted in the disintegration of the long-standing basis of Brazil's import substitution industrialization (ISI) developmentalist model, which was the *'tripé'* (or tripod) of state-owned, foreign-owned and domestic family-owned enterprises (Evans 1979).

Although most of these processes and policies pre-dated the 1994 Real Plan, price stabilization was the crucial condition necessary to round off the virtuous circle that was already creating a new dynamism in the economy with the promise of modernization, greater competitiveness and sustained growth (Mendonça de Barros and Goldenstein 1997). Globalization not only expanded access to technology, finance and markets, but also offered opportunities for Brazilian firms to integrate into global markets and participate in global productions chains. Regional integration not only expanded the size of the regional market, but also brought benefits in terms of reform lock-in (Devlin and Ffrench Davis 1999). Privatization not only divested the highly indebted public sector of productive assets, but also opened opportunities for investment in infrastructure and services that would contribute to increasing overall economic efficiency.

Market liberalization initially had a negative impact on the performance of local firms long accustomed to market reserves and high levels of protection. The rigors of competitive markets forced foreign and domestic owned firms to focus on reducing costs, upgrading technology and increasing productivity, all of which implied enhancing investment in order to survive. Trade opening also had a redistributive impact in that it transferred income from producers to consumers. Together, these changes ensured that market liberalization had a more positive impact on those firms that managed to restructure successfully. Finally, stabilization not only provided concrete benefits for the lowest income groups, thus increasing overall demand and consumption, but crucially had the lateral effect of increasing credit availability, which made it more feasible for firms to consider longer-term investments.

The massive restructuring of Brazilian industry in the 1990s was triggered by the above processes and policies, and not by financial crises. Private sector managers grappled with issues of productivity and competitiveness, while policy-makers were pre-occupied with macro-economic fundamentals, which meant that tight monetary (high interest rates) and fiscal (large primary surplus) policies were the order of the day.

In this type of policy setting, international capital flows were encouraged because of their beneficial impact on economic fundamentals.[3] Foreign capital (with its access to cheaper sources of financing in international financial markets) provided the dynamic for restructuring and modernization investment, and by 1998, FDI inflows accounted for 17 per cent of gross fixed capital formation (UNCTAD 2000). Meanwhile, many domestic firms were squeezed out of capital and credit markets. Given their difficulties of access to capital and its high cost, many domestic firms either entered into foreign partnerships/joint ventures or were forced to sell out (usually to foreign buyers). Again, contagion from international financial crises was less relevant to M&A activity than was the shifting profitability of firms forced to adjust to structural reform policies (especially trade opening).

In addition, given Brazil's fairly open investment regime for foreign manufacturing enterprises, the expansion of market opportunities (due to globalization, regional integration and the post-stabilization consumption boom) also attracted greenfield FDI (most notably in the automotive, consumer electronics and food processing industries). Rules were more restrictive in the financial sector and foreign bank entry could only be undertaken with prior authorization of the BCB or by Congressional decree. Although the 1988 Brazilian Constitution prohibited the installation of foreign banks, it allowed entry on a case-by-case basis through authorizations resulting from international agreements, from reciprocity or from the interest of the Brazilian government. Normally the objectives were to strengthen and to incorporate international experience of banking supervision into the domestic financial system.

To summarize, this section argued the need to take into account the wider context of change and the value of understanding the evolution of domestic economic policy-making. In the next two sections, we show that at the micro-economic (firm and industry) level, whether in the financial or productive sector, the above-mentioned domestic processes had a much greater bearing on the changing ownership structure and investment pattern than did the consequences of financial crises (e.g. currency devaluation, recession, etc.). We also show how the burden of adjustment in the aftermath of the various financial crises in the 1990s was more significant post-Mexican crisis than post-Asian crisis. Of course, this argument, while relevant at firm or industry level, was not applicable to the macro-economic scenario. Here, contagion from the Russian crisis not only led to a drastic devaluation, but more importantly, to a switch from an exchange rate anchor to an inflation-targeting monetary regime.

Finally, crises were not necessarily all bad news: some analysts argued that the 1999 devaluation even generated some favorable surprises for the Brazilian economy (Amann and Baer 2003), evidence of which could be gleaned from the quick recovery of the economy (growth was 4.4 per cent in 2000) with no 'explosion' of inflation (8.9 per cent in 1999 and 6.0 per cent in 2000). Furthermore, in macroeconomic terms, the 1999 crisis helped correct some of the downsides of the Real Plan. The devaluation not only contributed to boosting export competitiveness and expanding trade surpluses, but it also led to changes that reduced opportunities for speculation. This spelled longer-term benefits for Brazilian growth and development.

Foreign penetration in the banking sector

Banking consolidation, foreign entry and domestic resistance

In recent years, foreign bank entry increased significantly in emerging market economies (EMEs). Latin America and the transition countries of Central Europe were at the forefront, while progress towards foreign ownership of banks was more modest in Asia, Africa, the Middle East, and Russia. Financial deregulation and technological changes fostered the internationalization of the banking industry, while increased flexibility of domestic legal rules concerning the treatment of foreign bank entry increased foreign bank penetration particularly in EMEs. Benefits from foreign bank penetration came in terms of modernization and strengthening of the domestic financial system.

Banking consolidation in Latin America was the most advanced among the EMEs, where there was a remarkable rise in the quantity of banking institutions and a concomitant increase in banking concentration (IMF 2001b) in the aftermath of the 1994 Mexican crisis:

> Financial crises and the need to (re-)establish functioning banking systems created a one-time set of opportunities to invest in financial institutions and to expand business in EMEs in the second half of the 1990s. A standard response to crises by EME governments, encouraged by the international financial institutions, was to accelerate financial liberalization and to recapitalize banks with the help of foreign investors. This was the case in Latin America in the years following the 1994 Mexican crisis. (BIS 2004: 6)

In the 1990s, foreign ownership of the banking sector was substantially higher in Latin America and Central and Eastern Europe than in Asia (see Table 3.1 in this volume). In Central and Eastern Europe foreign banks controlled more than 60 per cent of total banking assets and in the major countries of Latin America, except Brazil, the share of assets owned by foreign banks was over 30 per cent. In 2004, in Mexico and Argentina, the market share of foreign banks (in terms of total assets) was 48 per cent and 82 per cent respectively.

M&A activity and domestic winners in the banking sector

In Brazil, as in other major Latin American EMEs (Argentina and Mexico), the 1994–95 'tequila crisis' triggered the liberalization of the financial system. All the same, Brazil was somehow a special case among EMEs in terms of domestic resistance to foreign banks penetration, especially when compared to other Latin American countries. Indeed, although three European banks (the British HSBC, the Spanish Santander and the Dutch ABN-Amro) made significant banking acquisitions during the 1990s, domestic banks remained dominant in Brazil.

The Brazilian banking sector had adapted very well to the pre-1994 environment of high inflation, taking advantage of inflationary revenues to make profits. It did this by applying non-remunerative deposits (sight deposits) in government securities, which combined liquidity with high interest rates. This was only possible due to the existence of a broader domestically-denominated indexed money and also the early development of a modern clearing system to support clients' demands for immediate information and the clearing of checks. Inflation made the Brazilian banking sector dynamic and technologically sophisticated. As a result, the decrease in M1 (cash plus sight deposits) – that is the conventional definition of the means of payment in an economy – did not result in a loss of funds in the Brazilian financial system as happened in the Argentine high inflation experience. In the latter case, an extensive process of dollarization was followed by an enormous decrease in financial deepening.[4]

Inflationary revenues accounted, on average, for 38.5 per cent of banks' value added between 1990 and 1993, but the Real Plan stabilization eliminated these revenues. Low inflation and re-monetization of the economy stimulated some increase in consumption spending, in spite of the increase in the BCB's interest rate. In this new context, banks earned most of their profits from credit operations (the rise in demand for loans and high interest rates). Therefore, when BCB sharply tightened monetary policy (short-term interest rate rose from 20 to 65 per cent per annum) in response to the 'tequila crisis', banks came under severe pressure as 'bad' loans increased quickly.

The 'tequila effect' threatened the banking sector as a whole, but in particular some of the national retail banks with problems that pre-dated the crisis; for example, Banco National and Banco Economico. In 1995, the likelihood of a systemic crisis in the banking sector increased when BCB, as regulator of the financial system, first decided to liquidate Economico (August 1995) and later Nacional (November 1995), the seventh- and the fourth-largest private banks, respectively. However, to avoid the spread of systemic risk, BCB implemented a special program in November 1995 – the Program of Incentives for the Restructuring and Strengthening of the National Financial System (PROER). This program aimed to preserve the solvency of the financial system by removing distressed banks and bolstering those that remained. An important feature of PROER was that the former controlling owners had to abandon their controls over the assisted bank. Furthermore, it provided a system of tax incentives and credit facilities to encourage rapid consolidation of the banking system through M&As.[5]

PROER financing backed some of the most important banking acquisitions in the following years, including the acquisition of Nacional by the domestic Unibanco, Economico by the domestic Excel, and the sale of Bamerindus to HSBC. PROER, and the provision of liquidity to the banking sector by BCB and other federal banks (BCB and Caixa Econômica Federal (CEF)) succeeded in averting a full-blown banking crisis.

The banking distress in 1995 provided the Brazilian federal government with an opportunity to privatize state banks and to allow the entrance of some foreign banks. However, as already noted, the 1988 Constitution restricted foreign bank entry, and financial liberalization after 1995 was carried out on a case-by-case basis, that is it depended on BCB authorization. Moreover, compared to Argentina and Mexico, banking sector opening was much less dramatic in Brazil. Comparing Brazil and Mexico, Martinez-Diaz (2005: 34) concluded that

> one of the most important differences between the two cases is that Mexican policymakers had clearly articulated beliefs about the nature and degree of liberalization they saw as desirable, while Brazilian official were more improvisational and had few a priori expectations of how liberalization should proceed. Brazilian policymakers also appeared less concerned with the ostensible long-term benefits of foreign bank presence and were far more interested in the short-term benefits of foreign participation, namely higher prices for privatized state banks and lower costs to the central bank for recapitalization.

The first foreign acquisition was the sale of Bamerindus to HSBC in April 1997. Bamerindus, one of the five largest private banks, had shown signs of severe distress in 1996–97, and BCB put it under intervention in March 1997. The transfer to HSBC was heavily assisted by PROER, which injected R$5.8 billion into Bamerindus. This operation triggered a wave of foreign bank entry: from 1997 to 2000, Santander of Spain bought the mid-sized banks Banco Geral do Comércio (1997), Noroeste (1997) and Meridional (2000) and, finally the big state-bank Banespa (2000), at the time the sixth largest bank in Brazil. This made Santander the major foreign bank in Brazil. The Italian–French Sudameris acquired America do Sul (1998); the Spanish BBV bought Excel-Econômico (1998); the Dutch ABN-Amro acquired Banco Real (1998), at the time the fourth biggest private bank. This last operation was the first instance when the government authorized the sale of a healthy bank to foreign investors. After 2000, foreign bank appetites slacked off, partly due to the impact of the 2001–2002 Argentine crisis as well as a global shift to risk-aversion post-2001. In Brazil, only foreign banks already present in the market made new acquisitions, as in the case of the sale of Sudameris to ABN-Amro, and the sale of Lloyds Bank (including Losango) to HSBC.

Of notable interest was the high level of M&A activity on the part of some of the domestic private banks in operations that involved state-banks and mid-sized domestic private and even foreign banks. For example, among others, Itau acquired the state-banks Banerj, BEMGE, BANESTADO and BEG, and the private banks Fiat and BBA; Bradesco acquired, among others, BCN/Credireal, Boavista, Ford, Mercantil de Sao Paulo and BBV Banco; Unibanco acquired Nacional, Bandeirantes and Fininvest. Some studies comparing efficiency (measured in terms of operational efficiency or profitability performance) between foreign banks and private domestic banks in the recent period showed that on the whole the latter performed better than the former (for instance, Guimarães (2002).

Table 7.3 shows market share in the Brazilian banking sector from 1994 to 2004. Between 1996 and 2004, foreign banks increased their market share rapidly from 4.4 per cent of total deposits, 9.8 per cent of total assets and 8.6 per cent of total credit in 1996 to 21.1 per cent, 27.4 per cent and 25.2 per cent, respectively, in 2000, but there was little change subsequently. Domestic private banks were still hegemonic in the Brazilian banking sector: they maintained more or less the same market share between 1994 and 2004, i.e. 39.4 per cent of total deposits, 41.7 per cent of total assets and 41.3 per cent of total credit. More interestingly, Bradesco, Itau and Unibanco were respectively the first, second and fourth biggest

Table 7.3 Market share in Brazilian banking sector

	1994	1996	1998	2000	2002	2004
			As % of total deposits			
Foreign-controlled banks	4.6	4.4	15.1	21.1	19.8	19.9
Private-sector domestic banks	39.4	34.1	33.1	33.9	36.6	39.4
Public-sector banks*	16.5	18.7	13.3	7.4	7.4	6.6
Caixa Econômica Federal	24.4	26.6	20.5	19.5	16.9	15.6
Banco do Brasil	15.1	16.0	17.4	17.1	17.7	17.1
Credit cooperatives	0.2	0.3	0.6	1.0	1.5	1.4
Total of banking sector	100.0	100.0	100.0	100.0	100.0	100.0
			As % of total assets			
Foreign-controlled banks	7.2	9.8	18.4	27.4	27.4	22.4
Private-sector domestic banks	41.2	39.0	35.3	35.2	36.9	41.7
Public-sector banks*	18.2	21.9	11.4	5.6	5.9	5.5
Caixa Econômica Federal	15.0	16.5	17.0	15.4	11.7	11.5
Banco do Brasil	18.3	12.5	17.4	15.6	17.1	17.4
Credit cooperatives	0.2	0.3	0.5	0.8	1.0	1.4
Total of banking sector	100.0	100.0	100.0	100.0	100.0	100.0
			As % of total credit			
Foreign-controlled banks	5.18	8.6	14.9	25.2	29.9	25.1
Private-sector domestic banks	35.35	32.7	31.0	34.5	39.7	41.3
Public-sector banks*	18.92	23.5	8.9	5.1	4.8	4.4
Caixa Econômica Federal	20.35	24.0	32.3	23.0	7.6	7.5
Banco do Brasil	19.87	10.6	12.1	11.0	16.2	19.4
Credit cooperatives	0.33	0.5	0.9	1.2	1.8	2.3
Total of banking sector	100.0	100.0	100.0	100.0	100.0	100.0

Note: *Excluding the two big federal banks: Banco do Brasil and Caixa Econômica Federal.
Source: COSIF/BCB.

private banks operating in Brazil. The two big federal public banks, Banco do Brasil and CEF, were still the largest banks, although their market share declined from 33.3 per cent of total assets in 1994 to 28.9 per cent in 2004. The biggest change was among state-banks, where as a result of the privatization program (PROES), their share in total assets shrank from 18.2 per cent in 1994 to 5.5 per cent in 2004.

It is also worth noting that even when Brazil suffered from the impact of contagion from successive currency crises in 1997–99, and even when capital inflows suddenly stopped in 2002, the banking sector continued to perform very well. Indeed, during periods of macroeconomic instability, the Brazilian government offered the banking sector (which was the main buyer of public securities) hedges against exchange devaluation and interest rate changes, by offering them securities indexed to the exchange rate and overnight interest rate. Consequently, notwithstanding severely restrictive macroeconomic conditions, the banks could adopt a conservative financial posture, i.e. a high proportion of government securities in their portfolio, low levels of mismatch between assets and liabilities and low leverage levels. The share of public securities in total banking assets was around 40 per cent on average in the 1998–2004 period (Table 7.4). Therefore, banks were able to afford risk aversion strategies, thanks to the availability of high-yielding, relatively risk-free government securities as an alternative to private sector lending. The Brazilian banking sector never faced the classical liquidity-versus-profitability trade-off, as the institutional–macroeconomic context afforded an environment with scope for banks to combine liquidity and profitability.[6]

To summarize, domestic winners and domestic resistance to foreign bank penetration can be attributed to a range of factors, including:

(i) high inflation, which helped make the Brazilian banking sector dynamic and technologically sophisticated; in particular domestic banks acquired the capabilities necessary to take advantage of the volatile macroeconomic environment;

(ii) the relatively less severe impact of the 1994–95 crisis on Brazil (compared to Mexico and Argentina);

(iii) the rapid response of BCB, which took action to avoid banking distress from becoming a systemic crisis;

(iv) relatively limited capital flight, because of the government's management of contagion from the financial crises after 1997, and the ability of the banking sector as a whole to re-allocate its portfolio to minimize the impact of capital flight.

Table 7.4 Banks portfolio, % share

End-of-period	Total loans on total assets (1)				Total securities on total assets (2)			
	Total	FB	DP	FE	Total	FB	DP	FE
Jun.98	41.8	55.1	39.9	39.5	36.5	24.3	34.6	37.3
Dec.98 (3)	43.6	55.2	41.2	44.0	31.0	35.9	38.9	36.7
Jun.99	43.0	54	39.4	42.2	38.2	31.9	35.8	35.1
Dec.99	44.0	53.5	41.8	42.2	37.9	29.7	36.4	36.6
Jun.00	47.1	55.1	45.0	46.7	37.8	30.8	35.1	36.0
Dec.00	47.8	56.5	47.2	38.4	37.5	26.0	36.0	48.1
Jun.01 (4)	46.9	46.9	49.7	46.4	37.2	32.7	31.5	39.4
Dec.01	44.2	37.3	49.9	46.4	43.1	46.0	33.3	43.3
Jun.02	43.9	42.5	43.1	46.6	42.1	39.8	35.7	41.0
Dec.02	41.7	33.7	47.4	48.7	43.2	45.8	35.4	38.4
Jun.03	42.6	35.5	49.2	49.7	41.8	45.0	32.7	35.9
Dec.03	40.6	33.6	47.5	50.7	45.4	48.7	36.4	36.6
Jun.04	42.6	35.4	51.1	49.9	42.4	44.7	31.2	37.5
Dec.04	43.5	38.0	50.1	50.1	41.5	43.2	31.4	36.8

Notes: (1) Data includes other loans besides normal loans.
(2) Data includes also interfinancial operations.
(3) Data excludes ABN Amro because of the incorporation of Banco Real.
(4) Data excludes Santander because of the incorporation of Banespa.
DP: 4 major domestic private banks (Bradesco, Itaú, Unibanco and Safra); FE: 6 major foreign banks (Santander, ABN Amro, BankBoston, HSBC, Citibank and Sudameris); FB: 2 major federal state-owned banks (Banco do Brasil and CEF); Total: includes all financial conglomerates, public and private ones.
Source: Authors' elaboration with data extracted from financial conglomerations' balance sheet in www.bcb.gov.br.

As a result, once domestic banks recovered and were performing well, they not only survived foreign bank competition, but also managed to lead in the wave of M&As.

FDI in the manufacturing sector

Industrial restructuring and foreign firms' uneven presence

Ever since the 1950s, the presence of foreign firms was part and parcel of Brazil's industrialization process.[7] Moreover, the characteristics of the Brazilian inwardly-oriented industrialization model, such as the *tripé*, placed emphasis on the different and complementary roles of domestic and foreign firms, as well as the state (including some state-owned firms in the production of intermediary goods and infra-structure) in the transformation of the economy. The typical configuration saw the foreign firm at the peak of the production chain, with backward linkages that encouraged the development of a network of local suppliers. The ideal type was the automotive industry chain, where foreign firms dominated vehicle manufacturing, but auto parts suppliers were often domestically-owned firms (Addis 1999).

Although ISI awarded domestic firms protection, subsidies and incentives, it was these very policies that subsequently disadvantaged them, because it led to market fragmentation (lack of scale economies as well as low levels of specialization) and a weak ability to deal with the realities of global competition. Hence, once policy-makers embarked on the process of market liberalization (discussed earlier), the high prices and generous profit margins of the ISI period actually became liabilities for firms. The manufacturing industry came under heavy pressure to restructure as a result of policies aimed at market opening and reduced state intervention in the economy.[8] Thus, already in the pre-crisis early years of the 1990s, domestic firms faced a number of challenges from the professionalization of their management to upgrading their technological capabilities and enhancing their productivity, efficiency and overall external competitiveness.

In the first instance, market opening had a differentiated impact on manufacturing firms present in the domestic market: it put foreign firms in a better position to respond quickly to the changing business environment. This was partly due to their easier access both to advanced technology as well as to low cost long-term capital for the investments necessary to restructure and modernize quickly (Mesquita Moreira 2000). Moreover, the foreign firm's initial advantage was subsequently consolidated precisely at the moment when domestically-owned firms came under even greater investment pressure. Sources of capital evaporated in the aftermath of international financial crises, resulting in higher interest rates, exchange rate devaluations, drying up of bank credit, and shrinking of local capital markets. This hurt domestic firms more, because they had few alternative sources of financing and technology. The private productive sector's problems were compounded by a hungry public sector, whose borrowing needs crowded out business access to debt and equity markets in addition to raising the cost of capital. Thus, although financial crises undeniably exacerbated the situation, it was the government's own macro-economic policy that actually further exposed the shortcomings of local firms.

It is worth emphasizing that unlike in the case of Asian firms, high debt-equity ratios were not a problem for most Brazilian firms. In Brazil, there was neither cheaply available credit nor over-investment and under-regulation nor the maturity mismatch in industrial firms' assets and liabilities that were typically blamed for triggering the Asian crisis in 1997 (Wade 1998; Chang 1999; Poon and Thompson 2001). In contrast, in Brazil, manufacturing firms suffered from lack of access to both debt and equity markets; under-investment and over-regulation were bigger problems; and macro-economic volatility rather than poor internal financial management was more likely to trigger financial distress. It was these features (and weaknesses) of domestic firms that provided MNEs with the opportunity for FDI, especially in the form of acquisition of already existing assets. Of course, there was also some limited market entry via greenfield investment.[9] Whatever the means of entry, the motivation remained largely market-seeking and inwardly-oriented, although the multi-national enterprises (MNEs) now operated in a new context of lower trade protection. These features of market entry and investment in turn had implications for the characteristics of Brazil's internationalization process.

Between 1994 and 2005, most indicators in the industrial sector pointed to an ever growing foreign presence. Thus, the stock of FDI expanded from US$42.5 billion in 1995 to US$164.1 billion in 1999 (UNCTAD 2000). FDI stock as a percentage of GDP also grew from 6 per cent in 1995 to over 33 per cent in 2000 (Sarti and Laplane 2002). The participation of MNEs in the top 500 firms in Brazil also expanded from 30 per cent in 1990 to 46 per cent in 2000. Since this internationalization process was seen as one-sided (i.e. there was no corresponding outflow of FDI by Brazilian firms), it was often declaimed as the denationalization of the productive sector. This trend, analyzed in the following section, raised much concern among local businesses as well as academics in Brazil in the early years of the new millennium (Gonçalves 1999; Lacerda 2000).

M&As and the impact of efficiency enhancing foreign investment

Having set out the general context favoring foreign firm entry and the low capacity for resistance from domestic manufacturing firms, this section examines trends and features of the capital ownership structure in the past decade with a special focus on the impact of financial crises. Although a number of industries experienced a significant increase in FDI, especially in the form of M&As, nowhere was the growing presence and impact of foreign firms more marked than in the automotive industry, especially in the auto parts sub-sector. The impact of foreign interests aroused heightened concern among more nationalist commentators, because of the symbolic importance of the automotive industry for Brazilian developmentalism. The automotive industry was considered the model for industrial development via the *tripé*, with a recognizable division of labor and a balanced presence of domestic (auto parts) and foreign (vehicle manufacturers) firms, while the federal government provided the infrastructure (roads) necessary for the development of the automotive industry. However, ten years of financial and trade liberalization eroded such distinctions, giving rise to a number of questions: Why did the automotive industry *tripé* disintegrate? What replaced it? Were international financial crises implicated in the process? Or were changes driven by other factors?

MNE capital had always dominated vehicle manufacturing in Brazil, where no local brands were developed under ISI. The more balanced capital ownership structure of the auto parts industry saw successful and competitive locally-owned firms emerge (Addis 1999), often hailed as evidence of the successes of ISI. However, from the mid 1990s, the auto parts supplier network in Brazil was completely transformed as a consequence of a mix of government policy (mainly economic liberalization) as well as global trends in the industry. In Brazil, the auto parts industry evolved from a sector comprised of many small and medium sized firms, mainly family-run enterprises with the presence of only a few MNEs, to a sector dominated by approximately 40 large MNEs, and the continuing presence of a number of smaller firms relegated to second and third tier supplier status. SINDIPEÇAS, the Brazilian auto parts industry association, reported that there were 648 firms spread over nine states in Brazil in 2005.

In 1994, asset ownership, sales revenues, and investment were roughly equal between foreign and domestically owned firms (Table 7.5). Between 1994 and 1997, from the Mexican crisis to the outbreak of the Asian financial crisis, there was already evidence of a big shift in ownership

Table 7.5 Internationalization of auto parts industry in Brazil

Assets	1994 (%)	2005 (%)
Foreign capital	48.1	79.2
Domestic capital	51.9	20.8
Sales Revenues		
Foreign capital	47.6	87.7
Domestic capital	52.4	12.3
Investment		
Foreign capital	48.0	76.9
Domestic capital	52.0	23.1

Source: Sindipeças (2006).

patterns. There were about 60 M&As involving auto parts firms, of which 40 resulted in a foreign firm acquiring a local firm (Gonçalvez 1999). Other forms of partnership were also attempted, including nine joint ventures and four technological partnerships. Perhaps the most emblematic case was the sale of Metal Leve[10] to the German/Brazilian firm Mahie/Cofap in 1996, which was later acquired by the Italian MNE Magnetti Marelli in 1997.

Data from a decade later, shows how the earlier balance, slightly tipped in favor of domestic firms, was overturned completely with domestic auto parts firms losing out to foreign interests. By 2005, 79.2 per cent of assets, 87.7 per cent of sales revenues, and 76.9 per cent of investment came from firms with total or majority foreign ownership. A mix of domestic and international factors contributed to this shift. The growing presence of MNEs was due to two trends: on the one hand, trade opening generated a competitive shock, which forced many traditional local producers to close, while others with more attractive assets (e.g. brand recognition or export presence) were acquired by foreign firms. In some cases, foreign firms with minority share holdings increased their participation to take control of management. By 1998, seven of the ten pre-1995 largest locally-owned auto parts suppliers were taken over by foreign buyers. On the other hand, a second trend favoring MNE entry was as a complement to the wave of new foreign entrants in vehicle manufacturing sector during the late 1990s (Doctor 2007). Vehicle manufacturers often demanded that their global suppliers follow them into new markets. These auto parts MNEs set up their Brazilian operations on a follow client basis, contributing to the rapidly changing capital ownership structure and the technological capacity of the auto parts sector.

Change was also driven by more general developments in the global automotive industry, specifically the trend towards transnationalization and modularization (Sako 2003). The growing importance of technological capabilities, scale and standardization of products spelled the end to idiosyncratic local relations between vehicle manufacturers and their suppliers. Although Brazil hoped to partake in the benefits promised to those economies that became involved in the global production chain, policy-makers and businesses seemed less prepared to acknowledge that this might be at the expense of a locally-owned auto parts industry. Moreover, even as Brazil became a prime location for experiments in new manufacturing processes and innovative types of client-supplier relations (Sako 2005), it was forced to accept that in most cases investments followed a market-seeking logic with only modest export orientation (Sarti and Laplane 2002).

Modular production also drove shifts in inter-firm relations globally, evidence of which emerged in Brazil when the number of direct suppliers to vehicle manufacturers fell from 500 to about 150. The greater technological and design capabilities required for modular production often disadvantaged local firms with their much weaker research and development and design capacity. Thus, trade opening and the auto parts required for the new vehicle models manufactured in Brazil, saw sales of locally produced parts fall from US$17.46 billion in 1997 to about US$10 billion in 2002. Although auto parts exports rose from US$2.3 billion in 1992 to US$3.88 billion in 2002, imports rose even faster from US$1.25 billion in 1992 to US$3.98 billion in 2002. By 2002, more evidence emerged on the early impact of change in the industry. Employment was down from 193,000 in 1996 to 168,000 in 2002 (SINDIPEÇAS 2006) and there was a noticeable loss in value added and local development capacity due to the changing production strategies and requirements of the vehicle manufacturers (ECLAC 2004).

Finally, in the longer-term and notwithstanding a rather grim start in the new millennium, the auto parts sector subsequently saw a sharp turnaround in its fortunes. This more favorable scenario became increasingly apparent from 2004 onwards. The recent boom in vehicle production and exports boosted demand for auto parts to record levels. In 2005, the auto parts industry generated sales revenues of US$24 billion, exports of US$7.5 billion and direct employment of 197,000. Anticipating further growth, auto parts firms invested some US$1.4 billion in 2005 alone, and were expected to invest another US$1 billion in 2006 (SINDIPEÇAS 2006). Although much of this was generated by the presence of foreign-owned firms, domestic capital also participated in and benefited from the up-swing.

Thus, the story of the 1990s in the case of manufacturing industry (as illustrated with the example of auto parts production) on the one hand highlighted domestic losses and weak ability to resist international pressures, and on the other hand, showcased foreign gains. Although foreign gains were apparent in a number of manufacturing industries (food processing, consumer electronics, domestic white goods, in addition to the automotive industry), these gains remained uneven since they were contingent on the specific dynamics of the sector in Brazil and on global conditions in that industry. Moreover, in most cases, increased foreign presence contributed to enhancing efficiency of the industry overall, not only due to MNE technology but also due to domestic efforts to keep up with the competition. Again, from the point of view of the main argument of the chapter, we noted that although the outcome in manufacturing industry in many ways differed sharply from the situation in the financial services/banking sector, there was a broad similarity in that foreign presence triggered modernization, efficiency enhancing business practices and greater investment in the relevant sector. Moreover, in the case of manufacturing industry, the driving forces were seldom related to the type of 'opportunism' referred to in the literature about foreign 'interests' taking advantage of financial crises to acquire cheap assets in emerging economies. If anything, the macro-economic volatility ensuing from the crises served to deter investment.

Conclusion

This chapter analyzed the position of foreign interests in Brazil in the aftermath of financial crisis from the mid-1990s onward. We studied the financial and manufacturing sectors more generally, but also used a closer examination of two specific cases – the banking sector and automotive parts industry – to get a more nuanced picture of the presence of and opportunities for foreign interests. Our analysis showed that foreign penetration in the years following financial crises had different impacts on the two sectors: in the case of the financial sector, domestic banks reacted to foreign entry by actively taking part in the M&As wave, thus, maintaining their hegemony in the Brazilian banking system; in contrast, in the automotive parts industry, there was a rapid process of 'denationalization' with the demise or foreign acquisition of many domestically-owned firms and the growing presence of MNEs. However, we found little evidence of foreign opportunism as a result of financial crises. Finally, we also noted that FDI (especially via M&As) had an uneven impact on manufacturing industries: some domestic firms in some industries (textiles, apparel, shoes, tiles and ceramics) successfully reacted to limit the scope for foreign entry; other domestic firms (food processing, household white goods) competed even with the growing presence of foreign firms.

Although different factors determined the reaction of domestic firms in each sector, it was clear that the management of economic policy in Brazil not only shaped opportunities for business (foreign and domestic) interests, but also had different impacts in each sector. On the one hand, the adoption of a very tight monetary policy – the main tool applied to protect against speculative attack on the domestic currency – favored the profitability and performance of the banking sector, including domestic banks. On the other hand, this tight monetary policy had highly negative effects on the manufacturing sector as a whole due to the impact of such policy on bank credit conditions. High interest rates affected both the supply and price of credit – that is the availability of funds and the loan rates. We also found that in many ways, an enhanced role for foreign interests coincided with a broadly similar positive impact across sectors, in that foreign presence triggered some modernization, efficiency enhancing business practices and greater investment in the relevant sector. Finally, we argued that notwithstanding these different fates for foreign interests, the financial crises themselves had much less influence on firm strategies and behavior than did macro-economic policy and the micro-economic investment climate.

Notes

1. For an analysis of the Real Plan, see Ferrari-Filho and Paula (2003).
2. GDP growth in China, India and Russia was in 2000–2004, on average, 6.8%, 5.7% and 8.5%, respectively (Ferrari Filho and Paula 2006). Recently revised methodology for calculating growth pushed growth up to 3.7% for 2006.
3. Sarti and Laplane (2002) note that increasing FDI and greater efficiency in manufacturing paradoxically resulted in aggravating Brazil's external vulnerability due to the tensions that arose between the macroeconomic and microeconomic logic of the internationalisation process. Thus, FDI improved the current account, but initially dampened the trade account via increased imports in the absence of a concomitant rise in exports.
4. According to Bresser-Pereira and Ferrer (1991:10), in Argentina both M1 and M4 (which includes M1 plus financial assets) decreased since the late 1970s. In February 1990, M1 was less than 3% of GDP, while M4 was less than 5% of GDP, because economic agents reallocated their portfolios to the dollar. Alternatively, in Brazil, accelerating inflation decreased M1 from the early 1970s, but M4 remained stable as a consequence of the supply of domestically-denominated indexed money. According to data from BCB, the ratio M1/GDP and the ratio M4/GDP were 9.2% and 25.1% in 1980, respectively, while in 1993 they were 1.3% and 23.1%, respectively.
5. The acquiring (healthy) bank took over all the deposits of the insolvent bank, and other assets that it chose to take with PROER credit making up the difference. All PROER credits were guaranteed using public bonds whose value exceeded the credit by 20%. The acquired (insolvent) bank was liquidated and its balance sheet included the PROER credit as a liability. For more details, see OECD (2001, Box 15).
6. For more on this analysis, see Paula and Alves, Jr (2003).
7. Amongst EMEs, Brazil had a long history as one of the most favoured host economies for large MNEs. This standing holds to date. For example, in 2003, Brazil was the most favoured host among developing countries/EMEs for the top 100 MNEs, 75 of which had affiliates in Brazil. To compare with other large EMEs: Hong Kong (67), China (60), S. Korea (42), India (38), Mexico (72) and Russia (45) (UNCTAD 2005).
8. See Suzigan and Furtado (2006) for a good discussion of industrial policy's development impact in Brazil.

9. Sarti and Laplane (2002) point out that the bulk (about 95%) of FDI inflows to China in the late 1990s were greenfield projects; while in Brazil almost 75% of FDI inflows were directed at M&A activity (mainly as a function of the government's privatisation programme).
10. Metal Leve's owner, José Mindlin, was strongly associated with the discourse of developmentalism and in many ways the firm was identified as a prime example of ISI success.

8
Central Europe: Predatory Finance and the Financialization of the New European Periphery
Or Raviv

The breakdown of the Communist Bloc in the late 1980s is perhaps the quintessential example of a crisis, followed by an expansion of Western economic norms and interests. In the aftermath of the collapse of communism, the former Communist states were plunged into a crisis, which in economic terms, rivaled the great depression of the 1930s (see Milanovic 1998 for an in-depth analysis of the crisis). More importantly however, this was a systemic crisis; a crisis of the system and all of its components. The ideological and institutional vacuum left in the wake of the delegitimization of actually existing socialism was quickly seized upon by Western public and private agents alike (de Boer 2000).

This is especially true in the case of the Central European new EU member states. Here the neoliberal principles of economic management, first introduced by the IMF in the early 1990s, were subsequently 'locked in' by the process of EU accession. Concomitantly, foreign private financial inflows have completely overhauled the ownership structures of the existing financial systems. If in 1994, immediately in the aftermath of the economic crisis of the early transition, an overwhelming majority of financial intermediaries and financial assets were still domestically (largely publicly) owned, by 2004, at the eve of EU accession, private foreign owners already controlled approximately 71 per cent of financial intermediaries and banks' assets in the new Central European member states (ECB 2005a: 11).[1]

Throughout the 1990s, the expansion of foreign financial interests, irrespective of where it took place, was universally legitimized and prescribed along broadly identical arguments. Easier access to global financial markets for individuals and corporations would lead to a more efficient allocation of capital at a reduced cost, and to improved investment opportunities for businesses and individuals alike, resulting in growth in output and employment. Access to foreign finance would further enhance the depth and liquidity of national financial systems, thus, reducing systemic risk and promoting financial stability. This (foreign) investment-led growth strategy was continuously backed up by a steady flow of studies, reports and recommendations emanating from the various international financial institutions (IFIs) as well as academia, lending credence to these theses and depicting foreign investment as a panacea to the problems of the developing world (see, for example, Levine 1996, 1999; Focarelli and Pozzolo 2000; Claessens *et al.* 2001; BIS 2004 amongst many others).

Conversely, a more critical analysis of financial expansion rejects outright this universal and ahistorical perspective. On the contrary, this chapter seeks to place the process of Western European financial expansion in its historical context, specifically by emphasizing the commonalities and differences between the current integration of Central Europe (CE) into the Western European circuits of capital and the previous episode of integration under the rule of the Austro-Hungarian Habsburg rule. Furthermore I reject the dominant view of financial expansion as a politically neutral process; rather I argue that the expansion of Western European finance was both facilitated and in large parts shaped by the political project of EU accession as it unfolded over the past decade.

This chapter aims to explore the actual motivations and strategies adopted by individual Western European financial intermediaries in their Eastward march. Thus, the expansion of global finance into peripheral economies will be addressed in the context of the structural contradictions facing credit institutions in their operations in the already financialized economies of the core. The recent and rapidly expanding literature on financialization has been instrumental in exploring the growing significance of debt-driven asset price inflation as a primary mechanism of capital accumulation in the contemporary global economy (to note but a few prominent examples, see Crotty 2000; Krippner 2004; Epstein 2005; Glyn 2006; Froud *et al.* 2006). However, the majority of this literature is primarily concerned with the Anglo-Saxon experience of financialization. By comparison, considerably less attention is afforded to the rest of the developed world, while the developing world has been overlooked almost without exception.

Thus this chapter expands the scope of this literature, by exploring the role played by Western European financial expansion in geographically diffusing the structural contradictions of financialization. I argue that the financial integration of Central and Eastern Europe (CEE) into the Western structures of accumulation was predatory in nature; it was never aimed at addressing the developmental needs of the host economies, but rather, redressing the structural contradiction faced by the already financialized economies of Western Europe. It will be demonstrated that thus far the financial integration of CEE has failed to generate the promised optimization of investment or to promote efficient economic management, let alone enhance general welfare levels in the region. Conversely, I argue that Western European financiers have emerged as a powerful foreign rentier class in the region, able to extract rent incomes far in excess of their profits in the west, whilst at the same time contributing to informal 'Euroization' and financialization of accumulation patterns in the region, resulting in increased indebtedness and risk to host societies.

The chapter begins by presenting a brief summary of financial relations between Western and CE in the context of the Austro-Hungarian Empire. The historical and institutional specificities that emerge from this summary are arguably significant for making sense of the rationale, dynamics and consequences of the current European Eastward financial expansion and accompanying finance-led social restructuring. The process of EU accession has constituted the primary political process underwriting financial Eastward expansion, thus, the second section of this chapter will focus on the role of the EU and of EU accession in facilitating financial expansion. Finally, the last section of this chapter will focus on the strategies of Western European financial expansion in CE, forming the basis for a firmer, more 'grounded' evaluation of the process of financial expansion, its motives and implications.

Banking in the Austro-Hungarian empire

Before addressing the current expansion of Western financial capital into CE it is important to note that the societies of CE have in fact, already constituted a part of the Western European political and economic order once before. In November 1995, at the eve of launching the accession negotiations, *The Economist* published a survey of Central European countries titled 'The return of the Habsburgs'. *The Economist* expressed enthusiastic support for the speedy integration of the five (the 'Visegrad four' and Slovenia) Central European countries on the basis of common heritage ('pedigree'). The countries of CE can

> trace their Western roots 1,000 years back-to a time when medieval German kings launched the Holy Roman Empire (headed, in due course, by the Habsburgs) and set about Christianising nearby Slavs by the sword. . . . They are the Hungarians, the Czechs, the Slovaks, the

Slovenes and, particularly, the Poles, . . . the Central European nations hold common credentials for entering the EU: they will be not so much joining Western Europe as coming home to it. (*The Economist*, 18 *November* 1995).

Indeed, Central European societies formed a part of the Austro-Hungarian Dual Monarchy, and thus, partook in the Western European political and economic order during the 19th and early 20th centuries. However, having established these so called credentials, *The Economist* displayed remarkably little interest in the nature of that previous integration, or in its effects on Central European societies. In fact, integration under the Austro-Hungarian Dual Monarchy took the form of military, political, economic and religious domination and subjection. Central Europe's previous 'Western experience' was a brutish imperialistic tale of exploitation and expropriation. In this section I examine the role played by Western financial capital in this previous episode of integration; arguably, this longer historical perspective will prove instrumental in promoting a more nuanced understanding of the dynamics, institutional features, and agents involved also in contemporary financial relations between Western and CE.

From the mid-19th century, the Austro-Hungarian Empire, much like the rest of continental Europe, entered a phase of rapid industrialization and economic development. This expansion led to a growing demand for credit. At the time, several private banks were already operating in the Austro-Hungarian Empire, however these were unable to satisfy the growing demand for credit.[2] Capital markets on the continent were similarly underdeveloped, mostly as a result of restrictive financial regulation, particularly, company and tax law which prior to their amendment in 1899 restricted the establishment of joint stock enterprises. The ensuing credit crunch prompted the rise of a new form of financial institution in Europe; the universal bank.[3]

In 1855, the first Austrian Universal Bank, K. k. privilegierte Osterreichische Credit-Anstalt (hereafter Credit-Anstalt), was founded. The main subscriber to the Credit-Anstalt's equity was the Viennese House of S. M. von Rothschild. Credit-Anstalt remained the only universal bank in operation in the Habsburg Empire until the establishment of Allgemeine osterreichische Boden-Credit-Anstalt (hereafter Boden-Credit-Anstalt) in 1863. In 1864 the Anglo-Osterreichische Bank was founded and in 1869, the Wiener Bank-Verein, an associate of the Boden-Credit-Anstalt commenced activities (Teichova 1997: 216). These universal banks represented the primary (almost exclusive) source of credit in the Austro-Hungarian

Empire. Indeed, during the period 1880–1913 bank credit to industrial enterprises quadrupled (Teichova 1997: 219). The bulk of this growth was in short-term credit which was later to be converted into shares.

The Austrian banks fulfilled the usual functions of financial intermediation as in other capitalist economies and offered a variety of services for business and private individuals such as deposit and investment banking, stock-broking, portfolio management, and acquisition of shares in joint-stock companies (on their own and on their clients' behalf). As in other countries close ties between banks and industrial enterprises developed. However, in the absence of alternative sources of credit, and of legal constraints to bank ownership of industrial enterprise shares, the big commercial banks of Vienna secured a more prominent control over the allocation of capital than their counterparts elsewhere in the continent. Bank ownership of shares entitled them to voting rights in joint stock companies and their supervision was further tightened through interlocking directorships and serving on the board of their client companies.[4]

The Viennese banks also played a dominant role in the penetration of CE. In 1918 the ten biggest Viennese banks operated some 143 branches outside of Austria. Ranki (cited in Teichova 1997: 219) has estimated that in 1913 only one Hungarian bank was of the same magnitude as the leading Viennese institutions – the Hungarian General Credit Bank – which itself was linked to the Austrian Credit-Anstalt. In Bohemia only one bank maintained significant capital resources, the Zivnostenska banka of Prague. Teichova (1997: 219) writes:

> By 1914 the eight great Viennese banks accounted for about two thirds of the total capital of all the financial institutions of the Empire. These institutions had secured strategic positions in almost all branches of industry and their influence radiated out from Vienna to encompass all the territories of the Dual Monarchy.

Thus, by the early 20th century, the imperially charted, universal banks of Vienna had seized control over significant shares of the corporate sectors of the newly industrializing economies of CE. This strategic position enabled them to also capture or expropriate a growing share of productivity growth in the region in the form of rentier incomes. This dominance of the Austrian banks continued unbroken right up until the dissolution of the Austro-Hungarian Empire at the end of World War One, as one by one the nations of CE declared independence. This left the Viennese banks in a precarious position, as they lost almost all of their branches outside Austria and consequently, their control over their most profitable clients which were now on the other side of the Czechoslovakian and Hungarian sovereign borders. This resulted in further concentration in the Austrian financial sector as banks merged or went under, and in ever increasing penetration of the weakened Austrian market itself by foreign interests, mostly British and French.

The politics of neoliberalism in Europe

While the concept of financial deregulation suggests the removal of the state from intervention in financial markets and sectors, in fact in CE the situation was quite the opposite; contrary to the popular yet simplistic beliefs underlying classical and neoclassical economics, markets, financial or otherwise, do not materialize spontaneously in the space vacated by the state. Rather the construction of markets as social institutions requires a significant amount of political commitment and action. This was particularly true in the case of post-communist CE, where governments introduced rapid and comprehensive regulatory reform with the explicit aim of bringing about regulatory convergence with the EU. Thus, the expansion of Western European financial capital into CE should be viewed as an inherently political project; one which was supported by intensive state action. This section examines the political process which framed and facilitated the current expansion of Western financial interests into CE, namely the process of EU accession.

The neoliberal restructuring of Central European economic and social governance began almost immediately after the fall of the Berlin wall in 1989. In the wake of the collapse of actually existing socialism, the political movement away from communism and towards rejoining the Liberal, Western political and economic order enjoyed extensive support amongst civil society and within the newly independent political systems. This is hardly surprising given the global hegemony of the neoliberal ideology, which was further compounded by the ideological legacy of the discourse of class in post-communist societies. The prospect of acceding into the EU, which was formally endorsed in the Council's Copenhagen Summit in 1993, lent further support to the neoliberal agenda even as the short-term prices of transition began to manifest themselves in the form of rising unemployment and deteriorating state and enterprise social provisioning. In turn EU membership itself was offered on the non-negotiable condition of adopting the entire existing catalogue of EU rules and achievements (the acquis communautaire). Consequently the EU has come to play a defining role in the political, economic and social restructuring of the Central European post-communist states.

The 1980s saw the broad introduction of neoliberal principles of privatization and market deregulation across the EU. The leading proponents of neoliberalism drew on classical ('Hayekian') economics in making the case for the universal benefits of free markets, low taxes and low inflation. At the core of the neoliberal transformation, stood the rejection of Keynesian principles of demand management and the 'embedded liberalism' of the welfare state, in favor of a supply-side, investment-led growth strategy. The goals of full employment and welfare, central to the post-war Fordist–Keynesian growth regime, were thus to be replaced by the pursuit of regulatory reform, aimed at facilitating increased capital mobility, and 'flexible' labor markets, deemed favorable to investment. Proponents of this view envisaged deregulated international capital markets, which would allocate credit based on efficiency and innovation, and equity markets which would distribute the corresponding efficiency gains and wealth throughout the economy (Montgomerie 2006).

Originally implemented by conservative governments, these principles were not fundamentally altered when these governments were replaced by nominally left/centre-left cabinets in the course of the 1990s. The EU in no small way was responsible for this continuity. The 1987 Single European Act (SEA) represented the first effort to amend the foundational treaties of the European Communities and re-launch European integration after almost two decades of so-called 'Eurosclerosis', with the aim of extending the internal market to allow the free movement of labor, services and critically, of capital. Thus, the renewed legitimacy of the European idea coalesced around a coherent vision for the institutional redesign and strategic reorientation of the European polity, in line with neoliberal principles of economic governance premised around notions of investment-led growth (Moravcsik 1998). The Treaty of Maastricht, ratified by the member states in 1993, paved the way towards European Monetary Union (EMU), and formally recognized neoliberal convergence (setting inflation targets and introducing constraints on national budget deficit levels) as the basis for any further integration. The Growth and Stability Pact (GSP) adopted in 1997 further entrenched these goals and also consolidated the role of European institutions in monitoring and enforcing national monetary and fiscal compliance with the targets set forth in Maastricht.

Since 1998, the EU agenda has been increasingly dominated by an emphasis on financial deregulation, as embodied by the Financial Services Action Plan (FSAP). The Plan has represented in the past few years the main tool for public action to further financial integration. In their Lisbon 2000 Summit, the Council identified the FSAP as being a 'prerequisite for the attainment of the EU's economic potential' and as such, an integral part of what has come to be known as the 'Lisbon Agenda', a plan to make the EU 'the most dynamic, innovative, knowledge-based economy in the world by 2010' (EU Commission 2000). FSAP legislation is procedurally based on the Lamfalussy process. Essentially, this process involves breaking down the decision making process into four levels. In Level 1 the key political aims are formulated by the Commission, and adopted and ratified by the EU Council and EU parliament respectively. The 'technical' details of implementation are than relegated to the EU Commission which in consultation with sector-specific national and European regulatory bodies decides on appropriate measures, while coordination between national regulators and compliance and enforcement are addressed in Levels 3 and 4 respectively.

In other words, significant aspects of financial legislation at the EU have been 'depoliticized', effectively removed from the regulatory control of the publicly elected representatives in the EU Parliament and the nationally elected members of the European Council (Weber 2006). This has prompted critics of the EU's neoliberal agenda to conclude that 'the leading political and economic forces in Europe present neoliberalism as a taboo that cannot be violated' (Milios 2005: 209). By equating neoliberal convergence with the goal of enhancing the economic, monetary and political unity among EU member states, the neoliberal strategy is effectively exempted from criticism and placed out of reach for 'any substantial revision or change' (Milios 2005). The process of European integration itself thus becomes a mechanism of imposing and observing neoliberal discipline; the deepening and broadening of integration a vehicle of conversion to neoliberalism.

Clearly, the EU has not been any less committed to neoliberal investment-led growth strategies than its Anglo-Saxon counterparts. Financial services and labor markets in the EU have been subject to similar regulatory reforms to the ones implemented across the Atlantic. This similarity is hardly surprising given the transnational character of the transformations in capitalist state organization. It was these disciplinary aspects that all new member states were directly confronted with; acceding into the EU implied a comprehensive restructuring of social and economic governance. This restructuring process was a necessary precondition for the expansion of Western finance which can only operate within the context of a Western based normative and regulative framework. The final section examines the strategies and performance of the Western European banks which have led the process of financial expansion into Central and Eastern Europe.

Banking strategies in the European Union

If one judges the success of Central European governments in reforming their weak and distressed financial systems by their ability to attract strategic foreign investors, then the reform must be considered nothing short of a staggering success. Since the mid – 1990s, foreign inflows have completely overhauled the ownership structures of the existing financial systems in CE. If in the early 1990s, an overwhelming majority of financial intermediaries and financial assets were still publicly owned, by 2005, private foreign ownership accounted for approximately 78 per cent of financial intermediaries and banks' assets in the region (Unicredit 2006: 13). This is especially striking when compared with just 25 per cent of foreign owned banking assets in the Euro Area (ECB 2005a). The three largest financial sectors in the region are no exception with foreign ownership reaching 96 per cent of banking assets in the Czech Republic; 84 per cent in Hungary; and 75 per cent in Poland (see Figure 8.1). In Poland, PKO, the last major state-owned bank represents nearly all of the remaining domestic owned banking assets. In Hungary, OTP Bank, considered domestically owned, accounts for almost all the remaining banking assets, however, almost 80 per cent of its shares, which have been free floated in the Hungarian stock exchange, are owned by foreign investors (The Banker 2005). In the Czech Republic all domestic banks are insignificant in terms of share of asset ownership.

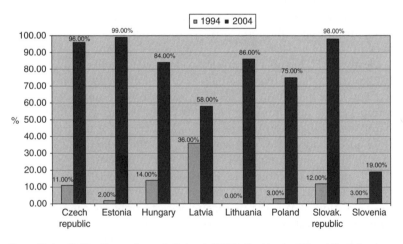

Source: Unicredit New Europe Research Network (2006), 'Banking in CEE and the Role of International Players', July, p. 13.

Figure 8.1   Share of foreign-owned banks in total banking assets, 1994–2004 (%)

The penetration of foreign banks into CE was legitimized on the basis of essentially neoliberal arguments. On the individual bank level, the entry of foreign banks was claimed to have positive effects, as the purchased bank would gain access to its new parent company's financial and knowledge resources. On the sectoral level, the entry of more efficient foreign players was argued to enhance market competition, forcing other actors to become more efficient (Claessens *et al.* 2001; Clarke *et al.* 2001). On a national level, a deeper, and more efficient financial intermediation system would in turn positively influence the private non-financial and household sectors, which would gain access to a wider choice of more sophisticated financial instruments at more competitive prices (Reininger *et al.* 2001). Finally, financial services FDI has been argued to contribute to the stability of the host economy. By improving the lacking risk management skills of local banks, foreign owners will contribute to enhancing macroeconomic stability and the systemic capacity of these economies to withstand shocks (Akbar and McBride 2004; Moreno and Villar 2004; Naaborg *et al.* 2004).

The neoliberal outlook on financial expansion was thus extremely positive. Opening Central European financial systems would allow a deepening of the intermediation system; enhanced access to credit for the public, private non-financial and household sectors would lead to a boost in investment resulting in growth in output and employment. On this basis many mainstream economists predicted in the late 1990s that convergence of living standards to EU levels would be achieved over the medium-to-long run (Dyker 2000).

Rather than privileging abstract, universal and ahistorical principles, this section addresses the actual motivations, and actual strategies, of individual Western European financial intermediaries. In what follows, I demonstrate that far from carrying out the above functions, the expansion of Western finance has thus far carried a transformative effect on the relationship between financial intermediaries on the one hand, and non-financial businesses, the state and societies in CE on the other. The penetration of foreign banks has resulted in reorientation of government corporate and household behavior in line with the imperatives of financially based accumulation strategies, resulting in increased transfer of property rights from local society to foreign investors, increased indebtedness, and increased risks, which are ultimately unsustainable in the longer run.

The financial expansion into CE was mainly channelled through financial intermediaries rather than equity markets; intermediaries account for approximately 85 per cent of financial sector assets in CE

(Racocha 2003; Backé and Zumer 2005). This is to be expected given the prominence of Western Europe in the region, both politically and financially. Corporate finance in Western Europe is similarly heavily bank based rather than market based as in the Anglo-Saxon model; in 2001, bank loans to the corporate sector amounted to 42.6 per cent of GDP in the Euro Area, but only 18.8 per cent in the US. Conversely, outstanding debt securities of non-financial corporations and stock market capitalization amounted respectively to 6.5 and 71.7 per cent in the Euro Area compared to 28.9 and 137.1 per cent in the US (ECB 2005b).

The reasons for this diversity are numerous and rightfully justify an entire chapter of their own; in this case I shall confine myself to discussing two major historical and regulatory differences that have played a crucial role in guiding these two systems along diverging paths. Perhaps the most significant regulation guiding the development of the US financial system towards market-based finance was the 1933 Banking Act (also known as the Glass Steagall Act). The aim of the Glass Steagall Act was to make banking safer and less prone to speculation as a direct reaction to the economic problems which followed the Stock Market Crash of 1929. The Act separated the activities of commercial banks and securities firms and prohibited commercial banks from owning brokerages. It also prohibited paying interest on commercial demand deposits and capped the interest rate on savings deposits. In effect, this legislation (along with the poor state of the banking sector during the 1930s), created a kind of 'capital vacuum' in the American financial system.[5]

This void was quickly seized by the ascendance of institutional investors in the US. One of the key elements contributing to the rise of institutional investors in the US (and the second point of difference from continental Europe) was the channeling of pension fund contributions into equity investment. From as early as the 1940s, defined contribution retirement plans began their ascent in the US. These plans do not guarantee a predetermined level of income, and consequently they can be channeled into (riskier) investment in equity markets rather than (safer but lower yield) government bonds (Langley 2004b).

Since the 1980s defined contribution plans have displaced defined benefit plans as the most popular form of retirement plan. The significance of pension funds to the rise of non-bank institutional investors in the US cannot be overestimated; it is estimated that in 2005 approximately 40 per cent of American common stock, or 12.9 trillion Dollars originated from pension and retirement funds (Fundamentals 2005). Similarly in 2003 institutional investors in the US accounted for approximately 75.9 per cent of the US leveraged loan market (Hickey 2003).

Meanwhile, in continental Europe the tradition of 'universal banking' originating in the 19th century continued unabated. European banks were unrestricted in conducting investment and securities businesses and consequently the European financial sectors did not experience the same 'capital vacuum' characteristic of the US. Furthermore, even to this day most EU Member States maintain predominantly state-financed pensions systems (with the exception of Ireland, the Netherlands and the UK). In Continental Europe, pensions have been largely state-run, pay-as-you-go schemes that essentially restrict investments to safe, low-yield domestic bond issues. This has further restricted the scope for the rise of non-bank institutional investors in Europe.

No doubt, over the past decade financial deregulation in the EU has contributed to the gradual strengthening and growth of European equity and debt securities markets. Consequently, the former have been increasingly replacing traditional bank lending in continental Europe, and while the recourse to market-based finance in Europe is still significantly below that of the United States, the gap is steadily narrowing. However, notwithstanding the increased competition from non-bank intermediaries, the importance of banks in Europe has not declined either. European banks have been able to exploit their extensive retail distribution networks in order to reach investors, thus gaining dominant positions as asset managers; in many EU countries the banking sector's combined asset management goes beyond 80 per cent of total collective investment (Padoa-Schioppa 2004). Thus, arguably by diversifying into this area, European banking groups have been able to 'internalize' the changes in their clients' saving and investment behavior, making the increased recourse to equity and securities markets compatible with the preservation and expansion of the role of financial intermediaries themselves (Seabrooke 2001).

Much to the surprise of some financial experts, the initial eastward drive was not led by German banks despite Germany being the region's biggest trading partner (and host to a sophisticated financial sector), but rather by its much smaller Austrian neighbour. While German banks were busy at home with the shocks and costs of the unification, their Austrian counterparts managed to build an early dominance in the region. Of course this is much less surprising given the historical background provided above, which emphasized the role played by the very same credit institutions in the region under the Austro-Hungarian Empire.

Indeed, it was the very same Creditanstalt that first entered the CE region in the mid 1980s, even prior to the breakdown of the communist bloc.[6] Creditanstalt (which has since than merged with Bank Austria in

1997 to form BA-CA) was quickly followed by Raiffeisen (RZB), a co-operative banking group, which penetrated Hungary as early as 1987. During the 1980s Austrian banks were only entitled to trade, finance and lend to the public sector – to companies controlled by the governments in the region. However, this initial presence has placed these banks in an advantaged position as the Iron Curtain came down, and indeed already by the early 1990s Austrian banks' relative share in Central and Eastern European business was large and growing rapidly; Austria was re-establishing itself as the most important financial hub for CEE region.

More recently, Central European financial sectors have been at the heart of the emerging trend towards pan-European banking conglomeration; the merger between Austrian CA-BA and German HVB was mainly aimed at facilitating increased penetration into the growth areas of CE. This was followed in 2005 by the acquisition of the HVB group itself by Italian UniCredit, which explicitly stated its intention in consolidating its position as the biggest player in the region. Further moves by other pan European bank-assurance groups which are highly active in the region such as Belgian KBC and French Société Générale are now also in the pipeline, and it is widely anticipated that the movement toward greater consolidation and conglomeration is likely to pick up pace in the near future (*The Banker* 2006; Ulst 2005).

What drives big credit institutions like UniCredit to penetrate the region by way of acquiring smaller so-called early movers such as Austrian BA-CA and RZB is the exceptional (and growing) levels of return on equity that these banks have been able to secure since they initially entered the region. For example the CE subsidiaries of RZB and BA-CA account for 20 per cent and 11 per cent respectively of the total group's assets in 2005, however approximately 40 per cent of RZB's and 54 per cent of BA-CA's annual profits were generated by their CE subsidiaries that year. For Erste Bank, another small Austrian bank which is nonetheless a big 'regional revolver', CE equity amounted to 23.7 per cent of the group's assets, and generated 61.4 per cent of the group's net profits in that same year![7]

In what follows the specific strategies employed by the foreign intermediaries in the region will be addressed; these strategies have evidently been extremely successful and generated phenomenal returns on equity, which are unheard of in mature markets. Let me note first that the speed of financial development has so far been rather slow, even in the three most financially advanced new member states (CE3). In Poland banking assets in 2005 accounted for approximately 152 billion Euros, or 60 per cent of GDP; in Hungary 75 billion Euros, or 87 per cent; and in the Czech

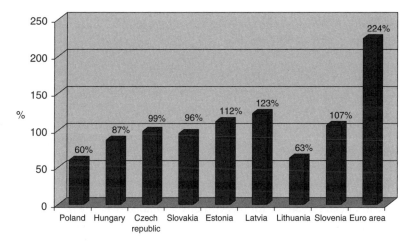

Sources: Unicredit New Europe Research Network (2006), July, p. 4, and ECB (2005), Occasional Paper 'EU Banking Structures'), October, p. 13.
Figure 8.2 Total banking assets as % of GDP, 2005

Republic 102 billion Euros, or 99 per cent. This is still considerably lower than the Euro Area average of 224 per cent (Barisitz 2005; UniCredit 2006).

Furthermore, despite the increase in bank capitalization and assets over the past decade, credit growth to the non-financial private sector (measured as the level of bank claims on the private sector as share of GDP, see Beck *et al.* 1999) has increased to a much lesser extent than total bank assets. In the Czech Republic, the ratio of private sector credit to GDP is slightly over 40 per cent while in Hungary and Poland the ratio is between 30 per cent and 40 per cent. The average share of credit to the private sector as share of total credit in all CE countries still hovers unchanged around 40–45 per cent of GDP similar to 1993 levels despite the massive influx of foreign-owned banks since then (Naarborg 2004).

To be sure this does not mean that Western capital has only achieved a weak position in the manufacturing sectors of Central European Economies. In fact well over 50 per cent of industrial assets in the region were already under foreign control by the late 1990s. This was secured, however, mostly through foreign direct investment rather than through the expansion of bank credit. What this does mean, however, is that so far the influx of financial capital into these economies has only scarcely been channelled into productive investment; the kind which results in increased employment and output growth.

The advantages of a bank-based financial intermediation system over a market-based one are supposedly in the specificity of bank–client relations which enables banks to gain 'insider' knowledge of their debtors and make risk judgments on the basis of an informal record of trust and reputation. Conversely, market-based financial intermediation is based on logic of homogenization, by rendering probability distributions of returns for standardized classes of financial products (Aglietta and Breton 2001). Arguably, therefore, a bank-based financial intermediation system is more suitable for Central European economies where a large number of small and medium enterprises (SMEs) enjoy limited access to equity markets and are dependent on bank credit.

However, foreign bank credit to SMEs as a share of total credit to the non-financial private sector has virtually stagnated over the past decade (Berger *et al.* 2001; Clarke *et al.* 2001). Whatever little increase in credit did accrue to the non-financial private sector was specifically targeted at foreign-owned enterprises and large and established domestic corporations. Evidently, banks have so far 'cherry picked' only the most credit-worthy clients. SMEs, on the other hand, although they form the backbone of the economy in terms of employment, are severely underrepresented in foreign-owned bank portfolios. The developmental value of foreign owned bank portfolios to the local non-financial private sector is thus confined to what Tilly (1986) called 'development assistance to the strong'; off course he was describing the previous expansion of Western finance under the Austro-Hungarian rule rather than the current one. As in the previous episode, the current foreign ownership in the banking sectors of CE has done little to promote productivity or employment-enhancing investment. The plausibility of the investment optimization thesis advocated by neoclassical economics encounters significant empirical difficulties.

If Western banks have indeed shunned the private non-financial sector thus far, then this immediately begs the question of where were financial funds directed to instead? De Haas and Van Lelyveld (2002; 2004) for example point out that foreign banks have so far opted to invest more in liquid securities such as government bonds. In the Euro area, private credit is about three times as high as public credit, whereas in the transition countries the share of private and public credit is roughly the same. Consequently foreign-owned banks play a central role in pricing public debt both as market makers in the primary markets and as major secondary markets investors.

This dominance of foreign ownership in the public debt markets of CE has proven instrumental in imposing foreign bondholder discipline over governments' fiscal policies, serving to further entrench and buttress their commitment to the neoliberal principles of economic governance. While the EU Commission has proven time and time again unable or unwilling to enforce the Growth and Stability Pact targets in the old Member states, market discipline is swift and unyielding in the case of the new member states. Poland has found this out in recent years, as it has not been able to meet EU public deficit requirements and is therefore required to maintain a comparatively high interest rate in order to stem financial outflow. Consequently foreign finance enjoys higher arbitrage income in Poland while domestic lenders face higher capital costs which under no circumstance can be judged as beneficial for promoting domestic economic activity and growth.

Even in Hungary and the Czech Republic, where public deficits are kept broadly within ERM requirements and interest rates are comparatively low, central banks are still incapacitated in controlling monetary aggregates. An interest rate hike will only serve to attract yet more speculative finance looking to cash in on interest rate differentials. These economies are in a constant state of 'structural liquidity surplus', and central banks are reduced to the function of 'sterilizing' excess liquidity from the market in order to maintain the 'health' of the financial systems and prevent overheating. Consequently central banks in these countries are victims of recurring speculative currency or interest attacks (Schmitz 2004). This is virtually risk-free for investors but imposes considerable costs on central banks, as when the Hungarian Magyar Nemzeti in January 2003 'sterilized' foreign currency to the tune of 4bn Euros before surrendering and slashing its interest rates by 1 percentage point twice in two days to fend off foreign currency speculators.

In contrast to the low and lagging growth in bank credit to the corporate sector, credit extended to households has been the main driver of credit growth in all the Central European economies. In 2004 credit to households has climbed to 38 per cent of total bank loans, compared to just 23 per cent in 2000 for the region as a whole (Coricelli *et al.* 2006). In the Czech Republic and Hungary, household lending as a share of total domestic lending has climbed from approximately 10 per cent in 1999 to over 30 per cent in 2004; in Poland household lending climbed from approximately 30 per cent to almost 50 per cent during the same time (Backé and Zumer 2005). Correspondingly household indebtedness for the region as a whole has nearly doubled, from 7 per cent of GDP in 2000 to 12 per cent in 2004 (Coricelli *et al.* 2006). This is off course still significantly lower than the corresponding levels of household indebtedness we have become accustomed to in the west; the average household debt across the OECD has reached 80 per cent of GDP in 2005, and for many EU member sates it is approaching or even exceeding 100 per cent of GDP (OECD Economic Outlook 2006).

The expansion of household credit in CE, much as in other countries, predominately took the form of mortgage lending; which is real-estate backed and is easily securitized and removed from the balance sheet of the creditor bank. Over the past five years foreign-owned banks have aggressively expanded into mortgage lending and mortgage-based debt consolidation. In Hungary for example, where government subsidies were introduced in 2001, mortgage lending has ballooned in recent years (+130 per cent in 2002, +70 per cent in 2003), albeit from a very modest point of departure (Barisitz 2005). Similar trends have been recorded in Poland, the Czech Republic and more broadly across the region, which on average has experienced an annual year on year growth rate in excess of 40 per cent in mortgage lending since 2000 (Unicredit 2006).

Thus, it is literally the homes of Central Europeans which form the primary target of Western financial expansion and where its biggest potential for profit lies. The reason for that lies in the comparatively high ratios of home ownership in the region; 69 per cent of households are homeowners in CE, a figure which compares favorably with the EU Area average of 70 per cent, especially given the extreme levels of household and mortgage debt in the EU (Coricelli *et al.* 2006). In CE mortgage debt is still comparatively very low, thus there is little doubt that this trend will intensify. Indeed, according to a Merrill Lynch study (2004), the new member states are considered 'seriously under-banked from a mortgage penetration perspective', and housing finance is identified as a potential growth area for years to come. In this sense the dominance of foreign owners in the financial system is in effect also spearheading a much wider transfer of ownership rights, through their aggressive expansion into mortgage lending.

Another troubling feature of credit growth in the new member states is the high (and rising) share of foreign currency-denominated loans. Whereas in Hungary and Poland foreign-denominated loans were virtually non-existent in the early 1990s, by 2004 foreign denominated credit to non-financials and household had surpassed 40 per cent in Hungary and 30 per cent in Poland and is growing fast (Backé and Zumer 2005).[8] Most of the loans referred to are euro-denominated, and have typically been granted to non-financial corporations, although recently their share in household loans has been soaring as well. In extending foreign denominated loans, foreign-owned banks have effectively 'externalized' their exchange rate risks to local businesses and households who have been motivated to borrow in foreign currency by the lower costs of borrowing. However, unlike foreign banks, local businesses and households who predominately rely on revenues (or wages) denominated in local currency are much less able to hedge against exchange rate risks, which makes any asset appreciation precarious (Szapáry 2005).

Furthermore, the dominance of foreign-owned banks in fact discourages personal saving in CE; as these banks are largely independent from the local deposit base, competition over deposit interest rates has failed to materialize. Indeed even in cases where the interest margins contracted, it was due to declining credit interest rates rather than rising deposit interest rates.[9] More recently, and especially as interest levels have gone down, foreign banks began to encourage personal investment through aggressively marketing their asset management services. This is of course because asset management yields fee-based income which in CE, much like elsewhere in Europe, accounts for a gradually growing share of banks incomes. Thus the expansion of foreign banks in the retail sector is in fact heralding significant transformations to household financial strategies, namely rising debt levels and transfer of ownership rights, increased foreign exchange risks and vulnerability to the discipline of financial markets.

Conclusions

The influx of foreign banks into CE has been spearheaded by banks which considered the region of CE be their 'second home market' due to their prior historical experience. Moreover, just like in the previous episode of financial expansion, the current financial integration of CE has thus far failed to deliver the promised optimization of investment and efficiency of economic management, let alone enhance general welfare levels. Reorienting patterns of accumulation whilst enjoying the advantages of corporate centralization, banks have instead prowled around to scoop up opportunities for interest income on asset-backed credit and risk-free lending, whilst passing on risks to the population at large. As a result foreign banks have been able to extract extremely high returns on their equity invested in the region. This I would argue lends support to an interpretation of Western European financial expansion as inherently predatory. That the Central European EU accession countries have also seen the regulation of their national financial systems, and by implication, their economies as a whole, alienated into foreign hands, was perhaps inevitable given the already established European structures. This realization will do little, however, to offset the evident pain incurred by the EU embrace.

Notes

1. For comparison at the end of 2004 the market share of foreign branches and subsidiaries stood at 24.7 per cent for the EU as a whole, and 15.5 per cent for the Euro area.
2. the Osterreichische National bank was founded in 1816 followed by the Niederosterreichische Escomptegesellschaft which received imperial permission to provide services to trade and industry in Lower Austria in 1853; Wurm 2006.
3. For a detailed account of the rise of Universal Banking in the Austro-Hungarian Empire see for example Teichova, 1997, 2005; Rathkolb *et al.* 2005; Wurm, 2006.
4. Hilferding (1910) was amongst the first to regard the relationship between industrial and banking capital as a power relationship. Through observing the development in Austria and Germany he concluded that banks directly and deliberately promoted further concentration through mergers and cartelization. Gerschenkron (1965) similarly recognized the growing power of banking capital particularly in 'latecomer' economies where capital is initially scarce.
5. The 1933 Banking Act was finally repealed by President Bill Clinton in 1999 (by the Gramm–Leach–Bliley Act).
6. In fact the first attempts of Creditanstalt to re-establish itself in the East reach back to the year 1975 when it opened the first representative office of a Western bank in Budapest under the communist regime.
7. Data is based on the respective annual reports of the above mentioned banks.
8. In the Czech Republic foreign-denominated credit on the other hand is relatively limited, and has in fact decreased to approximately 10 per cent in 2004 owing to the low interest rate levels.
9. The spread (or margin) between interest paid by banks on clients' deposits held with the bank and the interest charged on credit; a common measure of financial intermediation efficiency.

9
Indonesia and Malaysia: The Persistence of a Domestic Politico-Business Class

Ben Thirkell-White

The Asian financial crisis triggered significant changes in Malaysia and Indonesia. However, these changes are not well-characterized as a whole-scale take-over of domestic assets by foreign corporations or a dramatic re-working of domestic regulations to create a paradise for foreign investment. My main focus in this chapter is to draw out the resilience of domestic systems of political economy. However, I also argue that debates about 'globalisation' often obscure more than they illuminate when they are conducted at a very general level that paints false dichotomies between national and international, state and market.

The crisis experience in each country needs to be understood in the context of the pre-existing political economy. Both countries were quite open to FDI *before* the crisis struck, but there were also sectors reserved for politically well-connected domestic business. These politically connected businesses and the financial systems that supported them were the subject of market concern during the crisis. These relationships have been considerably altered by the crisis but not eliminated. There is little evidence that the outcome has been a windfall gain for foreign companies. Equally, for all the nationalist rhetoric attached to these 'national' businesses, there was not necessarily a strong domestic interest in the status quo. Many of the changes that took place as a result of the crisis have been positive from the point of view of domestic populations.

In both cases, I find that in emerging markets like Indonesia and Malaysia, creating an environment that is amenable to foreign investors requires active participation by the state and is therefore difficult to achieve through pure coercion. What would be required for a corporate take-over of Asian assets would be an alliance between external corporate interests and domestic political forces. Domestic forces in each country, though, were divided and external interests have been only partially successful in achieving market-enabling transformations.

I begin with an overview of the pre-crisis political economy of each country and an argument about how we should conceptualize the pressures for reform. I go on to a review of the reforms that have taken place and the current state of political economy in both countries, with particular reference to the issues that were at stake during the crisis. I conclude by drawing out the factors that explain the on-going importance of domestic political economy in shaping outcomes.

The crisis in context

It is not surprising that there was a tendency in Asia, and amongst academics with a long-standing research agenda in the region, to think of the crisis in terms of economic nationalism. Many Asian countries have never really had welfare states (the focus of Western concern about globalization). If anything, the crisis has created pressure for greater welfare provision than was previously available (Haggard 2005). The state's role has been much more important in promoting industrial upgrading and the development of a national capitalist class (Robison 1986; Amsden 1990; Wade 1990) and it was these roles that came under attack in the crisis period (Woo-Cummings 1999).

Different Asian states have gone about nationalist projects in different ways. Korean development relied heavily on the promotion of large domestic conglomerates. A variety of tools, including directed credit, were used to provide on-going incentives for industrial upgrading and export promotion (Woo 1991; Singh 1998). The system had been very successful in creating rapid growth and cutting-edge Korean business tended to be domestically owned. It was at least superficially plausible to see the crisis in terms of foreign take-over of the leading edge of Korean industry and an attack on the Korean development model (Wade and Venerosso 1998).[1]

There were some superficial similarities between the Korean model and Indonesian or Malaysian development. The state had been heavily involved in promoting domestic capital in ways that were supported by nationalist rhetoric. However, in Southeast Asia, there was a far greater role for foreign direct investment, particularly in the leading technological export sectors (Jomo *et al.* 1997). Domestic capital tended to be concentrated in non-tradeable sectors, like distribution and construction, or in utilities privatized in the late 1980s and early 1990s (Yoshihara 1988; Robison 1997; Gomez and Jomo 1999). The crisis would not result in selling off the most technologically sophisticated sectors of 'national' business, since those had always been foreign-owned. The normative terrain of any debate about the effect of crisis in Southeast Asia, then, was going to be different.

Instead debate in Indonesia and Malaysia revolved around the more ambiguous record of politically well-connected conglomerates operating, primarily, in domestic production. In both countries, these conglomerates were portrayed as representing attempts to promote indigenous business but (to different degrees in the two countries) that was never the whole story.

Malaysia

In Malaysia,[2] economic nationalist policy has always been unusual. It has partly been about the desire to promote modernisation and techno-logical upgrading and diversify the economy. However, it has has always been driven more strongly by a concern with *Malay* nationalism – the need to promote economic opportunity for the indigenous population, which was perceived as disadvantaged relative to more recent immi-grant communities. Controversy during the crisis was less about the for-eign takeover of 'national' assets than the likely impact on inter-ethnic economic power. The politics of response to crisis can only be under-stood on that basis.

At independence the population of Malaysia was made up of around 50 per cent indigenous Malays, 30 per cent ethnic Chinese and 20 per cent Indians. Malays had been predominant in government and the civil service during the colonial period but the majority of business and capital was in the hands of foreigners or the ethnic Chinese (Putucheary 1960; Ratnam 1965). The combination of Malay political power and Chinese economic power has profoundly shaped Malaysian politics ever since. Ethnic fragmentation has created a highly centralized political system, legitimated on the basis of economic policy designed to reduce ethnic inequality and promote stability.

Since 1969, every Malaysian election has been won by the Barisan Nasional (BN), an alliance of elite parties from each ethnic group, under the leadership of UMNO (United Malays National Organization). This inter-ethnic alliance has been difficult to defeat since, given the preva-lence of identity politics, the obvious opposition platform is to be 'more ethnic' than the corresponding Barisan party (the PAS,[3] the Malay oppos-ition, campaigns on an Islamic-nationalist platform, while the Chinese DAP[4] campaigns on a liberal, and implicitly anti-affirmative action, one). Only an inter-ethnic coalition can hope to win power at the national level but forming alliances with other ethnic groups risks undermining opposition parties' core support base.[5]

The economic manifestation of BN power has been the New Economic Policy (NEP), introduced following inter-ethnic riots in 1969. It was designed to 'reduce and eventually eradicate poverty, by raising income levels and increasing opportunities for all Malaysians, irrespective of race' and 'accelerate the process of restructuring Malaysian society to correct economic imbalance, so as to reduce and eventually eliminate the identification of race with economic function'. Specifically the government set three targets to be achieved by 1990: a reduction of poverty from 50 per cent to less than 20 per cent; restructuring of employment so that, in all sectors and occupations, it reflected the racial composition of the country; and restructuring of corporate ownership so that at least 30 per cent would be owned by *bumiputeras*[6] (Gomez and Jomo 1999).

Various means were employed to further those goals. Initially, inter-ethnic equity was pursued through a form of import-substituting industrialization, adapted to ensure that benefits accrued disproportionately to the *bumiputera* population. There were employment quotas for Malays and education quotas to ensure that they were qualified to fill posts. The government channeled funds into the new industries through '*bumiputera* trust agencies'. Most relevant in the current context is the Industrial Coordination Act (ICA), which imposed 30 per cent equity quotas for *bumiputera* ownership of most businesses operating in Malaysia.

In practice, the Malaysian government has been much more comfortable with the growth of foreign business than with business owned by the ethnic Chinese community. Alongside the promotion of domestic business to provide new employment for *bumiputera*, it has set up a number of Special Economic Zones and provided exemptions from ICA requirements for foreign firms in high-tech sectors or export manufacturing. These incentives were well-timed to catch the first wave of outsourcing in the early 1970s (Jomo *et al.* 1997; Gomez and Jomo 1999).

Up until the 1980s, NEP policy was strongly associated with state-owned businesses operating for the domestic market (while export growth was encouraged through FDI). From the mid-1980s, a combination of recession and ideological shifts pushed attempts at Malay betterment away from this broad-based strategy of employment creation through ISI, towards the creation of a symbolic class of millionaire *bumiputera* entrepreneurs, via a peculiarly Malaysian form of privatization. State corporations were sold off, licences were issued to firms to compete in sectors which had been public monopolies and infrastructure projects were contracted out to 'entrepreneurs' that were close to the government. This policy created a range of large conglomerates owned by a newly consolidated politico-business class, including some ethnic Chinese businessmen with strong ties to the Malaysian political elite. Restrictions on FDI were, if anything, reduced during the 1980s and Malaysian recovery in the early 1990s was partly fuelled by the influx of East Asian investment into the region following the Plaza Accord (Gomez 1999; Gomez and Jomo 1999; Searle 1999).

Politically, the NEP has been a key part of BN legitimacy, in its claim to be the only political grouping that can deliver inter-ethnic negotiation and harmony. During the early period, the NEP did head off mounting inter-ethnic conflict and deliver a significant increase in living standards for the Malays. However, it also tended to solidify ethnic identities and, particularly during the 1990s, to cloud the distinction between economic and political power. Arguably, by the late 1990s, the NEP was more closely tied up with elite level political patronage than any more socially justifiable redistributive policy. This shift from broad-based development towards the promotion of an elite politico-business class created considerable tensions within UMNO and growing public criticism.[7]

The crisis played into these tensions. Foreign market analysts' concerns revolved around the relationship between government policy and the large domestic conglomerates. The view was that these conglomerates were monopolizing capital and using it inefficiently. The government was squandering money on unproductive 'mega-projects' that did more to fuel crony corporate growth than improve economic conditions in Malaysia. The waste was something Malaysia could ill-afford when the country was facing growing pressure from lower-wage economies elsewhere in Asia. More self-interestedly, one can assume that foreign corporations had at least one eye on the potential for gaining access to lucrative government contracts and sectors of domestic business that were reserved for Malaysian business. Domestic reactions were partly about a perceived attack by foreign interests but they were also about the effects crisis would have on inter-ethnic balance and, relatedly, UMNO's popularity. For some, the potential to discredit UMNO and the newly created corporations was welcomed. For others, maintenance of Malay economic assets was a key goal in crisis resolution (Nesadurai 2000; Thirkell-White 2005a). The crisis, then, was not simply about foreign corporations versus the Malaysian national interest. It was also about the domestic politics of UMNO dominance and NEP redistribution.

Indonesia

Industrial policy in Suharto's New Order was even more problematic. It is difficult to disagree with the neoliberal view that Indonesian economic growth owed more to conservative macro-economic policy than adventures in economic nationalism.[8]

Analysts of Indonesian political economy have identified three forces driving policy: economic nationalism, a technocratic approach to promoting economic growth, and political patronage (Robison 1997). As in Malaysia, the economic marginalization of the domestic population was an issue at independence but foreign capital was higher on the list of threats than Chinese capital (Robison 1986). The difficult task of nation-building in the extraordinarily large and heterogeneous archipelago, combined with this sense of *pribumi*[9] marginalization, has kept economic nationalism on the agenda ever since (Robison 1986; Schwarz 1999).

In the Sukarno period, over-zealous pursuit of nationalist policies, in the context of an increasingly fragile political regime, proved economically disastrous. Suharto, his successor, had learnt the importance of producing economic growth for political legitimacy. From the start, he made a concerted effort to woo foreign investors and placed macroeconomic policy in the hands of a competent set of economic technocrats (the 'Berkeley mafia') (Winters 1996).

Nonetheless, economic nationalism continued to play an important role in policy, particularly when capital was plentiful (Winters 1996). High oil prices in the 1970s, for example, enabled measures to direct credit to *pribumi* business, reserve some markets for *pribumi* endeavour and encourage *pribumi* equity participation. Funds were spent on a variety of more or less ill-fated nationalist projects and a good deal was also directed to the agricultural sector (to head off the threat of communism and because it was a sector with comparative advantage). Much credit designated for promoting *pribumi* industry, though, was diverted to serve patrimonial interests and was often never repaid (MacIntyre 1993). Pressure to form joint ventures also had contradictory results since large Chinese firms or indigenous firms with strong political connections (rather than small *pribumi* enterprise) made the most attractive business partners (Robison 1986).

When the oil price fell in 1982, nationalist measures became more expensive and macroeconomic prudence began to take centre stage, returning power to the 'technocrats' in Bappenas (the state planning ministry) and Bank Indonesia, just as a shift towards free market policies was taking place in the wider world. Equally, some of the larger Indonesian conglomerates were becoming less reliant on the state and had come to see it as restricting their activities. While wishing to retain state protection, they were anxious to attract foreign investment and obtain access to sectors that had been state monopolies (Robison 1997). The result was: a good deal of privatisation in public utilities and infrastructure; some trade reform, particularly in sectors upstream to export-oriented industry; the opening of some previously restricted domestic sectors to foreign investment and the removal of some domestic equity requirements. Overall this package was not too unpopular with business. However, less popular tax reform and privatisation of the customs service were also introduced, emphasising Suharto's ability to reign in corruption when it threatened the medium-term stability of state revenues (MacIntyre 2000).

The reforms mobilized large amounts of capital and the banking sector grew rapidly. By 1996 there were 200 domestic banks, domestic private banks accounted for 12 of the 20 largest Indonesian banks, and the private banks commanded 53 per cent of funds in the banking sector (World Bank 1995). Foreign investment, particularly from East Asia, increased rapidly in low wage exports and more sophisticated upstream production of chemicals, paper, pulp, power generation and construction (Jomo *et al.* 1997; Robison 1997).

Contrary to the expectations of liberal reformers, the conglomerates' domination of the economy increased as a result. The politico-business families that had emerged during the late 1970s were best placed to take advantage of economic opening. Foreign investors' enthusiasm for politically well-connected conglomerates made the stock market a cheap source of funds: 'inadequate rules and enforcement capacity allowed companies to go public without adequate disclosure, insider trading was rife and fake share scandals occurred frequently' (Robison 1997).

Despite liberalisation, cartels, price controls, entry and exit controls, exclusive licensing and public sector dominance remained widespread (World Bank 1995). BULOG continued to control access to domestic food and even allocated new monopolies – notably the economically perverse clove monopoly awarded to Tommy Suharto in 1990 and a monopoly on fertilizer pellets granted to Suharto's grandson (Schwarz 1999). Equally important, as in Malaysia, was the state's ability to grant contracts for the construction of state 'mega-projects'. Finally the rise of Habibie as Suharto's political protégé invigorated industrial policy.

During the crisis, pressures to open protected domestic sectors were initially less prominent in Indonesia. The United States Trade Representative's annual report on restrictive trade practices in 1997 listed formal barriers to trade in the distribution system and financial services and cited joint venture requirements as an impediment to investment but it saw the principle problems as springing from informal barriers to entry and restricted competition, especially through patronage (United States Trade

Representative 1997). A good deal of foreign investment, though, relied on the patronage system to facilitate joint ventures with politically well-connected companies. These connections provided investment security and access to the protection and subsidies enjoyed by 'domestic' business (Robison and Rosser 2000). Indeed, there was an investment boom in the late 1990s that the government found hard to control. The banking sector appeared to be largely out of control, with growing levels of connected lending to conglomerates and large problems with non-performing loans.[10] Just as in previous periods of abundant capital, the technocrats were losing influence to political imperatives.

Given that foreign investors had found a way of doing business with Indonesia, we should perhaps not be surprised that early crisis commentary was reasonably positive. The general view was that Indonesia was simply feeling the effects of contagion. The government responded by allowing the exchange rate to depreciate and calling in the IMF to 'boost confidence'. However, the IMF joined forces with the Indonesian technocrats to propose a more extensive programme than Suharto had expected, pushing for a clean up of the banking system and other reforms that would attack the base of Suharto's patronage (Riesenhuber 2001; Thirkell-White 2005a). The botched implementation of bank closures and Suharto's apparent reluctance to do what was necessary to please the IMF started to turn economic sentiment against him. That boosted political opposition and, in combination with a health scare in December, made him look politically vulnerable. Given the reliance of virtually the entire economic system on structures of political patronage, it should come as no surprise that the result was economic meltdown (Robison and Rosser 2000).

By this time, it was clear to everyone that Suharto had to go. Foreign pressure was brought to bear to radically overhaul economic (and political) governance. Existing monopolies and cartels were broken up and a huge range of legislation introduced (including new laws on bankruptcy, corporate governance, competition, consumer rights and labour rights). There was direct foreign lobbying for the disbanding of the plywood cartel, which had been designed to prevent foreign access to unprocessed Indonesian timber products.

In the wake of the crisis there were efforts to re-organize Indonesian economic governance in ways that foreign investors would find easier to deal with. This included pressure for greater market access in particular sectors. However, these pressures only emerged relatively late in the crisis. Attitudes to the previous system were more mixed with many foreign investors benefiting from the 'irrational' system of economic and corporate governance in Indonesia. As we will see, the benefits of the pre-existing system have been particularly clear in contrast with investor attitudes to the turmoil of the post-crisis period. As in Malaysia, domestic interests were divided over the IMF agenda. The crisis was damaging for nearly everyone but many Indonesians had reasons to be relatively relaxed about foreign take-overs of large 'crony' corporations, given the likely knock-on effects on Suharto's power base.

The IMF, Western 'capital' and the goals of crisis intervention

Against this background, it is not surprising that nationalist rhetoric about corporate take-overs was prominent in Asia. The relationship between corporate interests and the state was under threat in both countries. Additionally, this relationship had been justified as part of broader nationalist political projects that were important in the legitimation of political regimes. Mahathir and Suharto both blamed the crisis on foreign speculators and tried to argue that the IMF would undermine the basis of their national political projects. Mahathir pointed to the economic and political stability the NEP had brought (Nesadurai 2000; Thirkell-White 2005a), while Suharto argued foreign markets were attacking Indonesian interests and the IMF was violating the Indonesian constitution in its calls for radical liberalization (Robison and Rosser 2000; Thirkell-White 2005a). As we have seen, these claims should be read within particular political contexts.

For now, though, I want to draw out the nature of the intentions behind foreign interventions during the crisis. I will suggest that the kind of foreign pressure exerted was more complex than a simple narrative of direct foreign corporate interest would suggest. There is little evidence of direct lobbying by particular corporations to shape the political programmes introduced by the IMF. The main exception was Congressional lobbying by domestic corporations operating in the US, concerned with 'unfair' competition from subsidized export industries in Asia (Thirkell-White 2005b).

There is far better evidence of a close correspondence between IMF perceptions of 'good corporate governance' and the views of financial interests in Wall Street. Indeed prominent liberal economists such as Stiglitz and Bhagwati, have argued that the IMF's interest in the financial, rather than real, sector is threatening international support for globalization (Wade 1996; Bhagwati 1998, 2001; Stiglitz 2002). It was a *Wall Street–Treasury*–IMF complex, that Bhagwati criticized, not pressure from would be foreign direct investors. That fits with long-standing patterns of institutional relationships in the US, in which the United States

Trade Representative (who deals with trade and investment issues, and is closely connected to corporate lobbies) has little input into IMF policy. The crisis was a *financial* crisis more than a corporate crisis and took place against a background of concerted US lobbying for global financial sector liberalization, including (ultimately abortive) efforts to have the IMF's Articles of Agreement modified to include an obligation for capital account liberalistion (Thirkell-White 2005b).

If IMF programmes served a particular interest, it was an interest in facilitating international financial transactions, rather than opening up the real sector. The emphasis was on the allocation of capital, particularly increasing the transparency of corporate accounting and the market-orientation of domestic bank lending (IMF 1997; Boresztein and Lee 1999). It was about creating a market for corporate assets to increase competition. That did imply an increase in foreign M&A activity, as part of an attempt to stimulate a return of investment to the countries concerned (Government of Indonesia 1998; Sohn and Yang 1998) but that was not the primary aim. The desire for a 'Westernisation' of Asian financial practices is influenced by Western financial interests through a variety of channels. It is Treasury officials and central bankers that sit on the Fund's Boards. These officials often have careers in the banking industry before or after their stint at the Fund and operate in the same cultural milieu. Even then, the dominance of neoclassical thinking in the economics profession, with its faith in investor rationality and competitive market discipline has at least as much influence on the thinking of Fund staff as direct lobbying (Wade 1996; Bhagwati 1998; Thirkell-White 2005b). If Asian crisis interventions were going to trigger fire-sales, that was more likely to involve investment bankers search for quick profits than transnational corporations interested in acquiring a longer-term domestic presence at discount prices (Robertson 2007). Indeed part of the criticism of economists like Stiglitz and Bhagwati has been over this emphasis on facilitating footloose capital, rather than more stable and (arguably) developmental FDI.

This emphasis on reorganizing the allocation of capital can be read in two ways. The difference between them has political significance domestically and internationally. The IMF justified its interventions on the basis that they would break up 'crony relationships' between government and domestic capital, increasing efficiency and creating opportunities for more efficient but less well-connected business (Thirkell-White 2003). Improved foreign access was one way of achieving these aims. Better foreign management techniques, particularly in the banking sector, would enhance the overall economic environment. Many at the IMF genuinely believed this to be the most effective way to rehabilitate the crisis economies. To be fair to the IMF, the Indonesian experience also lends some plausibility to this account. Historically, liberalizing reforms had been captured by large domestic conglomerates and other domestic interests had simply not been strong enough to break up politico-business dominance (Robison 1986, 1997). As we will see, the exclusionary nature of pre-existing corporate-government relationships meant that this view was also popular with some segments of the domestic population of both countries.[11]

On the other hand, whether sincere or not, this perspective on the crisis also had clear advantages to corporate interests in the IMF's leading shareholder countries. Officially, foreign investment was only one tool in a broader attempt to enhance efficient capital allocation and a more broadly competitive environment in crisis countries. However, reforms would also facilitate access for foreign direct investors and financial interests. The absence of direct lobbying does not mean that there are not indirect structural factors connecting IMF policy with corporate interest. After all, the crisis itself was one of massive capital flight. Even without the IMF's interventions, crisis countries had powerful reasons to think harder about how to satisfy the wishes of foreign capital.

Domestic opposition and the political economy of post-crisis reform

In the previous section I suggested it was possible to see IMF reform and international market pressures during the crisis in terms of an attempt to open up Indonesian and Malaysian markets to foreign take-overs. However, the history of the Malaysian and Indonesian political economies provides reasons to question any straightforward interpretation of such takeovers as an attack on *developmental* nationalism. Whilst there may have been a clear foreign interest in IMF-style reforms, domestic interests had mixed attitudes.

At one extreme, support came from those who saw liberalizing reforms as a way of challenging structures of political and corporate power that they viewed as elitist, inefficient and authoritarian. At the other, concerted opposition came from vested interests that would lose their access to captive banking institutions or political patronage. The most obvious proponents of the former view were businesses excluded from political patronage and relationship banking – either Chinese business in Malaysia or smaller businesses in both countries. The latter was popular with businesses in trouble during the crisis, trying to avoid break-up or take-over by foreign creditors or potential purchasers, including those with political connections.

Both sides then tried to influence those with less clear interests one way or the other through the political process. Existing corporate interests drew on the history of nationalist rhetoric. In Malaysia, the appeal was to Malay nationalism and less importantly the creation of national industry. In Indonesia, there were less successful appeals to the weaker tradition of *pribumi* nationalism. For reformers, the key was to talk less about industrial policy and more about cronyism, authoritarianism and corruption. Outside of official politics, the old politico-economic elite in both countries tried to use its ongoing power to protect itself from reform initiatives through direct pressures on politicians and the judiciary.

Crisis controversy, then, was not simply about foreign capital versus the 'national interest'. It was also about long-term domestic debates over what the national interest actually was. International pressure and international intervention interacted with those debates, adding pressure to those that wanted to see pre-existing systems dismantled, but it did not determine the outcomes.

In this section I will review some of the ways in which these political struggles have worked themselves out in the post-crisis reform period. International corporate power is sometimes portrayed in the globalization literature as something in opposition to the state. The post-crisis experience of Indonesia and Malaysia, however, illustrates how important it is for corporate interests to *use* the state to make the domestic environment safe and attractive for foreign investment. In Malaysia this attempt to capture the state was unsuccessful, due to the resilience of pre-existing political patterns, the limited severity of the crisis and, perhaps, Malaysia's adoption of capital controls. In Indonesia, by contrast, the state was strongly influenced by foreign advice and influence but did not have the capacity to create an environment that was significantly attractive to foreign investors.

Malaysia

Exactly what happened in Malaysian policy-making circles during 1997 and 1998 is difficult to determine because events have become so politicized. It appears that Mahathir was always torn between a tradition of broadly market-friendly Malaysian policy on the one hand and a populist anger with foreign speculators on the other. During the early period, his rhetoric was characterized by inflammatory economic nationalism but policy was often more orthodox (Thirkell-White 2005a). By December 1998, Malaysia was talking in terms of a 'virtual IMF' policy.

However, the perceived failure of this policy and concerns at its impact on politically well-connected corporations led to a change of course in 1998. Malaysia gradually eased fiscal and monetary policy and, in September 1998, instituted capital controls, designed to stem further capital flight.[12] At the same time, Mahathir sacked Anwar Ibrahim, who had been associated with more orthodox approaches, on distinctly questionable charges of sodomy and corruption. The dispute was about more than economic policy. Mahathir felt Anwar was trying to exploit popular dissent over elite corruption in an attempt to seize power (Funston 2000). For our purposes, though, what matters is that Anwar's dismissal triggered widespread political mobilization around calls for *reformasi* (which, for Mahathir, had dangerous echoes of the movement that had just overthrown Suharto). The official policy platform of the *reformasi* movement focused on executive dominance in Malaysia and called for a removal of repressive legislation, clean government and a rejuvenation of Malaysian democracy. However it also embodied straightforward anger at Mahathir's dismissal of Anwar, partly because it broke cultural taboos and partly because Anwar had been a key figure in the Malaysian Islamic resurgence movement (Khoo 2004).

Politically, Mahathir was faced with conflicting incentives. The crisis was harming his traditional project of Malay betterment and the political support that came with it. However, he was also under pressure from segments of the domestic population that showed dangerous signs of uniting behind an agenda of cleaner governance and a more level playing field. These domestic pressures explain Malaysian responses to the crisis at least as well as external corporate pressure. What we see is an attempt to steer a course between the imperative of on-going Malay accumulation on the one hand, and the need for 'cleaner' government on the other.

Capital controls gave the Malaysian authorities confidence to pursue modestly expansionary macroeconomic policy (Athukorala 2000; Jomo 2004). At the same time, there were widespread perceptions that they would provide a barrier behind which Mahathir could rescue 'crony corporations', preventing the increase in market discipline the IMF and the markets hoped would be forthcoming (IMF 1999). Econometric analysis shows that the markets attached a significant premium to firms perceived as having a connection with Mahathir in the immediate aftermath of the crisis (Johnson *et al.* 2006).

There were some high-profile bail-outs of powerful corporations – most notably the Renong corporation, Malaysian Airlines and Mirzan Mahathir's shipping business.[13] The government's tight control of bank restructuring was also controversial. It put pressure on the Malaysian banking industry to enter into consolidating mergers around key anchor banks. Whilst this consolidation made some economic sense (so that ailing banks would be merged with successful ones, reducing the need for refinancing and preventing closures), there were strong perceptions that the choice of anchor banks was driven partly by political considerations, with banks that were connected with Anwar receiving worse treatment than those connected with Mahathir (Chin 2004).

Political pressure over issues of cronyism and the government's disastrous performance in the 1999 elections also created pressure for cleaner governance (Khoo 2004). Despite Malaysia's limited democracy, the government's legitimacy is vulnerable to losses of electoral support. There is a long-standing pattern of responding to these pressures through modest accommodatory policy changes (Crouch 1996; Jesudason 1996). Fears that the capital controls were simply an attempt to avoid meaningful reform were unfounded. Corporate governance reforms began under Mahthir's leadership but really took off after his resignation in 2002. His successor, Ahmad Abdullah Badawi, stepped up the agenda of anti-corruption programmes and reform, making personal probity the basis of much of his appeal in the 2004 elections.[14] The result was a dramatic return of electoral fortunes for UMNO. Although a small number of high-profile bail-outs may have led the market to expect firms connected to the Prime Minister to prosper, there is no evidence that they actually did so (Johnson *et al.* 2006). Fears that the capital controls would be a means for avoiding post-crisis reforms, then, were misplaced.

However, it is notable that the changes in Malaysia were not strongly driven by market opening to foreign corporations, rather they involved modest changes within the existing parameters of the Malaysian political economy. A high-ranking member of the Prime Minister's National Economic Action Council, told me proudly that Malaysia had avoided selling off any of the 'national heritage'.[15]

If we look at figures for the early crisis period we see that acquisitions formed a much larger part of inward investment than in the pre-crisis era. However, looking at the largest 25 deals in Malaysia between August 1997 and March 1999 (which includes deals as small as US$1 million), we find the total value was a mere US$2.8 billion (Zhan and Ozawa 2001). In comparison, Danaharta managed over US$12 billion of assets during the crisis period[16] and the total market capitalization of the KLSE, by 2005, was over US$100 billion.

Instead, the focus of corporate governance reform and Badawi's attack on crony economic privilege has been on the efficiency of domestic banks and corporations. The primary agent for corporate restructuring was Danaharta, which acquired a huge portfolio of non-performing loans from the banking industry, becoming the principle creditor in large numbers of debt workouts (Danaharta 2005). Malaysian insiders hint at political influence in the process of asset resolution but there is little hard evidence (in comparison with the manipulation of bank mergers noted above).

Changes to corporate ownership during the crisis have reduced the ownership share of politically well-connected business and increased the influence of 'government linked corporations' (or GLCs) which account for 36 per cent of the market capitalization of the KLSE, 54 per cent of the composite index and more than 50 per cent of the top 25 stocks. A variety of forces promoted this outcome. The political allegiances of *bumiputera* corporate moguls in the pre-crisis period were divided between Mahathir, Anwar, and sometime finance minister Daim Zainuddin. Anwar's fall from grace and a later denouement between Mahathir and Daim provided political reasons for dispossession. In any case, the crisis was felt most severely in sectors that had been the province of the new Malay corporations, such as finance and construction. They were particularly likely to need government assistance, either through Danaharta or more directly and this provided the opportunity for partial government takeover or simply the declining influence of the company concerned. The details of this process are still only sketchily understood but, in a comprehensive empirical study of post-crisis ownership structures in the KLSE, Gomez (2004) demonstrates the increasing importance of the GLCs, a noticeable deconcentration of ownership amongst Malaysia's largest corporations, and the sharp (but by no means total) decline of the Malay politico-business class.

The newly-dominant GLCs have been the focus of government attempts to improve efficiency in the wake of the crisis. Assets have been transferred to an entity called Khazanah Nasional Bhd, which it hopes to convert into an investment arm along the lines of Singapore's Temasek. The government has also set up a high profile committee to promote 'high performance' in the GLCs. It began its first phase in May 2004 by encouraging GLCs to introduce key benchmarking performance indicators and performance related pay. It also relaxed restrictions that had restricted CEO posts to *bumiputera* executives.[17] Market reaction was initially positive (Kolesnikov-Jessop 2004) but fairly moderate progress has led to more mixed assessments recently, despite a second round of initiatives announced in 2006. The GLCs that have undergone a strong restructuring programme are now peforming better than the KLSE composite index but are very much a minority (Ang 2006). There are on-going doubts about Abdullah Badawi's political ability (and perhaps will) to drive through these reforms in the face of strong *status quo* interests in business and within UMNO.

There have been changes to the Malaysian corporate scene as a result of the crisis. However, if anything, they reflect increased state involvement, rather than a takeover by free-wheeling foreign investors. The same trend can be seen in the two Malaysia plans announced during the crisis. The 8th Malaysia plan, in particular, was interpreted as reflecting a reduced emphasis on foreign portfolio investment and FDI (Nagel 2004). The 9th Malaysia plan has much to say about fostering domestic industry on the basis of efficiency including, for instance, a more transparent and competitive approach to government procurement. On the other hand, this image of encouraging domestic competitiveness is undercut by an on-going emphasis on *bumiputera* preference (so, despite 'transparent and competitive' tendering, there continue to be quotas of projects that must be awarded to *bumiputera* companies).

Overall, the picture in Malaysia is one of continuity with modest changes at the margins. The crisis drove home messages about enhancing competitiveness and reigning in the worst excesses of the political business system. However, the limited scale of crisis and the continuing political strength of the BN left the Malaysian state firmly in control of post-crisis developments. There were some changes in the directions foreign investors hoped for. Restrictions were removed on foreign direct investment in manufacturing (but not the protected domestic service sector). Corporate governance and banking regulation reforms were introduced under Mahathir. His replacement has tried to drive forward anti-corruption initiatives and attempts to enhance the competitiveness of Malaysian business. However, these changes are taking place within a structural context that has changed little. UMNO still governs Malaysia and still sees Malay preference as a key part of its political role. Structures of politico-business power have been altered but the fundamentals of Malaysian political economy remain in place. The Malaysian state feels pressures to enhance competitiveness but it has also proven able to retain control of Malaysia's economic path through a strategic engagement with foreign capital.

Indonesia

In Indonesia, too, there has not been a radical convergence of corporate governance on a Western model or a large-scale take-over of domestic corporations. The reasons, however, are quite different. Since the fall of Suharto, all Indonesian Presidents have had to present a reformist image. Public intolerance of KKN (corruption, collusion and nepotism) continues to be one of the few certainties of Indonesian politics. Under electoral pressure and donor influence (Hamilton-Hart 2006), successive governments have introduced an enormous raft of new legislation on issues such as corporate governance, bankruptcy reform, banking regulation, central bank independence, labour rights, consumer rights and competition law. National and international political pressure for change has been far stronger than in Malaysia.

However, despite this activity, foreign investment (and, indeed, investment generally) in Indonesia has remained low. The fundamental problem is a lack of legal certainty. From the point of view of abstract orthodox principles, that is an unexpected result. Indonesia has shifted from a system of capricious authoritarian rule to one of regulatory liberal democracy. If one looks purely at changing power through elections, the transition to democracy has been successful (Rieffel 2004). Legislation protecting property rights is much stronger than it was under the New Order. One would expect investors to respond positively. Unfortunately, in practice, although state policy is far less likely to interfere with property rights, state capacity to enforce them remains weak. Under the Suharto regime, foreign businesses could find an appropriate political patron, who could be given a financial stake in their operations. Patronage provided political protection and facilitation that substituted for the legal certainties of orthodox liberal theory. So far, during the *reformasi* era, the Indonesian state has not had sufficient capacity to secure enforcement of new legislation in a way that is substitutes for the guarantees previously provided by political protection.

The problems are at two levels. First, the old oligarchy lost some of its formal political power with the fall of Suharto but less of its financial power. There is a struggle going on between the influence of this old money and the electoral importance of public opinion. Politicians face electoral incentives to act in the general interest but also personal and campaign funding incentives to pay more attention to old structures of financial power (Robison and Hadiz 2004).

Secondly, there are more mundane difficulties in getting state functionaries to behave as they are 'supposed' to do. Incentives facing officials do not yet align clearly with central policy makers' intent. The bureaucracy is in a difficult transition phase between a system in which incentives were driven by political loyalties and the ability to skim money off projects, and a new model driven by professional incentives and democratic oversight (McLeod 2005).

Informal corporate power was clearest in the ability of many (though by no means all) Indonesian conglomerates to survive the crisis. There were significant changes, particularly in the banking sector. Assets owned by state banks increased from 36 per cent of the total in 1996 to 50 per cent in 2000. The number of private banks halved and their assets fell from 52 per cent to 35 per cent. Banks associated with pre-crisis business groups were particularly affected (of 42 active in the pre-crisis era, only 7 survived without change in ownership). Former business-group banks that have been purchased by foreign (mostly Asian) companies after nationalization through IBRA now make up the second largest category of banks, behind state-owned banks (Sato 2005).

However, Robison and Hadiz have argued that changes in bank ownership mask the fact that corporate groups had already transferred banking assets to the rest of the group through connected lending transactions. Bank Indonesia Liquidity Assistance was used to pay off group debts in foreign currency (Robison and Hadiz 2004) echoing a broader pattern in which the inflow of capital to Indonesia in the run-up to the crisis was often invested overseas (Pincus and Ramli 2004). Corporations were often happy to sacrifice their banks and rely on their ability to avoid debt repayment obligations to save their wider corporate groups, given that the loans had largely been taken over by IBRA (the Indonesian Bank Restructuring Agency).

IBRA, along with foreign private creditors, has come up against enormous difficulties in enforcing debt or pushing companies into bankruptcy. Indonesia's original bankruptcy legislation was weak but, even after reform, it has not been enforced by the courts. During the Habibie era, the political influence of economic nationalism may have played a part. More recently, the state seems to have been unable to root out corruption in the judicial system. The weakness of legal remedies has undermined attempts at negotiation between conglomerates and foreign creditors, since there are few legal precedents to underpin negotiating positions (Linnan 1999). Overall, the process of corporate debt restructuring has been exceedingly slow and IBRA's ability to realize assets has been considerably weaker than that of similar institutions elsewhere in the region. It acquired assets at highly subsidized rates, based on book values, which were often fraudulent (rather than broadly market prices as in the case of the Malaysian Danaharta) (Tegara-Hagiwara and Pasadilla 2004). IBRA acquired assets worth a total of 57 per cent of GDP and political interference in its operation was rife, despite careful IMF-influenced institutional design that was supposed to keep it independent (Enoch *et al.* 2001; Robison 2001).

Attempts to remove Suharto-era monopolies made some initial headway. Particular successes included the dismantling of the plywood marketing system, Tommy Suharto's clove monopoly, the wheat monopolies that had belonged to Liem Sioe Liong and a range of BULOG monopolies in agricultural products. However, there were notable failures in attempts to unwind Suharto era preferential arrangements. When the government tried to re-negotiate extraordinarily generous dollar denominated electricity supply contracts, foreign corporations that had entered into partnerships with domestic corporations cried 'foul' and support from their home governments (particularly the US and Japanese) together with court action forced the government to back down. The Buloggate scandal surrounding president Wahid, the total failure to reign in illegal logging, and on-going bureaucratic turf-wars about control over lucrative institutions providing off-budget resources all indicate that the role of gate-keeping institutions in politico-business patronage has not been eliminated (Robison and Hadiz 2004; Kato 2005; Yonekura 2005).

Corporate resistance to dismantling such institutions and the sale of assets by IBRA were both boosted by economic nationalism. Centres of patronage, like Pertamina and BULOG, also had political purposes. They were symbols of national economic control over natural resources and performed a genuine social function as well as their problematic place in the murky world of corporate plunder. When it came to selling off assets, IBRA was caught between lack of interest from potential foreign investors (which triggered considerable political opposition over low prices) and its need to sell assets quickly for budgetary reasons on the other. The sale of Bank Bali to Standard Chartered failed because it aroused strong nationalist sentiment and a strike by bank staff. The sale of Bank Central Asia to a US financial firm, apparently owned by Asian interests, was only completed in the face of sustained opposition from the DPR (Sato 2005). Coordinating minister for the economy Kwik Kan Gie resigned in 2000 over opposition to the sale of IBRA assets to Suharto-era corporate interests at knock down prices (Robison and Hadiz 2004).

Finally, although large corporate groups had difficulties with their financial arms and heavily indebted infrastructure projects, the low Indonesian exchange rate meant they could make significant profits in forestry, foodstuffs and agriculture. Even if they could not entirely avoid losses, delaying tactics were often enough to preserve significant corporate wealth.

Overall, expectations in Asia and abroad that there would be large changes in ownership of the Indonesian corporate sector, including considerable fire-sales to foreign corporate groups, were not realized. There was more change of ownership than in Malaysia but, with the exception of the banking sector, there was hardly a significant transformation.

In terms of the formal political process, the sheer inability of the state to push through reforms and realize assets through the IBRA process already implies the on-going influence of Suharto-era elites. The glacial pace of prosecution for corruption and its limited success rate provide further evidence of the central state's weakness or inaction in the face of corporate interests (Robison and Hadiz 2004).

Corporate scandals also indicate the on-going existence of patronage in formal Indonesian politics. The Bank Bali scandal revolved around the expropriation of funds for Golkar and Buloggate implicated Wahid (and therefore presumably the PKB). More generally, Robison and Hadiz (2004) point to the wide range of Suharto-era elite actors that have found their way into new Indonesian political parties and the relative absence of representatives of some of the mass groups that mobilized in the *reformasi* demonstrations (labour, students or the peasantry).

The majority of new political parties are more like loose alliances of individuals than tightly disciplined organizations with a clear ideological position.[18] Proportional representation and fragmentation of the party system help to reinforce lack of clarity as presidents co-opt politicians from a wide range of parties into 'rainbow' cabinets (Slater 2004). It is very unclear how a vote for a particular party will translate into positions in the Executive. Party members may have little incentive to scrutinize government policy (since nearly all parties are, to some degree, part of the government) and the electorate is not presented with a clear choice between different policy programmes when voting. Additionally, particularly during the early period of tenure in the DPR, politicians are as much interested in recouping their 'investment' in acquiring political office as they are in genuine legislative scrutiny.[19] The electorate is left marginalized. If there are no obvious ways to link electoral results to performance, incentives to pursue a rational policy agenda are weaker than incentives to make relationships with wealthy corporate interests.

The result has been a fracturing of political power and a weakness of electoral oversight, encouraging either plain populism or bold statements of intent by Presidents that are rarely followed through (Slater 2004). That is particularly problematic given the sheer scale of changes that were supposed to take place in the Indonesian state. Suharto ruled by a combination of strong political discipline and carefully managed patronage-based incentives. The shift to bureaucratic discipline through managerial assessment of performance, measured against rules, was always going to be difficult to institute (McLeod 2005). In a context of weak electoral oversight and enormous corporate power, it is not surprising that success has so far been limited.

In terms of factors that affect corporate governance and foreign investment, the two key consequences are corruption and bureaucratic inertia. The unsavory certainties of the Suharto era have yet to be replaced by the legal certainties of a bureaucratic legalistic state on the Western model. At the same time, fragmentation of the political system means that it is no longer clear whose 'assistance' is required to get things done as a whole range of actors start to compete for resources in Indonesia's new political environment. The result is a noticeable increase in corruption as measured by the various international indices (McLeod 2005). Some of that increase may simply be perception as the media have gained new freedom to report scandals but that cannot be all that is going on.

Additionally, there are widespread complaints at the bureaucracy's inability to implement government policy, even when it is well defined and articulated. The clearest illustration being the government's inability to spend its budget, despite a desire for fiscal stimulus to overcome sluggish domestic investment and rising unemployment and the urgent needs of Indonesia's inadequate infrastructure. There are various reasons. One is the problems with DPR oversight that I have already discussed. Equally, where reforms have begun to bite, they may actually hamper the operation of a bureaucracy that is used to a rather different system. The capricious nature of the legal system and the need to produce results in high-profile corruption cases leaves civil servants that do want to do their jobs nervous. For others, the removal of the kick-backs that used to go hand in hand with project approval mean there is less incentive to drive through project implementation.[20]

Overall, change to formal political institutions has not yet created an environment in which foreigners (or indeed Indonesians) wish to invest. The feared influx of foreign capital has not materialized. The democratic system should have created space for the Indonesian technocrats to recover the influence they lost during the financial boom of the mid 1990s. There are large pockets of technocratic reformers within the bureaucracy who are being pursued by a swarm of foreign aid advisors and consultants. These forces have introduced a barrage of new legislation that should provide legal certainty and the basis for an economic system on the neo-liberal model. There are also strong voices emerging in civil society, calling for cleaner government and a more rational economic system (Tornquist 2006), though these voices often seek greater public action to deal with poverty, inequality, and the creation of labour-intensive industry (rather than the neo-liberal approach generally favoured by bureaucrats and consultants: get the property rights and macro-economic policy right and the rest will follow).

These voices often have some influence on formal policy but formal policy is by no means all that is going on in Indonesian politics. Traditions of patronage persist in new forms, adapting themselves to the new environment. Weak links between the party system and civil society create space for abuse and the reassertion of older patterns. It is possible that the growing vibrancy of Indonesian media and civil society groups will eventually translate into a more effective state that serves some kind of public interest. However, it currently seems at least equally likely that Indonesia is developing into a political system that serves the interests of a resurgent corporate elite.

Conclusions

In both Indonesia and Malaysia, it is largely unhelpful to conceptualize the recent crises in terms of the foreign plunder of domestic assets by transnational corporate interests. The crisis was, to some degree, driven by foreign investors' perception that 'crony capitalism' was undermining investment prospects. However, it was a crisis of the financial sector (short-term bank and portfolio investment). Discussion about the policies that would restore 'market confidence' were aimed at pleasing financial sector actors, rather than multi-national producers. Similarly, the IMF's approach to the crisis was driven by its financial market-centred approach, which is conditioned by a complex range of institutional factors. Pressure for reform was shaped by those institutional channels, so that it tended to focus on creating more transparent and less politically influenced relationships between investors and companies.

There were also some attempts to facilitate investment (i.e. enable foreign companies to buy into distressed corporations more easily) and to remove various monopolies and restrictive practices but these were justified as merely ancillary to the aim of increasing competition and efficiency. If this was merely a cloak for attempts to allow foreign companies to take over Indonesian and Malaysian companies and assets, those attempts have not been very successful. There were some acquisitions of domestic companies but these hardly constituted large-scale fire sales. In fact, inward foreign investment has been low in both countries since the crisis.

At the same time, it is important to be wary of assuming that attempts to break up pre-existing forms of political economy were necessarily against the 'national interest'. As we have seen, the kinds of systems that were under threat during the crisis period were, to varying degrees, controversial domestically. The IMF's insistence that breaking them up would be in the domestic interest cannot be dismissed out of hand. At the very least, one should be as skeptical of claims made by large politically-connected corporations about the national interest as one might be about the IMF's claims to be a neutral technocratic advisor. Both are contested and politically loaded claims that need careful assessment.

However, even if one is inclined to see government-business relationships in both countries as primarily authoritarian abuses, creating space for greater foreign access is not an automatic solution. The experience of Indonesia in the pre-crisis period and Johnson *et al.*'s research on market pricing of politically connected companies on the KLSE both suggest foreign corporations are quite capable of operating in environments characterized by high levels of rent-seeking. Rather, these kinds of abuses need be dealt with by concerted state action. There is no good *a priori* reason to think that openness to globalization will make states either more or less likely to carry out these functions. The shape of domestic politics is likely to be a far greater influence.

In Malaysia, the government has reacted to crisis by attempting to enhance the competitiveness of *domestic* business. The continuing strength of the Malaysian state has been used to resist pressure for greater foreign opening and continue Malaysia's pattern of strategic engagement with foreign capital. If anything, the state has become more reserved with foreign investors than it was before the crisis. Attempts to promote competitiveness through a mixture of orthodox market-based reforms and less orthodox state direction of the GLCs, though, continue to be hampered by continuities of political power in the country. It is only a changing balance of political power domestically that will alter the situation to put greater pressure on the relationship between the government and Malay 'entrepreneurs'. In short, under globalization, domestic politics and the state are not immune to pressure for competitiveness but choices remain over how to respond. It is possible to enter into strategic relationships with foreign capital in which the state remains in command.

In Indonesia, we also see the state's importance in regulating relationships with foreign investors but in a more negative way. It is a matter of interpretation whether or not the passing of reformist legislation and the strength of technocrats in the higher echelons of the bureaucracy allows one to say that the Indonesian *state* is attempting to pursue neoliberal reform. It is clear, though, that those attempts are currently failing and that, without the regulatory framework and guarantees of property rights a state can provide, foreign investors are unlikely to want to buy up domestic assets. As some have pointed out, neoliberalism does not require a weak state, rather it requires a strong state, intent on pursuing the neoliberal project. In Indonesia, it is the vestiges of corporate power from the Suharto era, rather than a clearly defined alternative political project, that have prevented widespread corporate take-over.

I would like to thank the ESRC for funding the research for this article, as part of Award RES156-25-0016 'Strategies for dealing with global crisis: distributional and political impacts'.

Notes

1. For a view that is more skeptical of the Korean state, see Lee (1997).
2. The accounts that follow are heavily condensed. For fuller versions, with more attention to the subtleties, see Jesudason (1989, 1996), Gomez and Jomo (1999), Milne and Mauzy (1999) and Searle (1999) on Malaysia and Robison (1986), Winters (1996) and Schwarz (1999) on Indonesia.
3. Parti Islam SeMalaysia.
4. Democratic Action Party.
5. Probably the best account is Jesudason (1996). The limited chances of electoral victory don't mean that opposition is irrelevant to Malaysian politics. In times of political difficulty, the central coalition has altered its policies to incorporate opposition demands or even whole political parties, hence Jesudason's characterization of Malaysia as a 'syncretic' state, or Case's (2005) description of it as a hybrid regime.
6. Descendents of the 'original' inhabitants of Malaysia (rather than Chinese or Indian immigrants)
7. On tensions within UMNO, see Shamsul (1987), on political authoritarianism, see Milne and Mauzy (1999).
8. The most prominent articulation of this position is World Bank (1993). For a dissenting voice, see Rock (1999).
9. The Indonesian equivalent of bumiputera (see note 6).
10. The Indonesian technocrats made several attempts to control foreign borrowing in the run up to the crisis. However, enforcement proved politically difficult and, in any case, to the extent that bank lending limits were able to bite, larger conglomerates were able to borrow directly on the international markets (Pincus and Ramli 1998).
11. The obvious weakness with the view that foreign competition would help to break up patronage relationships, of course, is that it assumes powerful foreign corporations will behave better than domestic ones. There seem to be few good reasons for taking this view.
12. Discussion of the effectiveness of the controls is largely outside the scope of this paper. They were not as disastrous as many observers expected but, since they were imposed so late on when other countries in the region were already recovering, it is not clear how much active benefit they provided – views depend crucially on the counterfactual assumptions one makes about what would have happened in Malaysia if the controls had not been in place (for the most pro-control view, see Kapstein and Rodrik (2001). For a review of different positions see Jomo (2004).
13. For a fuller list, see Haggard (2000).
14. For greater detail, see Case (2005).
15. Confidential interview, Prime Minister's office Putrajaya, June 2006.
16. Figures in Rupiah from Gomez (2003; Danaharta 2005), converted to US$ at the post-crisis exchange rate.

17. For a government perspective, see the website of the 'Putrajaya Committee' (http://www.pcg.gov.my/index.asp), including the April 2006 'transformation scorecard and update'.

18. This view was expressed to me by a wide range of observers interviewed in Jakarta in July 2006, including NGO activists, UNDP governance reform workers, economists and members of political parties.

19. Again, this is almost universally accepted in Jakarta. A high ranking Indonesian, working on UNDP's programmes for parliamentarians argued that much of the work he had done helping parliamentarians debate legislation during the DPR's first term was undone by the high turn-over of elected members. New members were not close enough to an election to concentrate on anything other than acquiring funds. Similar views were expressed by World Bank staff, NGO activists and bureaucrats, during interviews with the author in Jakarta, July 2006.

20. The view that capricious enforcement was making people nervous to make decisions was aired by a number of bureaucrats interviewed in Jakarta. The suggestion that the lack of kick-backs was also a problem was suggested to me by two economists of rather different political persuasion: Chatib Basri and Rizal Ramli.

10
Russia: Limiting the Impact of Crisis in a Post-Communist Transitional Economy

Neil Robinson

Introduction

Russia's experience of crisis would seem to be an enviable one. Crisis has not caused a loss of economic sovereignty nor did it presage a period of economic depression. Instead, the power of the Russian state has grown since 1998 and Russia has experienced near uninterrupted economic recovery since 1999 with GDP growth averaging 6.8 per cent per annum 1999–2005, growth in industrial production averaging 7 per cent per annum 1999–2005, unemployment falling from 13.2 per cent in 1998 to 7.7 per cent in 2005, and average wages rising from US$108 to US$301 a month. The role of foreign investors and institutions in this recovery has been small. The principal driver of change in Russia's post-crisis economy has been foreign trade, particularly oil exports, carried out by domestic forces.

This picture of prosperity masks a very large problem, however. The financial crisis of 1998 was not more devastating because of the peculiarities of Russia's post-communist system and the central problem of this system, the lack of capital to reform industry and produce a more competitive economy with a diversified export structure, remains. The influence of the August 1998 crash on domestic forces and the subsequent development of Russia's political economy have been shaped by three factors: the legacies of the USSR; the way that earlier reforms under President Boris Yeltsin benefited a small number of financiers and exporters; and the political fall-out of the crisis. Each of these was largely responsible for shaping one of the main segments of Russia's political economy: the 'national' sectors of the economy, i.e., those branches of the economy that produce mainly for domestic consumption and are not in receipt of any great level of foreign investment, the 'transnationalized' sectors of the economy, and the government/state.

Each of these segments of Russia's political economy has a specific relationship to the global economy. The national economy is isolated from it, receiving benefits second-hand from the general rise in national wealth caused by energy export price rises. The role of the national economy has been a passive one; its character and structure in the 1990s have meant limited foreign involvement in Russia's economy and little pressure to respond to the 1998 crisis in ways that would ensure continued capital inflows from abroad. The transnationalized economy and the state have more active international relationships and have been in competition to gatekeep Russia's relationship to the global economy. At the moment the state has the upper hand in this relationship. This might, if recovery carries on for long enough, eventually turn in to a successful response to Russia's problems. However, Russia's ability to grow over time depends on moving resources in to the national economy to modernize it. If it does not do this, then it will have to bear the cost of a large, unmodernized industrial sector at some point, just as it did in the 1990s. This will both perpetuate its isolation from the global economy and its dependency on hydrocarbons, and might lead to further crisis.

What does Russia's experience of crisis show us more generally? Russia, as a case study of how states respond to crisis, and of what is most salient in shaping their post-crisis development – domestic or international forces – is more an example of the influence of domestic forces having the upper hand. The argument presented in this chapter highlights the importance of different economic sectors and their relationship to the global economy, whether or not they are competitive in the global economy, and the relationship of the state to these sectors, in shaping a country's response to crisis. One conclusion that might be taken from this is that the way in which comparative advantage is revealed for a state shapes its experience of crisis, and comparative advantage is revealed by the 'directness with which world prices are transmitted into the domestic market' (Frieden and Rogowski 1996: 26). Russia was weakly penetrated by world prices because of its economic structure and this has allowed the state to gain the upper hand over those sectors of the economy that have a revealed comparative advantage after crisis because it was not under any general pressure to liberalize further from domestic constituencies since outside of the extractive industries – which are small employers even if they are major contributors to Russia's GDP – these constituencies were not disposed to more liberalization. Indeed, public opinion has been consistently hostile to foreign economic penetration of Russia and, therefore, against further liberalization. Crisis also eased some of the pressure on the state so that international forces that might have desired more liberalization were sidestepped.

There are limits to how far this conclusion – that domestic economic structure matters and that it matters because of how the relationship between the domestic economic structure and the international economy shapes the demands of social interests for openness – can be taken from the case of Russia. Whilst the Russian case shows that the power of international economic forces and agencies might on occasion be limited, the Russian case should not be taken as showing that this is always going to be the case for two reasons. The first reason is that Russia's developmental experience and economic structure might be different to the rest of the world. It experienced centrally planned state socialism longer than other states, over a larger territory, and emerged from this experience with a modern industrial economy that was shaped almost entirely from that experience. Russia's resistance to marketization and hence to the influence of global economy might be unique in scale because of these differences of economic history. Second, it is difficult to disentangle the influence that the energy boom has had from the some of the effects of economic structure and we should bear this in mind when comparing Russia to other cases. The boom in hydrocarbon prices came after crisis and after it had affected the balance of power in Russia. However, it might be the case that this influence would not have been locked in as it was if it had not been for energy price hikes and the way that they favoured the state at the moment that it had regained some strength because of crisis. In other words, another state might have a similar experience of crisis as Russia because of its economic structure and the relationship of that structure to the global economy but in the absence of oil wealth this similar experience might rapidly diverge from the trajectory Russia has followed.

Soviet legacies, the national economy and Russia's relative economic isolation

Soviet legacies have shaped the national economy because of two things: first, high levels of negative value added production, that is the production of industrial goods whose value as manufactured items is less than the worth of the raw materials that went into their production so that value has been subtracted from these materials during their transformation in to a manufactured good (McKinnon 1992; Gaddy and Ickes 1998); and second, capital deficiency in the Russian economy caused by high demand for investment during the Soviet period, when there were no constraints on borrowing because there was no such thing as bankruptcy, and because high investment was needed to deal with the demands of planners and their political masters.

Capital deficiency and negative value added production are difficult to distinguish as causes of firm behaviour. They interacted with reform to create what has been called a 'virtual economy' (Gaddy and Ickes 1998; 2002). This provided a bridge between the end of the Soviet era and the present that maintained the isolation of a large part of Russia's economy from direct influence from the global economy. Soviet industry developed in isolation from global economic pressures and prices because of central control over foreign economic relations (Evangelista 1996; Robinson 2004). This meant that changes in global supply and demand and pressures to be competitive did not impact on economic activity directly. Prices were set centrally and frequently for political reasons and so often bore no resemblance to costs. Soviet managers who could not break even were not faced with bankruptcy since they were judged by the ability to produce a set quantity of a good rather than by their profit margins. Losses were written off by planners and did not bar further investment. Controlling costs was further hampered by low labour productivity and by high levels of investment caused by the absence of self-restraint on employment or on demands for investment such as exists in capitalist economies (Kornai 1992: 162–3).

These factors combined at the end of the Soviet era to create an inefficient economy with high costs, high demand for investment and low returns on it. The goods produced by this economy were 'negative value added goods' in that they were unsaleable beyond the Soviet Union: by the late 1980s only about 7 to 8 per cent of Soviet production was of 'world standard', that is exportable to countries outside the USSR's trading bloc (Åslund 1989: 17). For reformers in the Russian government a key task was to expose this situation as economically unsustainable by subjecting the economy to commercialization through subsidy cuts.

For those engaged in negative value added production or in receipt of capital that they would not be able to access in a commercial environment, continuity was preferable to change since continuity meant the protection of livelihoods and of managerial power. The latter had come to resemble ownership as the power of the Soviet state declined (Johnson and Kroll 1991). Reform threatened this control directly by both redistribution and by removing the system of subsidies that supported it. Industrial interests therefore resisted reform. They did this by carrying on trading amongst themselves, building up huge inter-enterprise debts, or by barter, failing to pay taxes or paying them in kind, and through subsidies provided through lobbying both central and local governments. The latter were a particularly good source of subsidy especially since they were a conduit to energy suppliers, which under pressure from local authorities began to accept payment in kind or maintained supply where there was no payment. Capital deficiency was compounded by the shortage of credit caused by radical economic reform, which cut the supply of money going to industry as the state's budget was cut, and as banks found it more profitable to lend to the state and to finance arbitrage trading than to lend to industry.

Over the course of 1992–94 these different means of resisting reform created a 'virtual economy', a form of economy that is largely cashless and in which value subtracting production was protected. The continued existence of value subtracting production and the need of capital deficient enterprises for a new source of credit led to the development of a 'value pump', a means of infusing production with a value that it could not itself create, or of providing industry with capital that it could not get through the financial system (Gaddy and Ickes 2002: 5). The main sources of value pumped in to the national economy were the energy sector and labour. Transferring value from labour in the form of nonpayment of wages, or payment in (overvalued) kind was both a transfer of value and a means of perpetuating the systems of power and welfare in the economy at local level since it insured that workers remained 'dependent' on their enterprise (Crowley 1994). The transfer of value from the energy sector to the rest of the economy was based mostly on Gazprom, the state-owned gas monopoly. By mid-1996, it had 'practically replaced the [Central Bank] as the source of centralized credit' to industrial producers and was owed US$10 billion by its customers (*Nezavisimaya gazeta*, 4 June 1996).

The development of the 'virtual economy' after 1992 acted as a survival mechanism for Russian industrial interests (Nesvetailova 2004). It had two further related effects that are important for the analysis here. First, barter and inter-enterprise debt made it hard for outside interests to see whether an investment in an enterprise would yield a return. As a result, and in tandem with the other political and social problems that Russia faced during these years, the inflow of FDI to Russia before the 1998 crisis was very low. From 1989 to 1997, post-communist states in the former USSR and Eastern Europe received US$187 per capita in FDI, and in Eastern Europe (all post-communist states including the Baltic states minus the rest of the former USSR), the average was $439 per capita. Russia received just $63 per capita. In 1997, the year before the crash, the ratio of FDI to GDP as a percentage was on average 1.8 per cent for all post-communist states and 2.5 per cent in Eastern Europe. For Russia it was 0.8 per cent (Robinson 1999: 541). Most of this investment was concentrated in a few regions and in the energy sector so that the bulk of the Russian economy was untouched by foreign capital. This limited the impact that foreign demands for restructuring could have post-1998. Such demands were not matched by corresponding calls for reform from the bulk of Russian industry, which did not require governmental action to assuage foreign investors and maintain the inward flow of capital.

Second, this virtual economy resulted in the demonetization of the Russian economy. The demonetization took the form of payments in kind to workers (wages and welfare) and the state (tax), or non-payment of such, barter between enterprises and debt build-up. These actions forced the state to look for money elsewhere and after 1994 it increasingly began to raise revenue through the sale of short-term debt. This encouraged the banking sector to continue its neglect of the industrial economy and concentrate on speculative behaviour. Before 1994 the banks had engaged in currency speculation and loans to fund short-term commodity trades and arbitrage, rather than in loans to industrial producers. These actions generated very high profits because of inflation. As inflation fell after 1994 due to increasing demonetization of the economy these profits came from the new government debt market so that loans to industrial producers remained small: before August 1998 loans by banks to business were worth only 11 per cent of GDP (as against 82 per cent of GDP in the Czech Republic), and most loans were very short term, with only about 1 per cent of loans to business being for more than a year (Gustafson 1999: 88).

The result of this was that the financial crisis that hit the banking sector in August 1998 did not have any significant impact on many Russian businesses so as to leave them vulnerable to opportunistic outside investors. Crisis in the financial sector had an impact on that sector (a lot of the weaker banks just disappeared), and on the government, but it did not work through to the rest of the economy to cause bankruptcies or changes in lending because financial intermediation in the real economy was so small. This meant that the economic impact of crisis, while nasty, was short. In non-transitional emerging market economies, banking crises have depressed growth by one percentage point in the first year after the crisis and three the next before recovery on average (Eichengreen and Rose 1998). In Russia GDP dipped by just over 5 per cent in 1998, but this was immediately followed by growth in 1999 and thereafter (CBR 2006; Ahrend 2006: 1).

Russian industry thus survived the 1998 crash without being exposed to outside interference or having to respond to outside interests. In the short-run it even profited from crisis. The weakness of the rouble meant that consumers turned back to Russian producers because they could not afford foreign goods: the value of imports fell by US$17 billion in 1999 and continued to be relatively low in 2000–2002. Growth in demand for Russian goods boosted sales and the use of money, rather than payment in kind. The amount of barter in industrial sales fell from 46 per cent to 33 per cent between January 1999 and January 2000 and continued to decline thereafter as the economy remonetized (BOFIT 2000: 1).

Ironically then, a financial crisis made money more stable and usable because of the very weakness of money before the crisis. This remonetization is not the same as restructuring across the board. Some labour has been shed from industry and moved to the tertiary sector. However, industry has not yet recovered or reached a point where it is integrated into the global economy via external ownership or trade. Recovery has certainly not been based on foreign capital coming in and taking advantage of Russian weakness. There were net outflows of foreign capital in 2000, 2002 and 2003. There were high inflows in 2004 and 2005, but, again, relative to other states the amount was miniscule – US$15 per capita in 2004 in Russia against an average of US$97 for all post-communist transition economies (EBRD 2005: 55). Moreover, these inflows were concentrated on the energy sector, which has taken the lion's share of industrial FDI before and after 1999 and regularly accounted for about two-thirds of any increase in industrial FDI (and indeed domestic industrial investment), as well as on trade and catering (Goskomstat 2004: 620).

Russia's export structure is also unchanged: it still depends on hydrocarbon exports to generate its balance of payments surplus and fund imports, and has not been able to diversify exports. This points to continued fundamental weaknesses in the national economy. The terms of trade are beneficial to Russia because of high state spending to keep the rouble relatively undervalued. Despite the positive terms of trade, Russian industry is still uncompetitive and is likely to remain so as any comparative advantages that it has in terms of developing as a knowledge economy are eroded by developments in other emerging economies (Cooper 2006). In effect, and despite growth, the post-crisis Russian economy is still capital deficient as it was throughout the 1990s.

Russia's transnationalized economy and the state: shifting balances of power before and after 1998

If the relative isolation of much of Russia's economy and its largely 'national' focus is continuous from the Soviet era so too is the transnationalized sector of the economy. As for the USSR, Russia's main trade with the rest of the world is through the sale of energy, particularly oil and gas, backed up by sales of metals and some other raw materials. This pattern of trade developed from the 1960s and became deep-rooted in the 1970s as the USSR enjoyed high returns on its energy trade with the West after the OPEC oil price rises of the early 1970s and because the rest of Soviet industry began to lag technologically and competitively behind other industrialized states (Gustafson 1989; Kotkin 2001).

The difference between the Soviet era and the present is that control over hydrocarbons and other major exporting sectors is divided between the state and private business. This division occurred in the mid-1990s in response to the failure of reform in 1992–93. The failure of reform in 1992–93 placed severe constraints on the state's ability to raise revenue. Government fiscal difficulties contributed to a change of privatization policy as well as to the sale of government debt discussed above. The first rounds of privatization in 1992–93 were supposed to make citizens stockholders; people were allocated vouchers that they were to swap for shares, and enterprises were to be privatized in such a way as to allow their managers and workforces to gain control of them (Barnes 2006: 68–105). This form of privatization did not earn the state any revenue; property was transferred to 'new' owners (generally existing managers), rather than sold to them, by the state.

After 1994 the state hoped to raise revenue from privatization as well as to transfer it to 'efficient' managers. It did this through auctions. These auctions were dominated by Russia's commercial banks, sometimes with the assistance of foreign investors, and sometimes, and especially in the early and infamous 'share for loans' auctions, not. The banks used these auctions to turn some of the vast profits that they had made through currency speculation and arbitrage into assets. In the process they created large 'financial–industrial groups' (FIGs) (Johnson 1998). The leaders of these FIGs are often also labelled 'oligarchs', although their ability to construct an oligarchy was never that great, as the fate of some of them after 2000 was to show.

The types of enterprises that were auctioned to banks to create FIGs were those that had export potential and were attractive to foreign investors because of their revenue potential: oil producers, major producers of metals, and telecommunications firms, for example. The main ways in which these firms linked to the global economy was through trade. On average, just under 50 per cent of Russia's exports in the 1990s were hydrocarbons, and in particular oil, and just over 20 per cent were metals (Ustinov 2004: 111). Foreign investment did go in to these sectors, but its impact was limited by legal limits – until 1997 foreign ownership of stock in oil firms was capped at 15 per cent – and was, as we shall see below, often diluted by nefarious corporate governance. As a result, although foreign investment was larger in sectors like oil and was necessary for modernization, overall only 4.1 per cent of enterprises in the energy sector had some foreign investment by 1998; in ferrous and non-ferrous metals the figures were 1.5 per cent and 2.9 per cent of enterprises respectively. These were substantially higher than the overall industrial average of 0.7 per cent foreign involvement, but foreign capital was obviously far from dominant in the sectors that dominated Russia's export trade (Goskomstat 2000: 308).

The transnational sector of Russia's economy was thus largely formed as a response to the failures of the first wave of reform. Political actors protected this formation of the transnational sector of the Russian economy both nationally and regionally and in turn were granted support for their tenure. This mutually beneficial relationship lasted from 1994 through 1997. The relationship between the FIGs and their owners and the state began to change after 1997 because the cost of financing the state's deficit through the sale of short-term debt was too expensive (especially since privatization for cash had not been that lucrative and because FIGs were poor at paying their taxes). The government tried to improve its revenue situation by lowering the cost of its borrowing through opening up the government debt market to foreigners, and by improving tax collection. Both these policies threatened FIGs' profits. Their banking sectors would be hit if returns of government debt fell; their industrial wings would be less profitable if they had to pay their taxes on time instead of using unpaid tax to do things like buy government debt.

These actions were part of a general call by Yeltsin for the state to be autonomous of particular social interests and able to act in the general interest (see his 1997 state of the union address, *Rossiiskie vesti*, 11 March 1997). The push for more secure state finances did not work and was partially responsible for the August 1998 crash (Robinson 1999). The drive to isolate political power from particular social interests – in this case the interest of the FIGs – was successful to the extent that any semblance of a group interest between the FIGs disappeared as the competition between them for property became vitriolic under pressure from the state, and their relations with politicians became more conflictive (Robinson 2001). This too contributed to the build-up to the economic crisis because it led to government turnover and weakened credibility so that securing crisis prevention measures from parliament and from outside agencies such as the IMF became harder.

The impact of the 1998 crisis was filtered through these pre-crisis structures and processes. The linkage of banks to industry meant that although there were some casualties in the banking sector, many of the big banks, or at least their owners and the holding companies that they controlled, survived in one way or other. FIGs were hit by the losses they sustained when the government defaulted on some of its debt and devalued the rouble but they could fall back on the monies that continued to flow into their coffers from their industrial operations, in particular from their holdings in the oil sector as prices began to rise after 1998. Indeed, the weakness of the rouble in the immediate aftermath of the crisis made the export producing firms controlled by the banks even more profitable. Control over these assets and the profit that could be squeezed from them were secured by diluting the shareholdings of minority stockholders and transfer pricing operations that created rent for holding companies in which outside stockholders had no stake. Such actions were not new, nor were they confined to the oil industry (Moser and Oppenheimer 2001: 314–19; Adachi 2006). However, they do seem to have gathered pace in 1999, in part in response to the crisis and the need to tighten control over oil firms acquired in the 1990s. Control over oil industries was directly threatened in early 1999 when the government of Yevgenii Primakov, which was less committed to market solutions and less liberal in its political and economic orientation than pre-August 1998 governments, mooted the possibility of creating a new state oil company that would include those firms in which the state still had an interest and several that had been privatized (Lane and Seifulmulukov 1999: 43).

The form of privatization undertaken after 1994 thus shaped who was involved in the transnational sector and meant that the effects of the 1998 crisis were ameliorated for some of the banks. One result of this was that the gates were not opened to an influx of foreign banks as has been the case following other financial crises in post-communist states, and as was expected in some quarters at the time of the 1998 crash. The number of foreign owned banks has grown from 30 out of 1476 in 1998 to 41 out of 1329 in 2003. However, this growth mostly took place after 2000-2001, and the asset share of foreign owned banks has actually fallen since 1999 from 10.6 to 7.4 per cent. This is a very different picture to Eastern Europe. In 2003, Slovakia, for example, had 16 out of 21 banks foreign-owned with 96.3 per cent asset share, in the Czech Republic the figures were 26 out of 35 banks with 86.3 per cent asset share, and in Hungary 29 out of 38 with 83.5 per cent asset share (EBRD 2004; 2005).

If the impact of 1998 on Russia's FIGs was muted because of their particular mixture of financial and industrial operations, the impact on the state was more immediate. The crisis weakened Yeltsin's authority, his ability to command loyalty from regional leaders and some economic leaders, and threw open the question of his succession. Several elite groups began mobilizing early in 1999 with an eye to capturing support, competing in the December 1999 elections and starting a bandwagon that would last through the 2000 presidential election. Ironically, this political crisis allowed for an even more complete reassertion of state autonomy than Yeltsin had called for in 1997. By weakening Yeltsin and dividing the Russian political elite, particularly regional leaders from the centre, the 1998 crisis helped to separate the politics of succession from social interests. The divide between government and business and the weakening of the centre's control over the regions made them competitors in the succession struggle, rather than parties that negotiated as they had negotiated Yeltsin's 1996 re-election. Yeltsin was forced to find a successor from within his administration – Vladimir Putin – and use the extensive formal powers of the presidency to reclaim some degree of control over the political process.

Yeltsin and Putin were then lucky in that Putin's appointment as prime minister in August 1999 and Yeltsin's ceding of authority to him developed a bandwagon effect in late 1999 that swamped the efforts of his rivals. Putin's hard-line towards Chechnya when war restarted there at the end of September 1999 helped, as did the recovery of the national economy because of the shallow impact of the 1998 crisis (Sakwa 2004: 18–20). The net effect of these changes was that Putin won the presidency in 2000 in what turned out to be a non-contest – the only real question was whether Putin would secure a first round victory and he did – in which he essentially made no promises to any group, voter or vested interest. Once Putin had won the presidency in 2000 the effect of the 1998 crisis on politics reached its conclusion as he used his mandate to recreate central political authority.

This assertion of central state control took two forms in the first months of Putin's presidency: reassertion of central power over regional leaderships through curtailing the rights of regional leaders and weakening their tenure and voice in central decision-making (Hyde 2001); and an attack on major business interests that had media interests, particularly Vladimir Gusinsky and his Media-Most group, and Boris Berezovsky, who had a 49 per cent stake in ORT, the main Russian TV channel. The actions against the media interests of big banks and powerful business interests was accompanied by the opening of investigations in to the privatization and tax payments of several other FIGs and businessmen. Together the investigations and the takeovers of business media interests were a strong signal to FIGs that the political situation had changed and not in their favour. Putin made this signal even more explicit in a meeting that he held with business leaders in July 2000. At this meeting business leaders pressed for an end to the investigations and for guarantees that there would be no redistribution of privatized state property. Whilst Putin made some concessions on property redistribution he warned the oligarchs that interference on their part in politics would no longer be tolerated.

Putin's meeting with business leaders only marked a temporary ceasefire. The reassertion of central executive political authority soon developed to involve closer regulation of strategic sectors of the economy. The reason for this was to make the state the arbiter of the terms and condition on which major enterprises could link to the global economy. There is limited capacity to expand Russian energy production, or at least limited capacity to expand production without major outlay in the future (Dienes 2004; Gaddy 2004). After Putin's election this outlay was not forthcoming since oligarchs expanded production to deplete the resources without investing in future production, or they looked to foreign investors without taking account of the state.

The problem with foreign investment is that it potentially creates more stable property rights in the energy sector than before. For the state this is a trade-off. Whilst it welcomes the investment, the reinforcement of property rights in the oil industry gives it less control over the amount of oil pumped and the amount of rent that is received (Gaddy and Ickes 2005). This problem was an acute one in the early years of Putin's administration. Between 1998 and 2002 the export value of minerals (of which about 98 per cent are oil and related products) nearly doubled in dollar terms. Growth was particularly marked in 2000, when exports were 171.5 per cent of what they had been in 1999 (Ustinov 2004: 136–7). Six major private oil firms did the bulk of this exporting, with firms under state control barely expanding production (Ahrend 2006).

At the same time many of these firms began to reposition themselves to facilitate inward investment. Yukos, which had been one of the worst offenders against minority shareholders, did an about face and announced its intention to adopt international accounting standards. This was the beginning of a wave of re-engagement with international financial institutions by major Russian companies, with IPO launches on the London Stock Exchange a favoured method of expanding foreign participation. Actions against firms like Yukos, which began in 2003, were attempts to rein in this process. The attack on Yukos fit with the style of political management that had already begun to develop and been displayed in the attacks on Media-Most and Berezovsky. Besides tax evasion, Khodorkovsky's 'crimes' were political (support for civil society and opposition parties), as well as economic (championing a break-up of the state's oil transport monopoly, a major source of rent, and seeking to isolate his firm from influence by the state through international linkages).

Some analysts have described Russia under Putin as heading toward a form of state capitalism (Radygin 2004; Shlaapentokh 2004; Illarionov 2005). Yukos did mark a turning point, but whether it was of this magnitude remains to be seen. The Yukos affair has been followed by: moves to curtail foreign investment through legislation; blocking the sale of companies like equipment maker Siloviye Mashiny to foreign firms, in this case Siemens, and favouring sales to state-owned enterprises; attempts to place state representatives on more company boards, such as the board of Avtovaz (cars); the sale of Sibneft (Abramovich's oil firm) to Gazprom; the state's increasing its holding and control of Gazprom itself; and the rolling back privatization of major industrial units like Kamaz (trucks).

Yet whilst these and other actions support the view that there is centralization of economic power, and might be taken to indicate that intervention has developed a logic of its own, they have been tempered by the fact that the acquisition of firms like Yukos and Sibneft by state companies has seen them expand their foreign debts considerably to fund the purchases. Gazprom had to borrow US$7.3billion to buy Sibneft, for example, and Rosneft began to privatize, which included offering 13 per cent of its shares to international investors in July 2006, to pay for its takeover of Yukos (*The Financial Times*, 20 August 2005; *BOFIT Weekly*, 29, 21 July 2006). Increased political control has thus changed the way that the state manages the transnationalized Russian economy rather than rolling it back to some form of autarkic state-led development.

Crisis and the future

The limited impact of crisis on the national economy and the changed power of the Russian state over the transnationalized economy leaves open the issue of how far the crisis actually changed Russia's ability to develop as a part of the global economy. Foreign capital still enters Russia and has done so at an increased rate since 2000, but this does not mean that it has changed Russia all that greatly. Much of the foreign investment that Russia receives is still in the energy sector and it comes in to Russia in part because of the high profits that can be made in this sector and in part because of the desire of foreign energy firms to buy in to any oil reserves that they can as fewer new reserves of energy are discovered. It is not so much that Russia is a good place to invest in, more that these firms have no other choice but to take a chance on Russia even as the Russian state rolls back some foreign investment projects, like Shell's investment in the Sakhalin-2 gas field. Most of the rest of the foreign investment in to Russia goes in to its service sector. This was underdeveloped under the Soviet system so there are profits to be made here in virgin territory. Some of this money is also pulled in by high oil prices too as services develop to soak up high energy profits. Although many of these investments are large, they are relatively insignificant to the Russian state and do not influence much of the surrounding Russian industrial economy.

The limited impact of foreign investment and the upper hand that the state has with regard to the transnationalized economy post-1998 leave Russia to cope with the fact that its national economy is still capital deficient. Does it transfer wealth from the transnationalized sector of the economy to the capital deficient sector? If so, how does it do this? So far there have been few answers to these questions and few clues as to what the answers might be. Pressure to transfer resources from the transnationalized sector to the national sector of the economy is muted. This should not be surprising since there is a general rise in living standards caused by rising real wages. There are also effectively transfers already in place. Domestic energy prices are still charged at rates lower than international prices. This is backed up by a 'competitiveness' subsidy: the Central Bank's interventions in the currency market that have worked to hold down the appreciation of the ruble and hence the volume of imports. Foreign currency reserves have risen dramatically from $12 billion in 1998 to well over $200 billion in 2006. Purchases of foreign exchange were equal to 8–9 per cent of GDP in 2003–2005, and are equal to 70 per cent of domestic money supply (CBR 2006). If the Central Bank had not intervened in the foreign exchange market heavily the ruble would have already appreciated beyond its 1998 level.

The second reason that there has not been a move to transfer resources to the national economy and alleviate its capital deficiency is organizational. Putin believes that growth is possible and that there should be a strategy for a more activist use of Russia's natural resources to achieve this growth: hence the role of the state should grow in certain key sectors. This belief dates back to his PhD thesis (Balzer 2005), and has been expressed several times in his calls for the doubling of GDP within the decade. However, whilst there has been a growth in the power of the central executive the overall efficacy of public administration remains low. The effectiveness and competence of many state agencies is still poor, with corruption still a major problem. Indeed, corruption seems to be growing and despite efforts to control the growth of the state the number of bureaucrats continues to rise, having grown by a quarter since Putin took office. A more activist state approach is perhaps on hold whilst state reform takes place; this is likely to be a long process.

Finally, the strength of the central executive has meant that calls for resource transfers are not politically effective. Demanding more resource transfers would require channels through which demands could be made and actors willing to concede to demands. In the 1990s there was a willingness to make concessions and demands flowed through business associations and regional leaders. The influence of regional leaders has been curtailed by Putin, and business associations have over time become more market-orientated and the peak association has become more dominated by representatives from the transnationalized sector of the economy, that is from the group from whom resources would be transferred (Hanson and Teague 2005 and Pyle 2006). Consequently, only moderate sums were made available to a new Federal Investment Fund and for the completion of 'national priority projects' at the end of 2005. These do not represent major increases in state spending and fall far short of some of the demands that have been made to spend some of the monies in the Stabilization Fund (Paidiev 2006).

The lack of pressure to transfer resources has meant that the state has built up a large Stabilization Fund, some of which it now intends to invest abroad. This should act as a cushion for the state budget when the price of oil falls. Not planning major expenditure has also meant that the state can still run a surplus if the price of oil falls. However, whilst this means that falling oil revenues will not hit the state hard in the first instance there are still problems ensuring that growth continues even if the price of oil remains high. Further growth depends on either ever-higher oil prices, greater volume of oil production, or diversification. Even if Russia could pump more oil, which is far from certain, it would then have to get it to the areas where demand is high in Asia. Its pipeline network to Asian customers is still relatively undeveloped and will take several years to build.

To depend on oil for growth therefore leaves Russia vulnerable at the very least to problems with maintaining consistent growth. Price fluctuations might lead to temporary, short depressions of growth rates at the very least. Whilst these may not affect the state so much in the future because of the Stabilization Fund, they will encourage such things as capital flight and undermine business confidence, which will hit investment and perpetuate the problem of capital deficiency. The degree to which changing oil prices affects GDP is hard to pin down because of hidden effects like transfer pricing and the impact of oil production volumes rather than the price. However, the general view is that the impact is significant; Ruatava (2002: 18) estimates that a 10 per cent rise or fall in oil prices leads to a 2.2 per cent rise or fall in GDP. Moreover, industrial growth generally is heavily dependent on the oil industry. The steel industry, for example, relies on orders from the hydrocarbon extraction industries for orders. 80 per cent of the variation, and increase, in Russian industrial production in the first few years after 1998 when the effects of ruble devaluation of the economy were strongest, can be explained by the strengthened price of oil (Gaddy 2002: 130).

To balance out the effects that rising and falling oil prices and production levels might cause requires Russia to develop its other industrial sectors. This does not appear to be happening, or if it is happening it is at a very slow pace. Capital investment has gone up since 1998, reversing the trend of the 1990s when there was a massive reduction of investment. However, the share of the oil and gas industries in this investment has risen at a rate that accounts for virtually all of the percentage rise in industrial investment (Goskomstat 2004: 612). Overall, investment is low in Russia in comparison with other fast growing economies in Eastern Europe and Asia (Ahrend 2005: 603; 2006: 7). In official surveys the main factor reported as limiting business activity by industry has consistently been insufficient monetary instruments – capital and credit – both before and after the 1998 crisis, although the remonetization of the economy has lowered the overall number of respondents seeing it as a problem (see Goskomstat 2004: 531).

Whilst these problems remain and growth over time is uncertain, Russia is in effect still muddling through; it has not resolved the issue of what kind of capitalist economy it has become after 1998, and has remained permanently on the cusp of being something else. If it can develop state capacity, some form of developmental state could develop where resources would be harnessed through state capacity to produce growth. This growth would probably be different to that witnessed in other developmental states because Russia's starting point would be different, as would some of the problems that it faces because of geography and geopolitics. However, it would be a radical break with the past if development promoted a wider engagement with the global economy than solely through the energy sector.

If Russia cannot achieve this change then it runs the risk of developing in fits and starts according to the price of energy. Alternatively, if energy prices fall for a longer period of time, it may find itself back in the position that it was in pre-August 1998 of having to support the national economy in some way by resource transfers when money is scarce. If the latter is Russia's path, the question becomes: has the state accumulated enough power to bear depression without transferring resources from the transnationalized sector of the economy to the national? In other words, can a political regime survive a contraction of the national economy and restructuring via unemployment without using its new power in the economy to try to hide depression through subsidies? Neither the prospect of a more powerful Russian state controlling depression and unemployment nor allowing an unmodernized national economy to continue indefinitely is a very attractive proposition. The first option would marry Russia's devalued democracy to national poverty; the second would see Russia store up its problems and make their eventual resolution harder. If the former is Russia's future, developing in fits and starts according to the price of energy, it might just carry on muddling through much the same as it is now, depleting its Stabilization Fund when oil revenues are low, topping it up when they are high. It requires political will to be financially disciplined in good times and in bad, and such will might not outlast Putin. The danger then would be that Russia has to start to borrow again to cover downturns and lays itself open to another crisis, one that would be more destructive than 1998 because of the remonetization of the economy, and which would have the depressive effects that have characterized crises in other parts of the world.

Conclusion

The impact of the 1998 crisis was filtered through the developments of the 1990s in Russia, in particular the failure to develop a financial structure that was supportive and engaged with most of the industrial economy, the maintenance of negative value added production and capital deficiency in the national economy, and the linkage of banks to those few sectors of the economy that were capable of exporting or attractive to foreign capital. This in the first instance meant that the economy recovered rapidly after the crisis and that the most dramatic changes caused by crisis were in politics. These political changes have since influenced the way in which the transnationalized sector links to the global economy. Russia was thus protected by its weaknesses as a capitalist economy from some of the effects that financial crisis can have. Its experience of crisis, even the way and reasons for its being able to resist increased foreign pressure after crisis, might be relatively unique as a result. This might not be the case in the future since crisis has led to the remonetization of the Russian economy so that the crisis of 1998 might turn out to be a transitional one for Russia in more than one sense. The crisis of the late 1990s was part of Russia's transition, and the emergent political economy, heavily influenced by a resource-led economic boom, is founded upon a form of growth that is highly susceptible to future crisis.

11
Turkey: Risk-Conscious Foreign Firms and a Maturing Domestic Banking Sector

Korsan Cevdet

Power and politics are intensely debated topics in the study of international relations and political economy. These debates often focus on theories developed to explain the relational dynamics of states, IFIs, and corporations. This book provides readers with an opportunity to contrast theory with case studies to determine whether foreign interests exploit opportunities arising from financial crises. This chapter, in turn, focuses on Turkey's experience with financial crises and the impact these crises have had on the Turkish banking sector (TBS).

Like most other developing countries, Turkey's economy has been riddled with volatility. Financial instability created opportunities for some and marginalized the wealth of others. In the 1994–2001 period, Turkey experienced three major crises; the most damaging being the February 2001 episode. The 2001 crisis was marked by political turbulence, bank insolvencies, a 35 per cent devaluation of the Turkish Lira (TL), overnight lending rates of 5,000 per cent, and triple digit inflation. Turkey was in turmoil.

Five years onward, Turkey's economy and the TBS have changed. A stable, single party government and a strong opposition have replaced the fractured coalition government and divided opposition. The Central Bank is now independent and governs institutional accountability across the TBS. After 30 years of rampant inflation, the consumer price index (CPI) is down to single digits and the economy generates steady and stable growth. Recent oil price pressures and market shocks adversely affecting the world economy have not left Turkey unscathed. Inflation temporarily edged back above 10 per cent, the economy experienced a \$4 billion capital exodus (*Turkish Daily News* 2006a), and the New Turkish Lira or Yeni Türk Lira (YTL)[1] depreciated by approximately 30 per cent during 2006. Unlike past experiences, the Turkish government calmly advised onlookers that the fluctuations were a result of market forces and not deficiencies from within the economy. The government conceded that the 2006 inflationary target of 5 per cent would not be achieved; however, the goal of achieving inflation consistently below 4 per cent is unchanged.

Why did the 2006 experience differ from past crises? How did the Turkish government, Turkey's economy, and the TBS weather significant market volatility without panicking and maintain positive momentum? This chapter examines the consequences of the 2000–2001 crises and argues that the Turkish government implemented reforms to strengthen the TBS and increase confidence in a restructured and accountable financial system. The chapter proposes that while Turkey was vulnerable, neither the economy nor the TBS were exploited by foreign interests. Structural reforms implemented post 2000–2001 have strengthened the economy to effectively manage sudden systemic shocks and cyclical slowdowns. To confirm the proposition that the TBS was not exploited after the 2000–2001 crises, I examine the following areas: causes of the 2001 financial crisis, the crises's impact on the financial sector, and responses of domestic stakeholders and foreign firms. The analysis demonstrates that effective domestic policy implemented to address systemic deficiencies can foster sustainable growth. We see that the risk conscious and incremental expansion of foreign financial institutions into traditionally volatile markets is executed to control for instability and the risk of financial loss.

Qualifying concepts

Before delving into the impact financial crises had on the TBS, the interpretation of some concepts will be set out. Firstly, a common understanding of what is meant by exploited by foreign interests will be established. Exploitation captures the relationship between powerful and weak entities in which a powerful entity dominates, structurally controls, or expands self interest through the use of resources and markets within a weaker entity. The weaker entity is not provided with a fair level of return from the dominant entity's activities and extracts a disproportionate level of financial benefit. As a result of the exploitative activity, the weaker entity is less stable and more vulnerable to foreign interests and/or market fluctuations.

Traditionally, dependency theorists have examined core – periphery relationships in which the core, say the dominant state(s) and the companies therein, have disproportionate power over and exploit the political economy of peripheral states. The exploitation could be in the form of outright ownership, control of resources, or a weighted presence in peripheral markets. In the Turkish context, exploitation could have occurred if foreign financial institutions entered the TBS following the crises to dominate the TBS without providing material benefits to local interests. Exploitation could also occur if foreign assistance provided to Turkey was conditional on terms that created greater instability for the benefit of non-local interests or the domination of local markets by foreign entities.

The simple entry of foreign companies into a developing market cannot be considered exploitive. Competitive companies develop growth strategies that involve expansion of market share and the penetration of new markets. Profitable and competitive companies will have risk management systems that mitigate corporate exposure to unnecessary risks and situations that could adversely impact shareholder value. Expansion into foreign markets, particularly the economies of developing countries, is a risky venture that can quickly become a costly experience without favourable returns. Companies are therefore less likely to expose themselves to high risk scenarios that negatively impact long term profitability.

Companies considering expansion into developing markets perform due diligence to assess local risks. If the market provides a desirable opportunity, then the expansion is executed, usually with caution and often incrementally, limiting the potential for loss. In the post-Enron era, companies are held to higher standards of regulatory and corporate governance rigour. Haphazard corporate conduct, be it in a distant developing economy or a Western industrialized setting, can have devastating financial, reputational, and legal consequences. The potential of damaging prospects should be controlled for by executive management oversight and risk management systems that are accountable for the company's performance.

Another factor that should be considered is systemic or structural change that is sourced from abroad and implemented in a developing jurisdiction. Structural change and austerity programs are mandated by foreign aid providers to foster greater stability and accountability in the crisis ridden jurisdiction. IFIs are unlikely to provide support to governments that are not willing to make changes to the conditions that are believed to have caused the crisis or crises. Structural adjustment programs (SAPs) usually involve the IMF and the World Bank. These IFIs dictate strict terms and conditions for financial assistance.

The success of structural reform has varied over the past 60 years. When comparing the transformation of Africa, Latin America, and Asia to the countries of Eastern Europe, some episodes were systemically unsuccessful, while others led to modernisation. Unsuccessful cases are commonly viewed as exploitative or serving the interests of powerful foreign interests, whereas success stories are used as evidence for what can be achieved through restructuring and liberalization. Students of political development would be hard pressed to identify a single case of structural adjustment that did not result in popular resistance. The nature of structural reform involves the rationalisation of government spending, including reducing services and subsidies that adversely impact locals and disrupt the established order.

SAPs therefore have their share of critics. Some of the negativity is due to the ideological persuasions of critics because SAPs are often based on liberal economics and fiscal conservativism. Critics on the 'left' will often view such reforms as neo-colonial. On the other hand, to describe all SAPs as solely being exploitative or serving foreign interests is unfair and does not explain why SAPs fail. Each case should be evaluated according to its own merit and resultant outcome. Failed programs have multiple reasons underlying their ineffectiveness, including inadequate planning by the IFI policy reform advisors, domestic mismanagement, and a limited will to implement the required reforms by the local authority.

The Turkish case

Turkey's experience with SAPs is comprised of recent success and past failures. Since 1958, Turkey has had 18 separate IMF SAPs. Turkey's case demonstrates that success cannot be achieved in isolation and is dependent on a number of factors that affect the nation's economy. Simply adhering to interim fiscal discipline and restructuring cannot solve a country's systemic financial woes. Good governance and accountability, existing debt obligations, access to capital, and local inefficiencies need to be configured into SAPs. To place Turkey's case into perspective, a brief overview of the TBS and Turkey's economic development is provided below.

The Turkish economy developed through a statist approach. Statism was one of the principal tenants Mustafa Kemal Atatürk founded the Republic of Turkey upon. Statism was used to transform the remnants of a defunct Ottoman Empire into the economy of a modern nation-state. The central government engineered the development of the economy with funds sourced through the Central Bank and state-banks for distribution. State-banks supported the nation's agricultural, real-estate, commercial, and industrial growth. The state's role continued to expand throughout the 1960s and 1970s with the addition of more state-banks.

Throughout the 1970s, the Turkish economy was beleaguered by continued political and economic problems. Turkish politics was fragmented amongst the 'left' and the 'right'. Although the Turkish political spectrum had a 'right', the parties within this grouping did not have policies that were consistent with free market economics; the state centred economic policies dominated regardless of the ideological persuasion of the governing coalition. Admittedly, a handful of family-based conglomerates developed as private sector actors, for example the Koç and Sabanci families' holding companies. However, these market actors were indicative of an oligopoly and did not provide for economic dynamism to spur indigenous small businesses and an entrepreneurial spirit. Hence the early 1970s was a period of systemic economic inefficiencies, coupled with the oil crisis that added pressure on an already unstable economy.

Cyclical unproductiveness increased Turkey's economic risk exposure. Successive governments tried to stimulate the economy through increased spending. In the short-term, these activities provided for intermittent periods of expansion, but also caused serious balance of payments problems because of unaccountable government financing. Bad loans and an increasingly taxing debt burden left the Turkish government susceptible to economic volatility and with no alternative than to negotiate bail out packages with the IMF. 1970s SAPs focused on short-term objectives instead of targeting the economy's systemic deficiencies; that is, managing the balance of payments crisis (Pittman 2003), controlling the growing debt, and fighting inflation which increased from 50 per cent to triple digits in 1980 (Akyüz and Boratav 2002).

The relentless instability gave way to a military coup in September 1980. The Generals declared their aim was to stabilize Turkey's political, economic, and social crisis. For the first time Turkey's economic policy veered from statism. The architect of the liberal strategy was deputy prime minister and technocrat Turgut Özal. Özal was viewed as an outsider that could institute significant change to financial management in Turkey.

Control to a civilian government returned in 1983. Özal's new Motherland Party or Anavatan Partisi (ANAP) came to power during the elections with a clear reform mandate. Özal served as prime minister from 1983 to 1989 and pressed ahead with Turkey's economic liberalization program. Government reforms included Turkey's integration with global markets, encouraging private sector development, establishing a domestic free market, removing price controls and subsidies, reducing the state's interventionist role in commerce, stimulating private investments and savings, liberalizing foreign trade and foreign exchange rates, reducing tariffs, and the easing of capital transfer exchange controls

(Etkin *et al.* 2000). Turkey's liberalization process allowed for foreign currency deposit accounts and the liberalisation of capital accounts, including capital flows to external accounts (Celasun 1998). Özal managed to tame inflation and stimulated economic growth through an export led program. With the current account deficit being cut in half, public borrowing was reduced to a manageable level of four per cent of GNP (Akyüz and Boratav 2002).

Financial crises leading to economic collapse

Turkey's first major contemporary financial crisis occurred following the liberal reforms. Celasun (1998) explains that even though reforms were implemented, economic fundamentals in the early 1990s continued to deteriorate. For example, Turkey registered successive fiscal and external account imbalances. Imbalances were a result of mounting public sector borrowing that supported unproductive populist policies, inefficient state-owned corporations, a large, costly bureaucracy, and the management of an increasing debt burden. To support these activities, government borrowing became dependent on foreign sources, exposing Turkey to additional risks that were out of the government's control.

In response to poor fundamentals, the Central Bank restructured its balance sheet, limited credit to commercial banks, and created liquidity against foreign assets to increase macroeconomic confidence and counter the downward trend. There was also a move to source public financing domestically to reduce the dependence on foreign borrowing. As the government turned inward for financing, foreign borrowing was passed on to commercial banks. Commercial banks viewed the debt financing situation as an opportunity to arbitrage interest rate risks and make quick gains on foreign borrowings. Since local debt provided significantly higher yields when compared to the cost of borrowing abroad, private banks purchased local government debt with the low interest foreign borrowings. The weak regulatory environment allowed for the accumulation of large foreign exchange (FX) exposures without being accounted for by local authorities.

Debt financing fed a viscous risk cycle, earning solid returns for particular groups, while exposing the Central Bank, the Treasury, and Turkish financial institutions to increased FX risk. When the government presented its 1994 national budget, the lack of fiscal discipline exasperated the already low confidence level in Turkey's economy. To restore economic confidence, the Central Bank began selling foreign reserves to provide liquidity for Turkey's banks.

Turkey's Central Bank liquidated half its foreign reserves to no avail. Government debt was downgraded and the TL lost half its value against the US dollar (Celasun 1998). The crisis gave flight to approximately $19 billion and triggered the insolvency of eight banks (Akyüz and Boratav 2002). The government tried to restore confidence in the TBS by restructuring the Saving Deposit Insurance Fund (SDIF). The SDIF took ownership of the failed banks and provided for complete savings guarantees for deposits (Central Bank 2002). Unlike the full guarantee enacted by the SDIF (1994), banking systems of mature economies have limits. Take, for example, the Canada Deposit Insurance Corporation which guarantees eligible deposits. The guaranteed amount was only recently increased to CAD$100,000 from CAD$60,000. Unlike the Canadian practice, Turkey's full guarantee provides financial institutions with leverage to engage in high risk initiatives. Government guarantees secure deposits and reduce the incentive for management accountability. Banks that are unstable or poorly managed have security in relation to their depositors without having to be accountable.

Turkey's liquidity crisis forced the government back to the IMF. Unlike earlier SAPs, Turkey agreed to privatize state enterprises and reform social security and taxation. In spite of the government's commitments, none of the reforms were effectively implemented; reforms were not implemented until after the 2000–2001 crises. Some commitments that were achieved reduced public spending through restricting infrastructure projects, freezing public sector employee salaries and generating income through increased non-tax revenues (Celasun 1998). For the average citizen, the IMF appeared to be punishing low-to-middle income earners, instead of forcing discipline amongst the high-profiled profiteers that took advantage of the interest rate arbitraging activities and evaded taxes. Resentment towards the IMF can be appreciated as thousands lost their jobs and the cost of goods and services increased dramatically, whilst elites appeared to remain untouched. This round of IMF adjustment was highly questionable because the government did not implement structural change requirements and the average citizen beared the crisis.

The Turkish economy continued to grow during the inter-crisis period (1995–2000). However, economic fundamentals were not improving. Government fiscal irresponsibility led the IMF to withhold a standby facility in 1995; governments selfishly wasted resources to win electoral support instead of adhering to SAPs (Bodgenor 1996). Similarly, the implementation of Turkey's second Bank Act (June 1999) was to be a milestone for the strengthened financial sector, yet the SDIF took over five insolvent banks in December 1999 (Özatay and Sak 2003) indicating continued systemic weaknesses.

The revised Banks Act contained measures to improve the structure of Turkish banks, enhance the regulatory framework, and conform with EU standards. Since Turkey aspired to join the EU, Ankara needed to confirm the country's reform process was aligned to EU expectations. EU membership required a stable economy, including a functional banking and financial services sector. According to the new Bank Act, institutions with systemic deficiencies that were not viable would be taken over by the SDIF. The Act also established an independent Banking Regulation and Supervision Agency (BRSA) to increase the TBS's efficiency, competitiveness, and public confidence. The BRSA would be autonomous from the government to have the capacity to effectively mitigate systemic risks and identify government undertakings that were not sound or politically motivated. Turkey's traditionally weak regulatory framework was transformed into a significantly more demanding regime. Regulatory requirements provided rigour for the establishment and maintenance of banks, including stringent internal control and risk management systems (Central Bank 2002).

In spite of the Bank Act's enhancements, the government again failed to operationalize the changes. Instead, the government focused on quick fixes through attempting to improve economic indicators to demonstrate fiscal control. With the insolvency of five banks in December, liquidity warnings were sounded and the government again engaged the World Bank and IMF for another stabilization program as government priorities focused on countering rampant inflation. The 1999 inflationary forecast was 60 per cent and the government planned to reduce CPI to 25 per cent within a year, aiming for single-digit inflation in 2002. The deflationary strategy was based on aligning the TL to a crawling USD – Euro currency basket peg (Akyüz and Boratav 2002). Tackling rampant inflation was critical in stabilizing the economy, yet Özatay and Sak (2003) note that the government had to also address long outstanding structural deficiencies concerning pensions, agriculture, taxation, fiscal management, privatization and capital markets, and banking and financial services. Banking reform and systemic weaknesses across the TBS were again highlighted as successive governments failed to rectify risks that jeopardised the health of the economy. Enacting legislation without implementing the requirements could not solve Turkey's problems.

Within a year of enacting the second Bank Act and engaging the IMF, Turkey experienced another crisis. An inability to effectively implement structural reform, control the expanding account deficit, and tame inflation took its toll on the economy. The cumulative impact added upward pressure on interest rates and resulted in a liquidity crunch. Turkey's highly exposed local banks were unable to service their debt requirements and an additional 10 banks were taken over by the SDIF in December 2000 (Central Bank 2002; Derviş 2002; Liu 2003). Turkey's economy was on the brink of collapse and urgent attention was required to revive the ailing banking system. IMF emergency assistance provided interim relief which lightened the liquidity stress and eased pressure on the economy.

By February 2001, the TL was again under attack. This time the assault resulted in Turkey's worst financial crisis. On the first day of the crisis, the TL lost almost 40 per cent of its value and the government spent $US7 billion of its reserves to calm markets as capital took flight. Inter-bank interest rates fluctuated between 1,200–5,000 per cent and the Istanbul Stock Exchange lost almost 20 per cent of its value in a single day and another 40 per cent in the next two weeks. Standard and Poor (S&P)'s reduced Turkey's credit rating, making borrowing more costly and adding to the already strained financial crunch. The continuous decline of the TL made existing debt servicing significantly more costly as most of the government's debt was due in US$ (Morris 2001a) and many private banks were overexposed to FX risks – the days of recklessly profiting from interest rate arbitrage contributed to the collapse of the economy. Citizens were angered because the public experienced the hardships of austerity programs which were now compounded with the fear of losing their savings as a result of currency depreciation and bank insolvencies. Analysts accurately predicted that the consequences of crisis would 'cause massive damage to banks, which have large foreign currency debt and stocks of government bonds in TL' (BBC 2001a). The alarming rate of bank insolvencies continued, reaching 19 in a period of five years (Derviş 2002).

Past crises were triggered by economic volatility and poor fundamentals. In contrast, the February 2001 crisis began with a disagreement between late Prime Minister Bülent Ecevit and President Ahmet Necdet Sezer. During a February 2001 National Security Council meeting, Sezer accused Ecevit of being soft on corruption, resulting in Ecevit's prompt departure from the meeting. Unlike other politicians, Ecevit's integrity was impeccable; Ecevit's error was to acknowledge the dispute with Sezer in public which turned a difference of opinion into financial chaos (Morris 2001a).

Turkey's corruption problem was at the forefront of the public agenda and the crisis demonstrated how non-traditional factors threatened Turkey's economic stability (McKeeby and Geis 2000). Nearly 20 banks were taken over by the SDIF and banking irregularities led to the arrest of a former prime minister/president's nephew. This particular arrest demonstrated the depth of corruption in the Turkish economy and the publice demanded fundamental political change.

Post-crisis developments

An immediate consequence of the early 2001 crisis was the abandonment of the TL's currency peg. Markets moved too significantly for the Central Bank to maintain the peg; the currency peg no longer represented the true value of the TL. By floating the TL, the government allowed the market to re-value the TL and account for the fall-out. This crisis required real action and a revision of the failed SAP designed to tame Turkey's crisis ridden economy. Since the 1999 SAP rationale was based on the TL's peg, floating the TL negated the stabilisation program's rationale. Paul Rawkins, senior director at Fitch IBCA, suggests that Turkey had no alternative but to implement a high interest rate regime and tighten budgetary controls to alleviate the chaos; the implementation of such a plan, however, crippled domestic demand and produced an economic recession (BBC 2001b), further complicating Turkey's financial woes.

The dire sensitivities required the government to balance the countless economic and social interdependencies and considerations affecting the lives of citizens and the needs of the economy. Turkey's crisis put the government in a very difficult situation. The IMF immediately provided a $USD11 billion loan facility to support economic reform . The new 2001 facility was in addition to the $USD7.5 billion facility provided in December 2000.

Ironically, the February 2001 crisis coincided with the IMF first deputy director, Stanley Fischer's visit to Turkey. Fischer, an architect of the 1999 SAP, was immediately drawn into crisis negotiations. The situation was a serious embarrassment for the government as the IMF had only a few short months ago intervened to extend more loans to sustain the stabilization program. Similar to past episodes, the government gained a false sense of confidence with the IMF's expanded loan facility and did not adequately react to the November crisis. To spur on the restructuring effort, Fischer is said to have urged Ecevit to contact and appoint Kemal Derviş, a World Bank executive, as State Minister of the Economy (Aliriza 2001). Derviş would be responsible for developing Turkey's recovery plan and accountable for its implementation.

A relative unknown to Turkey's political establishment, Derviş had served as an advisor to Ecevit in the 1970s, joining the ranks of the World Bank in 1978. At the World Bank, Derviş developed a reputation for being an effective economic policy advisor. Local and international markets received Derviş's appointment as State Minister of the Economy positively, while Turkey's public greeted the newcomer with relief (Aliriza 2001). Along with the Derviş appointment, Süreyya Serdengeçti was appointed the new Governor of the Central Bank.

Derviş's priority was to set the reform agenda and deliver on expectations. From the onset, the focus was banking and the privatization of state enterprises. Within a month, emergency measures for Turkey's recovery were announced. The government committed to establishing a new board to control state-banks; transferring state-bank losses to the national budget; merging the state-owned Ziraat and Emlak banks; and privatizing Türk Telecom, Turkish Airlines, and other state-enterprises. Particular attention was given to the state-banks because four of the nation's largest state-banks accounted for an estimated $USD20 billion in losses. Since state-banks accounted for 33 per cent of the TBS's total assets, the depth of Turkey's banking troubles could be appreciated; both state and non-state banks were in serious difficulty. Without a viable banking sector, the economy could not stabilize.

In addition to the emergency measures, Derviş committed to severing ties between the Central Bank and the government. Political involvement in the economy led to corruption and the new Minister was taking measures to prevent the repeat of past problems. The clear separation and transparency of the Central Bank was an essential control to end the vicious cycle of debt financing that crippled the economy; the segregation of Bank and government was also a condition of international lenders to secure support for the recovery process (Morris 2001b). Derviş's effectiveness was evident as the required parliamentary legislation to provide the Central Bank with independence was enacted in April 2001.

Turkey's emergency recovery plan required financial soundness and discipline. Confidence from international markets was essential and the approach needed balance to maintain public support. Derviş organized meetings with the ambassadors of the G-7 in Turkey, the IMF, the World Bank, and representatives from upwards of 40 international banks (BBC 2001c, 2001d) to gain the confidence of major lenders. The structured approach was successful as the IMF agreed to make additional resources available in May 2001; Turkey's loan package was restructured to $USD 19 billion (IMF 2001c). With an additional $USD 16 billion in stand-by credit secured in February 2002, Turkey became the IMF's largest borrower (Arnold 2002). Öniş (2006) explains that Derviş demonstrated the importance of a credible policy maker that delivered on stringent programs. With a strong network of international bankers to support the SAP, Derviş managed a relatively smooth transition in the post-crisis environment and generated credibility in Turkey's reform program. Nevertheless, Derviş's popularity was not shared by opposition politicians and organized labour as both took every opportunity to protest the structural reforms.

2001 took a toll on the economy. Figures indicate that the economy contracted by 9.4 per cent (BBC 2002), a million people lost their jobs (Öniş 2006), and the crisis's depth demonstrated the structural weakness of the economy. In the TBS alone, more than 50,000 jobs were lost, accounting for 30 per cent of the sector's total employment (Şanli 2006). National unemployment rose from 6.3 per cent in 2000 to 8.2 in 2001 and to 10.1 in 2002 (Cotis 2006). The small business sector was hit hardest with extensive bankruptcies. Turkey's traditionally secure conglomerates also experienced sizeable reductions in their profit margins (Öniş 2006). Unlike past crises, this crisis affected everyone.

Notwithstanding the grim outlook, Turkey proceeded to implement its SAP. The program's strategy was based on robust structural reforms and prudent fiscal and monetary policies. The government and the BRSA worked to implement a BSRP that removed ambiguities and opportunities for irregularities in the governance of the sector and took on a significantly more robust regulatory framework (Pazarbaşoğlu 2005). By June 2001, the BSRP implemented a monitoring and reporting system to scrutinize profits–losses (P&L), liquidity, and interest rate margins, and appointed independent, external auditors to each of the state-banks. A reform law was passed to facilitate the closure of Emlak Bank, promote the operational restructuring of state-banks, and remove the government's ability to impose duty losses. Extensive progress was made to remedy the insolvent banks taken over by the SDIF. This process included the sale of viable entities, the closure of unworkable banks, and the establishment of transition banks to manage the salvageable pieces of the remaining institutions taken over by the SDIF. Action was also taken to strengthen the capital base of Turkey's private banks, identifying special terms for entities that would not be immediately compliant with the more rigorous requirements (Derviş and Serdengeçti 2001).

Interlocking EU and IMF reforms

Another element emphasized during the post-2001 crisis period was Turkey's ability to comply with the EU's requirements. As an EU candidate country, Turkish authorities worked diligently to ensure the reform process was consistent with EU requisites. Turkish banking legislation was thus being harmonized with EU and the Basel Committee on Banking Supervision's (BASEL II) requirements (Pazarbaşoğlu 2005).

Nazli (2004) argues that the establishment of a sound banking sector is a precondition of Turkey's EU candidacy. The TBS must ensure that conditions are conducive for reliable capital formation, maintain sustainable financial stability and promote long-term economic growth in order to fulfil EU expectations. Such a system will reduce risk and assist in averting the recurrence of the 2001 financial crisis. Turkey's EU finance related requirements and IMF conditionality led to the interlocking of two separate, yet shared interests. Incentives for IMF reform were provided by the prospect of EU accession. The difficult task of implementing IMF austerity measures was justified with reforms that fulfilled Turkey's Copenhagen criteria. Linking democratic and human rights reforms to an IMF austerity package may not have a natural connection, but Turkey's success in implementing EU reforms and harmonising policies boosted Turkey's international image and increased confidence in the economy. The reform program strengthened Turkey's banking sector and fulfilled both IMF and EU's expectations.

Since the 2002 elections, the Justice and Development Party, or *Adalet ve Kalkinma Partisi* (AKP), governed Turkey and continued with the IMF and EU reform programs. AKP's reforms brought Turkey to a level where it matched and/or exceeded the reforms implemented by member-states that joined the EU two years earlier (*The Economist* 2006b) and again in January 2007. Turkey now has the confidence of foreign analysts and the IMF alike, often being referred to as a robust economy that has effectively weathered the 2006 market fluctuations without experiencing a crisis that commonly rocked the economy in the past (Madslien 2006). According to a statement from the OECD Secretary-General, Turkey will no longer require IMF assistance and possesses geo-strategic significance. Turkey's role within the global economy has expanded due to its effective economic transformation (Anadolu 2006).

Turkey's country risk has declined with changes made to stabilize the crisis prone and volatile economy. Subsequent to the initial economic contraction of 9.4 per cent in 2001, Turkey's real gross domestic product (real GDP) registered gains of 5.8 per cent, 8.90 per cent, and 7.40 per cent between 2003 and 2005 (*Euromonitor* 2007). Similarly, FDI experienced sizeable growth, particularly in 2005, demonstrating greater confidence in the economy (see Table 11.1).

How has the TBS fared?

Since the 2001 crisis, a number of reforms were implemented. To determine whether this process worked, several matters need to be addressed.

Table 11.1   Turkey – FDI figures

	US$m					
	2000	*2001*	*2002*	*2003*	*2004*	*2005*
FDI	982	3,352	1,137	1,752	2,847	9,650

Source: *Foreign Direct Investment Information Bulletin* (2006).

How much has really changed in the TBS? Have the changes had a material affect on the economy? Are conditions more stable now than they were in the past or can crises still reap havoc across Turkey's economy?

Turkey's economy and the TBS have experienced fundamental change. Turkey, known for its lackadaisical approach to crisis management, surprised many critics. In the post-crisis period, the Central Bank was given independence and the SDIF no longer manages 20 odd financial institutions. The SDIF sold, liquidated, and/or restructured insolvent banks with only one entity remaining under the SDIF's supervision at the time of writing.[2] The BRSA is now accountable for overseeing the rigorous monitoring of the TBS. State-banks are consolidated and managed to limit the risk of financial leakage. Two of the largest state-banks, Halk Bank and Ziraat Bank, are slated for privatization. The structure and governance of the TBS have been strengthened.

The TBS is now closely followed by foreign financial institutions and a number of Turkish banks have been acquired by foreign entities. A 2006 Ankara Chamber of Commerce report indicated that foreign ownership of the TBS has increased to 28.3 per cent. Greater interest and targeted acquisitions indicates that foreign investors see Turkey as a growth market. When contrasting the foreign ownership figures of the TBS to those of Western industrialized nations, we see that the proportion of foreign ownership in mature markets is relatively low (see Table 11.2).

Mature markets in Western industrialized countries house the world's most powerful banks (see Table 11.3). Countries that are global or regional economic powers, that is, the 'core', have a strong correlation with being the home market of financial powerhouses. Having a stable and strong financial services sector provides countries, and companies therein, with the leverage to use sophisticated financial services and products to pursue their interests. This becomes more evident when the foreign ownership figures of emerging market economies and the EU's newest members are contrasted to the data from mature, industrialized markets (see Table 11.2 and Table 11.4).

Table 11.2   Foreign ownership of banking sector

	Country	%		Country	%
1.	Holland	2	12.	Turkey	28
2.	Germany	4	13.	South Korea	30
3.	Canada	5	14.	Brazil	30
4.	Italy	6	15.	Argentina	32
5.	Japan	7	16.	Peru	43
6.	Thailand	7	17.	Venezuela	43
7.	Switzerland	11	18.	Chile	47
8.	Australia	17	19.	Poland	69
9.	United States	19	20.	Mexico	83
10.	Malaysia	19	21.	Hungary	89
11.	EU Average	20	22.	Czech Republic	90

Source: CNN Turk (2006).

Table 11.3   World's largest banks by market capitalization

	Bank	Parent country	$USbn
1.	Citigroup	US	235
2.	Bank of America	US	230
3.	HSBC	UK	200
4.	JPMorgan Chase	US	155
5.	Mitsubishi-UFJ Financial Group	Japan	140
6.	Wells Fargo	US	120
7.	UBS	Switzerland	110
8.	Royal Bank of Scotland	UK	100
9.	China Construction Bank	China	100
10.	Mizuho Financial Group	Japan	95

Source: *The Economist* (2006c).

Turkey's foreign ownership figures are at a mid point between those of the mature markets and the EU's newest members. Although the TBS's foreign ownership is 9 per cent above the EU average, Turkey's figures are markedly less than those of the Czech Republic, Hungary, and Poland. On a separate measure, the market share of foreign financial institutions as a percentage of total banking assets in Bulgaria, Croatia, and Romania indicate that foreign entities control the vast majority of these countries' local sectors. In contrast to the former Eastern Bloc countries, Turkey's single digit figures have remained constant. The banking sectors of the former communist states have either been exploited or local liberalisation was unable to render sustainable local

Table 11.4   Market share of foreign owned banks (total assets as a %)

	1996	1997	1998	1999	2000	2001	2002	2003	2004
Bulgaria	9.5	18.0	32.3	44.7	67.0	70.0	72.0	82.3	82.5
Croatia	1.0	4.0	6.7	39.9	84.1	89.3	90.2	91.0	91.3
Macedonia	n.a	n.a	n.a	11.5	53.4	51.1	44.0	47.0	47.3
Romania	11.2	17.2	20.0	47.8	50.9	55.2	56.4	58.2	62.0
Turkey	2.4	4.3	4.3	5.3	5.2	3.1	3.1	2.8	3.4

Source: Hagmayr and Haissi (2006).

financial institutions, giving foreign financial institutions an opportunity to expand their market share. The same cannot be said for Turkey. Turkey's historic volatility likely explains why the market share controlled by foreign financial institutions has remained relatively low. Widespread losses resultant from economic volatility in a traditionally weak economy is often enough of a deterrent to keep foreign investors at bay or limit the amount of risk foreigners are willing to make.

The argument here is that the recent interest in the TBS can be attributed to progress in reforming a weak economy into a more versatile, robust structure. Material progress was achieved in establishing a generally more stable banking sector and economy, increasing the demand for foreign investment. Barring Croatia, the countries cited above are all relatively new EU member-states whose banking sectors are dominated by foreign actors. The prospect of a similar situation unfolding for Croatia and Turkey is apparent. Croatia and Turkey are EU candidates and the upward trend in foreign ownership is indicative of the experience witnessed by other new EU members. A review of recent acquisitions made by foreign institutions is also consistent with this assertion. Financial institutions from across Europe, the United States, and Asia have acquired Turkish assets in the post crisis period, with a higher frequency in the 2005–2006 timeframe (See Table 11.4). These acquisitions have increased Turkey's FDI and the proportion of foreign ownership in the TBS. Then again, when the stake and transaction cost columns of Table 11.5 are examined, we can confirm that the foreign investors are taking a gradual approach to expanding into the TBS. Most of these acquisitions are consistent with acquiring sizeable, measured interests in well-established and primarily profitable firms.

Turkey's track record of being a high risk and volatile economy is likely the reason why the M&A market is increasing at a moderate pace. The TBS has not seen the mass influx of private equity firms to acquire the once available insolvent banks controlled by the SDIF. HSBC and

Table 11.5 Foreign acquisitions of Turkish Banks

Foreign institution name	Parent country	Acquired Turkish bank	Stake (%)	Transaction Date	Transaction Cost $US Millions
HSBC	United Kingdom	Demirbank	100	October 2001	
		Byner Holding – cards/finance		August 2002	425
BNP Paribas	France	Türk Ekonomi Bankasi (TEB) Mali Yatirim	50	November 2004	217
UniCredito/Koçbank – joint venture	Italy/Turkey	Yapi Kredi	57.4	May 2005	1,530
Fortis	Belgium	Disbank	93.3	July 2005	€985
General Electric	United States	Garanti Bank	25.5	August 2005	1,560
National Bank of Greece	Greece	Finansbank	46	April 2006	2,770
Dexia	Belgium	Deniz Bank	75	May 2006	2,440
EFG Eurobank	Greece	Tekfenbank	70	September 2006	185
Arab Bank/Bank Med	Lebanon	MNG Bank	91	September 2006	n/a
Citigroup	United States	Akbank	20	October 2006	3,100
Turan Alem Securities	Kazakhstan	Şek er bank	33.98	December 2006	297

Source: Derived from various banking and media reports.

Koç Financial Services[3] were the only acquirers of financial institutions under the management of the SDIF with the purchase of Demirbank (2001) and Yapi Kredi (2005). Some analysts view the TBS as having 'enormous growth potential' and point to some of the recent acquisitions as indicative of aggressive bids and counter-bids amongst the world's largest financial institutions (Koh 2006). A competitive atmosphere has been amplified with Turkey's new universal mortgage system; a burgeoning population of more than 72 million provides local and foreign financial institutions with incentive to enter a new segment in the Turkish market and to compete for the potential windfall. These prospects correspond with the growing maturity of Turkey's reform process and successive, positive results in the post 2001 crisis era. Opportunities for greater foreign ownership will increase with the government's privatization of Halk Bank and Ziraat Bank. These two state-banks are well established and have the benefit of a five year restructuring exercise that has turned around the loss prone entities.

Future risks and challenges

The potential upside in the Turkish economy and the TBS sector is positive, but not without risk. Turkey successfully implemented a series of EU reforms and continues with the required program to advance its EU candidacy. With respect to political, economic, and social developments, Turkey is on par with or ahead of the EU's most recent members-states. Likewise, BSRP progress has comfortably brought the TBS in line with EU norms and BASEL II requirements, demonstrating that the environment in which the TBS is governed, regulated, and operates is of a high international standard. Although Turkey's risks include a large current account deficit, loan exposures, relatively high inflation, double digit unemployment, systemic corruption, and the prospect of political instability in the wake of future national elections, Turkey offers great potential for investors. Turkey's risks are real and although a reformed Turkey is better suited to manage volatility and the business cycle's natural fluctuations, the seriousness of Turkey's risks should not be overlooked.

Amongst priorities the government needs to tackle are unemployment, the current account-debt ratio, the informal economy, and a continuation with the economic reform and privatization efforts (AFX 2005). If the government maintains inflation at low, single digit figures, as is the case with most industrialized economies, then Turkey will further improve its macroeconomic management and become more competitive. Turkey's debt exposure is still a concern as external debt exceeds

50 per cent of the country's GNP and the gross public debt is greater than 75 per cent of gross national product (GNP). A significant proportion of the public debt is still indexed to foreign currencies or linked to short-term interest rates. A reduction in debt to GDP ratio and the balancing of Turkey's debt profile will reduce the country's vulnerability to global interest rate fluctuations and FX risk (Krueger 2005). The current account deficit continues to grow and is amongst the largest in emerging markets, exposing the Turkish economy to greater risks with respect to capital flows (*Turkish Daily News* 2006b). While the banking sector is in much better shape, interest rate sensitivities may expose Turkish banks to greater, unnecessary risks. Capital adequacy and reserves may now be in line with EU and BASEL II requirements, yet hundreds of millions in capital allocation to offset interest rate and market based risks is an inefficient use of capital. This money could be used more wisely to generate shareholder value instead of offsetting risks. Another factor that needs to be assessed as a possible source of instability is the cost of energy resources. Turkey is an energy importer and energy volatility can significantly affect the economies of developing countries which are dependent on importing energy from the Middle East and Russia.

Turkey's risks, both real and perceived, are likely the reasons why foreign interests have not exploited or further capitalized on discounted, post-crisis opportunities. Foreign interests could have aggressively pursued opportunities to extract an immediate profit from vulnerabilities within Turkey. Yet, the risks of investing aggressively in Turkey were too high to encourage this type of activity, which did not occur because of the possibility of loss due to systemic volatility in the short-term. Similarly, the en masse purchase of large enterprises as a long term strategy did not occur for the same reasons: the risks were simply too high and Turkey's history of volatility was too significant to encourage large scale acquisitions. Instead, foreign institutions opted for more conservative, integrated strategies that consist of strategic investments, partnerships and joint-ventures, or the acquisition of small-to-medium sized enterprises as means to enter the Turkish market in a risk conscious and incremental approach.

Despite the importance of economic fundamentals to Turkey's risk profile, arguably the most significant factor that will determine Turkey's risk over the next five year period will be the national elections of 2007. If Turkey returns to a fragmented legislature with a weak coalition government, then the risk of a slowing reform process will limit Turkey's growth potential. A slower reform process, compounded with a fractious government, may give way to inadequate fiscal discipline, inward party based patronage, and a return to political volatility. Such an environment will keep foreign interests at bay, limit Turkey's EU prospects, and reduce the likelihood of greater financial services competitiveness through foreign and local M&A activity.

Increased foreign ownership is another key consideration that needs to be assessed as a factor in systemic stability. If the percentage of foreign ownership continues with its current upward trend, then Turkey may gain the benefits of cutting edge products, services and processes, including risk management. These cutting edge elements will, however, be imported instead of produced domestically. This logic also applies to growth opportunities and benefits sourced through the spin-off of research and development advancements; Turkey will have limited opportunities to host the development of new technologies, products and systems. Greater foreign ownership results in less domestic control. As demonstrated by the figures in Table 11.2, mature Western economies have the lowest percentage of foreign ownership, meaning that powerful economies develop strong, locally based financial institutions. Finally, be it due to financial crisis scenarios or regular fluctuations in the business cycle, foreign companies have a natural tendency to 'cut their losses' in foreign markets during economic downturns and retreat to their national home-country base. If significant elements of the TBS were controlled by foreign financial institutions, then Turkey would also run the risk of a significant sector-based exit, leaving the TBS open to greater instability because foreign financial institutions may 'dump and run'. A sizeable exit from the TBS or other economic sectors, would then reduce confidence in the Turkish economy and cause greater panic and an outward flow of capital and decreased value for the sectors affected by the departure of foreign enterprises.

Strong local ownership in the TBS could reduce the risks posed by foreign ownership and capital flight from the Turkish economy. To control for the risks associated with foreign ownership of significant enterprises and the foreign domination of particular sectors, governments have a number of options that can be utilized. With specific reference to banking and financial services, both Australia and Canada have foreign ownership limits on their major, locally based entities. Foreign ownership restrictions are accompanied by limits placed on the percentage of equity investors can hold at any one time – the limit of equity permitted to be held by a single entity applies to both local and foreign investors. Governments can also provide local companies with incentives to encourage local mergers amongst traditional competitors. Such a policy would see the development of larger local actors which could seek to leverage operations of scale, increased resources to invest in stronger system and risk management platforms, expanding product portfolios and delivery capabilities, and generally building companies of greater mass that are better suited to ward off predator companies from abroad and within.

Conclusion

With Turkey's 2000–2001 financial crises came havoc and opportunity. Havoc due to the country's financial collapse, opportunity because a failed economy prompted rethinking about the structure and operations of the financial system. The seriousness of these crises, and the manner in which successive governments responded, demonstrated that positive results can be achieved if the people managing the reform program are committed to a sustainable and accountable recovery program. Turkey is now significantly more stable and economic growth is at a controllable level.

The TBS recovered from the collapse with a notable level of resurgence and, more importantly, sustainable profitability. Turkish banks are now held to a much higher level of regulatory rigour and governance. Foreign institutions have acknowledged the growth potential and are responding by investing in Turkey. The entry of new actors through the strategic, tactical and outright acquisition of Turkish banks will inevitably make the sector more competitive. Turkish regulatory authorities and the government should encourage the development of a more efficient and competitive TBS, but not lose sight of the importance of maintaining a strong local presence, as is the case with the world's most powerful economies. Foreign institutions customarily liquidate their assets in marginal markets during economic downturns; such a strategy during slowdown periods could potentially damage Turkey. A foreign dominated sector will also see a large proportion of the profit generated take flight to the home countries of parent foreign enterprises.

This chapter began by proposing that while Turkey was vulnerable in the post 2000–2001 era, neither the economy nor the TBS were exploited by foreign interests. Exploitation was defined as representing a disproportionate level of wealth extraction and financial benefit for foreign actors and/or foreign-imposed conditions that created greater local financial instability that worked to the detriment of locals and to the benefit of foreigners. Neither of these outcomes materialized. Instead, we witnessed that foreign banks taking gradual and incremental steps towards expanding in Turkey which were comprised of joint ventures and partnerships, and strategic investments in the form of purchasing small-to-medium sized actors or the acquisition of stakes in well established firms.

In the short-to-medium term, Turkey's high country risk is a deterrent for outright foreign domination. The deterrent is reduced when foreign companies contrast the growth potential of a stable Turkey. That said, the past decade provides plenty of hard evidence to demonstrate just how much can be lost. Foreign enterprises will likely continue to tap into the Turkish market through joint ventures and the purchase of significant stakes in profitable Turkish firms, making their investments in line with a risk based strategy. Based on the recent rate of foreign involvement, the TBS will experience a net marginal positive affect due to foreign investors gaining greater confidence in the increased frequency and size of M&A transactions. This activity will provide upward pressure on the size and cost of M&A transactions and further boost confidence in the economy. As confirmed by the increased cross border M&A activity, Turkish banks are being targeted by some of the world's largest financial institutions. However, the next test for Turkey will be when the regional or global economy experiences a major recession. This will test the structural strength of Turkey's reinvigorated economy as short-lived market shocks can be managed due to their relatively brief impact on the economy. The maintenance of economic stability in a prolonged recession will demonstrate the true underlying strength and maturity of Turkey's economy and especially its financial sector.

Notes

1. The Turkish Central Bank removed six zeros from the TL effective 1 January 2005 and the Turkish currency was transformed from the TL to the new Turkish lira or Yeni Türk Lira (YTL). 1,000,000 TL was redenominated to 1 YTL.
2. Birlesik Fon Bankasi (BFB) A.Ş. is the resultant merger of insolvent Bayindirbank A.Ş., Egs Bank A.Ş., Etibank A.Ş., Iktisat Bankasi T.A.Ş, Kentbank A.Ş., and Toprakbank A.Ş banks, respectively. BFB additionally includes segments of Demirbank, Sitebank, Sümerbank, Tarişbank, Bank Express, and Türk Ticaret Bankasi that were not a part their sale process.
3. Koç Financial Services was established in 2002 by Italy's UniCredi and Turkey's Koçbank – Koçbank was a subsidiary of the Koç Group. Koç Financial Services is an equal partnership between the two firms.

12
Conclusion: Contesting the Return to State-Led Economies

Justin Robertson

One decade after Thailand's currency crisis set in motion a broader set of economic crises in the developing world, a number of surprising patterns stand out. First, several leading emerging markets, in a striking reversal of fortune, have accumulated financial reserves equal to nearly half of their GDP. Secondly, some struggling and heavily subsidized companies have improbably turned the corner to profitability and expansion. Hynix of Korea is one obvious example. The economist would challenge the opportunity cost of the public funds devoted to these companies whereas the nationalist would claim that the investment paid off. Thirdly, with the power often attributed to global capital and the IMF, few observers would have foreseen Argentina successfully conducting cut-throat negotiations with the international economic community, and then both attracting financial flows and achieving growth during the mid-2000s. Finally, international policy-makers proved more self-reflective than normal. The IMF's quasi-independent review mechanism released a report noting that 'a crisis should not be used as an opportunity to force long-outstanding reforms, however desirable they may be, in areas that are not critical to the resolution of the crisis' (IEO 2003: 53), with particular reference to the costs of this policy in Indonesia, where the banking sector should have been the absolute focus (IEO 2003: 5).

While all of these examples might be read as forces of resistance in the international economy, the concluding chapter will suggest that the dominant post-crisis trend among emerging markets has, in fact, been continuing integration into the global economy, albeit at a moderate pace. The examples above are not strong enough to demonstrate disengagement from international economic relations. The argument in this chapter is that beyond the rhetoric of economic nationalism, countries do not tend to revert to protectionist policies after financial crises. More often than not, crises in emerging markets result in incremental changes that make these economies more open to foreign economic practices, as well as investments by foreign companies. Rather than the extremes of foreign-induced neoliberalism or the stubborn resistance of domestic political economies, crises are more commonly associated with small steps towards foreign investment liberalization and acceptance of global financial practices. This process can be fitful and uneven, but it is more representative of the developing world than the reappearance of state-directed economies, a process that appears to be unfolding in a select number of countries, such as Russia.

No closing to foreign investment

Is the place of foreign economic and commercial interests unresolved and potentially receding in leading emerging markets following the crises that engulfed these economies in the late 1990s and early 2000s? For those who believe so, Gilpin's observation (1987: 111) that 'the history of the world economy has been one of vibrant eras of liberalism, openness and free trade followed by eras of stagnation, protectionism and nationalist conflicts' provides theoretical and historical context. Economic crises, in this interpretation, hasten the transition to more closed national economies. My response would be that there has been no equivalent to Gilpin's reversion to nationalist conflicts in the current world economy. It is more accurate to say that the international trade and investment system is already largely liberal, except, of course, for agriculture. Barriers across countries have fallen significantly in the last twenty years enabling foreign firms to operate relatively freely in large parts of the world, even, for example, in China, where full foreign ownership is possible in most sectors. There may be a diminished appetite to go further and globally regulate domestic economic and social economic policy – the 'deep integration' agenda – yet there has been no retreat on the overall liberal orientation of foreign investment regimes, including in emerging markets.

One way to test this proposition is to examine countries where the position of foreign business has been put into question due to the fall-out from economic crises. Korea and Thailand are two such examples. Thailand's recent military government is another part of the country's adjustment to the crisis of the late 1990s. The government has pursued an independent economic policy and challenged aspects of global finance and global patents. It would be a mistake, however, to conclude that these steps represent a closing to foreign firms, as one might infer from reading *The Financial Times* where concern over Thailand's economic direction has made the front page regularly over 2006–2007. Too often the alarmist tone of business newspapers exaggerates the depth of foreign resentment in emerging markets. The military government's actions are bound up with political signaling to domestic constituencies and have affected only a restricted number of foreign firms.

Take Thailand's retail sector, in which the foreign presence has been depicted as at risk by the FT correspondent ever since the Asian crisis (e.g. *The Financial Times* 2002). In fact, the retail sector is a key example of change in Thailand with foreign superstores run by Carrefour and Tesco among the most visible illustrations of foreign firm entry. Consumers, moreover, have voiced their opinions on this issue through their purchasing decisions at these stores.[1] Despite justifiable concerns over the economic and cultural implications, the long-term decline of 'mom and pop stores' is a global trend. Perhaps the best example of the foreign business community's commitment to the Thai economy is that Carrefour recently increased its investment in the country, as reported in the inside pages of *The Financial Times* (2007), at a time when foreign retailers are allegedly deeply concerned about their legal status. Foreign investment has altered the landscape of the retail market in developing economies and Thailand's retail sector is an example of stable foreign ownership in post-crisis emerging markets.

In Korea, foreign private equity funds are under intense attack for the politics of their high profitability since the Asian economic crisis. While some of the nationalistic response is genuine, the practical impact is again concentrated on a handful of foreign companies, not foreign capital as a whole. The episode is better seen as a relatively minor irritant that will not derail the overall place of foreign business in the country. The greater irony is that private equity, as a business model, is not in decline today in Korea; rather, it is a burgeoning industry that is being pushed forward by new domestic and regional funds.

Korea's experience with private equity is telling for the argument that discourses of domestic resistance to foreign capital can conceal the degree to which practices pioneered in leading economies are found in an increasing number of countries. Returning to a theme introduced in the introduction, the latest international business and financial operations may be occurring below the surface and may ironically involve domestic actors copying Anglo-American practices. Several further Asian examples can be cited to make this point. Low FDI in Indonesia and Malaysia after the Asian crisis (Chapter 9) masks the adoption of foreign banking and business practices, some spearheaded by domestic capitalists and others by foreign companies. One close observer highlights how foreigners successfully restructured key Indonesian companies, such as Astra International, and generated high returns in doing so: 'there have not been many unhappy foreign investors in Indonesia over the last eight years' (Alexander 2006). This group of foreign firms included high-profile multinationals like Heinz and Philip Morris, but was led by lesser known new forms of global finance drawn from the worlds of distressed debt, hedge funds and investment banking. The point appears to be that foreign firms are driving market changes in Indonesia, even though the aggregate foreign investment flows are underwhelming.

In Thailand, there are now domestic bankers specializing in distressed assets and investment banking, many of whom gained their skill sets in 'new' finance at GE Capital and Goldman Sachs in Bangkok during the Asian financial crisis. In Northeast Asia, Japanese investment banks call themselves 'change agents' (Lincoln interview) and perform the same roles as Western investment banks, while Korea has become one of the most competitive investment banking markets in the world. Speaking to the changed Korean business environment, a Morgan Stanley official explained that 'the Koreans figured the game out and Koreans now regularly outbid US firms for non-performing loans' (Doran interview).

The emergent financial actors in Korea defy easy categorization. Consider the private equity fund MBK Partners and the challenges it poses for defining economic structures and processes as either domestic or international. MBK Partners is incorporated in Korea. It is led by Korean-Americans who left the senior ranks of American-owned Carlyle Corporation in Korea. Its operations are much more representative of global private equity than traditional Korean business practices, and it attracts global investment funds. Thus, at the same time as members of domestic society express their reservations about foreign capital in numerous developing countries, financial transactions characteristic of international capital are frequently being carried out by notionally 'domestic' capitalists. The growing role of these locally-based actors, such as MBK Partners in Seoul, suggests that today's emerging markets are operating differently than they were 5–10 years ago.

Incremental foreign business penetration

Neither a takeover spree by international investors nor blocked foreign investments by domestic groups represent the experiences of the developing world in recent decades. If the foreign power hypothesis held, we would observe dramatic shifts in ownership of capital in developing countries. As the rest of this section demonstrates, this has not been the case.

If the nationalist perspective guided emerging market policy-makers, global FDI flows to developing economies should not have been on the rise in recent decades. Using data from UNCTAD (2006), the annual FDI flows into developing economies and economies in transition increased to an average of over $240 billion for the eight years following the start of the Asian crisis, 1998–2005, whereas the annual average was just under $100 billion for the 1990–97 period.[2] Even three Asian economies known for their foreign investment restrictions, China, Japan and Malaysia, are pushing forward with incremental openings to foreign capital and private equity funds are taking their first real steps in each of these countries. In the case of Japan, the severity of its economic crisis forced its hand and it has reluctantly offered wider market access to foreign investors.

To simplify, emerging markets appear to pass through three steps in their relationship with foreign capital after crises with the ultimate outcome being an increased presence for foreign firms in these economies. These stages can be illustrated by the banking sector. At first, risk-based foreign investors steer clear of crisis-riven economies and domestic policy-makers struggle to design procedures to deal with distressed financial assets. The emphasis Cevdet (Chapter 11) places on risk as part of corporate decision-making in today's international economy is relevant here. Cevdet argues that most foreign firms have learned that expanding internationally entails substantial financial risks, as well as opportunities. His analysis implies that the risk management systems in place at leading multinationals would have slowed any aggressive moves to invest in crisis-affected assets in emerging economies. Cevdet's framework uses country risk as the variable that explains both historically weak foreign banking and the only moderate level of financial FDI in the aftermath of Turkey's recent economic crisis.

The proposition that follows is that in the first post-crisis stage, when developing economies open their investment markets in the wake of crises, strong foreign commercial interest is not assured. In fact, one analyst has quantified this relationship and finds that countries that negotiate support from the IMF receive 28 per cent less FDI than countries that do not do so (Jensen 2006: 130). This finding makes sense in the immediate aftermath of crises when asset disposition schemes are slow to take off (Claessens 2005: 25). There is clearly a process of learning at work since the management of failing assets is often a completely new public policy issue – domestic actors also only slowly recognize the importance of sending signals to the foreign investment community (Haggard and Maxfield 1996). However, within several years, sales to foreigners are realized, often at heavy discounts given the distressed nature of the assets. In this second stage, the private equity fund is a key international actor whereas global flagship banks approach emerging markets more hesitantly. Building on the introductory framework, this contrasting behaviour is intelligible through a disaggregated lens that captures how financial risks in crisis settings are interpreted differently by different factions of capital.

Only in the third stage, when recovery takes hold, do foreign commercial banks tend to enter emerging markets. Part of the reason, as Cevdet's analysis makes clear, is that foreign firms prefer to make investments in stable and growing domestic firms after crises, not distressed enterprises. Citibank's deal-making in post-crisis Korea, Mexico and Turkey illustrates the third post-crisis stage. Citibank has taken aggressive multi-billion positions in each of these countries but only did so after substantial time had passed from the crisis. Citibank did not acquire local banks through fire sales at the peak of crises. It took Citibank seven years from the Asian financial crisis and six years from the Mexican crisis to make major acquisitions in these economies. It also cost Citibank over $12 billion and nearly $3 billion to acquire a Mexican and a Korean bank, respectively. It is difficult to consider the timing of these transactions, and the high premium paid, as supporting an image of an opportunistic Citibank at the centre of financial crises in emerging markets. Citibank's recent $3 billion stake in Turkey's largest bank, Akbank, more than five years after its most recent crisis, is further evidence for the three stage model of foreign financial behaviour after crises.

Larger statistical trends are presented in Cull and Martinez-Peria's chapter to the effect that foreign banks do not overwhelm most emerging markets in crisis. Their calculations reveal a positive association between financial crises in developing countries and foreign financial participation, although not has high as critical analyses would have predicted. On average, foreign financial institutions gain control of an additional 7–10 per cent of banking assets after an emerging market crisis. Even where there have been rapid advances of foreign banking ownership, such as in Eastern Europe and Latin America, domestic owners still control over 50 per cent of financial assets and other regions, notably Asia and the Middle East, are starting from a minimal base of foreign penetration. Thus, while critics may be right to worry about foreign monopoly control of banks in Mexico, most developing countries cannot be fairly equated with Mexico. Turkey would be a more representative example. Turkey's crises have opened up the economy to foreign capital and yet the measured responses of foreign banks have left the financial sector three-quarters domestic-owned (Cevdet, Chapter 11).

Rather than foreign opportunism, one of the unresolved questions concerning the incorporation of developing countries into the international economy is how foreign capital will respond to the openings in countries that have so far been on the margins of global flows. Facing economic crisis and demographic challenges, many developing countries are liberalizing their foreign investment regimes. Looking into the future, will countries in this position, such those in the Middle East and North Africa, gradually and successfully incorporate into the international trading and investment system? The answer remains unclear and there is, of course, every chance that the liberalization process in these countries could lead to greater financial instability.

Argentina and Russia as exceptions?

Argentina, Russia and Venezuela are thought by some observers to be charting a revised economic course for developing states that downplays the role of foreign capital. Of the cases represented in this volume, Argentina and Russia feature among the most domestically-oriented economies. Are these two national experiences instructive for thinking about the politics of resistance to international economic integration in the world today? Argentina is a crucial test case since its financial sector policy was considered paradigmatic for foreign ownership (WB-Brookings 1999) before the country was subsequently called 'globalization's most stunning bust' in the wake of its devastating financial crisis (Blustein 2005: 12).

One analyst recently wrote of Argentina that 'the population has turned viscerally anti-American, anti-IMF and anti-globalization' (Steil 2007). There are several reasons why this statement is misleading. First, much of the nationalist rhetoric is politically managed by domestic elites while the remainder may by heartfelt but rests at a broad level of abstraction without significant influence on firm or government decisions. Second, I would strongly agree with Riggirozzi (Chapter 6) that Argentina 'forged a new space for dissent from global rules without falling into outdated, anti-capitalist economic autarchy.' While recognizing the boldness of Argentina's negotiating strategy with foreign creditors and the IMF, Argentina's dissent from global conventions on debt repayment does not justify the conclusion that it has remade its relations with global capital. Argentina achieved a domestic victory against international financial forces (Datz, Chapter 4) and the Argentine government has carried out effective national economic policy-making since the crisis (Riggirozzi, Chapter 6). Even so, is it really any more difficult for foreign firms to do business in Argentina today than it was during the 1990s, except for the reduced number of privatization opportunities? This is certainly debatable, which suggests that Argentina's conflictual international relations on debt are independent of its more regularized relations with foreign capital entering the country.

Russia has its own characteristics that diverge from the liberal economic model: the Russian state has intervened extensively into private ownership; there are almost Asian-like conglomerates bridging banking and industry; and a barter system is even present in some areas of the economy (see Robinson, Chapter 10). However, Russia can no more serve as a generalized model of resistance than Argentina. First, the size of Russia's oil wealth places it apart from most other developing countries. Second, despite recent growth rates, the economy is precariously balanced and the lack of industrial upgrading puts Russia in real danger of falling into future crises.

Looking to the future

Normal business cycles, globalized flows of capital and high debt levels around the world, combined with chance and accident, make national, regional and international economic crises a constant possibility. Nonetheless, despite a world economy fraught with risk and losses that have affected not only companies but also individuals, crises have failed to dent the commitment to capitalism itself. With surprising alacrity, the middle classes in crisis settings have accepted financial loss and re-engaged energetically with the financial system – examples range from Nortel shareholders in Canada to Korean consumers who overspent on credit cards not long after the country's economic crisis. Even in Argentina, where angry protestors during its crisis held signs reading 'I'll never forgive the banks nor the government,' the distrust of the market has passed and a functioning truce has been struck with global finance and the capitalist system. Crises may shift the tone of debate and engender nationalist rhetoric but capitalism's footing appears steady.

The Asian region, home to the world's fastest growing emerging markets, exemplifies this pattern. Ten years after the region's economic turmoil, the busy, air-conditioned malls of Asia and the emerging investment banking and private equity markets found in the financial capitals of richer and poorer Asian economies alike tell a story of recovery and adaptation – not economic nationalism. The world may be nowhere near the liberal ideal, but more and more countries and their mixed economies are engaging at a deeper level than ever before with both multinational corporations and international finance. To fully understand this unfolding process, past and future economic crises must be studied closely.

Notes

1. One personal anecdote would be of a Thai friend driving out of the way to buy marginally less expensive beer at a Carrefour superstore in Bangkok. This is textbook microeconomic behaviour.
2. Of course, there are issues concerning the concentration of this FDI in a select number of developing economies. However, if key emerging markets, such as Brazil and Russia, are receiving higher FDI flows, this in itself contradicts the argument that these countries are raising investment barriers against foreign firms. One important statistic is that all developing regions have experienced higher FDI flows since 1997.

References

Acuña, C. H. (1995) 'Politics and Economics in the Argentina of the Nineties', in W.C. Smith and E. A. Gamarra (eds), *Democracy, Markets and Structural Reform*. Florida: North–South Center Press.

Acuña, C. H. and Smith, W. C. (1996) 'The Political Economy of Structural Adjustment: The Logic and of Support and Opposition to Neoliberal Reforms', *Desarrollo Economico-Revista de Ciencias Sociales* 36 (141), April–June, 355–89.

Adachi, Y. (2006) 'The Ambiguous Effects of Russian Corporate Governance Abuses in the 1990s', *Post-Soviet Affairs* 22 (1), 65–89.

Addis, K. (1999) *Taking the Wheel: Auto Parts Firms and the Political Economy of Industrialization in Brazil*. University Park: Penn State University Press.

AFX (2006) 'IMF Urges Turkey To Cut Ratio of Debt To GDP, Take Action On Unemployment 2005', AFX News Limited, 6 May.

Aglietta, M. and Breton, R. (2001) 'Financial Systems, Corporate Control and Capital Accumulation', *Economy and Society* 30, 433–66.

Ahrend, R. (2005) 'Can Russia Break the "Resource Curse"?', *Eurasian Geography and Economics* 46 (8), 584–609.

Ahrend, R. (2006) 'Russia's Post-Crisis Growth: Its Sources and Prospects for Continuation', *Europe–Asia Studies*, 58 (1), 1–24.

Akbar, Y. H. and McBride, B. J. (2004) 'Multinational Enterprise Strategy, Foreign Direct Investment and Economic Development: The Case of the Hungarian Banking Industry', *Journal of World Business* 39, 89–105.

Akyüz, Y and Boratav, K. (2002) *The Making of the Turkish Financial Crisis*, The Financialization of the Global Economy Conference, PERI. Amherst: University of Massachusetts.

Alexander, P. (2006) *Presentation to 'Asian Venture Capital and Private Equity: Coming of Age'*, Hong Kong Venture Capital and Private Equity Association Conference, 9 October.

Aliriza, B. (2001) 'Turkey's Crisis: Corruption at the Core', *The Turkish Update*, The Center for Strategic and International Studies, 5 March.

Amann, E. and Baer, W. (2003) 'Anchors Away: the Costs and Benefits of Brazil's Devaluation', *World Development* 31(6): 1033–46.

Amsden, A. (1990) *Asia's Next Giant: South Korea and Late Industrialisation*. Oxford: Oxford University Press.

Anadolu (2006) 'OECD Says Turkey No Longer Needs IMF. Zaman – English Online Edition', Anadolu News Agency, 10 October.

Ang, E. (2006) 'Uphill Task for GLCs to Impress', *The Star*, 14 March.

Armijo, L. E. (ed.) (2001) 'Mixed Blessing: Expectations about Foreign Capital Flows and Democracy in Emerging Markets', in L. Armijo (ed.), *Financial Globalization and Democracy in Emerging Markets*. New York: Palgrave.

Arnold, J. (2002) *Analysis: Turkey's year of crisis*, BBC World Service, 21 February.

Asia Times (2006) 'Korea's Debate on Foreign Capital Rages On', 11 April.

Asiamoney (1999) 'Family Fortunes – The Winners and Losers', July/August.

Åslund, A. (1989) *Gorbachev's Struggle for Economic Reform*. London: Pinter.

Aspiazu, D. (2002) 'Privatizaciones en la Argentina: la Captura Institucional del Estado', *Realidad Económica* (189), 8–16.

Athukorala, P. C. (2000) 'The Malaysian Experiment' in P. Drysdale (ed.), *Reform and Recovery in East Asia*. London: Routledge.

Backé, P and Zumer, T. (2005) *Developments in Credit to the Private Sector in Central and Eastern European EU Member States: Emerging from Financial Repression – A Comparative Overview*, OeNB working paper Focus On European Economic Integration Series.

Baker, A (2005) 'The Three Dimensional Governance of Macroeconomic Policy in Advanced Capitalist States,' in A. Baker, D. Hudson, and R. Woodward (eds), *Governing Financial Globalization: IPE and Multi-level Governance*. London: Routledge.

Baker, A (2006a) *The Group of Seven: Finance Ministries, Central Banks and Global Financial Governance*. London: Routledge.

Baker, A (2006b) 'American Power and the Dollar: The Constraints of Technical Authority and Declaratory Policy in the 1990s', *New Political Economy* Vol.11, No.1.

Baldi-Delatle (2005) 'Did Pesification Rescue Argentina?', Paper presented at LACEA Conference, October 2005.

Ball, C.A. and Tschoegl, A. E. (1982) 'The Decision to Establish a Foreign Branch or Subsidiary: An Application of Binary Classification Procedures', *Journal of Financial and Quantitative Analysis* 17 (3), 411–24.

Balls, E (1998) 'Open Macroeconomics in an Open Economy', *Scottish Journal of Political Economy* 45 (2).

Balzer, H. (2005) 'The Putin Thesis and Russian Energy Policy', *Post-Soviet Affairs*, 21 (3), 210–25.

Barajas, A., Steiner, R. and Salazar, N. (2000) 'The Impact of Liberalization and Foreign Investment in Colombia's Financial Sector', *Journal of Development Economics* 63(1), 157–96.

Barisitz, S. (2005) *Banking in Central and Eastern Europe since the Turn of the Millennium – An Overview of Structural Modernization in Ten Countries*, OeNB Focus on European Economic Integration Series.

Barnes, A. (2006) *Owning Russia. The Struggle Over Factories, Farms, and Power*. Ithaca: Cornell University Press.

Barshefsky, C. (1998) Testimony of Ambassador Charlene Barshefsky, U.S. Trade Representative, House Ways and Means Trade Subcommittee, US Congress, 24 February.

Batten, J. Fetherstone, T. A. Szilagyi, P. G. (2004) *European Fixed Income Markets*, Chichester: John Wiley.

BBC (2001a) 'Turkish PM Defiant Amid Financial Chaos', 24 February.

BBC (2001b) 'Turkish Banks at Root of Crisis', 22 February.

BBC (2001c) 'Turkey Secures Banking Support', 12 June.

BBC (2001d) 'Turkey Asks Allies for Help', 18 March.

BBC (2002) 'Turkey's Ailing Leader Worries Markets', 20 May.

Beck, T., A. Demirguc-Kunt and R. Levine (1999), 'A New Database on Financial Development and Structure', Policy Research Working Paper, 2146, World Bank.

Beers, D. T., and John C. (2002) 'Sovereign Defaults: Moving Higher Again in 2003?', Standard & Poor's, Reprinted from *RatingsDirect*, September 24.

Beeson, M. (ed.) (2002) Reconfiguring East Asia: Regional Institutions and Organisations After the Crisis. London: RoutledgeCurzon.

Bello, W., Cunningham, S. and Poh, L.K. (1998) *A Siamese Tragedy: Development and Disintegration in Modern Thailand*. London: Zed Books.

Bello, W. (1998) 'East Asia on the Eve of the Great Transformation?', *Review of International Political Economy*, Vol. 5, No. 3, 424–44.

Berger, A., Klapper, L. and Udell, G. (2001) 'The Ability of Banks to Lend to Informationally Opaque Small Businesses', *Journal of Banking and Finance* 25, 2127–67.

Bergsten, F.C., Horst, T. and Moran, T.H. (1978) *American Multinationals and American Interests*. Washington: The Brookings Institution.

Best J. (2005) *The Limits of Transparency: Ambigui and the History of International Finance*. *Ithaca* Cornell University Press.

Bhagwati, J. (1998) 'The Capital Myth: The Difference Between Trade in Widgets and Dollars' *Foreign Affairs*, Vol. 77, No. 3, 7–12.

Bhagwati, J. (2001) *The Wind of the Hundred Days: How Washington Mismanaged Globalization*. Cambridge: MIT Press.

BIS (2004) 'Foreign Direct Investment in the Financial Sector of Emerging Market Economies', Committee on the Global Financial System, Working Paper 22, Basel: Bank for International Settlements.

Bleaney, M. (1985) *The Rise and Fall of Keynesian Macroeconomics*. London: Macmillan.

Block, F. (1987) *Revising State Theory: Essays in Politics and Postindustrialism*. Philadelphia: Temple University Press.

Block, F. (1991) 'Marxist Theories of the State in World Systems Analysis', in R. Little and M. Smith (eds), *Perspectives on World Politics*. London: Routledge.

Blume D. (2003) 'Experiences with the OECD Corporate Governance Principles', Middle East and North Africa Corporate Governance Workshop, 7 September.

Blustein, P. (2001) *The Chastening: Inside the Crisis that Rocked the Global Financial System and Humbled the IMF*. New York: Public Affairs.

Blustein, P. (2005) *And the Money Kept Rolling in (and Out): Wall Street, the IMF and the Bankrupting of Argentina*. New York: Public Affairs.

Blyth, M. (2003) 'The Political Power of Financial Ideas: Transparency, Risk and Distribution in Global Finance', in J. Kirshner (ed.) *Monetary Orders: Ambiguous Economics, Ubiquitous Politics*. Ithaca: Cornell University Press.

Bodgenor, J. (1996) 'A House of Cards', *The Banker*, London, Vol. 146, Issue 840, February.

BOFIT (Bank of Finland Institute of Economic in Transition) (2000) 'Russian Economy – the Month in Review' (5), (http://www.bof.fi/bofit).

Bonelli, M. (2004) *Un Pais en Deuda: La Argentina y Su Imposible Relacion con el FMI*. Buenos Aires: Planeta.

Boresztein, E. and Lee, J.W. (1999) 'Credit Allocation and Financial Crisis in Korea', *IMF Working Paper* WP/99/20, Washington, DC.

Borowski, J. (2004) 'Costs and Benefits of Poland's EMU Accession: a Tentative Assessment', *Comparative Economic Studies* 46, 127–45.

Bowie, A. and Unger, D. (1997) *The Politics of Open Economies: Indonesia, Malaysia, The Philippines and Thailand*. Cambridge: Cambridge University Press.

Bowles, P. (2002) 'Asia's Post Crisis Regionalism: Bringing the State Back In, Keeping the United States Out', *Review of International Political Economy* 9 (2): 244–70.

Braithwaite, J. and Drahos, P. (2000) *Global Business Regulation*. Cambridge: Cambridge University Press.

Bresser-Pereira, L. C. and Ferrer, A. (1991) 'Dolarização crônica: Argentina e Brasil', *Brazilian Journal of Political Economy* 11(1), 5–15.

Bresser-Pereira, L. C. and Nakano, Y. (2002) 'Uma estratégia de desenvolvimento com estabilidade', *Brazilian Journal of Political Economy* 22(3), 146–77.

Brimble, P. (2001) *The Effects of Cross-Border M&As in Developing Economies: Five Cases in Thailand*. Bangkok: The Brooker Group.

Buch, C. (2003) 'Information or Regulation: What Drives the International Activities of Commercial Banks?', *Journal of Money, Credit and Banking* 35(6), 851–69.

Buch, C. and DeLong G. (2004) 'Cross Border Bank Merger: What Lures the Rare Animal?', *Journal of Banking and Finance* 28(9), 2077–102.

Buch, C. and Lipponer A. (2004) 'FDI versus Cross-Border Financial Services: The Globalization of German Banks', *Discussion Paper Series 1*, Studies of the Economic Research Centre, No. 05.

Buckley, G. (2003) Interview, Financial Economist, US Department of the Treasury, Washington, DC, 16 September.

Calvo, G., Izquierdo, A. and Talvi, E. (2003) 'Sudden Stops, the Real Exchange Rate and Fiscal Sustainability: Argentina's Lessons', National Bureau of Economic Research, Working Paper No. 9828.

Calvo, G. and Mendoza, E. (2000) 'Rational Herding and the Globalization of Financial Markets', *Journal of International Economics*, vol. 51 (2000), 79–114.

Camdessus M. (1997) 'Asia Will Survive with Realistic Policies, Parts I and II', *The Jakarta Post* 8– 9 (5), December.

Cammack, P. (2003) 'The Governance of Global Capitalism', *Historical Materialism* 11 (2), 37–59.

Caprio, G. and Klingebiel, D. (2003) *Episodes of Systematic and Borderline Financial Crises*, The World Bank, mimeo.

Casaburi, G., Riggirozzi, M. P., Tuozzo, M. F. and Tussie, D. (2000) 'Multilateral Development Banks, Governments and Civil Society. Chiaroscuros in a Triangular Relationship'. *Global Governance*, 6 (4), 493–517.

Case, W. (2005) 'How's my Driving?: Abdullah's First Year as Malaysian PM', *Pacific Review*, 18(2), 137–57.

Cavarozzi, M. (1994) 'Politics: A Key for the Long Term in South America', in W.C. Smith, C.H. Acuna and E.A. Gamarra (eds), *Latin American Political Economy in the Age of Neoliberal Reform*, New Brunswick: Transaction Publishers.

CBR (Central Bank of Russia) (2006) *Statistics*.

Celasun, O. (1998) *The 1994 Currency Crisis in Turkey*, World Bank Policy Research Working Paper No. 1913, April.

Central Bank (2002) *The Impact of Globalization on the Turkish Economy*, 2002, Central Bank of the Republic of Turkey, June.

Chancellor, E. (1999) *Devil Take the Hindmost: A History of Financial Speculation*. New York: Plume.

Chang, R. (1999) 'Understanding Recent Crises in Emerging Markets', *Federal Reserve Bank of Atlanta Economic Review*, Second Quarter.

Cheung S. and Jang, H. (2005) *Evaluation of Corporate Governance in East Asian Economies*', mimeo.

Chin, K. F. (2004) 'Malaysia's Post-crisis Bank Restructuring' in K.S. Jomo (ed.), *After the Storm: Crisis, Recovery and Sustaining Development in Four Asian Economies*. Singapore: Singapore University Press.

Cho, K. R., Krishnan, S. and Nigh, D. (1987) 'The State of Foreign Banking Presence in the United States', *International Journal of Bank Marketing* 5(2), 59–75.

Cibils, A. (2003) 'Argentina's IMF Agreement the Dawn of a New Era?', *Foreign Policy in Focus*, 10 October.

Claessens, S. (2005) 'Policy Approaches to Corporate Restructuring Around the World: What Worked, What Failed?' in M. Pomerleano (ed.), *Corporate Restructuring: Lessons from Experience*. Washington: World Bank.

Claessens, S. and Laeven, L. (2003) 'What Drives Bank Competition?: Some International Evidence', *Journal of Money, Credit and Banking* 36(3), 563–83.

Claessens, S. and Lee, J. K. (2003) 'Foreign Banks in Low-Income Countries: Recent Developments and Impacts', in J. Hanson, P. Honohan, and G. Majnoni, (eds), *Globalization and National Financial Systems*. Washington: World Bank.

Claessens, S. and Van Horen, N. (2006) *Location Decisions of Foreign Banks and Competitive Advantage*, The World Bank, mimeo.

Claessens, S., Demirgüc-Kunt, A. and Huizinga, H. (2001) 'How Does Foreign Entry Affect Domestic Banking Markets?', *Journal of Banking and Finance* 25 (5), 891–911.

Clarke, G., Cull, R., Martinez Peria, M. S. and Sanchez, S. (2001) *Foreign Bank Entry: Experience, Implications for Developing Countries, and Agenda for Further Research*, World Bank Policy Research Working Paper No. 2698, October 2001.

Clarke, G., Cull, R. and Martinez Peria, M.S. (2006) 'Foreign Bank Participation and Access to Credit Across Firms in Developing Countries', *Journal of Comparative Economics* 34, 774–95.

Clarke, G., Cull, R., Martinez Peria, M. S. and Sanchez, S. (2003) 'Foreign Bank Entry: Experience, Implications for Developing Economies, and Agenda for Further Research', *The World Bank Research Observer* 18 (1), 25–59.

Clarke, G., Cull, R., Martinez Peria, M.S. and Sanchez, S. (2005) 'Bank Lending to Small Businesses in Latin America: Does Bank Origin Matter?' *Journal of Money, Credit, and Banking*, 37 (1), 83–118.

Cline, W. (2003) 'Restoring Economic Growth in Argentina', Working Paper N.9/03. Washington: World Bank.

CNN Turk (2006) *ATO: Bankacilik yabancilarin eline geçiyor*, 24 April.

Cohen, B. (2003) 'Capital Controls: The Neglected Option', in G. Underhill, and X. Zhang (eds), *International Financial Governance Under Stress: Global Structures Versus National Imperatives*. Cambridge: Cambridge University Press.

Coleman, W. D. (1996) *Financial Services, Globalization and Domestic Policy Change*. London: Macmillan.

Cooper, A. and Momani, B. (2005) 'Negotiating Out of Argentina's Financial Crisis: Segmenting the International Creditors', *New Political Economy* 10 (3), 305–20.

Cooper, J. (2006) 'Of BRICs and Brains: Comparing Russia with China, India and Other Populous Emerging Economies', *Eurasian Geography and Economics*, 47 (3), 255–84.

Coricelli, F., Mucci, F. Revoltella D. (2006). 'Household Credit In The New Europe: Lending Boom Or Sustainable Growth?' Discussion Paper 5520, Centre for Economic Policy Research.

Cotis, J. (2006) *OECD Economic Outlook No. 80*. Statistical Annex Tables, Wages, Costs, Unemployment and Inflation – Annex Table 13.

Crispin, S. (2003) Interview, Bureau Chief, Far Eastern Economic Review, Bangkok.

Crotty, J. (2000) 'The Structural Contradictions of the Global Neoliberal Regime', Political Economy Research Institute.

Crouch, H. (1996) *Government and Society in Malaysia*. Ithaca: Cornell University Press.

Crowley, S. (1994) 'Barriers to Collective Action. Steelworkers and Mutual Dependence in the Former Soviet Union', *World Politics* 46 (4), 589–615.

Crystal, J., Dages, G. and Goldberg, L. (2001) 'Does Foreign Ownership Contribute to Sounder Banks in Emerging Markets?: 'The Latin American Experience', in R.E. Litan, P. Masson, and M. Pomerleano (eds), *Open Doors: Foreign Participation in Financial Systems in Developing Countries*. Washington: Brooking Institution Press.

Cumings, B. (1999) 'The Asian Crisis, Democracy and the End of 'Late' Development' in T.J. Pempel (ed.), *The Politics of the Asian Economic Crisis*. Ithaca: Cornell University Press.

Dages, B. G., Damon, P. and Turney, S. (2005) *An Overview of the Emerging Market Credit Derivatives Market*, Federal Reserve Bank of New York, May.

Danaharta (2005). Final Report.

Datz, G. (2007a) 'Global–National Interactions and Sovereign Debt Restructuring Outcomes' in S. Sassen (ed.), *Deciphering the Global: Its Scales, Spaces and Subjects*. New York: Routledge.

Datz, G. (2007b) *Pension Funds and Sovereign Debt in Latin America*, paper presented at the International Studies Association Annual Convention, Chicago, IL.

de Boer, E. (2000). *The Global Economy and Post-1989 Change: The Place of the Central European Transition*. Basingstoke: Macmillan.

De Haas, R. T. A. (2002) 'Finance, Law and Growth during Transition: A Survey', *DNB Staff Reports* 74. The Netherlands Bank.

De Hass, R. and Van Lelyveld, I. (2006) 'Foreign Banks and Credit Stability in Central and Eastern Europe. A Panel Data Analysis', *Journal of Banking and Finance* 30, 1927–52.

De Mendiguren, J (2006) Interview. Vice-President of Union Industrial Argentina (UIA). 31 May.

Denizer, C. (2000) 'Foreign Entry in Turkey's Banking Sector, 1980–1997', in S. Claessens and M. Jansen (eds), *The Internationalization of Financial Services: Issues and Lessons for Developing Countries*. Boston: Kluwer Academic.

Derviş, K. (2002) *Special Policy Forum Report: Prospects for Economic Reform in Turkey – Summarised by Natan Sachs*, The Washington Institute for Near East Policy, 29 April.

Derviş, K. and Serdengeçti, S. (2001) *Letter of Intent of the Government of Turkey to the IMF*, 26 June.

Detragiache, E. and Gupta, P. (2006) 'Foreign Banks in Emerging Market Crises: Evidence from Malaysia', *Journal of Financial Stability* 2(3), 217–42.

Detragiache, E., Gupta, P. and Tressel, T. (2005) *Foreign Banks in Poor Countries: Theory and Evidence*, IMF Working Paper No. 06/18.

Devlin, R. and Ffrench D. (1999) 'Towards an Evaluation of Regional Integration in Latin America in the 1990s', *The World Economy* 22:2, 261–90.

Dhillon, A., J. Garcia-F., Ghosa S. and Mille, M. (2006) 'Debt Restructuring and Economic Recovery: Analysing the Argentine Swap', *World Economy* Vol. 29, No. 4, 377–98.

Dienes, L. (2004) 'Observations on the Problematic Potential of Russian Oil and the Complexities of Siberia', *Eurasian Geography and Economics* 45 (5), 319–45.

Doctor, M. (2007) 'Boosting Investment and Growth: the Role of Social Pacts in the Brazilian Automotive Industry', *Oxford Development Studies*, vol. 35(1), pp 105–30.

Domanski, D. (2005) 'Foreign Banks in Emerging Market Economies: Changing Players, Changing Issues', *BIS Quarterly Review* December, 69–81.

Doran, P. (2003) Interview, Senior Advisor, Morgan Stanley Real Estate Fund, Seoul, Korea, 8 April.

Doremus, P. N., Keller, W. W. and Pauly, L. W. (1998) *The Myth of the Global Corporation*. Princeton: Princeton University Press.

Dyker, D. (2000) *The Dynamic Impact on the Central–East European Economies of Accession to the European Union* 'ESRC' One Europe or Several Programme, Working Paper 06/00.

EBRD (2004) *Transition Report 2004, Infrastructure.*

EBRD (2005) *Transition report 2005. Business in Transition.*

ECB (2000). Occasional Paper: 'Structural Analysis of the EU Banking Sector'.

ECB (2005a). Occasional Paper: 'Banking Structures in the New EU Member States'. January.

ECB (2005b). Monthly Bulletin: May.

ECB (2005c). Occasional Paper: 'EU Banking Structures'. October.

ECB (2005d). Working Paper Series No. 547 November.

ECLAC (2004) *Foreign Investment in Latin America and the Caribbean*. Santiago: Economic Commission for Latin America and the Caribbean.

Eichengreen, B. and Rose, A. (1998) 'Staying Afloat when the Wind Shifts: External Factors in Emerging-Market Banking Crises', NBER Discussion paper 6370.

EIM Group (2006) *Hedge Fund Boom in Latin America*, 28 September.

Enoch, C., B. *et al.* (2001) 'Indonesia: Anatomy of a Banking Crisis Two Years of Living Dangerously, 1997–1999', IMF Working paper WP/01/52.

Epstein, G. (ed.) (2005) *Financialization and the World Economy*. Cheltenham: Edward Elgar.

Escude, G. (2002) 'Public Debt and Real Exchange Rate Dynamics in Argentina under Convertibility, Qué?', *Banco Central de la República Argentina*, May 2002, unpublished ms.

Etkin, L, Helms, M., Türkkan, U., and Morris, D. (2000) 'The Economic Emergence of Turkey', *European Business Review* 12(2).

Euromoney (2001) *Maturity of Hot New Market Faces Its Sternest Test,* December.

Euromonitor (2007) *Turkey: Country Fact File,* online edn.

Evangelista, M. (1996) 'Stalin's Revenge: Institutional Barriers to Internationalization in the Soviet Union', in R. Keohane and H. Milner (eds), *Internationalization and Domestic Politics*. Cambridge: Cambridge University Press.

Evans, P. (1979) *Dependent Development: the Alliance of Multinational, State and Local Capital in Brazil*. Princeton: Princeton University Press.

Fallows, J. (2005) 'Countdown to a Meltdown: America's Coming Economic Crisis: A Look Back from the Election of 2016', *The Atlantic Monthly* July/August, 51–64.

Ferrari-Filho, F. and Paula, L.F. (2003). 'The Legacy of the *Real* Plan and an Alternative Agenda for the Brazilian Economy', *Investigación Económica* 244: 57–92.

Ferrari-Filho F. F. and Paula, L. F. (2003) 'Regime cambial, conversibilidade da conta de capital e performance econômica: a experiência recente de Brasil, Rússia, Índia e China', in J. Sicsú, F. F. Ferrari (eds), *Câmbio e Controles de Capitais: Avaliando a Eficiência de Modelos Macroeconômicos*, Rio de Janeiro: Editora Campus.

Ffrench D. R. and Studart, R. (2001) 'The Regional Fallout of Argentina's Crisis', in A. Akkerman and J.J. Teunissen (eds), *The Crisis That Was Not Prevented: Argentina, the IMF, and Globalisation*, FONDAD.

Financial Stability Forum (2006) 'What We Do'. Available: <http://www.fsforum.org/about/what_we_do.html>.

Fisher, A. and Molyneaux, P. (1996) 'A Note on the Determinants of Foreign Bank Activity in London Between 1980–1989', *Applied Financial Economics* 6 (3), 271–7.

Focarelli, D. and Pozzolo, A. (2000) 'The Determinants of Cross-Border Shareholding: An Analysis with Bank-Level Data from OECD Countries', paper presented at the Federal Reserve Bank of Chicago Bank Structure Conference, May.

Focarelli, D. and Pozzolo, A. (2001) 'The Patterns of Cross-Border Bank Mergers and Shareholdings in OECD Countries', *Journal of Banking and Finance* Vol. 25 (12), 2305–37.

Foreign Direct Investment Information Bulletin (2006) T.C. Prime Ministry Undersecretariat of Treasury, February 2006.

Freeman N. (2005) 'Promoting Good Corporate Governance Practices in Vietnam: A New Element in the Economic Reform Agenda' in K.L. Ho (ed.), *Reforming Corporate Governance in Southeast Asia*. Singapore: ISEAS.

Fremond O. and M. Capaul (2002) *The State of Corporate Governance: Experience from Country Assessments*, World Bank Policy Research Working Paper 2858.

Frieden, J. and Rogowski R. (1996) 'The Impact of the International Economy on National Policies: An Analytical Overview', in H. Milner and R. Keohane (eds), *Internationalization and Domestic Politics*. Cambridge: Cambridge University Press.

Froud, J. Johal, S. Leaver, and A. Williams K. (2006) *Financialization and Strategy*. New York: Routledge.

FT (2002) 'Delicate Balancing Act Carries Great Risks', 6 December.

FT (2003) 'Losing Sleep Over a Rising Number of Deals', Special Report: South Korea, November 17.

FT (2007) 'Carrefour Plans for Growth in Thailand', 31 January.

Fundamental (2005) *Mutual Funds and the U.S. Retirement Market*, Vol. 14(4) August. Washington, DC: Washington.

Fungáčová, Z. (2005) 'Building a Castle on Sand: Effects of Mass Privatization on Capital Market Creation in Transition Economies', Centre for Economic Research and Graduate Education, Working Paper No. 256.

Funston, J. (2000) 'Malaysia: a Fateful September', *Southeast Asian Affairs 2000*. Singapore: ISEAS.

Gaddy, C. (2002) 'Has Russia Entered a Period of Sustainable Economic Growth', in A. Kuchins (ed.), *Russia After the Fall*. Washington: Carnegie Endowment for International Peace.

Gaddy, C. (2004) 'Perspectives on the Potential of Russian oil', *Eurasian Geography and Economics* 45 (5), 319–45.

Gaddy, C. and Ickes, B. (1998) 'Russia's Virtual Economy', *Foreign Affairs* 77 (5), 53–67.

Gaddy, C. and Ickes, B. (2002) *Russia's Virtual Economy*. Washington, DC: Brookings Institution Press.

Gaddy, C. and Ickes, B. (2005) 'Resource Rents and the Russian Economy', *Eurasian Geography and Economics* 46 (8), 559–83.

Galindo, A., Micco, A. and Serra, C. (2003) *Better the Devil That You Know: Evidence on Entry Costs Faced By Foreign Banks*, IDB – Research Department Working Paper No. 477.

Garrett, G. (1998) 'Shrinking States: Globalization and National Autonomy in the OECD', *Oxford Development Studies* Vol. 26, No. 1: 71–97.

Gelpern, A. (2005) *After Argentina*, Policy Brief in International Economics, Institute for International Economics No. PB05-2.

Gerchunoff, P. and Aguirre, H. (2004) *La Política Económica de Kirchner en la Argentina: Varios Estilos, Una Sola Agenda*, Boletín del Real Instituto Elcano de Estudios Internacionales y Estratégicos 48, 28 June.

Germain, R. (2003) 'Reforming the International Financial Architecture: The New Political Agenda' in R. Wilkinson (ed.), *Global Governance: Critical Perspectives*. London: Routledge.

Gerschenkron, A. (1966) *Economic Backwardness in Historical Perspective*. Cambridge: Cambridge University Press.

Gianneti, M. and Ongena, S. (2005) *Financial Integration and Entrepreneurial Activity: Evidence from Foreign Bank Entry in Emerging Markets*, ECB Working Paper No. 498, June.

Gill, A. (2001) *Saints and Sinners, Who's Got Religion?*, CLSA Emerging Markets Report.

Gill, S. (2005) 'Constitutionalising Capital: EMU and Disciplinary Neo-Liberalism' in A. Bieler and D. A. Morton (eds), *Social Forces in the Making of the New Europe* New York: Palgrave.

Gills, B. K. (2000) 'The Crisis of Postwar East Asian Capitalism: American Power, Democracy and the Vicissitudes of Globalization', *Review of International Studies* Vol. 26, No. 3, 381–403.

Gilpin, R. (1987) *The Political Economy of International Relations*. Princeton: Princeton University Press.

Glyn, A. (2006) *Capitalism Unleashed Finance Globalization and Welfare*. Oxford: Oxford University Press.

Goldberg, L. (2002) 'When is U.S. Bank Lending to Emerging Markets Volatile?' in S. Edwards and J. Frankel (eds), *Preventing Currency Crises in Emerging Markets*. NBER Working Paper No. 8209.

Goldberg, L.G. and Grosse, R. (1994) 'Location Choice of Foreign Bank in the United States', *Journal of Economics and Business* 46(5), 367–79.

Goldberg, L.G. and Johnson, D. (1990) 'The Determinants of U.S. Banking Activity Abroad', *Journal of International Money and Finance* 9 (2), 123–37.

Goldberg, L.G. and Saunders, A. (1980) 'The Causes of U.S. Bank Expansion Overseas: The Case of Great Britain', *Journal of Money, Credit and Banking* 12(4), 630–43.

Goldberg, L.G. and Saunders, A. (1981a) 'The Determinants of Foreign Banking Activity in the United States', *Journal of Banking and Finance* 5(1), 17–32.

Goldberg, L.G. and Saunders, A. (1981b) 'The Growth of Organizational Forms of Foreign Banks in the U.S.: A Note', *Journal of Money, Credit and Banking* 13(3), 365–74.

Goldstein, A. and Schneider, B.R. (2004) 'Big Business in Brazil: States and Markets in the Corporate Reorganization of the 1990s', in E. Amann and H.J. Chang (eds), *Brazil and South Korea: Economic Crisis and Restructuring*. London: Institute of Latin American Studies.

Goldberg, L., Dages, B.G., and Kinney, D. (2000) 'Foreign and Domestic Bank Participation in Emerging Markets: Lessons from Mexico and Argentina', *Economic Policy Review* 6(3). Federal Reserve Bank of New York.

Gomez, E. T. (1999) *Chinese Business in Malaysia: Accumulation, Ascendance, Accommodation*. London: Curzon.

Gomez, E. T. (2004) 'Governance, Affirmative Action and Enterprise Development: Ownership and Control of Corporate Malaysia' in E.T. Gomez (ed.), *The State of Malaysia*: Ethnicity, Equity and Reform. London: RoutledgeCurzon.

Gomez, E. T. and Jomo K. S. (1999) *Malaysia's Political Economy: Politics Patronage and Profits*. Cambridge: Cambridge University Press.

Gomez, T. (2003) 'Corporate Malaysia under Mahathir: Where Have all the Capitalists Gone?', *Aliran Monthly* No. 10.

Gonçalves, R. (1999) *Globalização e Desnacionalização*. São Paulo: Paz e Terra.

Goskomstat (2000) *Rossiiskii statisticheskii ezhegodnik*, Moscow: Federal'naya Sluzhba Gosudarstvennoi Statistiki

Goskomstat (2004) Rossiiskii statisticheskii ezhegodnik. Moscow: Federal'naya Sluzhba Gosudarstvennoi Statistiki.

Gourevitch, P. (1986) *Politics in Hard Times: Comparative Responses to International Economic Crises*. Ithaca: Cornell University Press.

Government of Indonesia (1998) *Memorandum of Economic and Financial Policies*. 15 January.

Gowan, P. (1999) *The Global Gamble: Washington's Faustian Bid for Global Dominance*. London: Verso.

Gowan, P. (2004) 'The American Campaign for Global Sovereignty' in Panitch *et al.* (eds), *The Globalisation Decade: A Critical Reader*. London: The Merlin Press.

Graham, E.M. (2005) 'Breaking South Korea's 'Too Big to Fail' Doctrine', *The Asian Wall Street Journal*, 11 April.

Graham, J. R. (1999) 'Herding Among Investment Newsletters: Theory and Evidence', *The Journal of Finance* Vol. LIV (1), 237–68.

Greenspan, A. (1998) *The Current Asian Crisis and the Dynamics of International Finance: Testimony of Chairman Alan Greenspan* before the Committee on Foreign Relations, US Senate.

Gregory H. (2000) 'The Globalisation of Corporate Governance', *Global Counsel*, September, 52–65.

Group of 20 (2006) *About G-20*, Available: http://www.g20.org/Public/AboutG20/index.jsp.

Grugel, J. and Riggirozzi, M P. (2007) 'The Return of the State in Argentina', *Journal of International Affairs*, 83:1, 87–107.

Guimarães, P. (2002) 'How Does Foreign Entry Affect the Domestic Banking Market? The Brazilian Case', *Latin American Business Review* 3(4): 121–40.

Gustafson, T. (1989) 'Crisis Amid Plenty', The Politics of Soviet Energy Under Brezhnev and Gorbachev. Princeton: Princeton University Press.

Gustafson, T. (1999) *Capitalism Russian-Style*. Cambridge: Cambridge University Press.

Haber, S. and Musacchio, A. (2005) *Contract Rights and Risk Aversion: Foreign Banks and the Mexican Economy, 1997–2000*. Stanford University, Mimeo.

Haggard, S. (2000) *The Political Economy of the Asian Financial Crisis*. Washington: Institute for International Economics.

Haggard, S. (2005) 'The Evolution of Social Contracts in Asia', in R. Boyd and T.W. Ngo (eds), *Asian States: Beyond the Developmental Perspective*. London, Routledge.

Haggard, S. and Kaufman, R. (1992) *The Politics of Economic Adjustment*. Princeton: Princeton University Press.

Haggard, S. and Kaufman, R. (1994) 'Democratic Institutions, Economic Policy and Performance in Latin America', in C. Bradford (ed.), *Redefining the State in Latin America*. Paris: OECD.

Haggard, S. and Maxfield, S. (1996) 'The Political Economy of Financial Liberalization in the Developing World', in H. Milner and R. Keohane (eds), *Internationalization and Domestic Politics*. Cambridge University Press.

Hagmayr, B. and Haissi, P. (2006) *Foreign Banks in Turkey and Other EU Accession Countries – Does Minority vs. Majority Ownership Make the Difference?* Europainstitut, Vienna, 7 May.

Hahnel, R. (1999) 'The Great Global Asset Swindle', *ZNet Commentary*, 23 March.

Haley, M. A. (2001) 'Emerging Market Makers: The Power of Institutional Investors', in L. E. Armijo (ed.), *Financial Globalization and Democracy in Emerging Markets*. New York: Palgrave.

Hamilton-Hart., N. (2006) 'Consultants in the Indonesian State: Modes of Influence and Institutional Implications', *New Political Economy* 11(2).

Hanson, P. and Teague, E. (2005) 'Big Business and the State in Russia', *Europe–Asia Studies* 57(5), 657–79.

Harvey, D. (2003) *The New Imperialism*. Oxford: Oxford University Press.

Hass, R. and Naaborg, I. (2005) *Foreign Banks in Transition Economies: Small Business Lending and Internal Capital Markets*, De Nederlandsche Bank, Monetary and Economic Policy Division, Amsterdam.

Held, D. and Mcgrew A. (eds) (2002) *Governing Globalization: Power, Authority and Global Governance*. Cambridge: Polity Press.

Hertz, N. (2004) *The Debt Threat: How Debt Is Destroying the Developing World*. New York: Harper Business.

Hickey, J. (2003) 'Spot the Difference', *The Banker*, 3 November.

Higgott, R. (1998) 'The Asian Economic Crisis: A Study in the Politics of Resentment', *New Political Economy* Vol. 3, No. 3, 333–56.

Higgott, R. (2004) 'US Foreign Economic Policy and the Securitisation of Globalisation', *International Politics* 41, Summer, 147–75.

Hilferding, R. (1910) *Finance Capital*. London: Routledge.

Ho, K. L. (2005) 'Corporate Governance Reforms and the Management of the GLCs in Singapore: Pressures, Problems, and Paradoxes' in K.L. Ho (ed.), *Reforming Corporate Governance in Southeast Asia: Economics, Politics, and Regulations*. Singapore: ISEAS.

Holman, O. (2005) 'The Enlargement of the European Union towards Central and Eastern Europe: The Role of Supranational and Transnational Actors', in A. Bieler and D. A. Morton (eds), *Social Forces in the Making of the New Europe*. New York: Palgrave Macmillan.

Hughes, C. (2000) 'Japanese Policy and the East Asian Crisis: Abject Defeat or Quiet Victory?', *Review of International Political Economy* 7 (2), 241–58.

Hultman, C. W. and McGee, R. (1989) 'Factors Affecting the Foreign Banking Presence in the United States.', *Journal of Banking and Finance* 13(3), 383–96.

Hutton, W. (2006) 'UK for Sale, One Careless Owner: The Takeover of Great British Companies by Foreign Buyers Raises Not a Whimper of Protest', *Observer*, 12 February.

Hyde, M. (2001) 'Putin's Federal Reforms and their Implication for Presidential Power in Russia', *Europe–Asia Studies* 53 (5), 719–43.

ICGN (1999) 'Statement on Global Corporate Governance Principles', 9 July. Available: <http://www.icgn.org/documents/globalcorpgov.htm>

ICGN (2001) *ICGNews*, No. 1(5), March.

IDB (2004) *Country Program Evaluation (CPE) Argentina 1990–2002*, Office of Evaluation and Oversight, OVE, Washington: Inter-American Development Bank.

IEO [Independent Evaluation Office] (2003) *The IMF and Recent Capital Account Crises: Indonesia, Korea and Brazil.*

IHT (2006) 'Asia Joins Europe and the US in Private Equity Boom', 21 December.

Illarionov, A. (2005) Press conference, 21 December. Avaliable:

IMF (1997) *World Economic Outlook Supplement: Interim Assessment.*

IMF (1999) Malaysia selected issues.

IMF (2001a) *Assessing the Determinants and Prospects for the Pace of Market Access by Countries Emerging from Crises*, Policy Development and Review Department.

IMF (2001b) *International Capital Markets: Developments. Prospects, and Key Policy Issues.*

IMF (2001c) *IMF Approves $3.1 Billion Disbursement to Turkey, Calls for Strong Economic response*, 2001, IMF Survey, 10 December.

IMF (2002) *Global Financial Stability.*

IMF (2004) *Letter of Intent*, available: <http://www.imf.org/External/NP/LOI/2004/arg/01/index.htm>.

IMF (2005) *The Standards and Codes Initiative: Is it Effective? And How Can it be Improved?'*. Washington, DC: IMF.

Jayasuriya, K. (2001) 'Southeast Asia's Embedded Mercantilism in Crisis: International Strategies and Domestic Coalitions', Southeast Asia Research Centre Working Paper Series No. 3.

Jayasuriya K. and Rosser A. (2006) 'Pathways from the Crisis: Politics and Reform in South-East Asia Since 1997' in G. Rodan *et al.* (eds), *The Political Economy of Southeast Asia: Markets, Power and Contestation*. Melbourne: Oxford University Press.

Jenkins, R. (2000) *Democratic Politics and Economic Reform in India*. Cambridge: Cambridge University Press.

Jensen, N. M. (2006) *Nation-States and the Multinational Corporation: A Political Economy of Foreign Direct Investment*. Princeton: Princeton University Press.

Jesover F. and Kirkpatrick G. (2003) 'The Revised OECD Principles of Corporate Governance and Their Relevance to Non-OECD Countries', *Corporate Governance*, 13 (2), 127–36.

Jesudason, J. (1989) *Ethnicity and the Economy: The States, Chinese Business, and Multinationals in Malaysia*. Singapore: Oxford University Press.

Jesudason, J. (1996) 'The Syncretic State and the Structuring of Oppositional Politics in Malaysia', in G. Rodan (ed.), *Political Opposition in Industrialising Asia*. London: Routledge.

Johnson, C. (2000) *Blowback: The Costs and Consequences of American Empire.* London: Little, Brown and Company.

Johnson, J. (1998) 'Russia's Emerging Financial Industrial Groups', *Post-Soviet Affairs*, 13 (4), 335–65.

Johnson, S. and Kroll, H. (1991) 'Managerial Strategies For Spontaneous Privatization', *Soviet Economy* 7 (4), 281–316.

Johnson, S. *et al.* (2006) 'Malaysian Capital Controls: Macroeconomics and Enstitutions', IMF Working paper WP/06/51.

Jomo, K. S. (2004) 'Were Malaysia's Capital Controls Effective?'in K.S. Jomo (ed.), *After the Storm: Crisis, Recovery and Sustaining Development in Four Asian Economies.* Singapore: Singapore University Press.

Jomo, K. S. *et al.* (1997) *Southeast Asia's Misunderstood Miracle*, Boulder: Westview.

Kager, M. (2002) *The Banking System in the Accession Countries on the Eve of EU Entry*, Department of Economics, Bank of Austria 2/2002.

Kapstein, E. and Rodrik D. (2001) *Did the Malaysian Capital Controls Work*, Harvard University, Department of Government, Mimeo.

Katada, S. (2001) 'Determining factors in Japan's Co-operation and Non Co-operation with the United States', in A. Miyashita and Y. Sato (eds), *Japanese Foreign Policy in Asia and the Pacific: Domestic Interests, American Pressure and Regional Integration.* New York: Palgrave.

Kato, G. (2005) 'Forestry Sector Reform and Distributional Change of Natural Resource Rent in Indonesia', *The Developing Economies* 41(1), 149–70.

Kaufman, R. and Stallings B. (1989) 'Debt and Democracy in the 1980s: The Latin American Experience', in B. Stallings and R. Kaufman (eds), *Debt and Democracy in Latin America.* Boulder: Westview.

Kay, S. J. (2003) *Pension Reform and Political Risk*, paper prepared for the LASA XXIV International Congress, Dallas, 27–29 March.

Khoo, B. T. (2004) *Beyond Mahathir: Malaysian Politics and its Discontents.* London: Zed Books.

Kindlberger, C. (1978) *Manias, Panics, and Crashes.* New York: John Wiley.

Kirshner, J. (2004) 'Currency and Coercion in the Twenty-First Century', paper presented at the International Studies Association Annual Meeting, Montreal, 17–20 March.

Koh, P. (2006) *'Turkey's Banks Put M&A Centre Stage, Euromoney*, May.

Kolesnikov-Jessop, S. (2004) 'Analysis: the Return of Malaysian GLCs', *The Washington Times*, 28 September.

Kornai, J. (1992) *The Socialist System. The Political Economy of Communism.* Oxford: Clarendon Press.

Kotkin, S. (2001) *Armageddon Averted. The Soviet Collapse 1970–2000.* Oxford: Oxford University Press.

Krippner, G. (2004) 'What is Financialization?', mimeo, Department of Sociology, UCLA.

Krongkaew, M. (2003) Interview, Professor of Economics, National Institute of Development Administration, Bangkok, 3 April.

Krueger, A. (2002a) 'Should Countries like Argentina Be Able to Declare Themselves Bankrupt?', *El Pais*, 18 January.

Krueger, A. (2002b) *Crisis Prevention and Resolution: Lessons from Argentina*, paper presented at National Bureau of Economic Research Conference, 17 July.

Krueger, A. (2005) 'Turkey's Economy – A Future Full of Promise', speech by the First Deputy Managing Director of the IMF. Istanbul Forum, Istanbul , Turkey, 5 May.

Krugman, P. (1999) *The Return Of Depression Economics*. New York: Norton, 1999.

Lacerda, A.C. (ed.) (2000) *Desnacionalização: Mitos, Riscos e Desafios*. São Paulo: Editora Contexto.

Lachman, D. (2004) 'Chasing Yield?', *International* Economy, Spring, 61–3.

Lane, D. and Seifulmulukov, I. (1999) 'Structure and Ownership', in D. Lane (ed.), *The Political Economy of Russian Oil*. Lanham: Rowman and Littlefield Publishers.

Langley P. (2004a) '(Re)Politicizing Global Financial Governance: What's 'New' About the 'New International Financial Architecture'?', *Global Networks*, 4 (1), 69–87.

Langley, P. (2004b) 'In the Eye of the 'Perfect Storm': The Final Salary Pension Crisis and Financialisation of Anglo-American Capitalism', *New Political Economy* 9(4), 539–58.

Larsen F. (2002) 'The Global Architecture in Transition', *The OECD Observer*, January, 10–12.

Lee, Y. H. (1997) *The State, Society and Big Business in Korea*. London: Routledge.

Lehman, H. and McCoy, J. (1992) 'The Dynamics of the Two-Level Bargaining Game: The 1988 Brazilian Debt Negotiations', *World Politics* 44(4), 600–44.

Levine, R. (1996) 'Foreign Banks, Financial Development, and Economic Growth' in E. B. Claude (ed.), *International Financial Markets*. Washington: AEI Press.

Levine, R. (1999) *Foreign Bank Entry and Capital Control Liberalization: Effects on Growth and Stability*. University of Minnesota, mimeo.

Levy Y, E. and Micco, A. (forthcoming) 'Concentration and Foreign Penetration in Latin American Banking Sectors: Impact on Competition and Risk', *Journal of Banking and Finance*.

Lincoln, E. (2005) Interview, Senior Fellow, Council on Foreign Relations, Washington, DC, 22 June.

Linnan, D. (1999) 'Insolvency Reform and the Indonesian Financial Crisis', *Bulletin of Indonesian Economic Studies* 35(2), 107–37.

Liu, H, (2003) 'How Turkey's Goose Was Cooked, *Asian Times*.

Lustiñg, N. (1997) 'Latin American Economic Policies', *Newsletter of the Office of the Chief Economist, Inter-American Development Bank*, Third Quarter. Washington: IDB.

Machinea, J. L. (2002) 'La Crisis de La Deuda, El Financiamiento Internacional y la Participación del Sector Privado', *Serie Financiamiento del Desarollo*, No. 117, CEPAL.

MacIntyre, A. (1993) 'The Politics of Finance in Indonesian Economic Development: Command Confusion and Competition', in S. Haggard, C. Lee and S. Maxfield (eds), *The Politics of Finance in Developing Countries*. Ithaca: Cornell University Press.

MacIntyre, A. (2000) 'Funny Money: Fiscal Policy, Rent-seeking and Economic Performance in Indonesia' in M. H. Khan and K. S. Jomo (eds), *Rents, Rent-Seeking and Economic Development: Theory and Evidence in Asia*. Cambridge: Cambridge University Press.

Madslien, J, (2006), *Robust Economy Raises Turkey's Hopes*. BBC World Service, 2 November.

Manzetti, L. (2002) 'The Argentine Implosion', *The North–South Agenda* 59, available: http://www.miami.edu/nsc/publications/Papers&Reports/Argentine Implosion.html.

Martinez Peria, M. S. and Mody, A. (2004) 'How Foreign Participation and Market Concentration Impact Bank Spreads: Evidence from Latin America', *Journal of Money, Credit, and Banking* 36(3), 511–37.

Martinez Peria, M. S., Powell, A. and Vladkova-Hollar, I. (2005) 'Banking on Foreigners: The Behavior of International Bank Claims on Latin America, 1985–2000', *IMF Staff Paper* 53(3). Washington, DC.

Martinez-Diaz, L. (2005) *Banking-Sector Liberalization in Mexico and Argentina: Explaining The Timing And Style Of Financial Opening*, paper presented for the 10th Annual Conference of the Latin America and Caribbean Economic Association.

Marx, D. (2003) *Sovereign Debt Restructuring: The Upcoming Case of Argentina*, Buenos Aires: AGM Finanzas.

Masnatta, M. (2005) Interview, Programme Officer. UNDP Latin America and Caribbean. Buenos Aires. 16 December.

Mathieson, D. J. and Roldós, J. (2001) 'Foreign Bank in Emerging Markets', in R.E. Litan, P. Masson, and M. Pomerleano (eds), *Open Doors: Foreign Participation in Financial Systems in Developing Countries*. Washington, DC: Brooking Institution Press.

McGovern, Daniel (2003) 'Different Market Windows on Sovereign Debt: Private-sector Credit from the 1980s to the Present', in V. Aggarwal and B. Granville (eds), *Sovereign Debt: Origins, Crises, and Restructuring*. London: Royal Institute of International Affairs.

McKeeby, D. and Geis, J., (2000) 'Tackling Turkey's 'Corrupt Quadrangle?', The *Turkish Update*. The Center for Strategic and International Studies, 14 December.

McKinnon, R. I. (1992) 'Taxation, Money, and Credit in a Liberalizing Socialist Economy', in C. Clague and G. Rausser (eds), *The Emergence of Market Economies in Eastern Europe*. Oxford: Blackwell.

McLeod, R. (2005) 'The Struggle to Regain Effective Government Under Democracy in Indonesia', *Bulletin of Indonesian Economic Studies* 41(3), 367–86.

Mendonça de Barros and Goldenstein, L. (1997) 'Avaliação do processo de reestruturação industrial brasileiro', *Revista de Economia Política* 17(2), 11–31.

Merrill Lynch (2004) *EU Enlargement Study*, March.

Mesquita, Moreira (2000) 'Capital nacional na indústria: reestruturar para sobreviver', in A. C. Lacerda (ed.), *Desnacionalização: Mitos, Riscos e Desafios*, São Paulo: Editora Contexto.

Mian, A. (2006) 'Distance Constraints: The Limits of Foreign Lending in Poor Economies', *Journal of Finance* 61(3), 1465–1505.

Micco, A., Panizza, U. and Yañez, M. (Forthcoming) 'Bank Ownership and Performance: Does Politics Matter?', *Journal of Banking and Finance*.

Milanovic, B. (1998) *Income, Inequality, and Poverty during the Transition from Planned to Market Economy*. Washington, DC: World Bank.

Milios, J. (2005) 'European Integration as a Vehicle of Neoliberal Hegemony' in A.S. Filho and D. Johnston (eds), *Neoliberalism: A Critical Reader*. Pluto London.

Miller, M. and Thomas, D. (2006) 'Sovereign Debt Restructuring: The Judge, The Vultures and Creditor Rights', *CSGR Working Paper 202/06*. University of Warwick, April.

Miller, S. R. and Parkhe, A. (1998) 'Patterns on the Expansion of U.S. Banks' Foreign Operations', *Journal of International Business Studies* 29(2), 359–90.

Millstein I. (ed.) (n.d.) 'Improving Corporate Governance', Comments at *Executive Policy Seminar Series*. Available: http://faculty.mb.edu/prog/cmrc/seminars/millstein.html.

Milne, R. and D. Mauzy (1999) *Malaysian Politics under Mahathir*. London: Routledge.

Ministerio, de Economia (2005) *Informe Económico*, Available: <http://www.mecon.gov.ar/analisis_economico/nro4/capitulo1.pdf> (accessed 11 July 2006).

Momani, B. (2005) 'Recruiting and Diversifying IMF Technocrats', *Global Society*, Vol. 19, No. 2, April, pp. 167–87.

Montgomerie, J. (2006). 'The Financialization of Consumption: Consumer Debt in a Finance-Led Growth Regime'. IPEG Working Paper.

Moravcsik, A. (1998). *The Choice for Europe: Social Purpose and State Power from Messina to Maastricht*. Ithaca: Cornell University Press.

Moreno, R. and Villar, A. (2004) 'The Increased Role of Foreign Bank Entry in Emerging Markets', *Bank of International Settlements*, Paper No. 23.

Morris, C. (2001a) *Analysis: Turkey's Costly Political Row*, BBC World Service, 20 February.

Morris, C. (2001b) *Turkey Frees Central Bank from Politics*, BBC World Service, 25 April.

Moser, N. and Oppenheimer, P. (2001) 'The Oil Industry: Structural Transformation And Corporate Governance', in B. Granville and P. Oppenheimer (eds), *Russia's Post-Communist Economy*. Oxford: Oxford University Press.

Mosley, L. (2003) *Global Capital and National Governments*. Cambridge: Cambridge University Press.

Murillo, M. V. (1997) 'Union Politics, Market-oriented Reforms, and the Reshaping of Argentine Corporatism', in D. Chalmers (ed.), *The New Politics of Inequality in Latin America*. Oxford: Oxford University Press.

Mussa, M. (2002) *Argentina and the Fund: From Triumph to Tragedy*. Washington, DC: Institute for International Economics.

Mussa, M. and Hache, G. (1998) 'Take the IMF Medicine and You Will Soon Mend', *International Herald Tribune*, 17–18, 6 January.

Naaborg, I. Scholtens, B. Haan, J. Bol, H. and Hass, R. (2004) 'How Important are Foreign Banks in the Financial Development of European Transition Countries', Journal of Emerging Market Finance 3:2, 100–23.

Nagel, S. (2004) *Country Report: Malaysia 2004. School of Advanced International Studies Country Risk Reports*. Washington, DC: John's Hopkins University.

Nazli, H. (2004) 'Banking on Turkey', *The National Interest*, Winter.

Nelson, J. (1990) *Economic Crisis and Policy Choice: The Politics of Adjustment in the Third World*. Princeton, NJ: Princeton University Press.

Nelson, J. (1994) *A Precarious Balance: An Overview of Democracy and Economic Reforms in Eastern Europe and Latin America*. San Francisco: International Center for Economic Growth and Overseas Development Council.

Nesadurai, H. (2000) 'In Defence of National Autonomy? Malaysia's Response to the Financial Crisis', *Pacific Review* 13(1), 73–113.

Nesvetailova, A. (2004) 'Coping in the Global Financial System: The Political Economy of Nonpayment in Russia', *Review of International Political Economy*, 11(5), 995–1021.

Nigh, D., Cho, K. R. and Krishnan, S. (1986) 'The Role of Location-Related Factors in U.S. Banking Involvement Abroad: An Empirical Analysis', *Journal of International Business Studies* 17, 59–72.

Noland, M. (2002) 'Economic Reform in South Korea: An Unfinished Legacy', Paper prepared for the conference 'Korea as a 21st Century Power'. University of Cambridge, 3–6 April.

Nölke A. (2004) 'Transnational Private Authority and Corporate Governance' in S. Schirm (ed.), *New Rules for Global Markets: Public and Private Governance in the World Economy*. London: Palgrave.

Norris F. (2004) 'Feud Over Workers' Role in Management Stalls OECD Project', *International Herald Tribune*, 27 March.

O'Brien, R. and Williams, M. (2004) *Global Political Economy: Evolution and Dynamics*. Basmostoke: Palgrave.

O'Donnell, G. (1994) 'Delegative Democracy', *Journal of Democracy* 5(1), 55–69.

OECD (1999) *OECD Principles of Corporate Governance*, Paris.

OECD (2001), *Brazil – OECD Economic Surveys*. Paris.

OECD (2003) *Experiences From the Regional Corporate Governance Roundtables*. Paris: OECD.

OECD (2004a) *Comments Received from Web Consultations*. Paris.

OECD (2004b) *OECD Principles of Corporate Governance*. Paris.

OECD (2006) *OECD Economic Outlook*, Vol. 2, No. 80.

Önis Z. (2006) *Beyond the 2001 Financial Crisis: The Political Economy of the New Phase of Neoliberal Restructuring in Turkey*. Available: <http://home.ku.edu.tr.>.-LOVE IDB (2004)

Özatay, F. and Sak, G. (2003) *Banking Sector Fragility and Turkey's 2000–01 Financial Crisis*, Research Department Discussion Paper, The Central Bank of the Republic of Turkey, Ankara, December.

Packer, F. and Chamaree, S. (2003) 'Sovereign Credit Default Swaps', *BIS Quarterly Review*, December, 79– 88.

Padoa-Schioppa, T. (2004). Member of the executive Board of the European Central Bank, Speech delivered at Colloquium Organized by Group Caisse Des Depots, Berlin, 22 March.

Paidiev, L. (2006) *Stabilizatsionnii fond. kopit' ili tratit'*. Moscow: Evropa.

Panzar, J. C. and Rose, J. N. (1987) 'Testing for "Monopoly" Equilibrium', *Journal of Industrial Economics* 35, 443–57.

Pastor, M. and Wise, C. (2004) 'Picking Up the Pieces: Comparing the Social Impacts of Financial Crisis in Mexico and Argentina', paper prepared for the CIGI-20 Meeting. Buenos Aires: Flacso, 20–21 May.

Paula, L. F. and Alves, Jr., A. J. (2003) 'Banking Behaviour and the Brazilian Economy After the Real Plan: a Post-Keynesian Approach', *BNL Quarterly Review* 227: 337–65.

Pazarbaşiğlu, C. (2005) 'Accession to the European Union: Potential impacts on the Turkish banking sector', in B. Hoekman and S. Togan (eds), *Turkey: Economic Reform and Accession to the European Union*. Washington: World Bank.

Peek, J. and Rosengren, E. (2000) 'Implications of the Globalization of the Banking Sector: The Latin American Experience', *New England Economic Review*, September/October. Federal Reserve Bank of Boston.

Peet, R. (2003) *Unholy Trinity: The IMF, World Bank and WTO*. London: Zed Books.

Perry, G. and Serven L. (2002) 'The Anatomy of a Multiple Crisis: Why Was Argentina Special and What Can We Learn from It?', background paper for the NBER Project on Exchange Rate Crises in Emerging Markets: the Argentina Crisis.

Peruzzotti, E. (2001) 'The Nature of the New Argentine Democracy. The Delegative Democracy Argument Revisited'. *Journal of Latin American Studies* 33(1), 133–55.

Peruzzotti, E. and Smulowitz, C. (2003) 'Societal and Horizontal Controls: Two Cases of a Fruitful Relationship', in G. S. Mainwaring, and C. Welna (eds), *Democratic Accountability in Latin Amreica*. Oxford: Oxford University Press.

Phillips, K. (1994) *Arrogant Capital: Washington, Wall Street and the Frustration of American Politics*. New York: Little Brown.

Phongpaichit, P. and Baker, C. (2001) 'Thailand's Thaksin: New Populism or Old Cronyism', *Report Prepared for the East Asian Institute*, 25 October.

Pincus, J. and Ramli, R. (1998) 'Indonesia: from Showcase to Basket Case', *Cambridge Journal of Economics* 22(6), 723–34.

Pincus, J. and Ramli, R. (2004) 'Deepening or Hollowing Out: Financial Liberalization, Accumulation and Indonesia's Economic Crisis', in K.S. Jomo (ed.), *After the Storm: Crisis, Recovery and Sustaining Development in Four Asian Economies*. Singapore: Singapore University Press.

Pirie, I. (2005) 'Better by Design: Korea's Neoliberal Economy', *Pacific Review*, 18, 3, 1–20.

Pittman II, P. M. (2003) *Turkey: A Country Study, US Library of Congress*, Washington, DC.

Poon, J. and Thompson, E. R. (2001) 'Effects of the Asian Financial Crisis on Transnational Capital', *Geoforum* 32, 121–31.

Porter, T. (2005) 'The Democratic Deficit in the Institutional Arrangements for Regulating Global Finance' in R. Wilkinson (ed.), *The Global Governance Reader*. London: Routledge.

Porzecanski, A. (2005) 'Dealing with Sovereign Debt: Trends and Implications', in C. Jochnick and F. Preston (eds), *Sovereign Debt at the Crossroads*. New York: Oxford University Press.

Porzecanski, A. (2006) 'Dealing with Sovereign Debt: Trends and Implications', in C. Jochnick and F. Preston (eds), *Sovereign Debt at the Crossroads*. New York: Oxford University Press.

Putucheary, J. (1960) *Ownership and Control in the Malaysian Economy*. Singapore: University of Malaya Press.

Pyle, W. (2006) 'Collective Action and Post-Communist Enterprise: The Economic Logic of Russia's Business Associations', *Europe–Asia Studies* 58(4), 491–522 and *Post-Communist Studies*, 35(2), 135–60.

Racocha, P. (2003) 'Joining the EU – Impact on the Financial Sector of New Member States', *National Europe Centre*, Working Paper No. 117.

Radygin, A. (2004) 'Rossiya v 2000–2004: na puti k gosudarstvennomu kapitalizmu?', *Voprosy ekonomki*, (4), 42–65.

Ranciere, R. G. (2001) 'Credit Derivatives in Emerging Markets', *International Monetary Fund Development Policy Paper*. Washington: IMF.

Rathkolb, O. Venus, T. and Zimmerl, U. (eds) (2005). Bank Austria Creditanstalt, 150 Jahre österreichische Bankengeschichte im Zentrum Europas, Viena Austria

Ratnam, K. (1965) *Communalism and the Political Process in Malaysia*. Singapore: University of Malaya Press.

Reinhart, C., Rogoff, K. and Savastano, M. (2003) 'Debt Intolerance', *Brookings Papers on Economic Activity* 1, 1–59.

Reininger, T., Schardax, F., and Summer, M. (2001) 'The Financial System in the Czech Republic, Hungary and Poland after a Decade of Transition', *Economic Research Centre, The Deutsche Bundesbank Working Paper* 16/01.

Rice-Oxley, M. (2006) 'Why Britain Welcomes Foreign Takeovers', *The Christian Science Monitor*, 19 May.

Rieffel, L. (2003) *Restructuring Sovereign Debt: The Case for Ad Hoc Machinery*. Washington: Brookings Institution Press.

Rieffel, L. (2004) 'Indonesia's Quiet Revolution', *Foreign Affairs* September/October.

Riesenhuber, E. (2001) *The International Monetary Fund Under Constraint: Legitimacy of Its Crisis Management*. The Hague, Kluwer Law International.

Robertson, J. (2007) 'Reconsidering American Interests in Emerging Market Crises: An Unanticipated Outcome to the Asian Financial Crisis', *Review of International Political Economy*, 14, 2, 276–305.

Robinson, N. (1999) 'The Global Economy, Reform and Crisis in Russia', *Review of International Political Economy*, 6(4), 531–64.

Robinson, N. (2001) 'The Myth of Equilibrium: Winner Power, Fiscal Crisis and Russian Economic Reform', *Communist and Post-Communist Studies* 34 (4), 423–46.

Robinson, N. (2004) 'Global Economy, the USSR and Post-Soviet Change', in N. Robinson (ed.), *Reforging the Weakest Link. Global Political Economy and Post-Soviet Change in Russia, Ukraine and Belarus*. Aldershot: Ashgate.

Robison, R. (1986) *Indonesia: The Rise of Capital*. Sydney: Allen & Unwin.

Robison, R. (1997) 'Politics and markets in Indonesia's Post-Oil Era', in G. Rodan, K. Hewison and R. Robison (eds), *The Political Economy of Southeast Asia*: Oxford: Oxford University Press.

Robison, R. (2001) 'The Politics of Financial Reform: Recapitalising Indonesia's Banks, Murdoch University, Mimeo.

Robison, R. and Rosser (2000) 'Surviving the Meltdown: Liberal Reform and Political Oligarchy in Indonesia', in R. Robison, M. Beeson, K. Jayasuriya and H.-R. Kim (eds), *Politics and Markets in the Wake of The Asian Crisis*. London: Routledge.

Robison, R. and Hadiz V. (2004) *Reorganising Power in Indonesia: The Politics of Oligarchy in an Age of Markets*. London: RoutledgeCurzon.

Robison, R., Beeson, M., Jayasuriya, K. and Kim, H.R. (eds) (2000) *Politics and Markets in the Wake of the Asian Crisis*. London: Routledge.

Rock, M. T. (1999) 'Reassessing the Effectiveness of Industrial Policy in Indonesia: Can the Neo-Liberals be Wrong?', *World Development* 27(4), 691–704.

Rodan, G. (2004) *Transparency and Authoritarian Rule in Southeast Asia: Singapore and Malaysia*. London: RoutledgeCurzon.

Rodan, G., Hewison, K. and Robison, R. (eds) (2001) *The Political Economy of South-East Asia: Conflicts, Crises and Change*. Melbourne: Oxford University Press.

Rodrik, D. (2004) 'Rethinking Economic Policies in the Developing World', Luca d'Agliano Lecture in Development Economics, 8 October, Torino, Italy.

Rosser, A. (2003a) 'Governance, Markets and Power: The Political Economy of Accounting Reform in Indonesia', in G.R.D. Underhill and X. Zhang (eds), *International Financial Governance Under Stress: Global Structures Versus National Imperatives*. Cambridge: Cambridge University Press.

Rosser, A. (2003b) 'Coalitions, Convergence and Corporate Governance Reform in Indonesia', *Third World Quarterly* 24(2), 319–38.

Rosser, A. (2005) 'The Political Economy of Corporate Governance in Indonesia', in K. L. Ho (ed.), *Reforming Corporate Governance in Southeast Asia: Economics, Politics, and Regulations*. Singapore: ISEAS.

Rozenwurcel, G. (2006) Interview, Profesor at School of Politics and Government, University of San Martin, Argentina and Researcher at CONICET (National Council of Scientific and Technical Research). 7 June.

Roubini, N. and Seltser, B. (2004) *Bailouts or Bail-ins?: Responding to Financial Crises in Emerging Economies*. Washington: Institute of International Economics.

Ruatava, J. (2002) *The Role of Oil Prices and The Real Exchange Rate in Russia's Economy*. Helsinki: Bank of Finland Institute for Economic in Transition Discussion Papers, 3.

Rubin, R. (1998) *Testimony Before the Committee on Banking and Financial Services Hearing on East Asia-Economic Conditions, Part 2*, US House of Representatives, January 30, Washington, D.C.

Rubin, R. and Weisberg, J. (2003) *In an Uncertain World: Tough Choices from Washington to Wall Street*. New York: Thomson Texere.

Sachs, J. D. (1995) 'Consolidating Capitalism', *Foreign Policy*, Spring: 50–64.

Sako, M. (2003) 'Modularity and Outsourcing: The Nature of Coevolution of Product Architecture and Organization Architecture in the Global Automotive Industry', in A. Prencipe, A. Davies and A. Hobday (eds), *The Business of Systems Integration*. Oxford: Oxford University Press.

Sako, M. (2005) 'Administrando Parques Industrialis de Autopeças no Brasil: Uma Comparação Entre Resende, Gravatai e Camaçari', *Caderno CRH* 19(46), 63–76. Salvador.

Sakwa, R. (2004) *Putin: Russia's Choice*. London: Routledge.

Şanli, K. (2006) 'Banking Competition to Bring 15,000 New Jobs', *Turkish Daily News – Online Edition*, 28 December.

Santiso, J. (2003) *The Political Economy of Emerging Markets: Actors, Institutions, and Financial Crises in Latin America*. New York: Palgrave.

Sarti, F. and Laplane, M. (2002) 'O investimento direto estrangeiro e a internacionalzação da economia brasileira nos anos 1990', *Economia e Sociedade, Campinas*, 11(1–18), 63–94.

Sassen, S. (2002) 'Globalization and the State', in R.B. Hall and T. Biersteker (eds), *The Emergence of Private Authority in Global Governance*. Cambridge: Cambridge University Press.

Sato, Y. (2005) 'Bank Restructuring and Financial Institution Reform in Indonesia', *The Developing Economies* 43(1), 91–120.

Schmitz, B. (2004) *What Role Do Banks Play in Monetary Policy Transmission in EU New Member Countries?*, Centre for European Integration Studies, University of Bonn.

Schneider, B. (2003) 'Implications of Implementing Standards and Codes: A Developing Country Perspective', in B. Schneider (ed.), The Road to *International Financial Stability: Are Key Financial Standards the Answer?*. London: Palgrave.

Scholte, J.A. (2000) *Globalization: A Critical Introduction*. Basingstoke: Palgrave Macmillan.

Schorr, M. (2005) 'La Industria Argentina: Trayectoria Reciente y Desafíos Futuros', paper presented at the seminar 'Hacia el Plan Fénix II. En vísperas del segundo centenario', Facultad de Ciencias Económicas (UBA), Buenos Aires: Argentina, 2–5 August.

Schorr, and Wanner, (2005).

Schulz, H. (2006) 'Foreign Banks in Mexico: New Conquistadors or Agents of Change?', *The Wharton School, Financial Institutions Center, Working Paper*, No. 06–11. University of Pennsylvania.

Schwarz, A. (1999) *A Nation in Waiting: Indonesia's Search for Stability*. Boulder, Westview.

Scott, H. S. (2006) 'Sovereign Debt Defaults: Cry for the United States, Not Argentina', *Washington Legal Foundation, Working Paper Series*, No. 140.

Seabrooke, L. (2001) *US Power in International Finance; The Victory of Dividends*. New York: Palgrave.

Searle, P. (1999) *The Riddle of Malaysian Capitalism: Rent-seekers or Real Capitalists?*. Honolulu: University of Hawaii Press.

Setser, B. and Gelpern A. (2004) 'Argentina's Pathway through Financial Crisis, Global Economic Governance Programme', *Working Paper 2004/02*, Department of Politics and International Studies, University College, Oxford.

Shamsul, A. B. (1987) 'The Battle Royal: The UNMO Election of 1987', *Southeast Asian Affairs 1988*. Singapore: Institute for Southeast Asian Studies.

Shlapentokh, V. (2004) 'Wealth Versus Political Power: the Russian case', *Communist and Post-Communist Studies*, 35(2), 135–60.

SINDIPECAS (2006) *Informativo SINDIPEÇAS*, São Paulo.

Singh, A. (1998) 'Savings Investment and The Corporation in the East Asian Miracle', *Journal of Development Studies* 34(6), 112–37.

Singh, M. (2003) 'Recovery Rates from Distressed Debt – Empirical Evidence from Chapter 11 Fillings, International Litigation, and Recent Sovereign Debt Restructurings', *IMF Working Paper*, No. 03/161.

Slater, D. (2004) 'Indonesia's Accountability Trap: Party Cartels and Presidential Power After Democratic Transition', *Indonesia* 78, 61–92.

Soederberg S. (2001) 'The New International Financial Architecture: Imposed Leadership and "Emerging Markets",' in L. Panitch and C. Leys (eds), *Socialist Register 2002: A World of Contradictions*. London: Merlin Press.

Soederberg S. (2003) 'The Promotion of "Anglo-American" Corporate Governance in the South: Who Benefits From the New International Standard', *Third World Quarterly*, 24(1), 7–27.

Soederberg, S. (2004) *The Politics of the New International Financial Architecture: Reimposing Neoliberal Domination in the Global South*. London: Zed Books.

Soederberg, S. (2005) 'The Transnational Debt Architecture and Emerging Markets: The Politics of Paradoxes and Punishment', *Third World Quarterly* 26(6), 927–49.

Sohn, C.-H. and Yang J. (eds). (1998) *Korea's Economic Reform Measures Under the IMF Program: Government Measures in the Critical First Six Months of the Korean Economic Crisis*. Seoul: Korea Institute for International Economic Policy.

Stallings, B. (1992) 'International Influence on Economic Policy', in S. Haggard and R. Kaufman (eds), *The Politics of Economic Adjustment*. Princeton: Princeton University Press.

Standard and Poor's (2004) 'Corporate Governance Scores – Frequently Asked Questions', Available: <www.standardandpoors.com>.

Steil, B. (2007) 'Digital Gold and a Flawed Global Order', *Financial Times*, 5 January.

Steil, B. and Litan, R. E. (2006) *Financial Statecraft: The Role of Financial Markets in American Foreign Policy*. New Haven: Yale University Press.

Stiglitz, J. (2002) 'Argentina, Shortchanged: Why the Nation that Followed the Rules Fell to Pieces', *Washington Post*, 12 May.

Stiglitz, J. (2002) *Globalization and its Discontents*. London: Penguin.

Strange, S. (1988) *States and Markets*. London: Pinter Publishers.

Strange, S. (1998) *Mad Money*. Manchester: Manchester University Press.

Sturzenegger, F. and Zettelmeyer, J. (2004) 'Haircuts', *Universidad Tocuato di Tella and IMF mimeo.*

Summers, L. (1996) 'US Policy Towards the International Monetary System on the Eve of the Lyon Summit', remarks to Emerging Markets Traders Association, 24 June.

Summers, L. (1999) 'Reflections on Managing Global Integration', Distinguished Lecture on Economics in Government, *Journal of Economic Perspectives*, Vol.13, No.2, Spring, 3–18.

Suzigan, W. and Furtado, J. (2006) 'Política industrial e desenvolvimento', *Revista de Economia Política*, 26(2), 163–85.

Svampa, M. and Pereyra, S. (2003) *Entre la Ruta y el Barrio. La Experiencia de las Organizaciones Piqueteros.* Buenos Aires: Editorial Biblos.

Szapary, G. (2005) 'Development of Credit Markets in New Member States and Implications for the Transmission of Monetary Policy', paper presented in Finance and Consumption Conference, IUE, Florence, October.

Tadokoro, M. (2003) 'The Asian Financial Crisis and Japanese Policy Reactions', in G. Underhill and X. Zhang (eds), *International Financial Governance Under Stress: Global Structures Versus National Imperatives.* Cambridge: Cambridge University Press.

Tedesco, L. (2002) 'Argentina's Turmoil: The Politics of Informality and the Roots of Economic Meltdown', *Cambridge Review of International Affairs* 15(3), 469–81.

Teen, M. (2005) 'The Singapore Experience', *Intheblack* 75(11), December, 60–2.

Tegara-Hagiwara, A. and Pasadilla, G. (2004) 'Experience of Asian Asset-Management Companies: Do They Increase Moral Hazard? Evidence from Thailand', *ERD Working Paper Series*. Manila, ADB. 55.

Teichova, A. (1997) *Central Europe in the Twentieth Century: An Economic History Perspective where?.* UK: Scolar Press.

Teichova, A. (2005) 'Banking and Industry in Central–East Europe in the First Decades of the 20th Century', in O. Rathkolb, T. Venus, and Zimmerl, U. (eds), *Bank Austria Creditanstalt, 150 Jahre österreichische Bankengeschichte im Zentrum Europas*, Vienna.

The Banker (2005) 'Boom Time for CEE Banking', 3 October.

The Banker (2006) 'Retail Drives Sector Growth', 2 October.

The Economist (1995) 'The Return of the Habsburgs', 18 November.

The Economist (2006a) *The Chavez Play*, 28 October.

The Economist (2006b) *Turkey and Europe: The Blackballer's Club*, 16–22 December.

The Economist (2006c) *The New Number One*, 27 July.

The New York Times (2006) *Junk Bonds May Yet Earn Their Title*, 17 November.

The Wall Street Journal (2006) *How a Good Aim at Risky Debt Scored Big*, 5 September.

Thirkell-White, B. (2003). 'The IMF, Good Governance and Middle-Income Countries', *European Journal of Development Studies* 15(1), 99–125.

Thirkell-White, B. (2005a) *IMF and the Politics of Globalization: From the Asian Crisis to a New International Financial Architecture?* Basingstoke: Palgrave.

Thirkell-White, B. (2005b) 'The Wall-Street-Treasury-IMF Complex After Asia: Neoliberalism in Decline?', in R. Robison (ed.), *The Neo-liberal Revolution: Forging the Market State.* Basingstoke: Palgrave.

Tilly, R. (1986) 'German Banking 1850–1914: Development Assistance for the Strong', *Journal of European Economic History* 15, 1.

Tomassi , M. (2002) 'Federalism in Argentina and the Reforms of the 1990's', *Working Paper 147*, Center for Research on Economic Development and Policy Reform, Stanford University.

Topowrski, J. (2005) 'Neoliberalism: The Eastern European Frontier', in A. Saad-Filho and D. Johnston (eds), *Neoliberalism: A Critical Reader*. London: Pluto.

Tornquist, O. (2006) 'Assessing Democracy From Below: A Framework and Indonesian Pilot Study', *Democratization* 13(2).

Truman, T. (2003) Interview, Former Assistant Secretary of the U.S. Treasury and Staff Director of the Division of International Finance, Federal Reserve, Washington, DC, 11 September.

Tsatsaronis, K. (2000) 'Hedge Funds', *BIS Quarterly Review*, November, 61–71.

Tschoegl, A.E. (2003) 'Financial Crises and the Presence of Foreign Banks', *The Wharton School, Financial Institutions Center Working Paper*, 03–35.

TUAC (2003) *Initial Statement on the Review of the OECD Principles of Corporate Governance*, 19 September.

TUAC (2004) *TUAC Evaluation of the 2004 Review of the OECD Principles of Corporate Governance*, October.

TUAC (2005) 'Workers' Voice in Corporate Governance – A Trade Union Perspective', *Global Unions Discussion* Paper, October.

TUAC (2006) *Personal Communication*, 5 September.

Turkish Daily News (2006a) *Forget About Hot Money and Political Tension*, online edition, 14 July.

Turkish Daily News (2006b) *Turkey's Current Account Deficit Up to $12.5 Billion in Four Months*, online edition, 8 June.

Tussie, D. (2006) 'Regionalism Adrift: The End of Collective Action?, paper presented at 'Responding to Globalisation in the Americas' Workshop, LSE, 1 June.

Tussie, D. and Tuozzo M. F. (2002) 'Shooting for Reform: The Interplay of Domestic and External Constraints in Argentina', in H. Hveem, and K. Nordhaug (eds), *Public Policy in the Age of Globalisation: Responses to Environmental and Economic Crisis*. Basingstoke: Palgrave.

Twining, D. (2006) 'America is Pursuing a Grand Design in Asia', *Financial Times*, 24 September.

US house of Representatives (1998) *Hearing on Asia Trade Issues, Subcommittee On Trade of the Committee on Ways and Means*, 24 February.

Uiboupin, J. (2004) 'Effects of Foreign Banks Entry on Bank Performance in the CEE Countries', *Working Paper* No. 33-2004, University of Tartu Faculty of Economics and Business Administration.

Ulst, I. (2005) *Linkages of Financial Groups in the EU: Financial Conglomeration Developments in the Old and New Member States*. New York: CEU Press

UNCTAD (2000) *World Investment Report: Cross-border Mergers and Acquisitions and Development*. Geneva: United Nations Conference on Trade and Development.

UNCTAD (2005) *UNCTAD Investment Brief*, No. 4., Geneva: United Nations Conference on Trade and Development.

UNCTAD (2006) *World Investment Report 2006, FDI From Developing And Transition Economies: Implications For Development*. New York: UN Publications.

Underhill, G. (1997) 'Private Markets and Public Responsibility in a Global System: Conflict and Cooperation in Transnational Banking and Securities Regulation' in G. Underhill (ed.), *The New World Order in International Finance*. London: Macmillan.

Unicredit New Europe Research Network (2006). 'Banking in CEE and the Role of International Players', July.

Union Industrial Argentina (UIA) (2001) 'La Vision de la UIA sobre las Causas de la Depresion', Presentation, Washington, October.

Unite, A.A. and Sullivan, M. J. (2002) 'The Effect of Foreign Entry and Ownership Structure on the Philippine Domestic Banking Sector', *Journal of Banking and Finance* 27, 2249–71.

Ustinov, I.N. (2004) *Mezhdunarodnie ekonomicheskie otnosheniya Rossii. Entsiklopediya statisticheskaya*. Moscow: Ekonomika.

USTR [United States Trade Representative] (1997) *Trade Estimate Report on Foreign Trade Barriers*.

Utting P. (2003) 'Promoting Development Through Corporate Social Responsibility – Does it Work?', *Global Future*, 3rd Quarter, 11–13.

Van Agtmael, A. (2007) *The Emerging Markets Century*. New York: The Free Press.

Vernon, R. (1998) *In the Hurricane's Eye: The Troubled Prospects of Multinational Enterprises*. Cambridge: Cambridge University Press.

Wade, R. (1990) Governing the Market. Princeton: Princeton University Press.

Wade, R. (1996) 'Japan, the World Bank, and The Art of Paradigm Maintenance: The East Asian Miracle in Political Perspective', *New Left Review* 217, 3–37.

Wade, R. (1998) 'The Asian Debt-and-Development Crisis of 1997-?: Causes and Consequences', *World Development* Vol. 26, No. 8, 1535–53.

Wade, R.H. (2002) 'US Hegemony and the World Bank: The Fight over People and Idea', *Review of International Political Economy* Vol. 9, No. 2, 215–43.

Wade, R. and Veneroso, F. (1998) 'The Asian Crisis: The High Debt Model Versus The Wall Street-Treasury–IMF Complex', *New Left Review* 228, 3–23.

Walter, A. (2000) 'Globalisation and Policy Convergence: The Case of Direct Investment Rules' in R.A. Higgott, G.R.D. Underhill and A. Bieler (eds), *Non-State Actors and Authority in the Global System*. London: Routledge.

Walter, A. (2003) 'Implementation in East Asia' in B. Schneider (ed.), *The Road to International Financial Stability: Are Key Financial Standards the Answer?* London: Palgrave.

WB-Brooking (1999) 'The Crisis in Emerging Financial Markets: A World Bank Group-Brookings Conference Report'. Washington: Brookings Institution.

Weber, B. (2006) 'The Construction of the Single Market in Financial Services and the Politics of Inclusion and Exclusion' in: P. Mooslechner, H. Schuberth and B. Weber (eds), *The Political Economy of Financial Market Regulation: The Dynamics of Inclusion and Exclusion*. Cheltenham: Edward Elgar.

Weiss, L. (1997) 'Globalization and the Myth of the Powerless State', *New Left Review*, 225, 3–27.

Weiss, L. (1999) 'State Power and the Asian Crisis', *New Political Economy* Vol. 4, No. 3, 317–42.

Weiss, L. (2003) 'Guiding Globalization in East Asia: New Roles for Old Developmental States', in L. Weiss (ed.), *States in the Global Economy: Bringing Domestic Institutions Back In*. Cambridge: Cambridge University Press.

Whitley, R. (1999) *Divergent Capitalisms: The Social Structuring and Change of Business Systems*. Oxford: Oxford University Press.

Winters (1996) *Power in Motion: Capital Mobility and the Indonesian State*. Ithaca: Cornell University Press.

Winters, J.A. (2000) 'The Financial Crisis in Southeast Asia' in R. Robison, M. Beeson, K. Jayasuriya, and H.R. Kim (eds), *Politics and Markets in the Wake of the Asian Crisis*. London: Routledge.

Wolf, M. (2004) *Why Globalization Works*. New Haven: Yale University Press.

Woo, Jung-en. (1991) *Race to the Swift: State and Finance in Korean Industralization*. New York: Columbia University Press.

Woo-Cummings, M. (ed.) (1999) *The Developmental State*. Ithaca: Cornell University Press.

Woodruff, D. (2005) 'Boom, Gloom, Doom: Balance Sheets, Monetary Fragmentation, and the Politics of Financial Crisis in Argentina and Russia', Politics and Society 33(1), 3–45.

Woods, N. (2000) 'Making the IMF and World Bank More Accountable', *International Affairs* 77(1), 83–100.

World Bank (1993) *The East Asian Miracle: Economic Growth and Public Policy*. New York: Oxford University Press.

World Bank (1995) *Indonesia: Improving Efficiency and Equity – Changes in the Public Sector's Role, Jakarta, World Bank, Country Department III*, East Asia and Pacific Region.

World Bank (1998) *East Asia: The Road to Recovery*, Washington.

World Bank (2000a) *East Asia: Recovery and Beyond*, Washington.

World Bank (2000b) *Country Assistance Strategy*, Report No. 20354, Washington.

World Bank (2001) *Report on the Observance of Codes and Standards: Corporate Governance Assessment, Republic of the Philippines*. Washington.

World Bank (2003a) *Report on the Observance of Codes and Standards: Corporate Governance Assessment, Republic of Korea*. Washington.

World Bank (2003b) *Indonesia Development Policy Report: Beyond Macroeconomic Stability*, Washington.

World Bank (2003c) *Indonesia: Maintaining Stability, Deepening Reforms*, Washington

World Bank (2004) *Report on the Observance of Codes and Standards: Corporate Governance Assessment, Republic of Indonesia*. Washington.

World Bank (2005) *Report on the Observance of Codes and Standards: Corporate Governance Assessment, Thailand*. Washington.

World Bank (2006a) *Global Development Finance*, Washington.

World Bank (2006b) *Promoting Corporate Governance for Sustainable Development*. Washington.

World Bank (2007) *Global Development Finance 2007*, Washington, DC: World Bank.

Wurm, S. (2006). 'The Development of Austrian Financial Institutions in Central, Eastern and South-Eastern Europe' Working Paper 31 University of Applied Science BFI Vienna.

Yonekura, H. (2005) 'Institutional Reform in Indonesia's Food Security Sector: the Transformation of BULOG into a Public Corporation', *The Developing Economies* 43(1), 121–48.

Yoshihara, K. (1988) *Ersatz capitalism in Southeast Asia*.

Zhan, J. and Ozawa T. (2001) *Business Restructuring in Asia: Cross-Border M & A in the Crisis Period*. Copenhagen: Copenhagen Business School Press.

Index